Confession of the Christian Religion

GIROLAMO ZANCHI

Confession of the Christian Religion

Girolamo Zanchi

Translated and introduced
by Patrick J. O'Banion

REFORMATION HERITAGE BOOKS
Grand Rapids, Michigan

Confession of the Christian Religion
© 2025 by Patrick J. O'Banion

All rights reserved. No part of this book may be used or reproduced in any manner whatsoever without written permission except in the case of brief quotations embodied in critical articles and reviews. Direct your requests to the publisher at the following addresses:

Reformation Heritage Books
3070 29th St. SE
Grand Rapids, MI 49512
616-977-0889
orders@heritagebooks.org
www.heritagebooks.org

Printed in the United States of America
25 26 27 28 29 30/10 9 8 7 6 5 4 3 2 1

Library of Congress Cataloging-in-Publication Data

Names: Zanchi, Girolamo, 1516-1590, author. | O'Banion, Patrick J., 1975- translator.
Title: Confession of the Christian religion / Girolamo Zanchi ; translated and introduced by Patrick J. O'Banion.
Other titles: De religione Christiana fides. English
Description: Grand Rapids, Michigan : Reformation Heritage Books, [2025] | Includes bibliographical references and index.
Identifiers: LCCN 2024035115 (print) | LCCN 2024035116 (ebook) | ISBN 9798886861402 (hardcover) | ISBN 9798886861419 (epub)
Subjects: LCSH: Reformed Church—Doctrines—Early works to 1800.
Classification: LCC BX9421 .Z3613 2025 (print) | LCC BX9421 (ebook) | DDC 230/.42—dc23/eng/20240801
LC record available at https://lccn.loc.gov/2024035115
LC ebook record available at https://lccn.loc.gov/2024035116

For Robert Petersen

And in memory of Josephine Petersen

Contents

Preface ix
Abbreviations xiii
Introduction xv

Confession of the Christian Religion

Dedicatory Letter... 3
Letter to the Reader... 31
  1. Holy Scripture, the Foundation of the Whole
     Christian Religion...................................... 41
  2. God and the Divine Persons and Properties 51
  3. Divine Foreknowledge and Predestination............... 55
  4. The Omnipotence and Will of God...................... 59
  5. The Creation of the World, the Angels, and the Condition
     of the First Man 61
  6. The Providence and Governance of the World 65
  7. The Fall of Man, and Original Sin and Its Fruits........... 69
  8. Man's Free Will after the Fall 75
  9. The Promise of Redemption and Salvation by Christ 79
10. The Law.. 83
11. Christ the Redeemer.................................... 89
12. The Actual Distribution of the Redemption, Salvation,
    and Life Deposited in the One Christ (and the Indispensable
    Union and Fellowship with Christ) 105

13. The Gospel and the Abrogation of the Law by Means
   of the Gospel 117
14. The Sacraments of the New Testament..................... 123
15. Baptism 135
16. The Lord's Supper 141
17. Faith, Hope, and Love 153
18. Repentance 157
19. Justification 161
20. The Regenerate Man's Free Will and His Power
    to Do Good 169
21. Good Works 175
22. Prayer and Oaths 181
23. Christ's Church in General 185
24. The Church Militant 191
25. The Governance of the Church Militant and
    Ecclesiastical Ministry 211
26. The Magistrate 239
27. The Ongoing Remission of Sins in Christ's Church 245
28. The State of Souls after Death and the Resurrection
    of the Dead 251
29. The Glorious Advent of Our Lord Jesus to Judge the Living
    and the Dead 257
30. Eternal Life 261

Zanchi's Own Observations on His Confession 265
An Appendix to Chapter Eleven 331
Certain Chief Articles of the Christian Faith Debated
   at Various Times at Heidelberg and Neustadt against
   Various Heresies 345

Bibliography 399
Scripture Index 415
Subject Index 427

Preface

Confession of the Christian Religion is the second recent translation of a work by sixteenth-century Italian Reformed theologian Girolamo Zanchi published by Reformation Heritage Books. This one, however, is substantially longer (and more complex) than the brief treatise on spiritual marriage that appeared in 2021. For all that, the *Confession* remains one of Zanchi's shorter works, dwarfed as it is by his massive treatments of the doctrine of God, the doctrine of man, and Christology; his many treatises on discreet doctrinal topics; and his commentaries on books of both the Old and New Testaments. It constitutes less than 0.25% of his entire theological corpus, and yet it is a strategic and significant book that I hope will be a blessing to Christ's flock and an aid to scholars, especially those who labor within the church.

In translating the *Confession*, I have tried to balance readability with fidelity to the original Latin and Greek text, perhaps leaning toward the former. This has entailed breaking up long sentences, clarifying pronouns by inserting their nominal referents, adding paragraph breaks, and so forth. In making these changes, I have sought to remain true to Zanchi's intent and arguments (as I understand them) and to help modern readers follow his thought.

Some words and phrases were a special challenge to translate. Here I mention only three examples that show up frequently, so as to prepare readers to encounter them. I chose to translate Zanchi's *fideles* (a word he used frequently to refer to those who are united to Christ) as "the faithful" largely because "those who have faith" (which is what the word meant for Zanchi) is inelegant. Accordingly, readers should not understand "the faithful" to mean "those who behave faithfully" (except in a secondary sense, as it were) but rather those who are "full of faith." Relatedly, an adjective often applied to *fideles* is *pius*, which might be rendered "godly," "devout," or even "faithful." I settled in this case on the English cognate "pious." This word is somewhat out of fashion, but it conveys that desired range of semantic meaning. Needless to say, neither Zanchi nor I mean for "pious" to bear any of the negative connotations—"sanctimonious," "hypocritical," or "self-righteous"—that it sometimes does nowadays. I could not quite bring myself to render *impius* as "impious," so I went with "wicked" instead.

Zanchi sought to tie his *Confession* into the warp and weft of the great tradition of Christian theology by frequently drawing not only from Scripture but also from the works of previous theologians, especially the church fathers. Direct quotations in the body of the text are indicated by italics. The rationale for this practice is that Zanchi liked to interpolate and interrupt quotations in ways that become confusing when the quotations are denoted by quotation marks. In the notes, however, the standard practice of using inverted commas to enclose quoted material is retained. In the body of the *Confession*, all translations are my own (based on the Latin or the Greek as written by Zanchi) unless otherwise indicated. Whenever possible, I have included in the notes at least one (and usually two) citations to standard English translations. When I determined that it would be useful for the reader, I have also placed in the notes appropriate excerpts from the works cited by Zanchi. I used modern English translations in the notes whenever possible and only provided my own translations if another one did not already exist.

I have endeavored to compare Zanchi's quotations against original sources and have indicated (the rare) discrepancies in the notes. He included citations for sources in the body of his *Confession*, so those have been retained in the body of the translated text as cited. In cases where he miscites or provides partial citations for biblical passages or extrabiblical works, I have corrected him or supplied full information in brackets within the body of the text. It should be said that Zanchi was working from the best sources available to him in the late sixteenth century. Hence, when he attributes a spurious work to a particular author or misattributes an authentic work to someone who did not write it, this does not indicate dishonesty or shoddy scholarship on his part but the fact that patristic studies have advanced over the last four centuries.

This translation of Zanchi's *Confession* is based on the 1586 Latin text, which is the first published version. Two previous translations exist. The first was published in 1599 by John Legat, printer for the University of Cambridge,[1] and the second appeared in 1659, the work of Ralph Winterton (1601–1636), a fellow of Kings College, Cambridge and Regius Professor of Physic.[2] The translator of the first work is unknown, but during this period Legat published several treatises, usually in translation, by Zanchi and other continental Reformed authors. Neither of these are bad translations, so to speak, but they are challenging to read on account of their dated style and vocabulary. They also lack significant portions of the *Confession* and are difficult (as well as very expensive) to access in print. The Legat volume contains a translation of most of the Latin text but omits the letter to the reader and several significant sections from the body of the text.[3] Less well-known than Legat's edition is Winterton's posthumously published translation, which omits all introductory materials (the dedicatory letter and the letter to the reader) as well as the appended materials (the observations, the appendix to chapter 11, and the eight theses) to the confession proper.

In preparing this translation, I benefited from the labors of Luca Baschera and Christian Moser, who published a two-volume critical Latin edition of Zanchi's *Confession* in 2007.[4] The notes in those volumes,

---

1. Girolamo Zanchi, *His Confession of the Christian Religion* (Cambridge: J. Legat, 1599). Legat became the university printer in 1598.

2. Jerome Zanchi, *The Whole Body of Christian Religion*, trans. Ralph Winterton (London: John Redmayne, 1659). On the translator, see Norman Moore and Michael Bevan, "Winterton, Ralph (1601–1636)," in *Oxford Dictionary of National Biography* (Oxford University Press, 2004–), https://doi.org/10.1093/ref:odnb/29776. Winterton apparently tackled bouts of depression ("melancholy") by translating works from Latin and Greek into English.

3. These omissions are indicated in the notes of this translation.

4. Girolamo Zanchi, *De religione christiana fides – Confession of Christian Religion*, ed. Luca Baschera and Christian Moser, 2 vols., Studies in the History of Christian Traditions 135 (Leiden: Brill, 2007). These volumes include the Legat translation on facing pages.

especially the ones that locate patristic references, saved me an enormous amount of time, and I have relied upon them extensively. On the infrequent occasions in which I discovered an error, I have corrected their citations. And, as noted above, I have added another layer to their work by providing references to English editions (when they exist) of all the works that Zanchi cites for readers who wish to dig deeper.

Finally, I would like to acknowledge the aid of my friend Dr. Robert Petersen, who graciously and patiently collaborated on this project by reading and providing feedback on drafts of each of the chapters as I completed them. His critical editorial eye, thoughtful questions, and gentle prodding kept the project moving, and his willingness to discuss the content has been a great blessing, but his humility and faithful service to his family and his church have been even greater encouragements. As Zanchi notes, "It is fitting for a book of good doctrine to have a good patron rather than a bad one,"[5] and while I am grateful for Robert's editorial help, it is on account of his Christlike spirit that I am honored to dedicate this volume to him and, in memoriam, to his beloved wife, Josephine.

---

5. Girolamo Zanchi, *Confession of the Christian Religion*, ed. and trans. Patrick J. O'Banion (Grand Rapids: Reformation Heritage Books, 2025), p. 27.

Abbreviations

ANF	*The Ante-Nicene Fathers: Translations of the Writings of the Fathers Down to A.D. 325.* Edited by Alexander Roberts and James Donaldson. 10 vols. Reprint, Peabody, Mass.: Hendrickson, 1999.
art./arts.	article/articles
b.	born
bk./bks.	book/books
ca.	*circa*
CB	*Correspondance de Théodore de Bèze.* Edited by Alain Dufour et al. 43 vols. Geneva: Droz, 1960–2017.
CCR	Girolamo Zanchi. *Confession of the Christian Religion.* Edited and translated by Patrick J. O'Banion. Grand Rapids: Reformation Heritage Books, 2024.
ch./chs.	chapter/chapters
col./cols.	column/columns
d.	died
dist./dists.	distinction/distinctions
ep./eps.	epistle/epistles
fl.	flourished
fol./fols.	folio/folios
FOTC	*The Fathers of the Church: A New Translation.* 145 vols. Washington, D.C.: Catholic University of America Press, 1947–.

hom./homs.	homily/homilies
NPNF1	*A Select Library of the Nicene and Post-Nicene Fathers of the Christian Church.* Edited by Philip Schaff. 14 vols. Reprint, Grand Rapids: Eerdmans, 1989–1994.
NPNF2	*A Select Library of the Nicene and Post-Nicene Fathers of the Christian Church.* Edited by Philip Schaff and Henry Wace. 14 vols. 2nd series. Reprint, Grand Rapids: Eerdmans, 1991.
obs.	observation
OOT	Girolamo Zanchi. *Omnia opera theologicorum.* 8 tomes in 3 vols. Geneva, 1619.
PG	*Patrologia Graeca.* Edited by J.-P. Migne. 162 vols. Paris, 1857–1886.
PL	*Patrologia Latina.* Edited by J.-P. Migne. 217 vols. Paris, 1844–1864.
PRRD	Richard A. Muller. *Post-Reformation Reformed Dogmatics: The Rise and Development of Reformed Orthodoxy, ca. 1520 to ca. 1725.* 2nd ed. 4 vols. Grand Rapids: Baker Academic, 2003.
q.	question
r.	ruled
v./vv.	verse/verses

Introduction

For the Reformed churches of late-sixteenth- and seventeenth-century Europe, the combination of two particular virtues made Girolamo Zanchi a notable figure. On the one hand, he was widely acclaimed for his devout life—"second to none in piety" was the way that memorialists put it after his death.[1] He was remembered for having shunned contention and loved concord, for being a man of singular modesty, and for pursuing the promotion of peace among churches.[2] On the other hand, he was equally renowned for uniting his pious life with deep learning.

His character struck his contemporaries as noteworthy, and his reputation outlived him. Seventeenth-century editors described him hyperbolically. One noted that Zanchi was not just one "Modern Divine" among many but that he was and "still is accounted, the very head of the chief…, the very flower of the prime choice."[3] Another drew a similar picture: Zanchi was "the flower of all new writers."[4] Two decades after his death, yet another author described him as "the previous generation's most brilliant theologian."[5] The Puritan Thomas Goodwin accounted

---

1. Patrick J. O'Banion, "Jerome Zanchi, the Application of Theology, and the Rise of the English Practical Divinity Tradition," *Renaissance and Reformation / Renaissance et Réforme* 29, no. 2–3 (2005): 97.

2. See the eulogy accorded him in Melchior Adam's *Decades duae continentes vitas theologorum exterorum principium* (Frankfurt, 1618), 152.

3. *The Whole Body of Christian Religion*, sig. a4v.

4. Robert Hill, "The Epistle Dedicatorie," in *Life Everlasting, or The True Knowledge of One Jehovah, Three Elohim, and Jesus Immanuel*, by Girolamo Zanchi (Cambridge, 1601), sig. ¶3r.

5. Sebastian Benefield, *Doctrinae Christianae sex capita* (Oxford, 1610), 21.

him "the best of Protestant Writers."[6] He was one of only seven authors whom John Owen cited more than five times.[7] Even Archbishop Richard Bancroft backhandedly complimented him as the most "moderate & learned" among those who inclined toward the rule of elders over the rule of bishops.[8] He greatly influenced the theology of the next generation of continental Reformed theologians who studied with him, read his writings, and carried forward his teaching—Philippe de Mornay (1549–1623), Jeremiah Bastinguis (1551–1595), Jean Taffin the Younger (1555?–1613), Sibrandus Lubbertus (1555–1625), Franciscus Gomarus (1563–1641), Antonius Thysius (1565–1640), Jacobus Kimedoncius (c. 1550–1596), Jean-Baptiste Rotan (d. 1598), and many others.

Nowadays, if Zanchi's theological reputation suffers relatively few direct attacks, this is largely because he is little known.[9] Zanchi's slide into obscurity is a consequence of multiple factors. The most important of them include the fact that his brand of scholastic theology came under attack during and went out of fashion after the Enlightenment; that his nomadic life meant no educational or civic institutions were invested in preserving his memory; and that, as latinity declined, so, too, did the ability of readers to access most of his writings.

In the late twentieth century, however, a reassessment and reappropriation of orthodox Reformed scholastic theologians like Zanchi began. The work of Richard Muller in the United States and Antonie Vos's Utrecht School in the Netherlands converged with other streams to produce a steady flow of research on figures who had formerly been

---

6. Thomas Goodwin, *The Works of Thomas Goodwin* (Grand Rapids: Reformation Heritage Books, 2021), 1:37.

7. Crawford Gribben, "John Owen, Renaissance Man? The Evidence of Edward Millington's Bibliotheca Oweniana (1684)," in *The Ashgate Research Companion to John Owen's Theology*, ed. Kelly M. Kapic and Mark Jones, Ashgate Research Companions (Aldershot: Ashgate, 2016), 101.

8. Richard Bancroft, *A Survey of the Pretended Holy Discipline* (London, 1663), 107.

9. For a recent overview of Zanchi's life, see my "Introduction" to Girolamo Zanchi, in *The Spiritual Marriage between Christ and His Church and Every One of the Faithful*, trans. Patrick J. O'Banion (Grand Rapids: Reformation Heritage Books, 2021), xv–xxvii. Older overviews include Giambattista Gallizioli, *Memorie istoriche e letterarie della vita e delle opere di Girolamo Zanchi* (Bergamo: Francesco Locatelli, 1785); and Charles Schmidt, "Girolamo Zanchi," *Theologische Studien und Kritiken* 32 (1859): 625–708.

consigned to the historical-theological dustbin.[10] Concurrent with this reassessment of the Reformed tradition's post-Reformation theologians, a parallel effort has sought to make their works available, both in their original languages and in translation. Hence, English-language editions of Francis Turretin's *Institutes of Elenctic Theology* and Wilhelmus à Brakel's *The Christian's Reasonable Service*, both of which appeared in the 1990s, now sit cozily on the shelf next to volumes of Petrus van Mastricht's *Theoretical-Practical Theology*, Leiden's *Synopsis of Purer Theology*, and many similar titles, which have appeared (and continue to appear) in the new millennium.[11]

Thanks to these efforts, the post-Reformation Reformed orthodox theologians have experienced a renaissance. They are no longer simply dismissed as betrayers of the devout, Christ-centered piety present in the movement's earliest figures but are celebrated as constructive figures in a developing theological tradition whose lives and writings eschew disjunctures between a supposedly dry, arid, and speculative scholasticism that controlled academic theology and the warm, pastoral heart that sought to comfort afflicted sinners and sufferers with the balm of the good news of Christ. In the main, contemporary scholars believe these authors and teachers presented that good news in ways that sought to be biblically grounded and warmhearted as well as academically precise and rigorous

---

10. A flavor of this scholarship can be found in Richard A. Muller, *Christ and the Decree: Christology and Predestination in Reformed Theology from Calvin to Perkins* (Grand Rapids: Baker Academic, 2008); and Willem J. van Asselt and Eef Dekker, eds., *Reformation and Scholasticism: An Ecumenical Enterprise*, Texts and Studies in Reformation and Post-Reformation Thought (Grand Rapids: Baker Academic, 2001).

11. Francis Turretin, *Institutes of Elenctic Theology*, ed. James T. Dennison Jr., trans. George Musgrave Giger, 3 vols. (Phillipsburg, N.J.: P&R Publishing, 1992–1997); Wilhelmus à Brakel, *The Christian's Reasonable Service*, ed. Joel R. Beeke, trans. Bartel Elshout, 4 vols. (Grand Rapids: Reformation Heritage Books, 1992); Petrus van Mastricht, *Theoretical-Practical Theology*, 4 vols., ed. Joel R. Beeke, trans. Todd M. Rester (Grand Rapids: Reformation Heritage Books, 2018–2023); Willem J. van Asselt et al., eds., *Synopsis Purioris Theologiae / Synopsis of a Purer Theology: Latin Text and English Translation*, 3 vols. (Leiden: Brill, 2014–2020). To this list we could add many more volumes by authors such as Vermigli, Olevianus, Cocceius, Heidegger, Junius, and Vitringa, among others. In addition to these translated works, digitization projects like Google Books and websites like Post-Reformation Digital Library (https://www.prdl.org/) have made it much easier to access digital versions of the original publications.

enough to hold their own against the pressing cultural, intellectual, and theological challenges of the age.

As his contemporaries and successors recognized, this happy conjunction of post-Reformation learning and piety particularly characterized Zanchi. Hence, when the Englishman Henry Nelson (fl. 1614) explained why he bothered to translate a series of treatises by the Italian scholastic, he offered the following rationale:

> In Argument and matter they are exceeding effectuall, befitting this sinfull and sottish Age.... They are fruitfull in many considerations; to prevent curiositie; to abandon securitie; to rowze up the drowsie Christian; to detect the Temporizer; to kindle zeale; to worke vigilancie; to enforce repentance; to minister consolation; to teach the wise; to hearten the weake; to confirme faith and hope of heaven and Happinesse; to da[u]nt ungodlinesse.[12]

Few could live up to Nelson's praise, but the careful reader of Zanchi will find him to be far more than an ivory tower figure and hardly an inconsequential thinker. He remains an important conversation partner for theological reflection in the twenty-first century, especially (but not exclusively) for those who belong to the Reformed tradition. Even so, Zanchi lived in a markedly different world than the one in which this book has been published, so some words about the context of his life and the content of his *Confession* are in order.

Zanchi's Life

Zanchi was born in 1516 in the northern Italian town of Alzano.[13] He was orphaned at age fifteen and grew to adulthood among the Augustinian Canons Regular of the Lateran Congregation in nearby Bergamo. He

---

12. Girolamo Zanchi, *Speculum Christianum: A Christian Survey of Conscience*, trans. Henry Nelson (London, 1614), sig. A7v–A8r.

13. The best accounts of his early life in Italy are Giulio Orazio Bravi, "Girolamo Zanchi, da Lucca a Strasburgo," *Archivio storico bergamasco* 1 (1981): 35–64 and "I riformati bergamaschi Girolamo Zanchi e Guglielmo Grataroli in Italia prima dell'esilio," in *Il dissenso religioso a Bergamo nel Cinquecento*, ed. Giulio Orazio Bravi (Bergamo: Centro studi e ricerche Archivio Bergamasco, 2018), 125–67.

was well educated and, by 1541, was a canon, priest, and public preacher for the Lateran Congregation. That same year, he was assigned to the Congregation's house in Lucca. There he came under the influence of the newly appointed abbot, Peter Martyr Vermigli (1499–1562), a noted Italian evangelical who soon fled north on account of inquisitorial attention, becoming a leading light of the Reformed Reformation unfolding in Europe.

Deeply influenced by Vermigli's teaching, Zanchi eventually followed his father in the faith into exile. He taught first at Strasbourg (1553–1563), where he found himself at odds with a contingent seeking to Lutheranize the city's school and church.[14] After much discussion, disagreement, and disappointment in Strasbourg, Zanchi accepted a call to pastor a Reformed congregation in Chiavenna (1563–1567), in the Alpine region of Rhaetia (also known as the Grisons).[15] He hoped to establish an academy there for the training of preachers and teachers to revitalize gospel ministry in Italy. Plague, congregational factionalism, and heresy combined to dim most of these hopes. In 1567, he accepted an invitation from Elector Frederick III (r. 1559–1576) of the Palatinate to teach at the University of Heidelberg, which he did with much success.[16] At the Elector's death in 1576, his Lutheran son and heir purged the university of

---

14. For more on Zanchi's time in Strasbourg, see Christopher J. Burchill, "Girolamo Zanchi in Strasbourg, 1553–1563" (PhD diss., University of Cambridge, 1979) and James M. Kittelson, *Toward an Established Church: Strasbourg from 1500 to the Dawn of the Seventeenth Century*, Veröffentlichungen des Instituts für Europäische Geschichte Mainz Abteilung für Abendländische Religionsgeschichte 182 (Mainz: Verlag Philipp von Zabern, 2000), esp. 89–111.

15. For more on Zanchi's pastorate in Chiavenna, see Lukas Vischer, "Girolamo Zancho, reformierter Prediger in Chiavenna," *Bündnerisches Monatsblatt* 10 (1951): 289–301.

16. Zanchi's Heidelberg and Neustadt years are not adequately covered in the secondary literature, but helpful details can be gleaned from Luca Baschera and Christian Moser, "Introduction," in *De religione christiana fides—Confession of Christian Religion*, Studies in the History of Christian Traditions 135 (Leiden: Brill, 2007); Charles Gunnoe, *Thomas Erastus and the Palatinate: A Renaissance Physician in the Second Reformation*, Brill's Series in Church History 48 (Leiden: Brill, 2010); and Christopher J. Burchill, *The Heidelberg Antitrinitarians: Johann Sylvan, Adam Neuser, Matthias Vehe, Jacob Suter, Johann Hasler*, Bibliotheca Dissidentium 11 (Baden-Baden: Koerner, 1989).

its Reformed professors for "teaching Calvinism up to this point."[17] Zanchi and others found refuge at a newly established Reformed academy in Neustadt an der Haardt. In declining health, he retired from teaching in 1584, although he remained active and received a stipend that supported him during his remaining years. He died in November 1590 while visiting friends in Heidelberg and was interred there at the university church.

The Historical Context of the Confession
Zanchi published his first book in 1554 (a Greek edition of Aristotle's *Physics* with a long Latin introduction) and his first theological treatise a decade later, at the age of forty-five. He did not hit his stride as an author until 1570.[18] His final years were marked by failing eyesight and, eventually, total blindness, which slowed his literary labors and made him completely reliant upon an amanuensis. Yet Zanchi proved a remarkably prolific writer and (thanks especially to the efforts of his heirs) published an astonishing amount of material. I estimate that his collected theological works in the definitive Crespin edition of 1619 comprise more than 5,500,000 words.[19] Through his teaching, writing, and social network, he exerted a tremendous influence on subsequent generations of Reformed ministers and theologians across the Continent and in the British Isles, as well as upon the future shape of the Reformed theological tradition more broadly.

---

17. Kenneth Austin, *From Judaism to Calvinism: The Life and Writings of Immanuel Tremellius (c.1510–1580)*, St Andrews Studies in Reformation History (London: Routledge, 2007), 170.

18. Referencing Zanchi's age when he began publishing in earnest, one commentator noted that "yo[u]ng vines bring forth the most grapes, but old the best grapes: so yo[u]ng wittes the most books, but olde the best books." Hill, "The Epistle Dedicatorie," sig. ¶3r.

19. By way of comparison, Aquinas's *Summa Theologiae* is around 1,800,000 words, and Petrus van Mastricht's *Theoretical-Practical Theology* is around 1,500,000 words. Zanchi's systematic treatises—sometimes referred to as his unfinished Reformed *summa*—which treat theology proper, creation, anthropology, sin and the law, and part of Christology amount to roughly 2,400,000 words. Aquinas, however, outpaced Zanchi in terms of total output; some 8,000,000 words of total written material are attributed to the Dominican over the course of his relatively short life (1225–1274).

Introduction xxi

De religione christiana fides, the work translated here, fits within the later part of Zanchi's career.[20] In 1577, during his period of transition from Heidelberg to Neustadt, Lutheran theologians and churchmen gathered to compose and approve the Formula of Concord, a statement of faith that established clear confessional boundaries for their churches. Johann Casimir (1543–1592), count palatine and Zanchi's lord following the death of Frederick III, believed that the Reformed ought to respond in kind and invited their churches to gather in colloquy at Frankfurt on September 27–28 of that year. The Palatinate, France, Navarre, Poland, Hungary, England, and the Netherlands were represented at the meeting.[21] Notably absent were the Swiss, who "declined to attend."[22] They stayed abreast of the proceedings, however, and subsequently became involved in a plan that was devised there to "formulate a confession of

---

20. Literally, *The Faith of the Christian Religion*. Faith (*fides*) is not merely knowledge or assent but a hearty trust that entails the believer's union with Christ. But as the biblical citation of Romans 10:10 on the title page of *De religione* suggests, this trusting faith necessarily issues forth in oral confession unto salvation. For Zanchi, religion (*religio*) or piety (*pietas*) is that which gives rise to worship. See Girolamo Zanchi, *De primi hominis lapsu, de peccato et de lege Dei* (Neustadt, 1597), cols. 263–362 (*OOT*, vol. 2, tome 4, cols. 263–362). Henceforth, the *OOT* will be cited with volume and tome separated by a slash, followed by the page, folio, or column number: *OOT*, 2/4, 263–362.

21. Baschera and Moser assert that this gathering took place in Neustadt. See "Introduction," in *De religione*, 1:14n88. Willem van 't Spijker contends with equal conviction that it met in Frankfurt. See review of *De religione christiana fides – Confession of Christian Religion*. [Studies in the History of Christian Traditions 135], by Girolamo Zanchi, edited by Luca Baschera and Christian Moser, *Church History and Religious Culture* 92, no. 2–3 (January 2012): 378. Irene Dingel explains that the colloquy in Frankfurt was followed by a December meeting in Neustadt. See *Concordia controversa: Die öffentlichen Diskussionen um das lutherische Konkordienwerk am Ende des 16. Jahrhunderts*, Quellen und Forschungen zur Reformationsgeschichte 63 (Gütersloh: Gütersloher Verlagshaus, 1996), 125.

22. Amy Nelson Burnett, "Basel, Beza, and the Development of Calvinist Orthodoxy in the Swiss Confederation," in *Calvin und Calvinismus: Europäische Perspektiven*, ed. Irene Dingel and Herman J. Selderhuis, Veröffentlichungen des Instituts für Europäische Geschichte Mainz 84 (Göttingen: Vandenhoeck & Ruprecht, 2013), 80n47, https://doi.org/10.13109/9783666101069.67. The Genevans received reports from Daniel Tossanus immediately afterward and read them aloud in a meeting of the Company of Pastors on October 16. See Dingel, *Concordia controversa*, 123.

faith acceptable to all Reformed churches, in order to demonstrate their doctrinal unity and orthodoxy."[23]

Initially, Zanchi and his colleague Zacharias Ursinus (1534–1583) were chosen to collaborate in drafting the confession, but when Ursinus (who had doubts about the project's advisability) backed out, the burden fell to Zanchi alone. Despite having his own qualms about the whole scheme, he felt obliged to accept the project and began work once his family's transition to Neustadt was complete.[24]

In order to bring the Swiss on board, it was agreed that drafts of Zanchi's confession would be reviewed by Theodore Beza (1519–1605) of Geneva and Rudolf Gwalther (1519–1586) of Zurich. Once they signed off, the document would be forwarded to an English envoy for further review before being distributed to the Reformed churches of Europe for discussion, feedback, and approval at the synodal and national levels. It was a cumbersome and ambitious project, but before Zanchi had submitted a word to his Swiss readers, Gwalther was already criticizing the final product. He assured Beza that he had no doubts about Zanchi's "learning and piety" but feared that, "in the Italian fashion," Zanchi would include "dubious, obscure, or even altogether unnecessary points" to showcase his theological acumen.[25]

As chapters began to appear, the critics multiplied. Daniel Tossanus (1541–1602) wrote to Beza that he had "repeatedly warned [Zanchi] to handle everything more briefly and clearly and less scholastically," but that he had "not succeeded nearly as much as he wished" in influencing the confession's author.[26] And Gwalther, writing to Beza, stated: "I expect you are aware of what is in Zanchi's confession. To me, it seems too long to be

---

23. Baschera and Moser, "Introduction," in *De religione*, 1:14–15. On the 1577 colloquy, the Reformed confession project, and Zanchi's role in it, see (in addition to Baschera and Moser's "Introduction," in *De religione*, 1:14–19) Irene Dingel, *Concordia controversa*, 115–29 and Amy Nelson Burnett, "Basel, Beza, and the Development of Calvinist Orthodoxy in the Swiss Confederation," 67–83.

24. Theodore Beza to Rudolf Gwalther, January 27, 1578, in *CB*, 19:17. See Zanchi to Lambert Daneau, June 11, 1580, in *OOT*, 3/8:198.

25. Gwalther to Beza, March 26, 1578, in *CB*, 19:79.

26. Tossanus to Beza, September 14, 1578, in *CB*, 19:171.

useful."[27] By mid-1578, some began to argue that a harmony of existing Reformed confessions would be more likely to gain widespread acceptance than the drafting of a new one.[28] And in early 1579, Beza suggested to Gwalther that Zanchi's project might instead be regarded merely as a "private confession."[29] Certainly by November of that year, Beza, Lambert Daneau (c. 1530–1595), and Jean-François Salvard (1530–1585) were working in earnest on a harmony that integrated eleven different confessions into a single document.[30]

Unaware of the course change, Zanchi soldiered on and continued to send drafts out for review. Only as his confession neared completion in May 1580, two and a half years into the project, did Daneau (with many assurances of esteem and respect) break the news.[31] Zanchi's reply was measured and diplomatic, recalling that at the Frankfurt Colloquy he himself had encouraged the Reformed churches to focus on drafting a harmony of the Second Helvetic Confession and the Augsburg Confession. He had only agreed to write a new one "against [his] will and under constraint."[32]

Yet having the confession project snatched from his hands was no trifling matter for Zanchi. Not only had he wasted a tremendous amount of valuable time and energy but, as he indicated in the introduction to his

---

27. Gwalther to Beza, January 11, 1579, in *CB*, 20:3.
28. Beza to Gwalther, May 27, 1578, in *CB*, 19:102.
29. Beza to Gwalther, February 7, 1579, in *CB*, 20:27.
30. This was published under the lead of Salvard as *Harmonia confessionum fidei orthodoxarum et reformatarum ecclesiarum, quae in praecipius quibusque Europae regnis, nationibus et provinciis sacram evangelii doctrinam pure profitentur* (Geneva, 1581). It has been published in English several times, originally as *An Harmony of the Confessions of the Faith of the Christian and Reformed Churches* (Cambridge, 1586). On the *Harmonia*, see Fritz Büsser, "Freedom in Reformed Confessions of the 16th Century (The 'Harmonia Confessionum Fidei' of 1581)," *Zwingliana* 16, no. 4 (1984): 281–300. As Andreas Beck notes, it "never achieved such significance as the *Formula of Concord*" and is largely forgotten nowadays. "Reformed Confessions and Scholasticism. Diversity and Harmony," *Perichoresis* 14, no. 3 (December 2016): 22.
31. Daneau to Zanchi, May 1580, in *OOT*, 3/8:197. Zanchi included part of this letter in his introductory comments to the observations in the *Confession* (p. 266).
32. Zanchi to Daneau, June 11, 1580, in *OOT*, 3/8:198.

observations on the confession, his personal and theological reputation suffered from the affair. He wrote,

> Although everyone can see that this confession was never published according to plan on behalf of those for whose sake it had been drafted, they do not fully grasp who did what or why it happened. Many people are astonished at what occurred, but they have no idea about the actual reasons behind it. Who could be ignorant of just how much suspicion is likely to arise as a result, not to mention the various assumptions that churches (let alone individuals) might make, either about me or about the confession itself? Lastly, who doesn't see how malicious rumors of many sorts might well be spread among the general public as a result? Hence, before I die, I had finally better respond to the malicious and depraved suspicions, judgments, and rumors about my doctrine.[33]

Partly to lay those rumors to rest and partly as a witness to his children, Zanchi did eventually publish the work as a private confession in his own name and that of his family. In 1586, four years before his death, it appeared with the press of Matthäus Harnisch of Neustadt.[34] The published work included not only the confession proper as originally drafted but also several additional elements. Zanchi wrote a lengthy dedicatory letter to Ulysses Martinengo (1537–1609), a friend and supporter during his time as pastor in Chiavenna.[35] A shorter letter "to the Reader" seems to have been added at the last moment, as Zanchi notes that the text had already gone to press. He also included a set of extensive observations that followed the confession proper. These were meant to "explain anything unclear and develop anything dubious" without introducing new material into the body of the confession in a way that would create confusion about what he had written in the first place.[36] To the observations, he also added an appendix to chapter 11, which further developed his

---

33. CCR, p. 265.
34. The publishing history of the earliest versions of CCR is handled in Baschera and Moser, "Introduction," in De religione, 1:19–20.
35. For more on Martinengo, see Baschera and Moser, "Introduction," in De religione, 1:22–25.
36. CCR, p. 265.

understanding of the person of the incarnate Christ. Finally, he included a series of theses against various heresies, which he had publicly defended in disputations conducted at Heidelberg and Neustadt between 1572 and 1582.

After its initial appearance, Zanchi's confession was reprinted several times in various editions into the mid-seventeenth century. In addition to the two early modern English translations noted in the preface to this work, it was reprinted in Latin in 1601 (Neustadt: Heirs of Wilhelm Harnisch) and 1605 (London: Jacob Rimeus). Finally, it was included in the various editions of Zanchi's collected theological works printed in Geneva (1605, 1613, 1619, and 1649).[37]

Through these media, the *Confession of the Christian Religion* influenced both the Reformed theological tradition generally and the development of Reformed dogmatics in particular. It represents a summary of the entire system of Christian doctrine as composed by a pious and vigorous theologian at the height of his powers during a critical moment in the history of the Reformed church. As I have suggested elsewhere, Zanchi helped to connect the earlier and later phases of the Reformation by guiding the Reformed churches toward theological maturity and formulating ways to communicate Reformed theology, piety, and practice through the formation of ministers from generation to generation.[38] Consequently, his labors provided the Reformed tradition with structure and content that far outlived him. And of his many works, none is a more useful and accessible overview of the entire Reformed theological system of doctrine than his *Confession*. It is of immense value both as a historical document and as a conversation partner in the church's effort—as Zanchi put it—to understand and explain the "apostolic doctrine contained in the Holy Scriptures...according to the orthodox interpretations of the ancient fathers."[39]

---

37. More recently, the confession has been translated into Italian as *La fede cristiana. Che precisamente ora, a sessantanove anni d'età, mise alla luce a nome suo e della sua famiglia*, trans. Emanuele Fiume (Rome: Edizioni GBU, 2011).
38. Zanchi, *Spiritual Marriage*, xv.
39. *CCR*, p. 9.

The Foundations and Structure of the Confession

Simply put, Zanchi's *Confession* is a confession. That is, it is a formal statement made on behalf of the catholic church concerning the "tradition" (παράδοσις) she has received on the basis of apostolic teaching (2 Thess. 2:15; 3:6). In general, the thirty chapters of the confession proper are patterned after the Apostles' Creed, giving it a broadly Trinitarian and redemptive-historical structure that emphasizes God's saving work for His people in His incarnate Son.[40] An initial chapter on Scripture, along with portions of the letter to Martinengo, serves as prolegomena to the rest. A series of relatively short chapters on theology proper, which address the being, nature, attributes, and acts of God, give way to lengthier chapters on anthropology, hamartiology, Christology, and soteriology. A series of chapters on ecclesiology follow, one of which (chapter 25, on church governance and ecclesiastical ministry) is the longest of all. Finally, the confession looks to the future hope by addressing eschatology, both personal and general.

Many confessions also played the important role of protecting the church against false teachings. To that end, most chapters of the confession end with a series of "errors" denounced by the church. As Zanchi noted in his dedicatory letter, however, the heretics who deny the foundations of the faith rarely do so directly or openly, opting instead to distort and reinterpret them.[41] Accordingly, he suggested that remaining faithful to Christianity's apostolic foundations meant hewing closely to the understanding of "the ancient church…in harmony with the Holy Scriptures and on the basis of the common confession, especially in the most excellent councils."[42] Hence, a confession is a communal document, drawing the voices of the whole church—past, present, and future—

---

40. On the relation of the *Confession* to the Apostles' Creed and the Second Helvetic Confession, see Baschera and Moser, "Introduction," in *De religione*, 1:27–28.

41. Zanchi believed that these foundations are expressed especially in the "outline of doctrine known as the Catechism," which includes the Apostles' Creed, the Lord's Prayer, and the Decalogue, along with the teaching about the sacraments—all of which are established and erected upon biblical revelation. CCR, p. 10.

42. CCR, p. 10.

into the united witness for that "faith which was once for all delivered to the saints," to the praise and glory of God (Jude 3).

As this suggests, theological tradition carried weight for Zanchi. He accepted the merit (even if only at the level of personal experience) of Augustine's famous claim that he "would not have believed the gospel, had not the authority of the church moved [him]."[43] Zanchi submitted his whole theological project to be judged by the "true catholic church" according to "the touchstone of the Holy Scriptures and the analogy of faith."[44] Repeatedly, he signaled that to diverge from patristic interpretations left his conscience uneasy. And he made it a point to "so reverence the ancient church and the ancient fathers and maintain such fellowship with those living on in heaven and have such communion with them" that he diverged from them in dogmas or exegesis only at length and when compelled to do so by the "evident words and testimonies of the Holy Scriptures, and…on the basis of necessary consequences derived from the foundations of the faith."[45]

The theology that the confession offers, then, was meant to be bound to and shaped by the long tradition of Christian reflection upon and response to God's holy Word. This is why so many of the paragraphs are stated in the first-person plural: "we believe." Zanchi took the ancient fathers, whom he so often cites, as reliable guides, especially as they confessed the faith in formal councils under the guidance of Scripture and the Spirit.[46] The medieval theologians, too, were part of that tradition, and Zanchi (with far less frequency than the patristic authorities) referred to

---

43. CCR, 1.7. Zanchi cites Augustine, *Answer to the Letter of Mani Known as The Foundation*, in *The Manichean Debate*, by Augustine, ed. Boniface Ramsey, trans. Roland J. Teske, The Works of Saint Augustine: A Translation for the 21st Century I/19 (Hyde Park, N.Y.: New City Press, 2006), 236 (*NPNF*1, 4:131).

44. CCR, p. 27. The title page of the confession, after quoting Romans 10:10, reads: "Let everything be submitted to the true judgment of the true catholic church."

45. CCR, p. 14.

46. Not surprisingly, Augustine is by far the most frequent extrabiblical source referenced, cited, or quoted in the *Confession*. After Augustine, Vigilius of Thapsus (whom sixteenth-century scholarship confused with Vigilius of Trent), Cyprian, John of Damascus, Tertullian, Ambrose, and Jerome appear most frequently, in descending order. In all, more than fifty different authorities (counting classical authors but not heterodox or heretical individuals or groups) are referenced.

and cited them accordingly.[47] Following the lead of the "Greek and Latin church," even the apocryphal books were not to be despised but received as witnesses to the faith of God's Old Testament people and granted the "first place" after the canonical books and the councils.[48]

Nevertheless, the authority accorded to extrabiblical sources in the *Confession* is always ministerial in nature. Unfolding his elaborate metaphor of the imperiled country in the dedicatory letter, Zanchi asserted, "Thus, nothing is safer than for everyone to secure themselves, as though in well-fortified cities, in these churches in which the Holy Scriptures are expounded according to the analogy of faith and according to the received interpretations of the ancient fathers. Accordingly, their faith is the same as the apostles' and that of the whole of the ancient church."[49] If Zanchi's approach cannot be characterized as a naive biblicism (that is, as recognizing the Bible as the only authoritative source of truth), it does acknowledge Scripture as the foundation on the basis of which all other (secondary, ministerial) authorities derive their stability and strength, and apart from which they cannot stand.

Creeds, councils, synods, church fathers, the long catholic consensus, individual theologians of note, the voice of the institutional church, ecclesiastical officers—all of these were authoritative for Zanchi, but only insofar as they reflected and conveyed the apostolic teaching of Scripture. To the extent that a church or any other authority lost those moorings, it was no longer to be heeded, for it had strayed from the apostolic faith. Fittingly, then, it is not "a perpetual succession of bishops" that entailed

---

47. His interaction with medieval sources in this work is generally positive. See his references to "the scholastics," Gratian, Anselm, and Aquinas. *CCR*, p. 31; 1.11 and 12, 16.17, 22.6, 24.18, 25.11; obs. 2.3, 11.6, 11.11, 11.13.8, 14.1, 19.19; and thesis 3 of the 1582 disputation. As John Patrick Donnelly noted, Zanchi was often indebted to Aquinas even when he did not explicitly cite him. See "Calvinist Thomism," *Viator* 7 (1976): 448. See also David S. Sytsma, "Sixteenth-Century Reformed Reception of Aquinas," in *The Oxford Handbook of the Reception of Aquinas*, ed. Matthew Levering and Marcus Plested (Oxford: Oxford University Press, 2021), 121–43.

48. *CCR*, 1.4 and obs. 1.4. On three instances, Zanchi cites the apocryphal books of Sirach and the Wisdom of Solomon as support.

49. *CCR*, p. 16.

true apostolicity but rather "a continuation of apostolic doctrine."[50] Such is the faith to which Zanchi's confession endeavored to bear witness with the church to God's glory.

But if the *Confession* is a confession, it is also something more. As Gwalther quipped, "It seems too long to be useful."[51] Indeed, Zanchi's confession is substantially longer than any of the confessions adopted by Reformed churches in the period, including the widely accepted Second Helvetic Confession, which Zanchi had previously suggested harmonizing with the Augsburg. It is debatable whether Zanchi's confession was too long to be useful for its intended purpose, but as a digestible, comprehensive, and systematic expression of late-sixteenth-century Reformed theology, it is altogether useful. While it is a fraction of the length of his scholastic treatises on the major heads of doctrine, "it can be read as a compendium of his theology and is surely more than a brief introduction of the faith to children."[52] Zanchi himself described the confession as a "summary of the whole of Christian doctrine."[53]

The Content of the Confession

Generally speaking, the *Confession* pursues catholicity by placing itself within the long tradition of Christian theology stretching back to the fathers of the Eastern and Western churches as well as within the developing Reformed theological tradition. For Zanchi, these were one, and he saw no reason to diverge from them so long as they converged with Scripture. He saw himself and was seen by others as part of a consensus, not as a lone theological genius. And yet, despite his effort to speak with that consensus, certain emphases, arguments, and conclusions in his *Confession* ought to be noted.

---

50. *CCR*, 24.6.
51. Gwalther to Beza, January 11, 1579, in *CB*, 20:3.
52. Beck, "Reformed Confessions and Scholasticism," 23. Along similar lines, Beck notes, "Indeed, the scholastic treatises arguably present with much more detail largely the same doctrine that is concisely summarized in [Zanchi's] confession" (p. 24). For the erroneous notion that the confession was intended for children, see Schmidt, "Girolamo Zanchi," 84.
53. *CCR*, pp. 26, 29.

Some readers, for instance, may be surprised at how little attention Zanchi devotes to the doctrine of predestination. The frequently reprinted eighteenth-century work *Absolute Predestination*, published by Augustus Toplady under Zanchi's name, has prepared centuries of readers to find the Italian's theology dominated by that topic.[54] And yet the *Confession*'s chapters on predestination, providence, and the freedom of the will are relatively short and less dominant over the whole system than Toplady's work might lead us to expect.

Similarly, in the second half of the twentieth century, Otto Gründler argued that Zanchi traded the warm, Christ-centered piety of Calvin for a cold, rationalistic systematizing. "Indeed," he averred, "it would be possible to present Zanchi's teaching on scripture, God, creation, providence, and predestination without ever mentioning Christ, and they would suffer little or no distortion from doing so." Further, "In the theology of Zanchi…one observes a clear shift from the Christocentric orientation of Calvin and Luther toward a metaphysics of causality that henceforth would characterize Reformed orthodoxy."[55] As the *Confession* demonstrates, however, this description misses the mark by a wide margin.[56]

In fact, rather than viewing the *Confession* as focused on predestination or a "metaphysics of causality," we ought to view it in terms of union and communion—the union of the eternal Son of God with man in His incarnation, His spiritual union with every one of the faithful, and consummately, the church's union, body and soul, with her Bridegroom at His return. Because God took on flesh for us and for our salvation, we can have fellowship with Him and, in Him, with one another. While the *Confession* does not have as many explicitly pastoral passages as do some of

---

54. Jerom [sic] Zanchi, *The Doctrine of Absolute Predestination Stated and Asserted with a Preliminary Discourse on the Divine Attributes*, trans. Augustus Toplady (London: Joseph Gurney, 1769).

55. Otto Gründler, "Zanchi, Girolamo," in *The Oxford Encyclopedia of the Reformation* (Oxford University Press, 2005), 305–6. Gründler wrote these words shortly before his death in 2004, but they reflect claims he had been making for over forty years.

56. For a devastating critique of Gründler's selective use of quotations in his 1961 dissertation on Zanchi, see Norman Shepherd, "Zanchius on Saving Faith," *Westminster Theological Journal* 36, no. 1 (Fall 1973): 31–47.

Zanchi's other works,[57] it is a richly devotional book insofar as it points readers toward Christ again and again. This, at least in part, is the reason why so many of the longest and most important chapters focus not on predestination or the divine decree but on Christ the Redeemer (ch. 11), union with Christ (ch. 12), the Lord's Supper (ch. 16), justification (ch. 19), and the church (esp. chs. 24–25).

Indeed, the *Confession*'s approach to ecclesiology deserves particular attention, not least because it proved unsettling to some of Zanchi's Reformed contemporaries. Lambert Daneau, for instance, wrote that the confession would satisfy him "altogether," if only Zanchi would remove the bit at the end about "archbishops and the hierarchy."[58] And in the 1599 Legat translation, the translator (or publisher) quietly removed several sections related to polity.

As was standard among the Reformed, Zanchi acknowledged that in the apostolic church, the "ministers of the Word were at first equally called shepherds, bishops, and elders since they were also of equal authority." Naturally, he viewed this as normative, asserting that "the closer we move toward apostolic simplicity, even in the ordering of ministers, the more we approve of it." Nevertheless, and despite being strongly opposed to papal supremacy, he defended "what was set up with regard to archbishops" and patriarchs in the pre-Nicene church.[59] His argument on this point was twofold. First, this structure was endorsed by the early church and the ecumenical councils, which gave it a weightiness that he could not easily ignore. Second, he argued that the origins of the ecclesiastical hierarchy are to be located not in Scripture but rather in custom. That is to say, he understood the hierarchy he described to be, at its best, an effort to implement 1 Corinthians 14—"Let all things be done decently and in order" in the churches, for "God is not the author of confusion but of peace" (vv. 40, 33)—rather than a direct command from God's Word.

---

57. For Zanchi's thoroughgoing pastoral application of the doctrine of God in one of his most densely scholastic treatises, see O'Banion, "Jerome Zanchi, the Application of Theology, and the Rise of the English Practical Divinity Tradition."
58. Daneau to Zanchi, May 11, 1580, in *OOT*, 3/8:197.
59. CCR, 25.11.

Although Daneau urged the removal of this material from the confession, Zanchi chose to defend and develop it instead. In an extended observation, he maintained a commitment to this position and argued that it fit within the mainstream of Reformed theology by quoting a lengthy section of Bucer's *Praelectiones in epistolam ad Ephesios* (Basil, 1562).[60] Therein Bucer endorsed not only patriarchs but also bishops, suffragan bishops, metropolitan bishops, and seven different clerical orders. In fact, Zanchi even suggested that many Protestant churches that had ostensibly rid themselves of bishops and archbishops had actually retained them under other names or allowed them to operate in an unofficial capacity. "Do you mean," he asked with mock astonishment, that some churches that eliminated the terminology of episcopy "are nevertheless accustomed to having a few who are of the first rank, to whom almost all the power generally belongs?"[61] It is a question worth pondering, especially in this age, when many seek influence in the church via "platforms" of informal authority.

Another noteworthy position within Zanchi's ecclesiology is his attitude toward the Roman Church. The Reformed had always recognized that a true church existed under the papacy and had continued even in Rome despite that church's many errors.[62] But Zanchi went a step further, recognizing as he did that the Roman Church continued to be Christ's.[63] Certainly he had no doubt that Rome, which once "outshone

---

60. See also Joannes à Lasco, *Opera, tam edita quam inedita*, ed. Abraham Kuyper (Amsterdam: Frederic Muller, 1866), 57; John Knox, "First Book of Discipline," in *The History of the Reformation of Religion in Scotland* (Glasgow: Blackie & Fullarton, 1831), 495–98.

61. CCR, obs. 25.10 and 11.

62. John Calvin, *Institutes*, 4.2.11; Heinrich Bullinger, *The Decades of Henry Bullinger*, ed. Thomas Harding (Cambridge: Cambridge University Press, 1852), 3:65, 72–76 (5th decade; sermon 2); Theodore Beza, *A Discourse of the True and Visible Markes of the Catholique Churche*, 1582, sig. g[3]v–4v; and Theodore Beza, *Tractationes theologicae* (Geneva, 1582), 3:192 (Beza to Andreas Dudith, June 18, 1570).

63. Zanchi was not the only Reformed theologian to make this point. See, for example, John Calvin and Jacopo Sadoleto, *A Reformation Debate: John Calvin & Jacopo Sadoleto*, ed. John C. Olin (New York: Fordham University Press, 2000), 75; Amandus Polanus, *The Substance of Christian Religion* (London, 1600), 388–89; Polanus, *Syntagma theologiae christianae* (Geneva, 1617), 535; Turretin, *Institutes of Elenctic Theology*, 3:122

all the churches on earth by her extraordinary example of Christian piety" such that she was universally regarded as "the mother of all churches, and with good reason," now "lies dead" in the darkness into which she has been cast by "God's just judgment."[64] Yet, he claimed that she was still "Christ's church," even if she resembles the Israelites under Jeroboam.[65] And, in a section of the confession that has not been included in any previous translation, he noted that much of what Rome taught was correct, especially as regards the doctrine of God, Christology, and eternal judgment. Even her teachings on the sacraments and salvation were not altogether wrong.[66]

Zanchi clearly recognized that the Protestant separation from the Roman Church was necessary, since the latter "rejects the faith, does not hold to the foundation of apostolic preaching, and does not continue in Christ's teachings."[67] But his reluctance to close the door on reconciliation is also apparent. In a uniquely personal moment, noting that Protestants had withdrawn from Rome only in the hope of returning to her if she returned to the apostolic foundations of the faith, Zanchi and his "entire family" begged "the Lord Jesus with all [their] soul that this might ultimately happen. For what could any pious person wish for more than to live out [their] lives to the end in that place where [they] were also reborn by baptism?"—but, of course, this was only desirable "in the Lord."

(topic 18, q.14, §3); and Petrus van Mastricht, *Theoretico-practica theologia* (Amsterdam, 1724), 873–74 (bk. 7, ch. 1, §25).

64. CCR, p. 5.

65. Zanchi makes a similar point in the preface to his *De natura Dei seu de divinis attributis libri quinque* (Heidelberg, 1577), sig. b3v.

66. CCR, p. 6. Richard Muller echoes Zanchi on this point, noting that "The Reformation, in spite of its substantial contribution to the history of doctrine and the shock it delivered to theology and the church in the sixteenth century, was not an attack upon the whole of medieval theology or upon Christian tradition. The Reformation assaulted a limited spectrum of doctrinal and practical abuses with the intention of reaffirming the values of the historical church catholic. Thus, the mainstream Reformers reconstructed the doctrines of justification and the sacraments and then modified their ideas of the *ordo salutis* and of the church accordingly; but they did not alter the doctrines of God, creation, providence, and Christ and they maintained the Augustinian tradition concerning predestination, human nature, and sin." PRRD, 1:97.

67. CCR, 24.18.

Zanchi's family then formally bore witness to this desire "to the whole of Christ's church for all eternity."[68]

Zanchi's desire for reconciliation with Rome is the more striking when we recall that he had fled Italy because that same Roman Church had sought his arrest and, potentially, would have facilitated his execution. By that point, many of his friends had already been driven into exile; others had been or would be arrested or killed. In this light, his desire for unity in the gospel, even with Rome, shows something of the sanctified refinement that a life of sojourning had worked in him.

A similar point can be made of his attempt to formulate language that he hoped would heal the breach in Christology and the sacraments between the Lutheran and Reformed churches.[69] Zanchi had suffered much in Strasbourg under the attacks of hard-liners. Johann Marbach, the city's chief preacher and Zanchi's academic superior, had openly questioned his reputation, orthodoxy, and salvation. Even after being exonerated of theological error, he still found it impossible to continue there. Yet he remained personally willing to "beg all Christians" by "the Lord Jesus Christ" to "put aside the vain dreams of individual men as well as the influences, hatreds, and enmities characteristic of the flesh," and instead to embrace "the ancient church's sure and wholesome doctrine and Christian love" in order that all might "unite in one faith and holy friendship, just as there is for us all one God, one Mediator, one baptism, one hope of our calling to God's glory, the church's edification, and our souls' salvation."[70] The path toward reconciliation with the Lutherans that he proposed proved unacceptable. Yet, considering the indignities Zanchi had suffered, his search for unity was no small thing and suggests the importance that he placed upon the Christian's obligation to seek unity within the household of faith.

---

68. CCR, 24.19.

69. CCR, obs. 16.9. It is notable that while Zanchi often criticizes theological positions with Lutherans in mind, he never mentions them by name (collectively or individually) in the confession. Only once (in thesis 65 of his 1581 disputation on Christ's resurrection, ascension, and session) does he refer to the "Ubiquitarians."

70. CCR, p. 344.

Zanchi was very conscious of his own fallibility, and he expected his theology to be engaged critically according to the touchstone of Scripture. But whatever its imperfections, much that he wrote is worthy of serious reflection. Amid the many errors and dangers besetting the church of his day, he offered Christian readers a picture of his living faith, hoping especially that it would stir up his own children "more and more to serious study of the Holy Scriptures, to growth in the knowledge of truth, and, consequently, to persevering in piety."[71] May this generation likewise be stirred up by Zanchi's "summary of the whole of Christian doctrine," and as we engage with this faithful elder in Christ's church who drew deeply from those who came before him, may we (like Zanchi) leave a faithful legacy of theological reflection wedded to godly piety for those who come after us.

---

71. *CCR*, p. 27.

The Confession of the Christian Religion

By Girolamo Zanchi

Which he has now, finally, at the age of seventy, arranged to bring to light in his own name and that of his family.

To
Ulysses Martinengo,
Count of Barco and Patrician of Venice

Rom. 10[:10]
With the heart one believes unto righteousness, but with the mouth confession is made unto salvation

Let everything be submitted to the true judgment of the true catholic church.

Confession of the Christian Religion
Dedicatory Letter

Girolamo Zanchi wishes grace and peace to Ulysses Martinengo, Count of Barco.

No one is unaware, noble Count, that the whole Christian world is confused and perturbed—neither how it is confused nor how great is that confusion—in this age of ours. This is not merely the case for everything in general but specifically for the church and with regard to religion, and there is not a good man out there who, astonished by these divine judgments, fails to mourn, nor is there a pious man who fails to lament.

Even as the sun shines down on us from heaven, so by God's singular kindness has a great light of truth shone forth from the Holy Scriptures upon our generation, spreading far and wide through several faithful servants of Christ.[1] Yet, how many and of what sort are the fogs

---

1. Although he does not name them, Zanchi certainly had in mind Luther, Zwingli, Calvin, and other reformers. Although Zanchi refused to be saddled with any "sectarian" label (e.g., Lutheran, Zwinglian, Calvinist), he had great esteem for these men. As he commented in the introductory letter to the second edition of his *Miscellaneorum libri tres* (Neustadt, 1582), "Certainly the spirit by which many are moved today to write, slander, defend errors, kindle fires anew, and disturb the churches is not the Spirit of Christ. Rather, I am convinced that it is a spirit—I will not say a Lutheran spirit (lest I ascribe this ignominy to that holy man, Luther) or a ubiquitarian spirit in the same way that they claim we are stirred by a Zwinglian or Sacramentarian spirit—but it is a spirit of dizziness whereby God punishes the very serious injury done more and more to Christ on a daily basis. Indeed, the Father willed that we should give this honor only to Christ: that we simply believe and acknowledge Him alone to be the only One among men and among all the spirits created by Him, who cannot err.… Every man (who is not

of errors? How many and how terrible are the clouds of heresies that have been whipped up and dredged out of the infernal abyss by more than a few scoundrels and diabolical ministers, that darkness might fall over this divine light?[2]

I am not speaking of tyrants right now, who have at all times advanced all of their weapons, all their power, and all the resources of their principalities. Even now they advance and strain toward this end: to use their iron for the destruction and utter overthrow of those candles that continue to display this light to some extent—albeit, of course, in *jars of clay* [2 Cor. 4:7]. This they do to overthrow and altogether extinguish all light of divine wisdom and in order that a hellish darkness called forth from the underworld might take its place, advancing and occupying everything everywhere.

All of us vividly recall everything that has been perpetrated and carried out in these wretched times of ours on this account. We recall the number and kinds of murders—almost too many to be counted—that have happened in many places and the frequent attempts made at other times. But you yourself know better than we do what the Devil recently attempted in your valleys and by whom he attempted it. Yet thanks to God's protection, that murder did not go according to the plan of the wicked. And the Lord Himself, who dwells in the heavens, and who, out of His incredible benevolence toward us, so often reduces the iniquitous counsels of the wicked to nothing (when doing so is expedient for the church and when tyrants least anticipate the frustration of their long and carefully concocted plans), and who is accustomed, as it were, to dispersing empty clouds in wonderful ways, knows what that Satan-of-a-thousand-artifices is currently and constantly devising for one and the same end. The Lord knows what counsels Satan is stirring up and what plans he is laying, what weapons he is preparing, what wars he is plotting against pious princes and magistrates who desire this heavenly light to

---

also God) is a liar. God, however, is (alone, simply) true. Christ alone is the Teacher we must honor, the only One who cannot err." *OOT*, 3/7: sig. ¶4r–v.

2. Zanchi's wordplay, which draws together the second half of this paragraph, does not come across in translation: fogs (*nebulae*) of errors, clouds (*nubes*) of heresies, and scoundrels (*nebulones*).

illuminate their own dominions all the more brightly and who, having banished the darkness, undertake to shine that light both far and wide.

Witness the Pharaohs, Sennacheribs, Hamans, Antiochi, Julians, Valenses, and other similar enemies of the church. For the promise stands that the gates of hell will not prevail against her [Matt. 16:18]. But let us set tyrants to one side and return to the wretchedly divided body of the Christian commonwealth. We observe that the body of all who profess and call upon Christ as true God and true man and sole Redeemer of the world has been torn to bits, with various groups stubbornly defending various errors—some, indeed, defending lots of errors, and serious ones at that; others defending fewer errors or lesser ones. On this account, each group persecutes the others with more hatred than for Vatinius and with more ferocity than Nero, and so they lay waste to one another.[3] I ask: can anyone see this, can anyone hear it and reflect upon it in his soul and, unless utterly devoid of piety, fail to be moved to the greatest of sorrow, lament, and shed tears?

Formerly and from ancient times, the Roman Church was much celebrated for the great splendor of her piety, heavenly doctrine, divine worship, Christian discipline, and constancy in faith against all heretics. And just as the sun outshines all the stars in heaven, so she outshone all the churches on earth by her extraordinary example of Christian piety. And she outshone them by such a margin that everywhere she was called the mother of all churches, and with good reason. But later, by God's just judgment, into what and how many kinds of darkness was she thrown, as if cast out of heaven? Even now, she lies dead therein. Whoever cannot see this, amidst such bright gospel light, is blinder than a mole.

Moreover, this is no novel turn of events, since we see that the same thing first befell the Israelite Church, and then the Christians in the East and in all of Greece as well.[4] Nevertheless, everyone (except those who

---

3. Publius Vatinius (b. ca. 95 BC) was a particularly despised Roman statesman whom Cicero harangued in his *Against Vatinius*. Nero (r. 54–68) was the Roman emperor who initiated the persecution that led to the deaths of the apostles Peter and Paul.

4. The remainder of this paragraph is not included in the 1605 English translation. The Ralph Winterton edition includes neither the dedicatory letter to Martinengo nor the letter to the reader.

refuse) sees this bit of good as yet preserved in the Roman Church by some special and unfathomable kindness of God: there is no doubt that she steadfastly continues constant and firm even now, as she always has, in the true doctrines of God and of the person of our Lord Jesus Christ, and that she baptizes in the name of the Father and of the Son and of the Holy Spirit, and knows and preaches Christ as the sole Redeemer of the world and as the future Judge of the living and the dead, who will take those who truly are faithful into eternal life with Him but who will cast unbelievers and the wicked into eternal fire with the Devil and his angels. It is for this reason that, even now, I will acknowledge the Roman Church to be Christ's church. But what kind of church is it? The same sort as the Church of Israel was under Jeroboam and the same sort as was subsequently described by Hosea and other prophets as well, for at no time did it recover from its fornications. So much for the Roman Church.

But as for those churches that were compelled to withdraw from the Roman Church on account of her pertinacity and tyranny in the matters wherein she ended up apostatizing[5] from the apostles, what horrendous heresies have Satan's ministers dragged out of hell and foisted upon some of them? Anabaptism, Libertinism, Arianism, Samosatianism, Marcionism, Eutychianism, Nestorianism, and what not? Yes, even atheism is advancing. Oh, what a pain! Christ's faithful ministers have withstood all of them and have restrained these diabolical doctrines in many places. Having reformed their churches on the basis of the pure doctrine of the gospel, they have kept (and, by God's blessing, continue

---

Excerpts of these comments were, however, included in Richard Hooker, *A Learned Discourse of Iustification, Workes, and How the Foundation of Faith Is Overthrowne* (Oxford, 1612), 46–47, which was based upon a sermon preached by Hooker in March 1586. If this reference to Zanchi's letter to Martinengo was included in Hooker's original sermon (as opposed to having been inserted later, before publication), then Hooker, like Johann Wilhelm Stucki (1542–1607) of Zurich, must have possessed an early version of the confession (one that still lacked the letter to the reader) by that date. On the earliest edition of the *Confession*, see Baschera and Moser, "Introduction," in *De religione*, 1:19–20. Stucki had a copy in hand by August 1586, and his feedback led Zanchi to add the letter to the reader. See Stucki to Zanchi, August 29, 1586, and Zanchi to Stucki, December 9, 1586, in *OOT*, 3/8:71–73.

5. ἀποστασίαν.

to keep) their churches immune to these plagues, so that no friendship exists between such sects and us.[6]

At the same time, it is nevertheless impossible to uproot all these weeds everywhere. Numerous plagues continue running riot everywhere, and many evil spirits enter the world on an ongoing basis. What, then, should the Christian man—one who sets his heart upon God's glory, upon the salvation of his own and his neighbor's souls, and upon a good reputation in the catholic church (for being known and reputed in the catholic church as Christ's true member is of some significance)—what should he do? What, I say, should that Christian man do amidst such confusion of matters, such differences of opinion, such a multitude of heresies, and such diversity of religions? If possible, I will employ a metaphor to demonstrate my way of thinking, which accords with the Holy Scriptures.

Imagine that a massive and overwhelmingly powerful enemy army advanced into a certain region and laid waste to the whole of it in such a way that there was no quick or easy way to drive it out. What course of action ought the region's inhabitants to pursue to keep themselves and their children safe?

1. First, they should retreat within and remain behind city walls until, with God's help, the whole region has been freed of enemies.

2. Next, everyone should immediately undertake to gather provisions— let them gather as much as possible—lest, being besieged, they either die of hunger or end up surrendering themselves to the enemy.

3. But *unless the Lord watches over the city, he who keeps watch does so in vain* [Ps. 127:1]. For this reason, everyone should call upon the Lord with fervent prayers so that He might daily attend to, protect, and preserve us.

---

6. The sects that Zanchi has in mind here seem to be those named above—Anabaptists, Libertines, Arians, Samosatians, Marcionites, Eutychians, Nestorians, and atheists. It is noteworthy that the roots of most, if not all, of these groups extended back to the early church; Zanchi sees their modern instantiations arising in continuity with their erroneous progenitors.

4. And to that end, they should take care that all citizens constantly cultivate brotherly faithfulness, love, peace, and concord among themselves. For, as the Lord Jesus was in the habit of saying, every kingdom divided against itself is desolate [Luke 11:17]. Even pagans testify that *Amidst harmony, small things flourish, but the greatest things go to ruin amidst disharmony* [Sallust, *The Jugurthine War*, 10].[7]

5. Nor should the citizens neglect good health, whereby, hale and hearty, they may be kept in reserve for the use and preservation of the republic to the greatest extent possible. For, especially in times such as this, the sick and unhealthy are of little use to the republic. The fact is that they are often a burden and a hindrance and of no service for prevailing in the fight against the enemy. Thus, everyone must see to his health.

6. To that end, a diligent and vigilant watch is necessary from here on out, lest the enemy—either by sudden force or through treachery and by secret devices—enter the city and attack us while we are carefree and unprepared.

7. But how can one be vigilant without sobriety? For drunkenness and intoxication induce heavy drowsiness, which leaves no place for vigilance. Thus, sobriety is necessary, lest our enemies overcome us while wine and sleep overtake us.

8. However, could anything be more necessary than for us always to have weapons both for defending and protecting ourselves from the enemies' darts as well as for slaying and repelling them? Consequently, in addition to strong city walls and well-defended bulwarks, the citizens themselves must also be armed at all times.

---

7. [Sallust, The Jugurthine War, 10]: Sallust, *Catiline's War, The Jugurthine War, Histories*, trans. A. J. Woodman (London: Penguin, 2007), 57. Here and following, all footnotes that refer to extrabiblical in-text citations—whether they be parenthetical citations original to Zanchi or bracketed citations inserted by the translator—will begin with an underlined citation label that reproduces the relevant portion of the in-text citation. This is meant to make the references as clear and accessible as possible, particularly when Zanchi includes more than one source within a given parenthetical citation.

9. But nothing more destructive and dangerous can befall a republic, especially in wartime, than to have friends of the enemy in the city, indisputably false and traitorous men whose words pretend friendship with the citizens and profess agreement in all matters but who, in fact, collude with the enemy. Therefore, every effort should be made to inquire diligently into who is in the city, what they are doing, what kind of life they live, and where they dwell. And if they are found to deviate from the citizens' joint profession, life, and customs, let them be noted, examined, corrected, punished, and expelled from the city.

10. But nothing can leave a greater stain of infamy upon citizens and better prove that they deserve intense suffering than rebelling against their prince, disgracefully allowing themselves either to be enticed by the enemy's promises and bribes or even to be terrified by his threats. Just so, there is conversely nothing that confers greater honor or is more useful and deserving of higher praise, more worthy of reward, than when, having publicly avowed your loyalty, you proceed resolutely to fight to the death for hearth and home in faithful service to your prince and patria. Thus, steadfastness in loyalty to your republic or prince and public profession of that loyalty unto death is necessary.

I liken these defended cities to the church, which, in time past, was *built upon the foundation of the apostles and the prophets* and, subsequently, was restored and truly reformed on the basis of the gospel [Eph. 2:20]. The church retains the firm foundations of apostolic doctrine contained in the Holy Scriptures and understands and explains those foundations according to the orthodox interpretations of the ancient fathers.

The church has always been inclined to summarize these foundations with the outline of doctrine known as the Catechism, which primarily includes the Apostles' Creed, the Lord's Prayer, and the Decalogue. The Creed briefly shows both what we should believe and in whom all hope of salvation must be placed. The Lord's Prayer lucidly teaches both whom we are to call upon and for what we should pray, as well as the reasons why we are to call upon God alone and why, whatever we ask for, we should ask only of Him—for His alone are the kingdom, power, and glory, which clause kindles faith for the asking. No less clearly than briefly, the Decalogue directs us how we should behave before God and with what form of worship we should honor Him. It also directs how we should live with our neighbor and how we must die to ourselves, which is to say, we must always deny our desire for anything that stands in opposition to God's law. To these three principal components of the Catechism is added a fourth: the doctrine of the sacraments, which is indicated synecdochally[8] by the word "baptism" in the Great Creed, as it is called.[9]

Along with the whole of the ancient church, we do not hesitate to call all these, which have been summarily gathered together on the basis of the Holy Scriptures and rendered into a brief compendium, the foundations of the entire Christian religion. Heretics, however, do not come right out and deny these foundations when they hear them. Instead, they make a practice of distorting them by interpreting components of the Catechism falsely in accordance with their heresies and twisting them besides. This is why we must understand and explain those heads of doctrine only in the way that the ancient church also explained them, in harmony with the Holy Scriptures and on the basis of the common confession, especially in the most excellent councils, so that the true church can be distinguished from the conventicles of heretics.[10]

I might ask, for the sake of example, what could or can be said more robustly, more reliably, and more clearly about the article in the Creed on the person of Christ than what was explained on the basis of the Holy Scriptures by the pious fathers at the Synods of Nicaea,

---

8. Συνεκδοχικῶς.

9. That is, the fourth-century Nicene (or, more properly, the Nicene-Constantinopolitan) Creed, which refers to "one baptism for the remission of sins."

10. Zanchi's point seems simply to be that, rather than denying the church's creeds outright, heretics pay them lip service in order to lay claim to a certain catholicity and fellowship with the true church while simultaneously "interpreting" and "twisting" those formulations in ways that strike at the foundations of the Christian religion. Zanchi's solution is to emphasize the importance of following not just the form of the words bequeathed by the fathers but also their interpretation of those words, especially as defined by the "most excellent councils" and, of course, in accordance with the Scriptures, so that true churches can discern these heresies (and rebut them).

Constantinople, Ephesus, and Chalcedon (with the addition of the fifth and sixth ecumenical councils[11]) against Arius, Paul of Samosata, Apollinaris, Nestorius, Eutyches, and the Monothelites? Therefore, we can be certain that whoever teaches something different about the person of Christ than what those councils teach does not rightly hold fast to this particular foundation of the Christian religion.

Again, consider that particular foundation of the Christian religion that is the grace and benefit of Christ. It begins with His eternal love toward us and His gracious election of us as participants of redemption and eternal salvation, but it progresses to the gracious provision of that very redemption—effectual calling, justification, sanctification, the gift of perseverance in faith, yes, even the glorious resurrection itself and eternal life—which is what was accomplished once for all on the cross. What could be more richly or reliably said about this foundation than what the Councils of Africa, Milan, Orange, and elsewhere explained against the Pelagians from the Holy Scriptures and what Augustine and others as well examined and set down in the many books they wrote against those same Pelagians?

With regard to the holy catholic church, what do you need to know that Augustine has not explained from the foundation of the Holy Scriptures in language that is both rich and clear, especially in his books against the Donatists but elsewhere as well? Yet, it is of the greatest importance to know what Christ's true church is and where it is, since *Outside of the church there is no salvation* [Cyprian, Letter to Jubaianus, §21],[12] so this is hardly the least important of the articles of the Christian faith.

Likewise, regarding the thing signified, if one is willing to be content with the simple truth, what is clearer than the doctrine taught by

---

11. That is, the second and third Councils of Constantinople (553 and 680–681). Zanchi notably does not recognize the second Council of Nicaea (787), which restored the veneration of sacred images and anathematized those who opposed them.

12. [Cyprian, Letter to Jubaianus, §21]: Cyprian, *Letters (1–81)*, trans. Rose Bernard Donna, Fathers of the Church 51 (Washington, D.C.: Catholic University of America Press, 1964), 281 (*ANF*, 5:384). This letter is variously numbered as either 73 or 74 in modern editions.

the ancient fathers—Justin, Irenaeus, Tertullian, Cyprian, and especially Augustine, on the basis of the sacred writings—which they have bequeathed to us in their writings? Someone says, *Just as Jesus Christ, having been made flesh by the Word of God, had flesh and blood, so also have we learned that, by the word of prayer and thanksgiving, the consecrated food is thereby made the flesh and blood of that incarnate Jesus, and this in accordance with Christ's own words, "This is my body"* (Justin Martyr, *The First Apology*, ch. 66).[13] And yet, Christ (that is, the Word[14]) was made flesh without any change to His flesh but only by hypostatic union. Therefore, neither is the bread made Christ's body by somehow being transubstantiated into His body. Rather, the bread is Christ's body only by union—indeed, not by a physical union of some sort or by a hypostatic union but merely by a sacramental union. Again, Justin says, *From that nourishment*, that is, of the blessed bread, *our flesh and blood is nourished by transformation*, that is, by its transformation *in Christ*, obviously.[15] Therefore, the transformation[16] that occurs in the Supper is not a transformation of the bread into Christ's body, as some have incorrectly understood it, nor is it a transformation of Christ into us. Rather, it is a transformation of us into Christ on account of engrafting.

---

13. Justin Martyr, *The First Apology*, ch. 66: Zanchi quotes here from the writings of Justin Martyr (d. 163), which had been marshalled by previous commentators to substantiate the patristic roots of the doctrine of transubstantiation. Zanchi intends to show that Justin was claiming that the bread becomes Christ's body not by transubstantiation but rather by sacramental union.

The modern translation of the pertinent passage in Justin's *First Apology* renders it as follows: "For we do not receive these things [that is, the elements of the Supper] as common bread nor common drink; but in like manner as Jesus Christ our Savior having been incarnate by God's logos took both flesh and blood for our salvation, so also we have been taught that the food eucharistized through the word of prayer that is from Him, from which our blood and flesh are nourished by transformation, is the flesh and blood of that Jesus who became incarnate." Justin Martyr, *The First and Second Apologies*, trans. Leslie W. Barnard, Ancient Christian Writers (New York: Paulist Press, 1997), 70 (*ANF*, 1:185; *FOTC*, 6:105–6).

14. Λόγος.

15. ἐξ ἧς (τροφῆς) αἷμα καὶ σάρκες κατὰ μεταβολὴν τρέφονται ἡμῶν. Zanchi provides the Greek original for the passage from Justin, supplying the word τροφῆς (nourishment). The phrase "in Christ" is emphasized in the original.

16. Μεταβολήν.

This accords with Augustine's reading of what Christ said when he discusses the reception of the Eucharist: *I will not be changed into you but you will be changed into Me* [*Confessions*, 7.16].[17] And again, referring to the Eucharistic meal, Justin says, *No one is admitted to it except he who believes that our doctrine is true, who has been washed in the laver of regeneration unto the remission of sins, and who lives accordingly, as Christ taught* [*First Apology*, ch. 66].[18] Therefore, neither infidels nor heretics should be admitted to the Supper, nor those who have yet to receive the baptism of Christ, nor those who live in such manifest sins that they give the church no indication of their repentance.

Another church father says that the eucharist consists of two things: one terrestrial, the other celestial. Yet he calls the bread terrestrial, even though it is sanctified. Why so? Because it is from the earth and because it exists on the earth and because it is eaten with a terrestrial mouth. But Christ's body is a celestial thing, not on account of its substance being from heaven but partly because it was assumed into the unity of the person of the Word and partly because it is endowed with celestial qualities (Irenaeus[, *Against Heresies*], bk. 4, ch. 34 [that is, ch. 18.5]).[19] For although it is everywhere by hypostasis, which is *the Word* itself, nevertheless, by its own essence,[20] Christ's body is only in heaven and not on earth. From this it also follows that it is eaten neither by terrestrial men nor with the body's terrestrial teeth but only by those who are begotten

---

17. [*Confessions*, 7.16]: Augustine, *The Confessions*, ed. John E. Rotelle, trans. Maria Boulding, The Works of Saint Augustine: A Translation for the 21st Century I/1 (Hyde Park, N.Y.: New City Press, 1997), 173 (*NPNF*1, 1:109).

18. [*First Apology*, ch. 66]: The modern translation renders the passage: "And this food is called among us eucharist, of which no one is allowed to partake except one who believes that the things which we teach are true, and has received the washing that is for the remission of sins and for rebirth, and who so lives as Christ handed down." Justin Martyr, *The First and Second Apologies*, 70 (*ANF*, 1:185; *FOTC*, 6:105–6).

19. Irenaeus[, *Against Heresies*], bk. 4, ch. 34 [that is, ch. 18.5]: *ANF*, 1:486 renders the pertinent passage: "For as the bread, which is produced from the earth, when it receives the invocation of God, is no longer common bread, but the Eucharist, consisting of two realities, earthly and heavenly; so also our bodies, when they receive the Eucharist, are no longer corruptible, having the hope of the resurrection to eternity."

20. Οὐσία.

from on high,[21] who bear the image of the heavenly Man, and who eat in a celestial manner—by mind and spirit.[22] And yet the very bodies of the faithful, although they eat only that which is terrestrial, also participate in that which is celestial unto their own glorious resurrection and are nourished by it, as Irenaeus himself clearly explains in that same passage [1 Cor. 15:40–49].

Such is your piety, learning, and prudence, Count Ulysses, that I do not doubt but that, based on what I said from the Creed about the four distinct components of Christian doctrine, you are easily able to grasp what ought to be concluded about the whole. The sum of it is this: Christ's true churches (and, thus, what we rightly call the walled cities of Christ's kingdom) are those that, professing the Holy Scriptures in general and the Catechism universally received in particular, so reverence the ancient church and the ancient fathers and maintain such fellowship with those living on in heaven and have such communion with them that they are prone to diverge from them neither in dogmas[23] altogether necessary to the faith nor in their interpretation of the Holy Scriptures. Rather, they do so only at length, when they are compelled to dissent from the fathers by the most evident words and testimonies of the Holy

---

21. ἄνωθεν.

22. Rendering *mente* as "mind" does not really capture the full scope of the word. With reference to Augustine's use of *mente*, Edmund Hill comments, "God being truth and goodness, we really have to say that he is the very mold or structure, the very cast of the human self, of what Augustine calls the mens or mind." Edmund Hill, "Introduction," in *The Trinity*, by Augustine, ed. John E. Rotelle, trans. Edmund Hill, The Works of Saint Augustine: A Translation for the 21st Century I/5 (Hyde Park, N.Y.: New City Press, 1991), 25. In other words, for those who followed in the Augustinian tradition, the *mens* is the deepest part of humanity that, in some particular sense, bears the imprint of God's image.

23. The word translated here—*dogmatibus*, as opposed to *doctrinabus*—suggests not just teachings ("doctrines") but teachings that are to be obeyed according to command, or "a doctrine or teaching absolutely necessary to the faith, in the strictest sense a doctrine established by an ecumenical council of the church of the first five centuries." Richard A. Muller, *Dictionary of Latin and Greek Theological Terms: Drawn Principally from Protestant Scholastic Theology*, 2nd ed. (Grand Rapids: Baker, 2017), 97. *Dogma* here seems synonymous with the phrase used by Zanchi later in the dedicatory letter when he refers to "doctrine [*doctrina*] that is necessary for salvation."

Scriptures, and moreover, they do so on the basis of necessary consequences derived from the foundations of the faith.

At any rate, the reason chiefly alleged as Nestorius's defect and depicted as the reason for his great heresy is this: out of contempt for the fathers and confidence in his own genius, he interpreted the Holy Scriptures according to his own inclinations. But why speak only of Nestorius? If the length of this letter permitted, I could easily demonstrate from ecclesiastical histories and councils that the same contempt for the fathers and confidence in personal genius and knowledge was the real reason why a great many other men fell into various heresies as well.

For where, I wonder, did all the heretics come from who suddenly appeared in the wake of the most holy Council of Nicaea? Some of them attacked Christ's true and eternal deity; others His true and perfect humanity; others attacked the true and personal union of both natures in one and the same person; and yet others the true nature of their proper distinction. Truly, it arose from that same original error. For, once they dismissed the explanations and interpretations of Holy Scripture concerning the person of Christ given by the Nicene fathers and, conversely, became convinced of their own insights and puffed up by human erudition or eloquence, they presumed to expound—that is, to distort—the Holy Scriptures and the foundations of the faith, each one according to his own interpretation.

What Vigilius wrote about the origins of heresies has bearing here. He said, *But these clouds of empty accusations are, especially, sent forth by those afflicted either by the fault of ignorance or by the vice of contempt. And, having been raised up by the haughtiness of an impudent soul, solely on that account, they look down upon the rules of faith that the fathers handed down long ago so that they can introduce ill-conceived opinions of their own fickleness to the church* (*Against Eutyches*, bk. 1[, §2]).[24]

---

24. *Against Eutyches*, bk. 1[, §2]: Sixteenth-century scholarship understood that the Vigilius who wrote *Five Books Against Eutyches* was the fourth-century martyr Vigilius of Trent. In fact, the author was the African bishop Vigilius of Thapsus (fl. 484). See *PL*, 62:95D, which corresponds with Zanchi's quotation, except that he reads the word *mobilitatum* (fickleness) in place of the *PL*'s *novitatum* (novelty).

My point is proved by the counterbalancing character, trajectory, and words of the orthodox fathers, who, having explained the Holy Scriptures and the foundations of the Christian faith as defined by the ancient fathers, defended the truth of the Christian religion no less happily than faithfully and held onto what was confirmed in the church. Therefore, they attend to those words in the authoritative pronouncements of the fathers: *following in all things the definitions and the rule of the holy fathers, we ourselves also assert the same thing* (Council of Chalcedon[, canon 28]).[25] Thus, nothing is safer than for everyone to secure themselves, as though in well-fortified cities, in these churches in which the Holy Scriptures are expounded according to the analogy of faith and according to the received interpretations of the ancient fathers. Accordingly, their faith is the same as the apostles' and that of the whole of the ancient church.

1. I said that the first duty of the Christian man who desires to keep himself and his family safe from the enemy unto eternal happiness was for him to withdraw into the walled cities of Christ's kingdom and remain there resolutely until, at length, our King arrives in noble fashion after conquering all our enemies, wherever they might be, in order to liberate us and make us safe.

---

25. Council of Chalcedon[, canon 28]: Zanchi quotes elliptically here from canon 28 of the Council of Chalcedon, which granted the see of Constantinople (the "new Rome") equal authority with that of "older" Rome. The decree reads in part: "Following in every way the decrees of the holy fathers and recognising the canon which has recently been read out—the canon of the 150 most devout bishops who assembled in the time of the great Theodosius of pious memory, then emperor, in imperial Constantinople, new Rome—we issue the same decree and resolution concerning the prerogatives of the most holy church of the same Constantinople, new Rome. The fathers rightly accorded prerogatives to the see of older Rome, since that is an imperial city; and moved by the same purpose the 150 most devout bishops apportioned equal prerogatives to the most holy see of new Rome, reasonably judging that the city which is honoured by the imperial power and senate and enjoying privileges equaling older imperial Rome, should also be elevated to her level in ecclesiastical affairs and take second place after her." Norman P. Tanner, ed., *Decrees of the Ecumenical Councils*, vol. 1, *Nicaea I to Lateran V* (Washington, D.C.: Georgetown University Press, 1990), 99.

2. But lacking supplies, who can sustain his life for such a long a time? Our supplies are the daily hearing, reading of, and meditating upon the divine Word, and the receiving of the Lord's Supper when it is offered. For we are nourished, fostered, and do live by both of these—and that on account of Christ our life, whom the Word and sacraments offer and hold forth to us. He who eats this bread, whether through the Word or through the reception of the sacrament, will never die. In Acts [2:42], Christ's disciples were persevering in the apostles' teaching and in the breaking of bread (that is, in the communal love-feasts[26] at which the Lord's Supper was customarily celebrated). Certainly, such heavenly provisions are not ordinarily absent in well-defended cities, but if you do not eat and drink—and thereby sustain your life—what will it benefit you to be behind city walls? Hence, one ought to attend sermons and receive the sacraments and apply oneself to reading the Holy Scriptures.

3. It is also necessary that constant prayers, both public and private, be offered to God, that we might thereby request that which the Lord Jesus commanded us to ask of the Father: everything that tends to His glory or to our and our neighbor's salvation, and that we might be defended from all types of enemies and kept safe in the truth. The Lord says, *"In the day of tribulation, you will call upon Me"* [Ps. 50:15]. But is it not especially in the days of affliction that heresies run riot and tyrants attack the truth? That, then, is the time when the Lord should especially be called upon, and let it be done from faith. And, therefore, says the apostle, *Pray ceaselessly* [1 Thess. 5:17]. And Christ says that one *ought always to pray and not give up* [Luke 18:1]. Moreover, he who prays in that way and who prays from faith, how shall he not receive? Therefore, God adds through the prophet, *And I will hear you* [Jer. 33:3]. *Ask and you shall receive*, as the Lord Jesus likewise said. *Seek and you will find; knock and it will be opened unto you* [Matt. 7:7].

4. But how can one live contentedly in a place where the citizens do not cultivate bonds of friendship among themselves? And, lacking that, how can the city be preserved? Therefore, brotherly affection, peace,

---

26. ἀγάπαις.

and concord must be cultivated. Nothing can be sweeter, nothing more pleasing to God, nothing more effective for the preserving of churches than that affection. Conversely, nothing more quickly destroys churches and all fellowships than jealousy, hatred, pretense, enmity, discord, and domestic disputes. Certainly, love does not flourish where faith is absent, since true faith, as the apostle testifies, *works through love* [Gal. 5:6], and brotherly affection has always been the mark of true Christians. As Christ said, *By this shall men know that you are My disciples, if you love one another* [John 13:35]. The Acts of the apostles teaches this when Luke describes the faithful as having in them *one soul and one heart*, namely, in the Lord [Acts 4:32]. And Tertullian writes that the Romans regularly said of the Christians, *See how they love one another* (*Apology*, ch. 39).[27] For they all assert that Christians are distinguished from non-Christians by this brotherly affection—a genuine sign, as it were, of Christian piety.

5. Moreover, the extent to which it is necessary for the citizen abiding in such a city to maintain good health—both in order to protect themselves against the enemy and, indeed, for the sake of the whole city—has already been stated. In this context, when I refer to spiritual health, what I mean is a good conscience, which is both born from faith and also protects faith, lest faith altogether perish. It is like how bodily life produces good health, and, in turn, good health keeps the body alive.

This is why a good conscience should be maintained. But how in the world does one do that? First, subsequent to proper sorrow, there should be a sturdy trust that the sins we have committed have been freely forgiven on account of Christ. Next, there follows true repentance, that is, an earnest zeal to avoid sins in the future and keep God's commands. Finally, there is a firm resolution that if we stumble on account of our weakness, we will get back up and flee to Christ for forgiveness.

By this method, a good conscience is preserved at all times. Let him who consistently maintains his good health in this way know with

---

27. *Apology*, ch. 39: Tertullian, "Apology," in *Tertullian, Apologetical Works and Minucius Felix, Octavius*, trans. Rudolph Arbesmann, Emily Joseph Daly, and Edwin A. Quain, Fathers of the Church 10 (Washington, D.C.: Catholic University of America Press, 1962), 99 (*ANF*, 3:46).

certainty that God will by no means allow him to perish eternally, that is, he will not ultimately go astray and be ruined with regard to doctrine that is necessary for salvation.[28] For the apostle says to Timothy, *Preserve faith and a good conscience, which some, when they rejected it, made a shipwreck concerning the faith,* meaning, the doctrine of faith [1 Tim. 1:19].

Thus, they who preserve a good conscience will not make a deadly shipwreck of that doctrine that is necessary for salvation, because, on account of His grace, the Lord bestows upon them such things as the treasure of a good conscience and, thus also, the benefit of perseverance in the faith and heavenly doctrine. Therefore, the most prudent thing always—and especially amidst all this religious dissension—is to apply oneself to hearing God's Word and receiving the sacraments, to call upon God, to cultivate friendship with brothers, and to preserve a good conscience for oneself by remaining in churches where God's pure Word resounds and where the solid foundations of the faith are retained according to the interpretations of the fathers.

6. Moreover, who but a complete ignoramus could be ignorant of the critical role that vigilance plays in all this? Where there is nothing whatsoever to fear—as, for example, in heaven—there is no need for vigilance. Instead, one can and ought to live an absolutely carefree life. But who is ignorant of just how dangerous carefree living and idleness are when thieves, bandits, swindlers, flatterers, imposters, traitors, foes, and enemies are about? Therefore, Christ, foreseeing the evils that threatened, told the apostles, *Watch and pray that you do not enter into temptation* [Matt. 26:41]. And Peter says, *Be sober and watch because your adversary the Devil is going about, seeking whom he may devour* [1 Peter 5:8].

But what is this vigilance that the Holy Spirit demands? Everyone knows what it means to be vigilant in soul. Therefore also, insofar as a man is possessed of reason, he is said to be vigilant, when, having banished all idleness of mind and keeping his eyes wide open, he carefully considers what is proposed and sensibly distinguishes between good and

---

28. *Doctrina ad salutem necessaria* (here and below) corresponds to the notion of *dogmata*, which Zanchi previously used to refer to those foundational doctrines that, having been established by the church on the basis of Scripture, must be believed.

bad, between advantages and disadvantages in such a way that his will thereafter rejects what should be rejected and chooses what should be chosen, keeps clear of and wards off what should be avoided and urges on and pursues what should be permitted. So, having shaken off every dream of carnal carelessness, we must vigilantly and diligently be on our guard against the Devil's snares, the charms of the world and the flesh, and the doctrines and tricks of heretics. The Lord Jesus said, *Watch out for false prophets who come to you in sheep's clothing but inwardly are ravaging wolves* [Matt. 7:15].

7. But how can anyone who is dead drunk and intoxicated be vigilant? Hence, sobriety is altogether necessary. Thus, the apostle Peter first said, *Be sober*, before adding, *and be vigilant* (1 Peter 5[:8]). And Paul: *Let us be sober and let us be vigilant* (1 Thess. 5[:6]).[29] But *sober* is the opposite of *intoxicated*, and when we say *sobriety*, we mean *without intoxication*. (The word *intoxication* includes drunkenness itself by way of a synecdoche. For sobriety is the moderate use not only of drink but also of food, so that we might be contented with the quality and portions that suffice for sustaining life and maintaining good health.) Therefore, the Lord Jesus, exhorting unto sobriety, advised against both drunkenness and intoxication when He said, *Lest your hearts be weighed down with drunkenness and intoxication*, clearly exposing with one word how dangerous is intoxication (Luke 21[:34]). For here hearts are so weighed down and sunk into the earth and so choked that they cannot be raised toward heavenly things; toward sincerely calling upon God; toward serious contemplation of divine matters; toward attentive reading, hearing, and true meditation upon the Holy Scriptures; and finally, toward consideration of a divine mystery like the Lord's Supper.

They who are given over to this vice of intoxication have been rendered altogether unfit for all training in piety. And how many falter from the truth on account of their bellies? As many as lack either the desire or the ability to remain vigilant against their enemies and to guard themselves against false prophets and who must, therefore, wretchedly perish

---

29. Here Zanchi reverses the Pauline injunctions ("let us watch and be sober"), presumably for emphasis.

at last. But Christian sobriety extends itself further and wider. Concerning this the apostle says, *Let us be sober, and let us be vigilant* [1 Thess. 5:6], not only in moderating our eating and drinking but also in using everything else that pertains to this age. For God does not want us to be intoxicated with an excessive love for riches, pleasures, honors, friendships, children, wives, indeed our very lives, as though with the sweetest wine. Rather, He wants *those who have wives to be as though they had none, and for those who weep to be as though they wept not, and for those who rejoice to be as though they rejoiced not, and for those who acquire as though they possessed nothing, and for those who make use of this world as though they did not consume* (1 Cor. 7[:29–31]).

Truly, testimony that these sobrieties are needed to preserve faith and true piety is given by those who habitually falter from the faith, because they have an excessive love for the world and the things of this age. Some falter absolutely, so that they never repent, and others do so in part, so that God grants them repentance, as with Demas, concerning whom the apostle wrote, *Demas has abandoned me, loving this present world* (2 Tim. 4[:10]).[30] And the Lord Jesus, after he said, *Beware, lest your hearts be weighed down by drunkenness and intoxication*, then added, regarding another sort of intoxication, *and by the cares of this life, and the last day come upon you* [Luke 21:34]. For where do these cares come from if not from an excessive love of this life?

Yet, there is a third intoxication, which, being the more subtle, is worse than the others, and it pertains to the mind more than to the flesh, namely, the intoxication of carnal wisdom, vain eloquence, and worldly philosophy. For those who, scornful of the simplicity of Christian doctrine, are addicted to, delighted by, and reliant upon such things (as if to wine that has been sweetened and adulterated to improve its color), have little trouble making a shipwreck of their faith. Concerning this matter, the apostle wrote, *Beware lest someone pillage you by means of philosophy and empty deception* (Col. 2[:8]). For while we long with

---

30. The mention of Demas here is curious, as it seems to suggest that Paul's former fellow-laborer, who abandoned the incarcerated apostle in Rome, was among those to whom God granted repentance. Yet there is no scriptural witness of Demas having repented or of his being restored. Cf. Col. 4:14 and Philemon 24.

our carnal speculations to peer into God's mysteries, which the Holy Spirit delivered to us in a simple style and method, and to measure them by the laws of human wisdom, yet, being overwhelmed by divine glory that we cannot bear, we are thrown headlong into an abyss of various heresies—as happened to Arius, Marcion, and almost all heretics—since the wisdom of the flesh is enmity against God [Rom. 8:7] and *the natural man does not perceive those things that are of God, nor can he perceive them, for they are foolishness to him* [1 Cor. 2:14].

From what I have said—as briefly as this letter would permit me—regarding that threefold intoxication, I believe that you, my dear Count Ulysses, who are the best of us, can grasp better than anyone else regardless of his desire, how necessary is the counterbalancing sobriety for withstanding the enemy and preserving the treasures of divine wisdom. What would happen if a disproportionate, blind love for the teachings of men and our own instructors (with whom we often become so intoxicated—contrary to the apostolic injunction, *Test all things; hold fast to what is good* [1 Thess. 5:21]) were to lead us to embrace and hold tenaciously to whatever they say or write, without any trial or inspection, as if they were utterances of the Holy Spirit? Let us, then, be sober, and let us be vigilant.

8. Indeed, as the apostle teaches, *Our weapons are not carnal but spiritual* [2 Cor. 10:4], and they are of two sorts: some are suited to protecting us and others to slaying the enemy. The helm, breastplate, belt, and shield are of the first sort; the sword and javelins are of the latter.[31]

First, then, the head of the interior man should be protected by the helmet of salvation, that is, by a sure hope of salvation—that, just as salvation has begun in us already through Christ on the basis of grace alone, so, too, will it be completed through Him on the basis of that same grace. For can anyone make a stand in the battle or continue in it without this sure hope? The chest, where the vitals are located, ought to be protected all around by the breastplate of righteousness—preeminently, I say, the breastplate of the righteousness of faith and of a good conscience as well.

---

31. *Missilia* (javelins or some other missile weapon) are not among the elements of the armor of God mentioned by Paul in Eph. 6:11–17.

For who can fight in a battle against so many and such great enemies except he who is persuaded that God stands favorably with him and supports him against the enemy? Likewise, who can fight in such a battle except the one who hates the wickedness against which and loves the righteousness for the sake of which the battle is joined?

The loins ought to be encircled by the belt of truth, and the feet shod with the knowledge of the gospel of peace. That is, it behooves us that our every part be defended by the knowledge, love, and strength of truth so that we are ready and prepared to fight for the gospel at a given moment, holding fast with our left hand the shield of faith, whereby we intercept and extinguish all the Enemy's flaming darts, and, with our right, the sword of God's Word, whereby we drive back and strike down the Enemy. Indeed, we will wield the shield of faith if we preserve the firm foundations of the faith against all the previously mentioned sophistry of heretics, no matter how ignorant we might be of how to refute those very tricks. And, truly, we will wield the sword of the Word if we conquer the Enemy by the clear testimonies of the Holy Scriptures and with reasoning that follows by necessary consequence from them.

To this end, we will also find it quite useful to have launched sharp javelins and arrows at the Enemy out of the quivers of the most ancient fathers, just as we observe later generations of fathers having done, advancing the testimonies and arguments of earlier times against heretics. Therefore, we should take up this whole suit of God's armor,[32] along with very fervent prayers to Him, so that we can stand during this unfavorable and tumultuous time against so many, so diverse, and such powerful adversaries and ultimately triumph over them.

9. Once the city has been purged of enemy sympathizers and of mercenaries, collaborators, and traitors, the citizens will obviously need to live more prudent and quieter lives. Who could possibly be unaware of this, except someone totally ignorant of both history and current events? Therefore, above everything else, let those placed in authority over the church and the magistrates see to it that everyone's profession of doctrine

---

32. πανοπλία.

and lifestyle is diligently overseen according to the apostolic discipline. And let those who have been instructed and admonished but who refuse to repent be made known publicly to the whole church and separated from the holy gatherings and from the common life of the faithful who remain, so that no one else gets infected by their disease. Otherwise, as the apostle says, *a little leaven corrupts the whole lump* [Gal. 5:9].

Moreover, let all the faithful regard obstinate men of that sort as pagans and publicans, and let what John said be observed: *If someone comes to you who does not bear this doctrine*—meaning that doctrine handed down by the apostles concerning the Son of God and the foundations of the Christian religion—*neither receive him into your house nor greet him* [2 John 10]. This discipline, about which Tertullian writes in his *Apology*, is perpetual for the church (ch. 39[, §§3–5]).[33] Moreover, afterward, let the magistrate attend to the nature of their crimes and blasphemies on the basis of God's command.

10. The tenth point that we made regarding the ultimate duty of each citizen is easy to grasp. (If only it were also easy to perform.) We must, therefore, guard the faith given to us in baptism by Jesus Christ our Prince unto the end, even to the shedding of blood and the pouring out of our lives if necessary. And so, with absolutely steadfast faith, we must hold onto the doctrine that we know for certain is the doctrine of Christ—based on the prophetic and apostolic writings, on the clear foundations of the faith, and, indeed, on the whole of the ancient church's common confession as well—against all novel dogmas.[34] Nor ought we only to hold onto that doctrine in our heart, but we should also confess it frankly with our mouths. We should never wish to turn ourselves from it but profess it freely. And moreover, this obligation is such that, unless we do it, we can plainly have no hope of salvation. *For with the heart one believes unto righteousness, but with the mouth makes confession unto salvation* [Rom. 10:10].

---

33. ch. 39[, §§3–5]: Tertullian, "Apology," 99 (*ANF*, 3:46).

34. That is, against all novel claims about what constitutes a doctrine necessary to salvation.

To be sure, faith alone will suffice before God who sees the heart, but the free confession and profession of that doctrine is also necessary before men and for their sake. *He who is ashamed of Me before men, I will be ashamed of him before My Father*, said the Lord Jesus [Matt. 10:33; cf. Mark 8:38]. For, in this world, we must promote God's glory, Christ's name, and our neighbor's salvation, and it is proper for us to proclaim to the entire church what sort of religion it is that we follow and with what faith we have been endowed by God's grace, so that every one of its members will avoid being manifestly ignorant. Thus, the Lord Himself, urging us on to this confession, added, *He who will confess Me before men, I will also confess him before My Father* [Matt. 10:32]. Therefore, we should not be lured by bribes to abandon Christ nor deterred from freely confessing Him by bugbears of the mind or sufferings. Instead, with our attention focused on Jesus Himself, *the commander and perfecter of our faith, who, for the joy displayed to Him, endured the cross, paying no heed to the dishonor, and sat down at the right hand of the throne of God*, let us resolutely run our race [Heb. 12:1–2]. For, *He who will persevere to the end, he will be saved* [Matt. 10:22].

With these ten headings, my dear Count Ulysses, I judge that I have explained the true method whereby each one can provide for his own salvation and for those who are his amidst such disagreement of opinions about the path of salvation, amidst the incursions (and even assaults) made among us by evil spirits, and amidst such diabolical tyranny.

By God's blessing, I have devoted myself to following this method for thirty-four years, and I have learned from many years of experience—not to mention from the Holy Scriptures, which very clearly teach that it is derived from the will of God—that it is truly an admirable and excellent method. This is the reason why, having forsaken a Babylonian captivity, I charted a course for the free churches of Christ's kingdom (unto walled cities, as it were): first to Rhaetia for eight months or more, then to Geneva, where I spent another nine months more or less. From there I came to Strasbourg, where the French church was flourishing. I lived and taught there for eleven years, albeit not without struggle following the death of Jacob Sturm, that ornament of the whole republic and father of the school, and the gradual waning of the experienced elders.

Later, called to Chiavenna, I served as pastor in that church for about four years. And you, generous Count, who always attended to me and who, by your words and authority, helped not a little to promote Christ's kingdom, know very well how fruitfully I served, although not without a cross. Afterward, during the reign of that great and incomparable Prince Frederick III, I was a professor in the Heidelberg Academy for ten years. And, finally, I came to Neustadt, the town of the most illustrious and mighty Prince Johann Casimir, where a new school was established at which I taught for seven years and more. And there, thanks to the generosity of my prince, I live still, a worn-out old man, but, nevertheless, in good health by God's grace.

And as I die to the world, as is certainly the case in my body little by little, so I devote myself as I am able to do the same in my soul every day more and more. Truly, that is what I want. For *the world passes away and the lusts of it* [1 John 2:17]. And it did not take long for the worm in the book of Jonah to so gnaw the root of the gourd plant under the shade of which he was dwelling carefree that the good prophet, with the plant dried up, found himself unprotected from the sun's great heat [Jonah 4:5–8]. I long for my children to follow this same course.

And this is the chief reason why I undertook to bring this summary of the whole of Christian doctrine—which I had formerly composed with another, more public purpose in mind—to light at this time not only in my own name but in that of my family as well, so that I might also bequeath to my children the pattern of my own Christian faith in that same Christ for them to follow alongside of the doctrine that they daily hear resounding in our churches. For although, as regards the substance of Christian doctrine, I teach nothing different in this confession of mine than what our churches preach, nevertheless, I am aware of how much weight the authority and example of parents carry with children. For that reason, I decided it would be a very useful thing to have done for them if I were to leave behind in Christ's church some image of myself— I don't mean of my face but rather of my faith. For they might often consider it and, thereby, be stirred up more and more to serious study of the Holy Scriptures, to growth in the knowledge of truth, and consequently, to persevering in piety. I am also aware that what the apostle wrote to Timothy particularly pertains to this point: *He who does not care for his own, and especially for those of his household, has denied the faith and is worse than an unbeliever* [1 Tim. 5:8].

To this is added another reason that pertains specifically to me and to my situation. I longed to collect in a single, comprehensive volume everything that I have, up till now, believed in my heart and confessed with my mouth and publicly taught for many years in the church, both verbally and in print. I wanted to do this so that all posterity would know what my faith has been and so that all the faithful—both those of the present and of the future, and so the whole of the true catholic church—might clearly understand that I never consented to any of the heresies that are even now spreading all around or that spread at any previous time. In particular, if I have perhaps been deceived in anything, I submit that error to be properly judged according to the touchstone of the Holy Scriptures and the analogy of faith, whereby I wish to be examined and corrected.

Furthermore, I was persuaded to dedicate this my book to you, my dear Count Ulysses, for many well-deserved reasons, which I am sure neither you nor any other good man will reject.

It is fitting for a book of good doctrine to have a good patron rather than a bad one, who will protect it for piety's sake, who can protect it for learning's sake, and who will, indeed, do so steadfastly. Long experience has taught us how much nobility of blood and generosity of soul can help to accomplish this, if they are joined with true piety. For it is characteristic of a noble man to be steadfast in a matter that is laudable and worthy of honor and not to allow himself to be hindered from his worthy intention either by favorable or adverse circumstances. Sincerity and steadfastness are the kind of virtues that cannot come into the possession of provincial and slavish minds.

Add to this the fact that I judged it to be proper and necessary for some memorial to exist for the ages of my regard for you and of our Christian friendship. For both before God and before men, the sort of friendship that is character based—and that is therefore genuine and lasting—is a thing worthy of all the highest praise, like the friendships between David and Jonathan, Peter and John, and Paul and Barnabas. In fact, according to the apostle, just as *not all have faith*, so not every friendship is true [2 Thess. 3:2]. And as faith is of God, so too is love, according to John, and it is born of true piety and character [1 John 4:7].

To be sure, it was not flesh and blood that established our friendship but rather Christ, piety, religion, and love for the same religion, to which was subsequently added similarity of minds, enthusiasms, and habits as well as several years of most pleasant intimacy that strengthened our friendship, and strengthened it to such a degree that it could not be diminished or undermined by great geographical separation, not even over many years. What? Has it not only remained rock steady and resolute to this point but even appears to have grown and daily to grow as the Holy Spirit kindles more and more holy fraternal love[35] in our hearts? Certainly, that is my experience insofar as I long to see you, speak with you, and embrace you in the Lord. And, in turn, I easily grasp from your letters to me and your kindnesses on my behalf how much you care for my affairs. That is how true friendships, which are formed on the basis of the Holy Spirit, are preserved and promoted in the normal course of events.

The things that are from God are good and can also be used for the benefit of others, and they should be proclaimed and celebrated unto His glory and the edification of the brothers in every way. Thus, just as God willed that the Holy Scriptures commend specific friendships of certain saints, so our friendship should not be laid to rest in perpetual silence.

Add to this the fact that you have always pursued with singular goodwill not only me but also mine, as they say, and the whole upright and Christian family of the Lumaga (my most dear relatives).[36] Such things were and are your service and kindness unto me. For these reasons, unless I was planning to be altogether ungrateful, I absolutely had to come up with something, if not to completely balance accounts, then

---

35. φιλαδελφίαν.
36. The family of Zanchi's second wife, Livia Lumaga, came from Piur in the Valtellina and was associated with the Reformed congregation there.

at least as the worthy sign of a grateful soul, especially since true friendship cannot exist between the ungrateful. But what could I give that would be more agreeable to you or more suited to your piety, character, and nobility than to dedicate to your name this little book within which I have included the summary of the whole of Christian doctrine as briefly and clearly as I could?

For, according to custom and propriety, the sort of works that each person gets dedicated and commended to him depends on who he is and accords with the skill, knowledge, and religion that he professes. Thus, Luke dedicated Acts both in its substance and in its name to Theophilus. Thus, Caecilius Lactantius dedicated his *Divine Institutes* to the most Christian Emperor Constantine. Thus, Ambrose dedicated his pious books on faith and the Holy Spirit to the most pious Emperor Gratian. Thus, to get finally to the point, every discerning author has chosen patrons for his books that suited the books themselves, so that the titles of the books corresponded with the public profession of him to whom they were dedicated. Therefore, since I am unable in the slightest to repay your kindnesses toward me in any better way than by the dedication of this little book, please accept it, such as it is, with an obliging spirit as a lasting testimony of my love for you. In turn, I ask and pray that you continue to love my children truly, as you do, and to have them commended unto you, particularly after my death—Titus Cornelius, Ludwig, Girolamo Robert, Laelia Constantia, Anna Lydia, and Violanthis, along with the most loving mother of all our children, the venerable Livia, who is to me my most dear wife in the Lord.

Truly I pray, Count Ulysses, that the Lord grant you as many years as me so that you might remain useful for many years to yours and mine and, indeed, to our churches, as you have been up to now. But I pray that you might arrive at my age and beyond without any of those inconveniences that usually accompany feeble old age, for which reason Menander, who said, *Old age is lovely*,[37] also added, *but being old a second*

---

37. Καλόν γηρᾶνν.

time is not, for old age does not come alone.[38] I mean to say that, for the elderly, to live is itself often a heavy burden,[39] as they must constantly muse on death and the grave rather than on life. On this account also we always remember that the very word *old man*[40] derives from *one who pays heed to the ground*.[41]

Besides, to pray that someone might have a long life is not wrong since, although it is impossible for old age to be devoid of all evils, nevertheless, *to live* is itself a very great gift of God. And since it can be of use to many others, and, finally, since the very inconveniences of the flesh that accompany old age are also of spiritual advantage to pious men, therefore, may the greatest and best God preserve you in good health, and may He deign to grant you, out of His good will, a good long life with many blessings. *Health and a sound mind are two blessings in life.*[42]

At Neustadt on the first of April, 1585.

---

38. καὶ μὴ γηρᾶν πάλιν, τὸ γὰρ γῆρας, οὐκ ἔρχεται μόνον. This appears to be a composite quotation from sayings attributed to Menander. See Menander, *Menandri sententiae. Comparatio Menandri et Philistionis*, ed. Siegfried Jäkel (Leipzig: Teubner, 1964), 55, 79 (lines 396 and 802).

39. χαλεπόν βάρος. Euripides, *Hippolytus*, in *Euripidis Fabulae*, vol. 1, *Cyclops, Alcestis, Medea, Heraclidae, Hippolytus, Andromacha, Hecuba*, ed. Gilbert Murray (Oxford: Oxford University Press, 1902), sig. G9r.

40. Γέρων.

41. τήν γῆν ὁρῶν.

42. Ὑγιεία καὶ νοῦς ἐσθλά τῷ βίῳ δύο. This is another saying attributed to Menander, which Zanchi probably cites from Erasmus's *Adages*. See Desiderius Erasmus, *Collected Works of Erasmus*, vol. 34, *Adages: II vii 1 to III iii 100*, trans. R. A. B. Mynors (Toronto: University of Toronto Press, 1992), 218 (3.1.90). See Menander, *Menandri sententiae*, 79 (line 779).

Letter to the Reader

Kind reader, I had no desire to alter this confession, which I wrote some years ago for a specific purpose, either in substance or in words. However, in cases where it seemed something ought to be explained more clearly or developed more fully, I judged that it was better for those comments to be stated and set forth on their own rather than for all of it to be merged in such a way that the confession itself—of which there had already been more than ten copies made and which had come into the hands of many people—was modified.

Instead, we used this little star * to indicate whatever we found in the confession itself that seemed to require correction or confirmation, each in its own place. When you see that mark, you should turn back to the observations and consult the corresponding heading and aphorism.

Reader, be advised of the following as well. As publication of the entire book was nearing completion, I was informed that I should not neglect those who disapproved of what I wrote in chapter eleven, aphorism fifteen—that *Christ merited eternal life not only for Himself but also for us*—as if I had been disrespectful in alleging that He merited eternal life *for Himself*. I admit that I am amazed, and not just a little, since nothing was clearer than this doctrine according to the fathers, from whom the scholastics also received it. But at that very moment it occurred to me that the sense of taste differs from man to man. Indeed, some—like the young—enjoy the taste of wine that is new and sweet, while others—like the elderly—esteem an older vintage as the more wholesome. Immediately, I ceased to be amazed.

The antiquity of the above-mentioned doctrine is evident from the ancient fathers, who expounded Philippians 2[:9]—*On account of which God also exalted Him…*—in such a way that they said Christ merited that exaltation for Himself by His humility, obedience, and death.

Expounding the words of the apostle in Philippians 2, Augustine says, *His humility begins at "He emptied Himself…" but His glory begins at "on account of which God also exalted Him…" Humility is the merit of glory; glory is the reward of humility. However, He did this in "the form of a servant"; to be sure, in "the form of God" there always was and always will be glory* (*Homilies on the Gospel of John*, vol. 9, hom. 104, ch. 17, col. 505).[1] Bede commended these same words of Augustine, for he repeated them in his notes on Philippians 2.[2]

Ambrose [that is, Ambrosiaster], commenting on the same words of the apostle—*on which account God also…*—said that it *showed what and how much humility merited*.[3]

---

1. *Homilies on the Gospel of John*, vol. 9, hom. 104, ch. 17, col. 505: Note that the word rendered "glory" here is *claritas*. The modern translation of this entire section of Augustine's homily on John 17:1 helps to clarify Zanchi's usage of that word and his argument: "This is the glorification of our Lord Jesus Christ, which took its start with his resurrection. In the words of the apostle, then, his humility begins at the place where he says, 'He humbled himself, taking the form of a slave, and goes as far as death on a cross' (Phil. 2:7-8). But his glorification begins at the place where he says, 'Because of which God also exalted him,' and goes as far as 'to the glory of God the Father.' For even the noun itself, if the Greek edition were to be examined (it was from that language that the apostolic epistles were translated into Latin), which is read here as *gloria*, is read there as δόξα. The Latin translator says *clarifica*, although he could also have said *glorifica*, which is where the word comes from that appears in Greek as δόξασον, which means the same thing. And therefore in the apostle's epistle, too, *claritas* could have been put down where *gloria* appears. If that had been done, it would have meant the same thing. But, so as not to miss the sound of the words, "glorification" comes from *gloria*, just as "clarification" comes from *claritas*.

"And so, in order that 'the mediator between God and man, the man Christ Jesus' (1 Tim. 2:5), might be glorified by his resurrection, he was first humbled by his Passion, for he wouldn't have risen from the dead if he hadn't died. Humility merits glory; glory rewards humility. But this took place in the form of a slave, whereas in the form of God there always has been and always will be glory." Augustine, *Homilies on the Gospel of John 41–124*, ed. Allan D. Fitzgerald, trans. Edmund Hill, The Works of Saint Augustine: A Translation for the 21st Century III/13 (Hyde Park, N.Y.: New City Press, 2020), 408 (*NPNF*1, 7:395).

2. *PL*, 92:871D.

3. The modern translation renders this sentence thus: "Paul shows what and how

Jerome, commenting on the same passage, writes, *Because the assumed humanity condescended to humble itself, the divinity, which cannot be humbled, exalted Him who had been humbled.*[4] Take note of the word *because*.

Vigilius says, *According to His human nature, Christ received honors on account of merit* (*Against Eutyches*, bk. 5[, §10], p. 130).[5]

Again, Vigilius points out that *to be raised in honor* is something that cannot be attributed to Christ according to His divine nature but only according to His human nature. Among other things, he writes the following:

> Is it possible that His (divine) nature needed to be both raised up in honor and increased by progress of dignity in order that, by merit of His humility and obedience and death, He might be worthy of possessing the peak of exalted rewards and of receiving rule over heaven and earth of the sort that He previously lacked? Or will they perhaps deny that all things have been united in the Lord Jesus Christ on account of the merit of His suffering and death? Let them read what the apostle says about this: *He humbled Himself, becoming obedient unto death, even the death of the cross, on which account God exalted Him, and gave Him a name that is above every name, that at the name of Jesus every knee should bow of those in heaven, of those on the earth, and of those under the earth* [Phil. 2:8–10]. And David says, *He shall drink from the rushing stream in the way;* that is, He shall drink from the river of human death;

---

much humility earned, so that we will suppress our pride and seek it more." Ambrosiaster, *Commentaries on Galatians–Philemon*, trans. and ed. Gerald L. Bray, Ancient Christian Texts (Downers Grove, Ill.: IVP Academic, 2009), 70.

4. This is from a commentary on Philippians (*Commentarius in epistolam ad Philippenses*) that was long believed to have been written by the fourth-century church father Jerome but that is now regarded as the work of a later pseudo-Jerome. No English translation exists. See *PL*, 30:845D.

5. *Against Eutyches*, bk. 5[, §10], p. 130: The longer passage in Vigilius from which Zanchi is drawing reads as follows: "And Christ Himself, therefore, is one and the same in such a way that He is both created and uncreated, has a beginning and is without beginning, increases in knowledge and age and receives no increase of either knowledge or age, endures death and is not subject to death's rules, receives honors on account of merit and requires no honors at all" *PL*, 62:139C.

therefore, He will lift up the head because He partook of death [Ps. 110:7]. And, in the gospel, Jesus Himself says, *For that reason, My Father loves Me, because I lay down My life for My sheep…* [John 10:17] ([*Against Eutyches*, bk. 5, §11,] p. 132).[6]

And a little later, Vigilius adds: *As yet, therefore, let us pursue every gift of His blessedness, which He acquired on account of His meritorious suffering. By these, He will be visible with a brighter light—not possible for Him according to the nature that is God but suitable according to the nature that was made man* [*Against Eutyches*, bk. 5, §11].[7] Let them read what follows. I could advance many other testimonies, but doing so makes writing short letters impossible, nor is it necessary. There is no doubt that this doctrine of the church is ancient. I ask my guests, therefore, not to be irritated with me if, having set both old and new wine out on the table, I leave the new for others to drink and, being an old man, partake myself of the old. In fact, for the sake of my health I am mindful, as I should be based on God's command, to drink new wine with pleasure when it is good rather than old wine that is bad.

This should be noted as well: while reviewing the already-printed book, I discovered an error in the observations on page 248, line 25 [that is, observation 15.6]: the word Ἰωάννης should have been set before the word μέν, so it should read: *that* Ἰωάννης μέν. For I meant the text to include not only that little μέν but the whole of Paul's statement, as is clear from what follows thereafter.

I will add this as well. In the appendix to chapter eleven concerning the person of Christ, at the end of the observations, I sought to point out, on the basis of Vigilius, a brief method whereby the quarrel concerning the communication of the properties could be reconciled. To that end, I said that Christ's flesh could be said, without any contradiction, to be both omnipotent and not omnipotent, present everywhere and not present everywhere—but obviously in different respects. For

---

6. [*Against Eutyches*, bk. 5, §11,] p. 132: *PL*, 62:141A–B. Note that the adjective "divine" in the first sentence of the quotation, which Zanchi set off within parentheses, is a clarifying interpolation to Vigilius's text.

7. [*Against Eutyches*, bk. 5, §11]: *PL*, 62:141D.

what is shared with the divine nature is not the essence[8] of Christ's flesh in particular but the hypostasis[9] itself.[10] So, note this explanation here, lest the sophists perpetrate some kind of sham hereabouts.

When we say that Christ's flesh is not present by its essence,[11] that statement can be understood in two different ways. First, it could be understood in this sense: according to what is called a *What?*[12] question, someone might say that the very substance of Christ's flesh is really present, not with reference to its knowledge or authority nor even merely according to the hypostasis,[13] but rather really and properly with reference to its essence.[14] This is the sense in which the Word[15] is declared to be everywhere according to His essence,[16] since by His essence[17] He fills everything.

The other way the statement can be understood is in this sense: according to what is called a *Why?*[18] question, we ask the reason why Christ's flesh might be said to be present everywhere according to its essence[19]—whether this is the case on account of its nature (or essence[20])

---

8. οὐσίᾳ.
9. ὑποστάσει.
10. Zanchi's distinction here draws upon a patristic interpretive tradition to explain that, in the hypostatic union, Christ's human nature was not joined to the divine essence generally but rather to the person of the Son in particular. He develops this line of thought at the end of his observations in the appendix to chapter 11. On this topic generally, see K. J. Drake, *The Flesh of the Word: The Extra Calvinisticum from Zwingli to Early Orthodoxy*, Oxford Studies in Historical Theology (New York: Oxford University Press, 2021); and Andrew M. McGinnis, *The Son of God Beyond the Flesh: A Historical and Theological Study of the Extra Calvinisticum*, T&T Clark Studies in Systematic Theology 29 (London and New York: Bloomsbury T&T Clark, 2014).
11. οὐσίᾳ.
12. τό ὅτι.
13. τῇ ὑποστάσει.
14. οὐσίᾳ. To be clear, Zanchi is not advocating for this position—he is simply noting that someone *might* say that Christ's flesh is really present in the same way that the Word is essentially present everywhere.
15. λόγος.
16. οὐσίᾳ.
17. οὐσίᾳ.
18. τοῦ διότι.
19. οὐσίᾳ.
20. οὐσίᾳ.

or whether, in fact, it is the case by grace and the bounty of the hypostatic union.[21] This, furthermore, is the sense in which the Word[22] is said to be God and omnipotent according to His essence,[23] because the Word[24] has these things not by grace but by His nature and essence.[25]

Up to now, many have waged fierce debates about the first question in order to defend an affirmative answer, that Christ's flesh is everywhere according to its essence.[26] And they do this for the following purpose: to conclude that Christ's flesh really exists in the bread by its essence.[27] We resolutely and altogether deny both these points.[28]

As regards the *Why?* question, those same disputants deny (correctly and without anyone contradicting them) that, according to its natural essence,[29] Christ's flesh possesses the following quality: it is present everywhere. But, on the basis of the hypostatic union, they assert

---

21. The distinction here between a question that asks *what a thing is* and one that asks *why a thing is the way it is* was a regular tool in medieval theology and was derived from Aristotle.

Thomas Aquinas described this distinction as follows: "Besides, the problem of why something is so is related to the problem of whether it is so, in the same way that an inquiry as to what something is stands in regard to an inquiry as to whether it exists. For the question why looks for a means to demonstrate that something is so…likewise, the question what is it seeks a means to demonstrate that something exists, according to the traditional teaching in [Aristotle's] Posterior Analytics II [§1]. Now, we observe that those who see that something is so naturally desire to know why. So, too, those acquainted with the fact that something exists naturally desire to know what this thing is, and this is to understand its substance. Therefore, the natural desire to know does not rest in that knowledge of God whereby we know merely that He is." Thomas Aquinas, *Summa Contra Gentiles: Book Three: Providence, Part 1*, trans. Vernon J. Bourke (Notre Dame, Ind.: University of Notre Dame Press, 1975), 173 (3.50.4).

22. λόγος.
23. οὐσία.
24. λόγος.
25. οὐσία.
26. οὐσία. The disputants in view here are those so-called Gnesio-Lutherans who held to the doctrine of the ubiquity of Christ's flesh on the basis of the *communicatio idiomatum*.
27. οὐσία.
28. That is, the Reformed deny, first, that Christ's flesh is everywhere essentially and, second, that Christ's flesh really exists in the bread essentially.
29. οὐσία.

that Christ's flesh has undoubtedly gained this: that, if desired, it could be everywhere and, in fact, that since its resurrection and glorification, His flesh really has been existing everywhere by its essence.³⁰

We earnestly maintain both these assertions to be false. This means that we agree with those disputants about the first assertion and that we oppose them on the second.³¹ And this is the reason we deny the second of these claims: because the hypostatic union occurred *unchangeably and without confusion*,³² as the Council of Chalcedon asserted, that is, without any change or confusion of either nature (or of the essences³³) or of essential properties.³⁴

If *unchangeably*,³⁵ then Christ's flesh did not undergo any change as a result of the union—much less from glorification—in its οὐσίᾳ or its essential properties. Rather, with reference to its essence,³⁶ Christ's flesh remained created, finite, and circumscribed. If, however, it was either able to be or really was present everywhere (and, indeed, according to the whole person), then Christ's flesh did not remain unchanged, since it is not possible for that which has a divine nature to die, unless that which is infinite and most simple in its essence³⁷ can also die.

---

30. οὐσίᾳ.

31. That is, the Reformed deny, first, that Christ's flesh naturally (or essentially) possesses the quality of ubiquity and, second, that Christ's flesh became ubiquitous as a result of the hypostatic union subsequent to Christ's resurrection and glorification. The latter was accepted as true by Lutheran theologians.

32. ἀτρέπτως καί ἀσυγχύτως.

33. τῶν οὐσιῶν.

34. The pertinent section of the Chalcedonian Creed regarding the hypostatic union read as follows: "One and the same Christ, Son, Lord, Only-begotten, to be acknowledged in two natures, inconfusedly [ἀσυγχύτως], unchangeably [ἀτρέπτως], indivisibly, inseparably; the distinction of natures being by no means taken away by the union, but rather the property of each nature being preserved, and concurring in one Person and one Subsistence, not parted or divided into two persons, but one and the same Son, and only begotten, God the Word, the Lord Jesus Christ." Philip Schaff, ed., *Creeds of Christendom, with a History and Critical Notes*, 6th ed. (Grand Rapids: Baker Books, 1984), 2:62.

35. ἀτρέπτως.

36. οὐσίᾳ.

37. οὐσίᾳ.

If *without confusion*,[38] then those things whereby the divine essence[39] is distinguished from the human cannot be attributed to the human nature, otherwise confusion follows whereby one nature cannot be distinguished from another. This is true whether these things are applied to Christ and predicated of Him according to His divine nature or, on the other hand, according to His human nature. The Council of Chalcedon hurled that little phrase *without confusion*[40] against this sort of Eutychian confusion. And the fathers laid out this principle, which we read everywhere: Whenever you read something about Christ that is more exalted and divine, it is to be attributed to His divine nature; that which is humbler and human is attributed to His human nature.

Writing in Greek, Justin says: *Therefore, since you will hear various expressions from the one Son, conveniently divide what you hear according to the two natures. If something is great and divine, attribute it to the divine nature. If something is small and human, credit it to the human nature. For thus you will both escape the discordance of the expressions—with each nature receiving that which corresponds to it—and you will confess the one Son to have existed before all ages and not to have long existed, according to the Holy Scriptures* ([*The Exposition of the True Faith*, §10,] fol. 178).[41]

In his *Dialogues* [*on the Trinity*], Cyril of Alexandria indicates something not dissimilar (bk. 2, dialogue 5 with Hermias, col. 320).[42]

---

38. ἀσυγχύτως.
39. οὐσίᾳ.
40. ἀσυγχύτως.
41. [*The Exposition of the True Faith*, §10,] fol. 178: Zanchi quotes the Greek text of *The Exposition of the True Faith*: Ὅταν ἀκούσῃς περί τοῦ ἑνός υἱοῦ τὰς ἐναντίας φωνάς, καταλλήως μέριζε ταῖς φύσεσι τὰ λεγόμενα, ἂν μέγα τι καὶ θεῖον, τῇ θείᾳ φύσει προσνέμων, ἂν δέ τι μικρὸν καὶ ἀνθρώπινον, τῇ ἀνθρωπίνῃ λογιζόμενος. Οὕτω γὰρ καὶ τὸ τῶν φωνῶν ἀσύμφωνον διαφεύξῃ, ἑκάστης ἃ πέφυκε δεχομένης φύσεως, καὶ τὸν υἱὸν τὸν ἕνα καὶ πρὸ πάντων αἰώνων καὶ πρόσφατον κατὰ τὰς θείας γραφὰς ὁμολογήσεις.

From the seventh century, this treatise (Ἔκθεσις ἀκριβὴς τῆς ὀρθοδόξου πίστεως/*Expositio rectae confessionis*) was received as a work of Justin Martyr, but, since the eighteenth century, it has been widely regarded as a work of a Pseudo-Justin (probably Theodoret of Cyrus [c. 393–c. 458]). No English translation of the work exists, but see *PG*, 6:1225A.

42. bk. 2, dialogue 5 with Hermias, col. 320: Cyril of Alexandria, *Dialogues sur la*

Moreover, in *On the Orthodox Faith* (bk. 3, ch. 4[, §48]), John of Damascus admirably explains all of this in opposition to the Eutychian confusion: *Therefore, when we are speaking of the divinity, we do not attribute to it the properties of the humanity (for we do not say that divinity is passible or created), nor do we attribute to the flesh, that is to say, to the humanity, the properties of the divinity (for we do not say that flesh, that is to say, humanity, is uncreated).*[43] Subsequently, he indicates at greater length how those things that are properly said to belong to one nature or the other are predicated of the person.[44]

These are two invincible reasons whereby it is demonstrated that Christ's flesh received the ability to be everywhere by its essence[45] neither as a result of union nor of glorification. If, then, this way of speaking—*the body of Christ is present everywhere*—must be granted (which, even so, we do not approve), we teach that it is to be granted in no other sense

---

Trinité, trans. Georges-Matthieu de Durand (Paris: Éditions du Cerf, 1977), 2:277–79 (*PG*, 75:938D–939A).

43. bk. 3, ch. 4[, §48]: θεότητα μέν οὖν λέγοντες, οὐ κατονομάζομεν αὐτῆς τὰ τῆς ἀνθρωπότητος ἰδιώματα. οὐ γάρ φαμεν θεότητα παθητὴν ἢ κτιστήν. οὔτε δὲ τῆς σαρκὸς, ἤτοι τῆς ἀνθρωπότητος κατηγοροῦμεν τὰ τῆς θεότητος ἰδιώματα. οὐ γάρ φαμεν σάρκα, ἤτοι ἀνθρωπότητα ἄκτιστον. Zanchi quotes the Greek. The translation is from John of Damascus, *On the Orthodox Faith*, trans. Norman Russell, Popular Patristics Series 62 (Yonkers, N.Y.: St Vladimir's Seminary Press, 2022), 171–72 (*NPNF2*, 9:49; *FOTC*, 37:276).

44. The passage quoted by Zanchi continues thus: "But in the case of the hypostasis, whether we are speaking of it in terms of one of the combination, or whether we are speaking of it in terms of one of its parts, we attribute the properties of both natures to it. For Christ—the name that expresses the combination of the two—is called both God and man, both created and uncreated, both passible and impassible. But when he is named from one of the parts and is called Son of God and God, he receives the properties of the nature that forms a unity with the other part, that is to say, the properties of the flesh, and is named passible God and crucified Lord of glory, not in respect of being God but in respect of the same being also human. And when he is named as Man and Son of Man, he receives the properties and glorious distinctions of the divine essence, eternal child and human being without beginning, not in respect of being a child and a human being but in respect of being eternal God, yet becoming a child in these latter days. And this is the manner of the exchange, each nature exchanging with the other its own properties through the identity of the hypostasis and the mutual interpenetration of the natures." John of Damascus, *On the Orthodox Faith*, 172 (*FOTC*, 37:276).

45. οὐσία.

than with reference to its hypostasis,[46] or even its knowledge, power, and authority, but by no means according to its own created and finite essence.[47] For this is a truly diabolical monster, thoroughly destroying Christ's true humanity, which is like us in all things except for sin.

We can also slip in here another explication of the proposition that we are considering from John of Damascus. For, in the fourth book of his *On the Orthodox Faith*, near the end of the third chapter, explaining how we might adore Christ's flesh, he wrote these words: *We do not say that we worship mere flesh but God's flesh, that is to say, God incarnate* [§76].[48] Therefore, we also find ourselves able to explain the proposition in this way: Christ's body (that is, Christ incarnate) is present everywhere, but according to which part thereof? Or according to what nature? It was God who did it, so that we might know and speak all things in the Lord.

But you, Christian reader, whoever you are, I beg you Christianly (that is, sincerely and from the heart) that if perhaps you find something wanting in my little book here, feel free to let me know about it and instruct me in a friendly spirit. Once I am persuaded, you will have done me an exceedingly great favor. For I want nothing more than, before I die, to leave behind in the church the kind of confession of faith that, having been diligently examined according to the touchstone of the Holy Scriptures, is approved by every pious and learned man and, consequently, by the whole of the truly catholic church.

Farewell. And I beg for true reconciliation and fellowship between all the churches that call upon Christ's name and for union under one and the same Head, Christ, that God the Father might be with us, through the same Lord Jesus Christ. And do not forget to remember me in your prayers. *The effective prayer of a righteous person has much power*[49] [James 5:16].

---

46. ὑποστάσει.

47. οὐσίᾳ.

48. [§76]: καὶ οὐ φανεμ, ὅτι σάρκα προσκυνοῦμεν ψιλήν, ἀλλὰ σάρκα θεοῦ ἤτοι σεσαρκωμένον θεόν. Zanchi quotes the Greek text. The translation is from John of Damascus, *The Orthodox Faith*, 230 (NPNF2, 9:74–75; FOTC, 37:337).

49. Πολὺ ἰσχύει δέησις δικαίου ἐνεργουμένη.

Chapter One

Holy Scripture, the Foundation of the Whole Christian Religion

1. *When it comes to God and matters pertaining to religion, we should only believe God unconditionally.*
With regard to God and the divine matters that pertain to Christ's kingdom and our salvation, we believe that no one can teach us better or with more certainty than God Himself, who can neither be deceived nor deceive (Ambrose, ep. 31).[1] *No one has ever seen God; the Son, who is in the Father's bosom, He has interpreted Him to us* (John 1:18).

2. *God speaks in the writings of the prophets and apostles.*
God has made Himself and His eternal power and deity known—and not in any miserly or obscure way—to men all over the earth by means of those things which He has made, so that all those who do not glorify God are without excuse. Nevertheless, we know that God has revealed His will clearly and fully in a special way, namely, by means of Spirit-inspired prophets and apostles, and by means of their writings. And, therefore, the prophetic and apostolic writings are the very Word of God (Rom. 1:19–20; Heb. 1:1; 2:3; 1 Peter 1:21; Matt. 10:20).

---

1. Ambrose, ep. 31: In 384, Ambrose wrote to Emperor Valentinian: "Let God Himself, who established the mystery of heaven, teach me about it, not man who does not know himself. Whom more than God shall I believe concerning God? How can I believe you who admit that you do not know what you worship?" *FOTC*, 26:40. Zanchi's citation of this as epistle 31 is based upon the numbering in Erasmus's edition of Ambrose's works. *Divi Ambrosii episcopi Mediolanensis omnia opera* (Basel, 1516), vol. 3, fol. 33v.

3. The prophetic and apostolic writings alone are the canonical books.

Yet we doubt not that the prophetic and apostolic writings are those which the church of God is accustomed, for that reason, to call canonical books. For, knowing with certainty that these books are God-breathed[2] (2 Tim. 3:16), the church has always and only acknowledged them as the canon of all Christian piety, according to which all religious controversy must be tried. She nevertheless calls other writings apocryphal because, although they are included alongside the holy books, they are less evidently from the Holy Spirit than are the others.

4. Which are the canonical and which the apocryphal books.

Together with the whole church, both before Christ's coming and since, we therefore acknowledge and embrace, without any doubt, the following books from the Old Testament as most certainly the Word of God (Council of Laodicea, canon 59).[3]

>   Five books of Moses
>   One of Joshua
>   One of Judges
>   One of Ruth
>   Two of Samuel
>   Two of Kings
>   Two of Chronicles
>   The first two of Esdras[4]
>   Nine chapters of Esther and the first three verses of chapter 10
>   Job
>   Psalms
>   Proverbs
>   Ecclesiastes

---

2. θεόπνευστος.

3. Council of Laodicea, canon 59: The Council of Laodicea (360) pronounced that "no psalms composed by private individuals, nor any uncanonical books may be read in the church, but only the Canonical Books of the Old and New Testaments." NPNF2, 14:158. A list of the canonical books (excluding Revelation) was subsequently appended to canon 59. See Lee Martin McDonald, *The Formation of the Biblical Canon*, vol. 2, *The New Testament: Its Authority and Canonicity* (London: Bloomsbury T&T Clark, 2021), 122.

4. That is, Ezra and Nehemiah.

The Song of Songs
Isaiah
Jeremiah with Lamentations
Ezekiel
The first twelve chapters of Daniel, except the song of the three youths
The twelve Minor Prophets

We do not, however, receive these others as canonical:
Judith
Tobit
The third and fourth of Esdras
The Wisdom of Solomon
The Wisdom of Jesus, son of Sirach, which in Latin is called Ecclesiasticus
Baruch
The Epistle of Jeremiah
Chapters 13 and 14 of Daniel
Again, the song of the three youths, which is affixed to the third chapter of Daniel
The remainder of Esther, after the third verse of chapter 10
Both books of the Maccabees

These are the books of the Old Testament.

But from the New Testament we except none, for although there are others about which there formerly was doubt, nevertheless, later they were acknowledged no less than the others as having been written by the apostles, to which judgment we also subscribe.

Of the former kind are:
The Gospel according to Matthew, Mark, Luke, John
The Acts of the Apostles
The epistles of Paul
First Peter
First John

Of the latter are:
> The Epistle to the Hebrews
> The Epistle of James
> Second Peter
> Second and Third John
> The Epistle of Jude
> Revelation

Although those about which there never was any doubt may seem to have some greater kind of authority than those about which there was doubt, nevertheless, we believe the one as well as the other certainly to be the Word of God. And, with regard to the apocryphal books that are included alongside the holy books, we assign them the first place after the canonical books.

5. *The dogmas*[5] *of the faith can be proved only with the canonical books.* And, therefore, we use only the canonical books for proving the dogmas of the faith, and, with the fathers, we teach that they must be used. However, we think that the others have no little authority for subsequently confirming the dogmas once they have been proved (Jerome's "Prologue to the Books of Solomon"; Cyprian's, *A Commentary on the Apostles' Creed*, §38; Council of Laodicea, canon 59).[6]

---

5. *Dogmata*. On this word, see Muller, *Dictionary*, 97. As noted previously, for Zanchi, the word *dogma* appears to be synonymous with what he calls doctrine (*doctrina*) "necessary for salvation" in the dedicatory letter.

6. Jerome's "Prologue to the Books of Solomon": "Therefore, just as the Church also reads the books of Judith, Tobias, and the Maccabees, but does not receive them among the canonical Scriptures, so also one may read these two scrolls [i.e., Ecclesiasticus and the Wisdom of Solomon] for the strengthening of the people, (but) not for confirming the authority of ecclesiastical dogmas." Jerome, "Jerome's Prologue to the Books of Solomon," trans. Kevin P. Edgecomb, *Biblicalia* (blog), August 13, 2006, https://web.archive.org/web/20220309114224/https://www.bombaxo.com/2006/08/13/jeromes-prologue-to-the-books-of-solomon/ (*NPNF2*, 6:492).

Cyprian's, *A Commentary on the Apostles' Creed*, §38: "At the same time we should appreciate that there are certain other books which our predecessors designated 'ecclesiastical' rather than 'canonical.' Thus, there is the Wisdom of Solomon, as we call it; and another Wisdom, ascribed to the son of Sirach. This latter is known by the general title Ecclesiasticus among Latin-speaking people, the description pointing not to the

Holy Scripture, Foundation of the Christian Religion 45

6. *The canonical books do not receive their authority from the church.*
For this reason, we also hold the following to be beyond controversy, and we think it must be held. The church, having been taught by the first fathers (that is, the prophets and apostles who received their doctrine directly from God and committed it to writing), and having been convinced by the Holy Spirit, has indicated to posterity by a perpetual and unbroken tradition which books are canonical and which are not and has offered (and perpetually offers) testimony to the church of their divine and heavenly truth. The former points having been granted, these writings nevertheless neither receive nor derive their authority from the church, but only from God, who is their author, properly speaking. Therefore, because they are the Word of God, they have authority on their own over everyone and deserve to be believed and obeyed by everyone unconditionally.

7. *Nevertheless, the church's authority is of no little use in bringing men to trust Holy Scripture.*
At the same time, however, we do not deny that the authority of the church has great weight for persuading men to hear and read the Holy Scriptures as the Word of God. As Augustine said on the basis of his own experience, *I would not have believed the gospel, had not the authority of the church moved me* (*Against the Letter of "The Foundation"*, vol. 6, ch. 5).⁷ Nevertheless, that same Augustine declares everywhere that he did not believe on account of the church but rather on account of the Holy Spirit, whose gift is faith.

---

author of the book, but to the character of the writing. The Book of Tobias belongs to the same class, as do Judith and the books of the Maccabees. In the New Testament we have the little work known as The Book of the Shepherd, or Hermas, and the book which is named The Two Ways, and The Judgment of Peter. They desired that all these should be read in the churches, but that appeal should not be made to them on points of faith." Rufinus of Aquileia, *A Commentary on the Apostles' Creed*, trans. J. N. D. Kelly, Ancient Christian Writers (New York: Newman Press, 1954), 73 (*NPNF2*, 3:558). This work by Rufinus (d. 410) had previously been attributed to Cyprian of Carthage (d. 258).
    Council of Laodicea, canon 59: *NPNF2*, 14:158.
    7. *Against the Letter of "The Foundation,"* vol. 6, ch. 5: Augustine, *Answer to the Letter of Mani Known as The Foundation*, 236 (*NPNF1*, 4:131).

8. *The church has no authority over Holy Scripture.*
But we judge it to be utter sacrilege to argue about whether the church's authority is greater than that of Holy Scripture—and all the more to offer an affirmative answer. It is not as though the church, in addition to the gift that she has of knowing the Spirit and discerning the canonical writings from the others and testifying concerning them and interpreting them, also has authority either to add something to or to take something away from them, or to dispense with them. For God commanded that no one add or take away, that none should turn aside to the right or to the left, but rather that everyone should unconditionally obey Him in everything that He says in His Holy Scriptures (Deut. 4:2; 5:31; 12:32; Rev. 22:18–19).

9. *Holy Scripture is so perfect that we can neither add to nor take away anything from it.*
For Scripture is so holy and perfect, containing in abundance whatever is necessary for salvation, that nothing can be added to it, and it is also so perfectly and prudently composed that nothing can be taken away from it.

10. *That we must, therefore, submit to Holy Scripture.*
Thus, we submit to the teaching of the Holy Scriptures, just as all the devout ought to do, holding to what the apostle said: *All Scripture inspired of God is useful for teaching* (2 Tim. 3:16).

11. *With regard to religion, nothing should be established apart from God's Word, but everything should be corrected by it.*
For this reason we also think that nothing should be established in God's church related to religion that lacks clear testimony in the canonical books or that does not follow thereupon by manifest and necessary consequence (Gratian's *Decretum*, dist. 9[, ch. 10]).[8] And if at any time

---

8. Gratian's *Decretum*, dist. 9[, ch. 10]: The *Decretum* is the great medieval collection of canon law compiled by the jurist Gratian in the twelfth century. The pertinent section is the following: "'Equal authority should not be ascribed to the canonical Scriptures and commentaries on them.' Nor ought we to hold to any arguments, no matter

either teachings or worship have crept into the church that are inconsistent with the Holy Scriptures, they should, in some legitimate way, be entirely removed or corrected according to the rule of the Word of God. Again, all controversies pertaining to religion should legitimately be judged and settled on the basis of those same Holy Scriptures.

12. *Truly apostolic and catholic traditions should be retained in the church.* Nevertheless, we judge that traditions known by all to have proceeded from the apostles and always to have been observed by the whole church—such as keeping holy the Lord's Day in place of the Sabbath, and other things—should be retained in the churches, even if no command for their observance exists in the Holy Scriptures (Augustine, *On Baptism, against the Donatists*, vol. 7, bk. 4, ch. 24[, §31] and his letter to Januarius, vol. 2, ep. 118 [i.e., ep. 54, §§1–2]; Gratian's *Decretrum*, dist. 11, ch. 8).[9]

---

how Catholic and praiseworthy their authors, as if they were sacred Scripture. Nor are we forbidden, on account of the honor we owe such men, from condemning or rejecting anything in their writings, if perchance we find them to have a sense contrary to the truth as we or others have understood it with divine help. As I treat others' writings, so I want interpreters to treat mine." Gratian, *The Treatise on Laws (Decretum DD. 1-20) with the Ordinary Gloss*, trans. Augustine Thompson and James Gordley, Studies in Medieval and Early Modern Canon Law (Washington, D.C.: Catholic University of America Press, 1993), 32.

9. Augustine, *On Baptism, against the Donatists*, vol. 7, bk. 4, ch. 24[, §31]: In this passage, Augustine argues for infant baptism despite the absence of an explicit biblical (or even conciliar) command. Augustine does this, in part, because he understands the apostles to have handed down the practice to the church. However, Zanchi does not note that Augustine also grounds that tradition in Scripture by connecting it to the divinely ordained practice of circumcision in the Old Testament. Augustine writes: "The universal Church maintains what was handed down to it in the case of baptism of small infants.... Suppose someone asks about the divine authority for this. Although what the universal Church maintains that was not established by councils but has always been held is most rightly believed to have been handed down only by apostolic authority, we can still obtain a true sense of what value the sacrament of baptism has for small children from the circumcision of the flesh." Augustine, *The Donatist Controversy*, vol. 1, ed. Boniface Ramsey and David G. Hunter, trans. Maureen Tilley and Boniface Ramsey, The Works of Saint Augustine: A Translation for the 21st Century I/21 (Hyde Park, N.Y.: New City Press, 2019), 496 (*NPNF*1, 4:461).

13. Scripture is perspicuous in those things that are necessary for salvation and, therefore, should be read by all.

Indeed, we think and know that the whole doctrine of salvation is not only abundantly but also perspicuously delivered in the Holy Scriptures, since God did not speak to His people except in their own language, which they all understood. Thus, it is a great iniquity and tyranny to forbid the reading and, consequently, the translation of those books (which God has willed and judged should be read by all for the sake of their

---

Augustine, letter to Januarius, vol. 2, ep. 118 [i.e., ep. 54, §§1–2]: Zanchi refers to a portion of Augustine's first letter to Januarius in which he discusses those Christian practices that were universal, as opposed to those that varied from place to place. He suggests that the universal practices could be established either directly by Scripture or by apostolic tradition or conciliar pronouncement. He writes, "First of all, then, I want you to hold onto what is the principal point of this discussion, that our Lord Jesus Christ, as he himself says in the gospel, has made us subject to his gentle yoke and light burden. For this reason he bound together the society of the new people by sacraments very few in number, very easy in their observance, and most excellent in what they signify. They are, for example, baptism made sacred by the name of the Trinity, the partaking of his body and blood, and any other that is mentioned in the canonical scriptures, with the exception of those about which we read in the books of Moses and which imposed a heavy servitude upon the old people, such as was suitable to their heart and to a prophetic time. But we are given to understand that those practices we observe which are not in scripture, but in tradition, and which are observed throughout the whole world, are maintained as taught and established either by the apostles themselves or by plenary councils, which have an authority in the Church most conducive to salvation: for example, the passion and resurrection of the Lord, his ascension into heaven, and the coming of the Holy Spirit from heaven that are celebrated solemnly each year, and any other occurrence that is observed by the universal Church wherever it is spread." Augustine, *Letters*, vol. 1, 1–99, ed. John E. Rotelle, trans. Roland J. Teske, The Works of Saint Augustine: A Translation for the 21st Century II/1 (Hyde Park, N.Y.: New City Press, 2001), 210 (*NPNF*1, 1:300). Zanchi cites from Erasmus's edition of Augustine's works: *Opera Divi Aurelii Augustini episcopi Hipponensis*, 10 vols. (Basel, 1528–1529).

Gratian's *Decretrum*, dist. 11, ch. 8: The medieval jurist Gratian described Scripture and tradition as independently authoritative sources for Christian practice. He writes, "'The Church is ruled by authority and by universal and local traditions.' The Catholic Church throughout the world lives by three things. For all her observances clearly come either from scriptural authority or universal tradition, unless they are a particular and local arrangement. Now, by an authority the whole is bound, and by universal tradition of previous generations, nothing less than the whole; but each, according to the diversity of place, submits to and is ruled by enactments particular to their own establishment, as anyone can see." Gratian, *Treatise on Laws*, 40.

salvation and handled day and night by all) into the particular language of any nation (Ps. 1:2).

14. *The faithful interpretations of the devout and learned should not be condemned.*

Indeed, although the Holy Scriptures are perspicuous in those things that are necessary for salvation, we nevertheless do not reject the interpretations and explications of devout men who are both learned and skillful, whether they are ancient or more recent, namely, their interpretations and explanations that are pursued on the basis of those same Holy Scriptures and insofar as the Scriptures are explained by the Scriptures and in accordance with the first foundations of the faith (1 Thess. 5:21).[10] The sum of these is contained in the Apostles' Creed as well as in the creeds of the truly ancient and holy ecumenical councils convened against prominent heretics.

15. *The Word of God alone is the support of the faith and foundation of religion.*

For our faith cannot and should not lean upon anything other than the Word of God, handed down in the Holy Scriptures, that faith might always be from hearing, but hearing by the Word of God (Rom. 10:17). We reject whatever is opposed to that Word of God in the books of any man. We embrace whatever accords with it. But we admit or reject that which is neither opposed to nor in accordance with the Word of God depending on whether it is expedient for churches, and we make them aware whether something should be admitted or rejected.

---

10. *Primis fidei principiis*. Zanchi harkens back to the principle he affirmed in his dedicatory letter to Martinengo, where he notes, "The church retains the firm foundations of apostolic doctrine contained in the Holy Scriptures and understands and explains those foundations according to the orthodox interpretations of the ancient fathers. The church has always been inclined to summarize these foundations with the outline of doctrine known as the Catechism, which primarily includes the Apostles' Creed, the Lord's Prayer, and the Decalogue." See also, Zanchi, *De natura Dei*, sig. b2r, b3r–v (*OOT*, 1/2:ℂℂiiiiv–iiiiir).

Chapter Two

God and the Divine Persons and Properties

1. There is only one God, distinct in three persons.
* Having been thus instructed by God in the Holy Scriptures, which are His Word, we believe that there is only one God (Deut. 4:6 [that is, 6:4]), that is, one most simple, indivisible, eternal, living, and most perfect essence subsisting in three subsisting ones[1] or (as the church usually says) persons—namely, the eternal Father, the eternal Son, and the eternal Holy Spirit, truly distinct among themselves but without any division, the source and cause of all things (Matt. 28:19; 1 John 5:7).
[* Observation 2.1][2]

2. Each person is true God on His own in such a way that there are, nevertheless, not three gods.
For we believe and have learned from the Holy Scriptures that the Father is true and perfect God on His own, that the Son also is God on His own, and that the Holy Spirit is God on His own. Yet, this is in such

---

1. ὑφισταμένοις. Richard Muller (*Dictionary*, 155) defines ὑφιστάμενον as "something placed or set under something else; a subordinate thing." Here and elsewhere, Zanchi uses it without clearly differentiating its meaning from ὑπόστασις. Throughout this text, I have rendered the former as "subsisting one" and the latter as "hypostasis." Bernardus de Moor, *Compendium theologiae christianae didactico-elencticum* (Leiden, 1761), 1:700 (ch. 5, §II) suggests that, in many cases, "perhaps ὑπόστασις and ὑφιστάμενον no less than *personalitas* and *persona* can be distinguished as abstract and concrete."

2. As indicated in the letter to the reader, an asterisk points to the observations appended to the confession proper. They are identified with reference to the chapter and section that they address from the confession. Hence, observation 2.1 refers the reader to ch. 2, §1 of the confession.

a way that there are not many but only one Jehovah,[3] from whom and by means of whom and in whom all things exist [Rom. 11:36].

3. *One person is distinguished from another person by personal properties, but they differ in essential properties from all creatures.*
* To be sure, the Holy Scriptures speak about God in such a way that they attribute to Him many properties—both essential as well as personal—and, indeed, they teach that by His essential properties He differs from all created things, but that one person is distinguished from another by personal properties. For this reason, we also believe that, as it is proper to the Father to beget the Son, it is therefore appropriate neither for the Son nor the Holy Spirit to do so. We also believe that to be begotten is appropriate to none but the Son, and so forth concerning the rest. So, likewise, to be most simply eternal, immense, and everywhere present, simply omniscient, simply omnipotent, simply good, and other things of this sort, is so proper to God that they cannot really be communicated to any creature in such a way that (for the sake of example) a creature is good with the immense goodness or omnipotent with the same omnipotence with which God is good and omnipotent.
[* Observation 2.3]

4. *The essential properties in God do not really differ from His essence.*
For we acknowledge that, in God, on account of His simplicity,[4] essential properties do not really differ from essence and, so, that they cannot be communicated to any creature without His essence being communicated. Therefore, no creature can truly be or be said to be (for example) simply omnipotent, simply good, just, wise, and other similar things.

---

3. Although modern scholarship tends to regard "Jehovah" as an incorrect pronunciation of the tetragrammaton, Zanchi was convinced that it was correct. Consequently, his preferred reading is maintained here. See, Zanchi, *De natura Dei*, 40–41 (bk. 1, ch. 13; *OOT*, 1/2:31–32).

4. Zanchi's use of "simple," "simply," and "simplicity" here and elsewhere refers to the attribute of divine simplicity, that God is not composed of parts but that all that is in God is God.

This is as our Lord Jesus also taught, speaking of one attribute, saying, *No one is good* (simply) *except God* (Matt. 19:17).

5. *Nothing is or can be made simple as God is, unless it can also be God simply.*

For this reason, those who allow that any created substance could or can become a partaker of the divine properties in such a way that the substance thereby also becomes as God is (simply omnipotent and so forth) must also confess that the created substance is or can be consubstantial[5] with God, since neither the Son Himself nor the Holy Spirit is simply omnipotent, except as He is consubstantial[6] with the Father.

6. *A confirmation of the previous judgment.*

From this we also understand how it is that we, nevertheless, do not say that there are three almighties, since the Son (and, likewise, the Holy Spirit) is not less omnipotent than the Father. Rather, with Athanasius and the whole church, we confess only one Almighty because there is no doubt that all of them have only the one and the same essence[7] (Athanasian Creed[, §14]).[8] Accordingly, since no created thing has one and the same essence as God, but rather some other and very different essence, it would be necessary for there to be more than one Almighty for the essence of the created thing also to become omnipotent by communication of the divine omnipotence. We do not believe this can be said without blasphemy.

7. *Errors.*

Therefore, we condemn and abhor all the heresies that have risen up or are revived from hell against this first article of the faith and were condemned by the holy fathers in legitimate councils: Cerinthus, Ebion, Valentinus, Marcion, Mani, Arius, Eunomius, Sabellius, Praxeas, Fotinus, and, likewise, Servetus and the tritheists, as well as the blasphemies

---

5. ὁμοούσιον.
6. ὁμοούσιος.
7. οὐσία.
8. Athanasian Creed[, §14]: Schaff, *Creeds of Christendom*, 2:67.

of the Jews and the Turks, and, finally, all heresies contrived by the Devil either against the unity of the divine essence or against the true Trinity of persons. And, thus, we condemn those who either deny that the Son is the true and eternal God (and, accordingly, the Holy Spirit) or confound these persons and say that they are one and the same subsisting one[9] but are called by the various names of Father, Son, and Holy Spirit on account of various considerations.

We also condemn all those errors that separate the properties of God from the divine essence. This, it seems to us, is what they are doing who teach that the properties of God actually can be communicated (or, rather, that they are now already communicated) to any creature without imparting the divine essence as well.

---

9. ὑφιστάμενον.

Chapter Three

Divine Foreknowledge and Predestination

1. From eternity, God has foreknown and foreseen all things.
We believe that, before God created the world, even from eternity, He foreknew all things by His boundless wisdom, both the good things that He Himself would do and also the evil that He would permit to be done by others, such that nothing was ever or could be hidden from Him. Rather, we do not doubt that all things—not only those that have been done and will yet be done but also those that might be done even if they never are—are and always have been naked and exposed before His eyes (Heb. 4:13; Acts 15:18).

2. In His eternal council, God has predetermined all things and foreordained them to the best ends.
We believe not only that God foreknew all things and had them present in His sight but also that, in His most wise and eternal council, He predetermined whatever pertained or pertains to the creation and governance of the world. The same is true of His gathering of the church out of the muck of other men, her redemption, and her eternal salvation (Acts 4:28). And, likewise, we believe that He foreordained all the evils that He would permit to be done unto the best ends and according to His infinite goodness, such that not even a hair falls from our head apart from the will of our Father and without cause (Matt. 10:29–30).

3. Out of all men, some are predestined to life and others to death.
For this reason also, we do not doubt that God, having foreseen that everyone He created righteous in Adam would sin in Adam as well,

elected some in Christ, that they might be holy and blameless in His sight, and, so, in love predestined them unto eternal life merely on the basis of grace and according to the purpose of His will (Eph. 1:4–5). (Note that, at this point, we are not speaking of the angels.) To others, however, He was unwilling to grant this grace and, therefore, prepared them for destruction as vessels of wrath according to His just judgment. He did this so that His infinite mercy might be revealed to the whole world by the former and His justice by the latter, unto His glory (Rom. 9:22).

4. The election of the saints is a free gift.
Calling unto Christ, and justification in Christ, is an altogether free gift and not a result of our own works. Just so, do we understand that every element of the saints' predestination is a free gift because it was done in Christ and its execution was commanded on account of Christ, so that no one could glory in himself. Rather, *He who glories, let him glory in the Lord* (Eph. 2:9; Titus 3:5; Eph. 1:4; Rom. 9:11; 1 Cor. 1:31).

5. We are predestined not only unto the end but also unto the means.
For which reason we also believe that, since God has elected us in Christ in order to be faithful and holy and blameless in His sight, we are predestinated not only unto the end (that is, unto eternal life and glory) but also unto the means by which we attain to that end. Especially, we are ordained unto faith whereby we are grafted onto Christ and unto regeneration and true repentance whereby, having been made new creatures in Christ, we live holy lives to His glory and for the edification of our neighbor (2 Cor. 5:17; Gal. 6:15; Matt. 5:16).

6. Those who are never grafted onto Christ by His Spirit and by living faith are not elect and cannot be saved.
So then, they are shamefully deceived to their own destruction who reckon themselves to be elect (and who, on that account, reckon that they shall be saved) but who have never been grafted onto Christ by faith, nor repented of their sins, nor applied themselves to doing the will

of God and good works (Titus 1:16; Eph. 2:10). For they separate what God wills to be joined.

7. Everyone ought to be confident of his election in Christ, but we can be more assured of it on the basis of our experience of faith in Christ.
Here also it is evident that, generally speaking, no one should exclude himself from the number of the elect, since Scripture does not do so. Instead, each one should trust that, when he is called unto Christ, he is called according to the eternal purpose and election of God. Nevertheless, if someone wants his own certainty of his election to grow, he should hasten unto faith and the testimony of conscience to observe whether he discerns himself truly to believe in Christ and to be moved by sincere love toward God and neighbor (2 Cor. 13:5). And if he does not discern this in a sound way and to good effect, let him nevertheless not despair but rather ask God to help his unbelief, hoping that he will come to greater certainty (Mark 9:24).

8. The reasons why the Holy Scriptures teach the doctrine of predestination.
The doctrine of eternal, gratuitous, immutable predestination is not taught in the Holy Scriptures in order for us to neglect Christ or despair about our salvation, nor is it taught so that, feeling secure, we might give free rein to concupiscence,[1] nor, finally, in order for us to grow proud. Rather, it is taught for the following reasons:

First, that we might know that, outside of Christ, no one can be saved, since the foundation of our whole salvation was established and fortified in Christ Himself before the world's creation (Acts 4:12; 2 Tim. 2:19).

---

1. *Concupiscentia.* Zacharias Ursinus, whom Zanchi succeeded at Heidelberg and who was his colleague in Neustadt, defined concupiscence as "an inordinate desire or corrupt inclination, coveting those things which God has forbidden." He goes on to comment that "concupiscence, although it is without doubt born in us, is both an evil and sin; for we are not to judge according to nature, but according to the law whether a thing be sin or not. Whatever is opposed to the law is sin, whether it be born in us, or not." *The Commentary of Dr. Zacharias Ursinus on the Heidelberg Catechism*, trans. G. W. Williard (Phillipsburg, N.J.: Presbyterian and Reformed, 1985), 606.

Second, that, when facing temptation, we who believe in Christ might sustain ourselves in the certainty of salvation and neither despair nor distrust, since salvation is certain and secure in God's eternal decree (Romans 8 [esp. vv. 38–39]).

Third, that we might be stirred up by the doctrine of predestination to pursue faith in Christ, holiness, and good works. For we are elect in order that we might be faithful and holy and blameless in His sight and walk in good works (Eph. 1:4; 2:10).

Finally, that, if we believe in Christ and live holy lives, we might not grow proud but rather credit everything solely to divine grace in Christ, so that he who glories might glory in the Lord, since, by means of His eternal grace in Christ, God decreed these things for us from eternity (1 Cor. 1:31).

Chapter Four

The Omnipotence and Will of God

1. God's omnipotence is such that He can do more than He wills to do.

We believe that God's omnipotence is such that He not only did and does whatever He willed or wills but that He also is able to will and do an infinite number of things that He does not will. In this we also follow the teaching of John the Baptist, who said, *God can raise up sons to Abraham from these stones*, although He did not will it (Matt. 3:9). Likewise, we follow the judgment of the apostle, who wrote, *God shows mercy to those whom He will*, whereas He could show mercy to all, *and hardens not all, as He could, but rather those whom He will* (Rom. 9:15, 18). So, it is very wicked to be willing to conclude that anything is, was, or will be done only by God's omnipotence without also being ordained by His will (Tertullian, *Against Praxeas*[, §10.8]).[1]

2. The fact that there are certain things that God cannot do does not impugn His omnipotence.

Since the apostle writes that God is not able to deny Himself, we believe that it does no injury to God's omnipotence if one says that there are

---

1. Tertullian, *Against Praxeas*[, §10.8]: "Certainly nothing is difficult for God: but if in our assumptions we so rashly make use of this judgement, we shall be able to invent any manner of thing concerning God, as that he has done it, on the ground that he was able to do it. But we must not, on the ground that he can do all things, for that reason believe that he has done even what he has not done, but must enquire whether he has done it." Tertullian, *Tertullian's Treatise against Praxeas: The Text Edited, with an Introduction, Translation, and Commentary*, ed. and trans. Ernest Evans (London: SPCK, 1948), 142 (*ANF*, 3:605).

many things that God cannot do, namely, those things that oppose His nature and imply contradiction (2 Tim. 2:13).

3. A confirmation of the previous judgment.
For since He is the highest good, He certainly cannot become evil or do evil. And since He is the essence of truth, He cannot lie. Since He is the essence of justice, He is unable to do anything unjustly. Since He is life itself, how can He die? Finally, since He is the one and only God and is uncreated and eternal, subsisting in only three persons, we believe and confess that He cannot assume to Himself any creature in such a way that it becomes consubstantial[2] with Him and such as He Himself also is, or in such a way that it constitutes a fourth person. And we are persuaded that nothing of God's omnipotence is decreased or diminished by this confession. Certainly, what has been done cannot be done without having been done, just as it is equally certain that God, who is the highest truth, can do nothing that results in a contradiction. For if we were to take that approach, the very omnipotence of God whereby those things were done would be openly denied.

4. The will of God should be sought only in the Holy Scriptures.
Furthermore, since the councils of God are infinite and secret—indeed, they are not disclosed to the angels themselves (Mark 13:32)—we believe that, when there is a question concerning the will of God, it should be sought nowhere but in the Holy Scriptures, wherein God abundantly and perspicuously supplied and supplies us with everything necessary for salvation, and wherein God, by His mercy, has revealed through His Spirit what He wills for us to do (John 15:15; 17:29 [that is, 17:26]).

---

2. ὁμοούσιον.

Chapter Five

The Creation of the World, the Angels, and the Condition of the First Man

1. All things were made by God, and they were made very good (Genesis 1–2).
We believe that, through the Son and together with the Holy Spirit, God the Father created all things, visible and invisible, that are encompassed in the term *heaven and earth* by the Holy Spirit in the Holy Scriptures (Col. 1:16). And they were created very good, in the space of six days, out of nothing. And we believe that God intended all things to be used by man and for His own glory. Therefore, we acknowledge the Son and the Spirit as well as the Father as the world's creator, since He is one and the same God.

2. Heaven is distinguished from earth, and the heaven of the blessed differs from the other heavens.
* We neither confound heaven with earth nor confuse one heaven with another. Rather, with the Holy Scriptures, we distinguish them, just as we see the elements and animals of all kinds and other things distinguished (2 Cor. 12:2; Matt. 6:10). And therefore, when we refer to that heaven in which the souls of the blessed wait with Christ, where the bodies of all the godly will be, which Christ called paradise, the house of His Father, and which the apostle called the city having a foundation whose builder and maker is God, we confess that it is to be distinguished from the other heavens, and all the more from earth and hell (John 14:2; Luke 23:42; Heb. 11:10). Paul likewise alluded to this when he said that he was *caught up to the third heaven*, meaning, above

the atmospheric heavens as well as all the visible and movable spheres (2 Cor. 12:2).

[* Observation 5.2]

3. *All the angels were created good, although they did not all persevere in the truth.*

Accordingly, we also believe that all the angels were created good and righteous, as spiritual and immortal substances provided with intelligence and free will. Nevertheless, not all of them continued in that goodness and righteousness nor, as the Lord Jesus says, *persevered in the truth* (John 8:44). Rather, we learn from the Scriptures that, even from the beginning, many of them willingly sinned and became enemies of God, of everything that is good, of human beings, and, especially, of God's church. They became liars and, of themselves, speakers of lies, murderers, devils, evil spirits. For this reason, they were cast down from heaven into Tartarus[1] and delivered into chains of darkness, to be reserved unto condemnation (John 8:44; 2 Peter 2:4).

4. *The reasons why many heavenly spirits were permitted to sin and become evil.*

But we learned from the Holy Scriptures that divine wisdom did not permit this to happen without reason. For, besides the fact that God willed to use these matters to reveal His judgment and wrath against the sins of all kinds of creatures, He also ordained their works for testing and stirring us up in the faith, for spiritual battle, for patience, and, consequently, for promoting our salvation (Eph. 6:12). Finally, He also willed them to be executors and administrators of His judgments against human wickedness, that they who refuse to receive the love of truth (whereby they

---

1. This section uses the Greek word *Tartarus*, which is often translated into English as "hell" in its single appearance in the New Testament (2 Peter 2:4). Elsewhere (CCR, 28.7 and 29.6) in the confession, *Tartarus* is equated with *infernus*, that is, that place where demonic spirits are chained until the day of judgment about which Zanchi appears to be speaking here. (Compare Jude 6.) To distinguish Zanchi's use of *Tartarus* from his use of *infernus* in this translation, the former is left as "Tartarus" while the latter is rendered "hell."

might be saved) might follow the doctrines of demons and believe their lies and perish (1 Kings 22:21; 2 Thess. 2:12).

5. Good angels were preserved by God's grace so that they might be His ministers and ours.
Again, we believe that innumerable heavenly spirits were preserved out of the total number by God's grace and on Christ's account, so that they did not sin with the rest but persevered in truth and obedience (Dan. 7:10). These were made God's messengers and administrators, who are devoted to the welfare of the elect and protect them from the devils and advance Christ's kingdom (Heb. 1:7; Ps. 103:20). They love us and look after us to such an extent that they rejoice exceedingly at our salvation (Luke 15:7). They refuse, however, to be worshiped by us. Instead, they remind us that God alone should be worshiped and say of themselves that they are our fellow servants, those with whom we will spend our eternal and blessed life in heaven (Rev. 22:9; Matt. 22:30).

6. Man was created in the image of God.
We believe that God, having already created everything else, at last also created man after the image and likeness of God, forming his body from the earth and his soul, a spiritual and immortal substance, from nothing, and He breathed into that body. Shortly thereafter, a wife was added unto him. As concerns her body, she was forged from his bones, and she was formed according to the same image of God (Genesis 1–2).

7. Wherein that image of God especially consists.
But we believe God's image to have been especially located in this: that, as God is the absolute Lord of all things, so all things were subject to man—the birds of the heavens, the fish of the sea, and the beasts of the earth—such that he would be king of the whole world (Gen. 1:28; Ps. 8:6–8). And even more especially in this: that, as God is most holy and righteous, so also man was created upright in true righteousness and holiness, just as the apostle explains (Eph. 4:24).

8. Adam was truly free before the fall.
And hence, we believe that man in that first estate was gifted with such

liberty that he could not will anything against his own will, which liberty always has remained and does remain in man. However, he was also given such power accompanying that liberty that, if he had willed, he could have not sinned and not died but rather persevered in righteousness and avoided death, such that his losing both is to be attributed to him and to no one else (Eccl. 7:30 [that is, v. 29]; Sir. 15:18).

9. Errors.
God is none other than He who consummately does good and who is the sole creator of all things. We, therefore, condemn the Valentinians, the Marcionites, the Manicheans, and whomever has taught or left behind any writing against this article of the faith, whether they contrived that all things were fashioned by a god other than the Father of Christ or that good things were made by a good god but that evil things were made by a different wicked one. We also condemn all those who either teach that man's soul is of the divine substance or deny its immortality and perpetual action or who locate the image of God only in dominion or, finally, who deny that the first man was truly created free.

Chapter Six

The Providence and Governance of the World

1. The world and everything in it and that is done in it are ruled by divine providence.

We believe that God, having created all things, rested from all His work that He had completed in such a way that He, nevertheless, never stopped or stops providing for, ruling, and governing the world and everything in it. This is true for both great and small things and, especially, for humankind and for each individual person, such that nothing happens (or might happen) in the world that is not ruled by divine providence (Gen. 2:2; Wisd. of Sol. 14:3; Matt. 10:29–30).

2. The church of God is ruled over with particular care.

Although each and every thing is subject to divine providence, we nevertheless believe that God's church, each one of the elect, and their wills and actions are ruled over with a certain special care and prudence. This is the case since He particularly calls, justifies, and sanctifies them, which He does not do for everyone. Moreover, He works in them *to will and to accomplish* and says that He will dwell in them, which He does not do in everyone. Furthermore, He leads them unto eternal life but allows the rest *to walk in their own ways* toward His just judgment and to charge into eternal ruin (Rom. 8:30; Phil. 2:13; 2 Cor. 6:16; Acts 14:16). He also does this particularly so that He might appropriately command us *to cast all our cares upon God, for He cares for us*—and He cares for us in particular (1 Peter 5:7).

3. *God ordinarily rules the world by means of secondary causes.*
We learn this also from the Holy Scriptures: although God executes many decrees of His eternal providence on His own, without any external helper—and, indeed, sometimes does so by contravening the ordinary means—nevertheless, the usual way that He ordinarily commands the execution of most things is by means of secondary causes, both in the governance of the whole world and in the church. For He says, *He will hear heaven, and heaven will hear earth, and earth will hear the grain, and the grain will hear Jezreel* (Hos. 2:21–22).

4. *The means to the end should not be disregarded, since God, by His providence, wills the one no less than the other.*
We also understand from this that we are assured that, although God cares for us, the means ordained by God unto the salvation of both souls and bodies should, nevertheless, not be disregarded, nor should God be tested. Rather, we should follow the apostle, who—despite being fully persuaded of the safety of all those who were in the boat—nevertheless, told the soldiers and the centurion *you cannot be saved* unless those sailors who were considering flight remained in the boat (Acts 27:31). For God, who determines everything unto its own end, has also ordained the origin and the means whereby that end is attained.

5. *With regard to God, all things are necessary; with regard to us, many things occur contingently.*
Indeed, in His providence, God maintains and even moves the secondary causes that He ordinarily uses to govern the world, each one according to its own nature. Some of these are determined unto specific consequences by their own nature; others are indeterminate. For this reason, we understand and confess that, with regard to God (without whose foreknowledge and will nothing in the world happens), all things are necessary.[1] Yet, with regard to us and to secondary causes, all things are

---

1. Beck notes that Zanchi does not "explain whether he understands the necessity of secondary causes in respect to God in the sense Aquinas did in S[*umma*] *Th*[*eologiae*], I, q. 19, a[rt]. 8, or rather in terms of Scotus's interpretation of the necessity of the

not necessary. Rather, most things happen or come to pass contingently (Matt. 10:29–30). For what can be more contingent and, indeed, more a matter of chance to the woodcutter and the passerby than the axe of the one flying from his hand and killing the other? Yet the Lord says that the woodcutter is the one who killed the passerby (Ex. 21:13). And although the Lord Jesus died voluntarily, nevertheless, He said, *the Christ should suffer* (Luke 24:46). Again, although Herod and Pilate condemned Jesus of their own free will, the apostles say they did only that which the hand and council of God decreed to be done (Acts 4:28).

6. *God is not the author of the sins that are committed in the world.*
From this, we also understand and confess that, although much wickedness is committed in the world by men, it cannot be charged to God and His providence. For God, indeed, moves all things and, by His providence, supplies strength to each one for working, but He does not instill in anyone the wickedness whereby he commits wicked acts (1 John 2:16). Thus, as the earth cannot be blamed for providing nutrients for bad trees as well as for good ones—for it is the bad tree that produces bad fruit—so, far less does God deserve to be called either the author or the cause of our sins, despite His sustaining, conveying, conducting, and ruling all things by the hand of His providence, even the wicked (Heb. 1:3). *In Him*, says the apostle, *we live and move and exist* (Acts 17:28); evidently, what we are is what we are moved by Him to be—unless He makes us different than we are by His grace.

7. *We should adore, but not pry into, God's hidden counsel in governing the world.*
At the same time and with all due reverence, we admire and adore God's hidden and marvelous counsel. Thereby we see innumerable things accomplished to which we cannot assign or even discern a reason. Yet we are content with this sure knowledge: nothing is done in this world outside of God's will, and His will is so just that it is the rock-solid standard

---

consequence and its compatibility with true contingency of the consequent (see *Lectura* I, d. 39, n. 48, 162–65)." "Reformed Confessions and Scholasticism," 23n1.

of all justice (Matt. 10:29–30; Rom. 9:14). And thus, we should always hold onto what the apostle said: *Oh, the depths of the riches, of the wisdom, and of the knowledge of God; how incomprehensible are His judgments and unsearchable His ways* (Rom. 11:33).[2] Again this: *Is there any injustice with God?* (Rom. 9:14). But yet, *Of Him and by Him and in Him are all things. To Him be glory forever. Amen* (Rom. 11:36).

8. Errors.

We, therefore, condemn all scoffers and all those philosophers who either remove God's providence from the world altogether or who deny that God attends to humans and every detail. We likewise condemn those who, abusing God's providence, dismiss it as a means ordained by Him for the salvation of both our souls and bodies as well as those who argue that everything happens necessarily in so simple a way that they remove all contingency and eliminate all human liberty. Finally, we condemn those who want God to be working all things in such a way that they also blasphemously make Him to be a coworker[3] and author of sins.

---

2. Although Zanchi quotes Rom. 11:33 from the Vulgate, he amends the word translated here "unsearchable" (for the Greek ἀνεξιχνίαστοι). The Vulgate translates this with *investigabiles*, but Zanchi uses *impervestigabiles*, as do Erasmus (in Eph. 3:8), Calvin, Beza (in his *Novum testamentum*), and others. See Desiderius Erasmus, *Collected Works of Erasmus*, vol. 56, *Annotations on Romans*, ed. Robert D. Sider (Toronto: University of Toronto Press, 1994), 317–18; John Calvin, *Commentaries on the Epistle of Paul the Apostle to the Romans*, ed. John Owen (Edinburgh: Calvin Translation Society, 1849), 443.

3. σύνεργον.

Chapter Seven

The Fall of Man, and Original Sin and Its Fruits

1. Adam sinned of his own accord through disobedience.
We believe that the first man was created after the image of God—righteous, upright, and truly free, so that he was able not to have sinned nor to have died any kind of death if he had willed (Genesis 1–2; Eccl. 7:30 [that is, v. 29]; Sir. 15:18). Subsequently, being persuaded by the Devil and not being prevented by God (but rather God leaving him to his own counsel), he sinned by means of disobedience with his own truly free will. The first man did this in such a way that he neither could nor ought to ascribe the guilt of his sin to the nature he received from God nor to God Himself, nor should he blame any other creature but himself alone, because he was the one who willed thus (Gen. 3:1; Sir. 15:14; Rom. 5:19).

2. What and of what sort was Adam's sin.
For we understand the sin of Adam to have been (as Moses describes it) the voluntary transgressing of the divine mandate not to eat of the forbidden fruit (Genesis 2; 3:6), and that, therefore, (as the apostle says), it was disobedience, which consisted not so much in the external act as in his soul's voluntary resolution whereby he refused to obey God (Rom. 5:19).

3. What kind and how manifold a death followed Adam's sin.
Thus, we acknowledge that, by his own fault, man was then destitute of God's grace, his mind darkened, his will distorted, and all integrity of his nature utterly lost. He ruined that life which he had formerly lived

in a holy way unto God, namely in those things that pertain unto God and a life pleasing to Him. Man became a servant of sin, a slave of Satan, and truly dead unto God (John 8:34; Eph. 2:1). Moreover, he incurred the death of the body (which is now common to all men, along with all the misfortunes of the body) and, especially, the eternal death of the whole man (that is, a most wretched, most miserable, and most unhappy life with the Devil in eternal punishment—a life beyond all comparison and worse than any death). He cannot be liberated from this except by Christ (Rom. 5:12; 1 Cor. 15:22).

4. *All men sinned in Adam.*
But because all humankind that was to be propagated from Adam by means of natural generation was in his loins—whence the commandment, along with its threat, pertained not only to the person of Adam but also to all humankind—therefore, with the apostle, we believe and confess that all men sinned by sinning in Adam. Thus, Adam's disobedience was not his alone but also became common to all humankind, since the guilt of that one man involved all men who were thereafter procreated carnally of his seed as well as those who are procreated today. This is the same thing that the apostle taught openly to the Romans, and he also confirmed it most strongly by contrasting Adam's disobedience with Christ's obedience (Rom. 5:19). Because we are born again of Christ's incorruptible seed and Spirit, His obedience is ours by means of imputation just as it is His own by means of His own personal action. And if this is true, then it follows that Adam's disobedience is also imputed to us and that we bear his guilt because we are begotten of his flesh and by his seed as the father of us all.

5. *Adam's disobedience resulted in the corruption of the entire nature of all men.*
Moreover, by God's just judgment, the corruption of the whole nature—called concupiscence by the apostle, which was the punishment proceeding from the sin, and sin, and the cause of other sins (Rom. 7:7 [that is, v. 8])—soon overtook the person of Adam on account of the actual disobedience (Augustine, *Against Julian the Pelagian*, bk. 5, ch.

3[, §8]).[1] So, having been taught out of the Holy Scriptures, we also believe and with the whole church confess that all men, who are conceived by natural propagation from Adam's seed, are in like manner born infected by the same pollution of corrupt nature. For all sinned in Adam, and all are held fast, bound by the guilt of that same disobedience.

6. *What we call original sin, properly speaking.*
This is the reason why we say that this inherited defect and contamination of nature in all men is sin, and why we usually call it original sin. But we do so in such a way that we separate the guilt of this first disobedience from its imputation in no way whatever. Just so, conversely, we do not doubt that the righteousness of Christians consists not so much in the regeneration of their nature (which is accomplished by means of Christ's Spirit and which it is customary to call inhering righteousness) as in the imputation of the perfect obedience and righteousness of Christ, whose members we are.

7. *The contamination of nature is truly sin.*
But although this contamination of nature was inflicted not only upon Adam in punishment for that first transgression of the divine mandate but also upon the whole of his posterity, nevertheless, on the basis of the Holy Scriptures, we consider this to be the most certain thing in the world: not only is original sin a punishment for sin and the cause of subsequent sins, but it really is sin as well, such that it suffices on its own for condemnation (Rom. 7:7 [that is, v. 8]).

8. *Even in the regenerate themselves, concupiscence is, by its nature, sin.*
Indeed, we have learned that concupiscence is, by its nature, sin to such

---

1. Augustine, *Against Julian the Pelagian*, bk. 5, ch. 3[, §8]: "In the same way, concupiscence of the flesh against which the good spirit has its own desires is a sin because it involves disobedience against the rule of the mind. It is a punishment of sin, because it is retribution that the disobedient deserve, and it is the cause of sin by reason of the failure of one who consents or the infection of one who is born." Augustine, *Answer to Julian*, in *Answer to the Pelagians*, vol. 2, by Augustine, ed. John E. Rotelle, trans. Roland J. Teske, *The Works of Saint Augustine: A Translation for the 21st Century* I/24 (Hyde Park, N.Y.: New City Press, 1998), 437 (*FOTC*, 35:249).

an extent that it fights against the law of God and delivers all guilty men unto damnation (unless they are set free by means of Christ). Consequently, even in the regenerate, to whom guilt is no longer imputed since it has been removed on account of faith in Christ, nevertheless we have absolutely no doubt that concupiscence truly, in and of itself, is sin and, therefore, that it is worthy of eternal death. For it is lawlessness[2] and is condemned by God's law, as the apostle also teaches (1 John 3:4; Rom. 7:7).

9. Sin perpetually flows forth from our innate concupiscence.
In addition, we believe this natural crookedness to be such an inexhaustible fountain of all kinds of sins that the utterly putrid waters of evil affections, impious thoughts, and crooked desires perpetually flow from it. Unless they are restrained by the Spirit of Christ, they ultimately burst forth in open wickedness and disgrace, some worse than others, so that there is no one who is so holy that he does not bear within him this cesspool of all defects, who is unaware that he is constantly exhaling its putrid vapors, and who is not perpetually splattered and befouled by its filth. *Every man*, says James, *is tempted by his own concupiscence, being drawn away and allured, but concupiscence, when it has conceived, gives birth to sin, and when it is completed, sin begets death* (James 1:14–15).

10. God is not the author of sin.
Still, from all of this we are confirmed in the confidence whereby we believe that God is in no way the author of sin, since He did not create Adam evil or with an inclination toward evil but rather righteous and upright; nor did He impel or move Adam toward evil. Rather, Adam sinned by his own voluntary and free will. Even this willful sinning was not a natural crookedness from God but followed the disobedience of Adam, who was deprived of righteousness. God justly permitted this and thus inflicted an appropriate punishment upon man for his sin (1 John 2:16).

---

2. ἀνομία.

11. Errors.

Therefore, with Irenaeus and the whole church, we condemn all those who make God the author of sin. We condemn all Pelagians as well, both the new ones and the old, who either deny that all men sinned in Adam and bear the guilt of that first sin, or who contend that this inborn concupiscence is only a disease and sin's punishment but not actually sin itself, or who, at least, want it to be unworthy of being called genuine sin in the regenerate.* We also condemn those who teach that original sin is a substance, because this opinion either makes God the author of sin or denies that He is the creator of all substances and confirms the doctrine of the Manicheans concerning two first principles—the greatest good and the greatest evil—whereby all things were made and proceed, the good things from the good principle, obviously, and the bad things from the evil one. Additionally, we condemn the Stoics and those like them who teach that all sin is equal, that none is more serious than another. Finally, we condemn those who contend that there is anyone in this world who is entirely devoid of all sin.

[* Observation 7.11]

Chapter Eight

Man's Free Will after the Fall

1. What we mean by the term "free choice."[1]
All men, since and on account of Adam's fall, are conceived in sin and born children of wrath, not at all disposed toward good but altogether toward evil. In view of that fact, this is our faith and confession concerning the nonregenerate man's freedom of choice (Eph. 2:3; Gen. 6:5; 8:21). By the term *free choice* we understand man's free will in such a way that we yet do not divorce it from the faculty of the intellect whereby we judge things and decide what is good and evil or what we should choose and what we should refuse.

2. The question is twofold: one concerning the nature of free will and the other concerning its power.
However, we distinguish the question about the power of free will as a whole from the question about the nature of man's freedom of choice. We designate *nature* an inherent[2] and essential property of the

---

1. Zanchi generally equates "free choice" (*libera voluntas*) with "free will" (*liberum arbitrium*). His understanding of these terms is explored in Roelf T. te Velde, "Always Free, but Not Always Good: Girolamo Zanchi (1516–1590) on Free Will," in *Reformed Thought on Freedom: The Concept of Free Choice in Early Modern Reformed Theology*, ed. Willem J. van Asselt, J. Martin Bac, and Roelf T. te Velde (Grand Rapids: Baker, 2010), 51–93. Later Reformed scholastic theologians distinguished more precisely between free will, free choice, and other related terms. See, for example, Dolf te Velde and Rein Ferwerda, eds., *Synopsis Purioris Theologiae / Synopsis of a Purer Theology: Latin Text and English Translation*, vol. 1, *Disputations 1–23*, trans. Riemer A. Faber, Studies in Medieval and Reformation Traditions 187/5 (Leiden: Brill, 2015), 346–47 and 406–31.

2. *Naturalem*, that is, inherent to the very nature of the will.

will imparted by God. It is that whereby the will chooses whatever it chooses—whether good or evil—freely, on its own, voluntarily, and always apart from any constraint. By the term *power*, however, we understand the power, whether innate or bestowed, whereby we are able not only to distinguish with our minds what is good from what is bad but also to choose the one and refuse the other with our will.

3. *Free will is always free of constraint.*

Thus, just as the substance of free will did not perish on account of sins (for the intellect, the will, and the whole substance of the soul endured) neither do we believe that its nature perished, since whatever it yet wills—whether good or evil—it wills freely and apart from any constraint. Indeed, as Augustine said, *Free will is always free* from constraint, but is not always good.[3]

4. *The three kinds of matters and actions that engage the power of the human will.*

But with regard to the power to choose the good or refuse the evil, we think thus. We distinguish good and evil things into three kinds: those that pertain to animal life, those that pertain to human life, and those that pertain to divine (that is, Christian) life. Among the first kind are those things that we share, in a broad sense, with the beasts and that belong to the vegetative and sentient soul.[4] Among the second kind are reckoned those that are proper to man and that pertain to the human mind, such as all arts, mechanical as well as liberal, moral and political virtues, and lastly, all knowledge and the whole of philosophy. But the third kind of life includes only those good things and good actions that are properly ordained unto the kingdom of God and the Christian life,

---

3. Augustine, *Grace and Free Choice*, in *Answer to the Pelagians*, vol. 4, by Augustine, ed. John E. Rotelle, trans. Roland J. Teske, The Works of Saint Augustine: A Translation for the 21st Century I/26 (Hyde Park, N.Y.: New City Press, 1999), 92 (*NPNF1*, 5:457).

4. According to Aristotelian philosophy as it was appropriated through Thomas Aquinas, a variety of types of souls exist and are distinguished hierarchically according to their vital functions. A vegetative soul accounts for nutrition and reproduction; a sentient soul accounts for motion; a rational soul accounts for the ability of humans to reason and speak. See, for example, *Summa theologiae*, I, q. 78, art. 1.

such as true knowledge of God, faith, and its effects: regeneration, obedience, charity, and other things of this kind.

5. *The power pertaining to human life is very weak in the unregenerate man.*[5]

Thus, let us say nothing about the power of humans after the fall as regards knowing, seeking, and (if the opportunity were to present itself) choosing, and pursuing that which has to do with sustaining our physical life and spending it happily and fleeing what opposes it, for these have nothing to do with religion and morality. (Yet, as for these, experience teaches on a daily basis how corrupted man is about such things in both his judgment and his appetite.) We believe that, by God's mercy, a certain light remains in the minds of humans—partly for making judgments between equity and inequity, good and evil, in human affairs; partly for gaining knowledge of many things, of the arts, of teaching, and of the various virtues. Yet so meager is that remaining light in the human mind and so distorted is the human will that, unless it is aided by heavenly light, and unless the will is inclined by special grace to choose the good that is set forth and to reject the evil, man cannot gain what he lacks in knowledge or practical skills or any virtues, all of which may exist in the unregenerate. Augustine was not wrong when he wrote that all the knowledge and virtues (or, rather, the appearance of virtue) that were in the Romans and other unbelievers were also God's singular gifts (*Against Julian the Pelagian*, vol. 7, bk. 4, ch. 3[, §32]).[6]

6. *A confirmation of the previous judgment.*

God does not provide all unbelievers with the same or equal virtues and knowledge. This is so that it might thereby be obvious that they do

---

5. For a survey of this topic in the theology of Calvin and later Reformed theologians, see Luca Baschera, "Total Depravity? The Consequences of Original Sin in John Calvin and Later Reformed Theology," in *Calvinus Clarissimus Theologus: Papers of the Tenth International Congress on Calvin Research*, ed. Herman J. Selderhuis, Reformed Historical Theology 18 (Göttingen: Vandenhoeck & Ruprecht, 2012), 37–58.

6. *Against Julian the Pelagian*, vol. 7, bk. 4, ch. 3[, §32]: "From this it follows that even those good actions which unbelievers do belong not to them, but to him who makes good use of bad persons." Augustine, *Answer to Julian*, 399 (FOTC, 35:196).

not possess such things naturally but that these are God's gifts added to nature.

7. In matters that pertain to God and true piety, an unregenerate man can do nothing.

However, in matters pertaining to God and Christian piety, religion, and life, we believe that the mind of the unregenerate man is so blind and his heart so crooked and all his remaining powers so weak that he can neither truly know God or the things of God, nor can he love Him and aspire to things that please Him. How can the unregenerate man obey God's will as he ought? If the apostle says, *The natural man does not perceive the things that are of God, nor can he perceive them* (1 Cor. 2:14), then how can he will them or do them? And Christ says, *Apart from Me, you can do nothing* (John 15:5).

8. A confirmation of the previous judgment.

For just as a man who is dead with respect to nature and men cannot do anything that pertains to nature or men, so neither can he who is dead in sins to God truly become aware of or do those things that are of God and true piety. Rather, he brings forth only sin, and he rots unless freed from it by Christ on the basis of grace and restored to life. But all men who are outside of Christ and who have not been regenerated by Christ's Spirit are truly dead. Thus, those who are freed by means of faith in Christ from sin are truly said to be made alive, resurrected, reborn, and grafted onto Christ (Eph. 2:3 [that is, v. 1]; John 5:21).

9. Errors.

Therefore, we condemn all Pelagians, who teach otherwise and extol the power of free choice against the grace of Christ. Likewise, no less do we detest the Manicheans and others who make man to be but a block of wood that, even in civil matters, has been granted no judgment or freedom of will.

Chapter Nine

The Promise of Redemption and Salvation by Christ

1. It was promised on the basis of grace that Christ the heavenly man would save us.

The first and earthly man fell into so miserable an estate by his own fault, and it was the same for all of his posterity who sinned in him and were indeed conceived in sin and born children of wrath. Therefore, we believe that God, out of His mere grace and mercy to Adam and Eve (and, in them, to all humanity), promised another Man, a heavenly one (Gen. 3:13 [that is, v. 15]; 1 Cor. 15:47–48). He, indeed, would be conceived of the true substance of true man but apart from the seed of man and, therefore, would be born of a virgin and without sin. This would happen so that, in Him—as in another head of humankind consisting of both a divine and a human nature, the true image of God the Father, full of the Holy Spirit—the very thing might be accomplished that the first head, Adam, had failed to accomplish by his own fault (Matt. 1:20; Luke 21:34 [that is, 1:34]; Heb. 4:15; Isa. 7:14). Namely, He, the second man, would perfectly and completely obey God the Father on behalf of all of us who would be grafted onto Him by means of His Spirit and who would become flesh of His flesh and bone from His bones by spiritual regeneration. And furthermore, by His obedience and death, He would bear away our sin, appease God's wrath, redeem us, justify us, sanctify us, govern us by His Spirit, truly free us, empower us to do good, and, ultimately, save us unto eternal life and glorify us (Rom. 6:5; 11:17; John 3:6; Eph. 5:29 [that is, v. 30]; Phil. 2:8; Rom. 5:19; Eph. 2:13–14 [that is, vv. 12–13]).

2. *The promise of redemption by Christ was necessary.*

Adam received righteousness not as a private person but rather as the parent and source of all of humanity, so that he might propagate that righteousness unto all his descendants as an inheritance, so to speak. (For that reason, this righteousness is usually called original righteousness.) In the same way, by his disobedience, Adam transmitted the most profound iniquity—the source of all sins—unto all men instead of righteousness; instead of eternal life, he transmitted eternal death. For this reason, we needed another Head, all of whose members might receive true and heavenly righteousness, holiness, and life on account of His obedience. This is Christ.

3. *Why that promise was made immediately after the transgression.*

Therefore, we also believe that this promise was made at the world's beginning immediately after the sin was committed. Thereafter, the promise was frequently repeated, set forth, confirmed, and sealed to the holy patriarchs in various ways, signs, and sacraments, so that we who would exist after the Messiah's advent, along with everyone from the world's creation who believed in this promise and embraced this coming Savior with true faith, might become partakers of the future redemption, that they might be justified and saved.

4. *Even from the creation of the world, everyone who believed in the coming Christ was saved.*

Thus, we believe that, even from the creation of the world, everyone who believed in the promised and coming Christ was grafted onto Him by faith. They became partakers of His future obedience, passion, death, and redemption. They ate His body (the body that would be given) and drank His blood (the blood that would be poured out) [Matt. 26:26–28]. In a word, all those who believed were Christians, were granted Christ's Spirit, and were saved unto eternal life no less than we are.

5. *Errors.*

* And so, we condemn and detest those who say that none were saved before Christ's advent, along with those who say that the patriarchs received no promises concerning eternal life but only concerning temporal things.

[* Observation 9.5]

Chapter Ten

The Law

1. *The law of Moses came between the promise of redemption by Christ and its fulfillment, and the reason why it came.*[1]
Yet between the promise of redemption by Christ that was first made to Adam and later clearly set forth to others, especially to Abraham, that was sealed with the sacrament of circumcision, that was confirmed (as it were) in the offering of Isaac the firstborn as a sacrifice, and that was established by an everlasting covenant—between this promise and its fulfillment, the law given by Moses was interposed. This happened so that—the descendants of Abraham (from whom also Christ would be born) having already been gathered, miraculously increased, and spectacularly freed from Egyptian servitude—a specific and visible church might exist unto God distinct from other nations and gathered in a certain place; so that the promise concerning Christ given to the patriarchs might be preserved in that people; and so that pleasing worship might be presented unto God until the advent of the true and promised Redeemer.

That is to say, the law God gave through Moses to His church, which came between the promise and its fulfillment, contained three types of precepts: moral, which molds the piety and life of everyone; ceremonial, which directs the church in her external worship and religious life; and judicial, which pertains to the governance of the whole commonwealth

---

1. Zanchi explored the law at length in *De primi hominis lapsu, de peccato, et de Lege Dei* (*OOT*, 2/4:185–872; chs. 10–28). A small part of that discussion has been published in translation as *On the Law in General*, trans. Jeffrey J. Veenstra, Sources in Early Modern Economics, Ethics, and Law (Grand Rapids: CLP Academic, 2012).

in political and domestic matters. By means of the law, God's people (from whom Christ would come) were to be restrained from the profane habits and idolatries of wicked nations, continue in service of and obedience to the divine will, and, ultimately, be sustained in their faith and in the hope of the fulfillment of the promise of true redemption by Christ. Thus, daily—more and more—they would be prepared to receive Christ, and God would thus be glorified in His people.

2. *Whatever is necessary for accomplishing salvation is contained in God's law.*
Let us say nothing more about the ceremonial and judicial parts of the law, which do not pertain to us. We believe, however, that the moral part of the law—as set forth in the books of Moses, the prophets, and the apostles (2 Tim. 3:16)—has displayed and revealed in so perfect a manner what is necessary for salvation and what God wants us to do in this world that it would be impossible for anything to be added to or subtracted from it (Deut. 2:4 [that is, 4:2]; 5:22; 12:32).

3. *The law of the Decalogue is an explication of the law of nature and a picture of the image of God.*
In fact, we believe that this law is the explication of the law of nature, which was inscribed perfectly on the hearts of the first people but imperfectly and in part on the hearts of others. And thus, it condemns anything that is contrary to God's image after which man was created and, conversely, commands whatever is consistent with it. That is to say, by this law, God willed to publicly proclaim what man was like in his first estate, what he became in his second estate, how excellent he ought to be, and what he would eventually be like—in part in the third estate but perfectly in the fourth estate through Christ.[*2] Thus, the law of God is nothing other than a true and lifelike picture of the image of God after

---

2. Zanchi follows the Augustinian tradition here. The first estate was in the garden before the fall. The second was after the fall but before Christ. The third is after Christ but before the parousia. The fourth will be in the glory of the eschaton. See *The Augustine Catechism: The Enchiridion on Faith, Hope, and Charity*, ed. Boniface Ramsey, trans. Bruce Harbert (Hyde Park, N.Y.: New City Press, 1999), 139–40 (*FOTC*, 2:468–69).

which man was created and by which we are reminded what we were like, what we are like, what we ought to be like, and even what we will be like if we believe in Christ.

[* Observation 10.3]

4. The summary of the law is restricted to the love of God and of neighbor.
But we believe and confess, because Christ taught it, that the sum or substance of the whole law is contained in these two precepts: *Love the Lord your God with your whole heart, with your whole mind, with your whole soul, and with your strength,* and, *Love your neighbor as yourself* (Matt. 22:37[–39]). The first of these is the substance of the first table of the Ten Commandments, while the second one is the substance of the second table.

5. If God alone is to be loved with the whole heart, then He alone should be adored.
However, the substance of the first table, which contains the entirety of the devotion owed to God, consists solely in the perfect love of God alone. From this and God's other express commands that explain this one, we conclude and believe that He alone should be adored, invoked, and worshiped with religious devotion, and that oaths should only be sworn in His name. For this conclusion is comprehended within the command to love the one God with the whole heart, not to mention that the image of God (of which the law is a picture) taught Adam the very same thing.

6. Concupiscence itself and the corruption of nature are also sin.
But if the divine law condemns as sin anything out of harmony with that first image of God in which man was created (that is, with righteousness, holiness, and uprightness), then we understand that, not only are consensual actions of man's will against God's law to be taken as sin but so, too, is the stirring of concupiscence and even concupiscence itself and the whole corruption of the nature, and they are condemned by God's law. For they fight against the uprightness and righteousness in which

man was created and in which he should have kept himself and could have if he had so willed (Rom. 7:7).

7. Although the law cannot be kept, nevertheless, it was not given in vain or without purpose.

Moreover, we believe that, although God's law is so perfect that no mortal was or is able to keep it wholly or always or as it should be kept, nevertheless, it was not given in vain or to no purpose.[3] For God does nothing in vain but rather does everything out of His exceeding wisdom, to His glory, and for our profit and salvation (Rom. 7:10; 8:3).

8. The threefold usefulness of the law of the Lord.

For, first, this law's perfect displaying of the divine will enables and enabled men to understand what pleases God—what is good, what is bad, what should be done, and what should be avoided—better than they could merely from the remnants of the law of nature that linger in the human mind. Consequently, more than any other nation, the Jews, being deprived of every pretext of ignorance, were rendered inexcusable for failing to keep the law. This results in God's greater glory, since men thereby understand that His judgment against us is most righteous.

Second, because men feared the curses added against transgressors, the law served as a brake, helping to restrain them from giving into sin. And the hope of blessings for those who observed the law acted as a goad that encouraged them to follow it, if not perfectly then at least in part and in external works. Thus, they were better kept within the bounds of their duty. Everyone knows how useful it is not only for the whole republic but also for each individual man to conduct himself in such a way.

Third, because of what men observed in their daily life—that they were always sinning against this perfect law and unable to keep it as they should and, therefore, that they daily became more and more subject to

---

3. In view of what was said in the previous section about Adam's ability to keep the law before the fall, Zanchi presumably intends this sentence to refer only to human beings after the fall. Hence, his reference to mortality. In other words, he has returned to his previous discussion of the moral law contained in the Decalogue, which Jesus summarized as love of God and neighbor.

God's wrath and liable to eternal death—it happened that, despairing of themselves and of their own strength, they were moved toward a greater desire for the promised redeemer and liberator. And so, they increasingly came to know their sins and their weakness through the law, and they experienced God's wrath more vividly. Consequently, they hungered and thirsted more ardently after righteousness and were disposed and prepared to receive Christ by faith. Thus, the apostle truly says both that *knowledge of sin comes through the law* and that *the law was our pedagogue unto Christ* (Rom. 2:20 [that is, 3:20]; Gal. 3:24).

9. *The law still retains the same uses, even in men who are regenerate.*
Moreover, we believe that, so long as we are in this world, these same uses of the law are perpetual, not only for the unregenerate (as was already said) but even for the regenerate. For our minds are as yet shrouded by great darkness, and our memory is slippery, such that we can neither perfectly grasp the things of God nor keep in mind what we do understand. For this reason, we continually have need of this mirror of divine law in which we may daily contemplate what God desires us to do and may understand it more clearly from day to day.

Second, our heart is not perfectly purged of all depravity such that it could be wholly inclined toward doing God's will; rather, the flesh always struggles against the spirit. On that account, we need the law, which intimidates us with its threats, restrains us from sins, and with its promises goads us toward obedience and the doing of righteousness (Gal. 5:17).

Finally, the law is also useful to us because no one is as yet so holy that he does not sin in many ways or that he has in himself no indwelling sin, which is weak toward good and always inclines toward evil (1 John 1:8). For, as we discern our sins and weaknesses through the law more and more day by day, we realize how impossible it is for us ever to be justified and saved through our own work. And thus, we are moved all the more by a desire, hunger, and thirst after Christ's righteousness, and we embrace Him by faith. Therefore, while the law was never able to justify, at least it always leads those of us who are to be justified nearer and nearer to Christ, the one who justifies.

10. *As regards its substance, Christ did not intend to abrogate the moral law.*

For we know and believe that Christ did not intend to abrogate the law about which we are speaking as regards the substance of its teaching and its wholesome use. Nor was it abrogated except as regards cursing and condemnation, because *there is no condemnation for those who are in Christ Jesus, who do not walk according to the flesh but according to the Spirit* (Rom. 8:1[, 4]). Yet, even in its condemning, the law was always useful (and remains so) for those who are not yet in Christ insofar as it drives them unto Christ, that they might not be condemned.

11. *Errors.*

Therefore, we condemn those who cast this law away from the church as useless and not pertinent to Christians as well as those who teach that, either in whole or in part, man can be justified by the law, for it was rather given in order to confine everyone under sin and lead to Christ, who alone bears the sin of the world (John 1:29[; Gal. 3:22]). And this is our brief confession concerning the law delivered by God through Moses and explained by the prophets, which prepares man for, disposes him toward, and leads him unto Christ. And, so, as the apostle writes, *Christ is the end of the law* (Rom. 10:4).

Chapter Eleven

Christ the Redeemer

1. *The substance of the faith regarding the person and office of Christ the Redeemer.*

> *Therefore, when in the fullness of time, God sent His Son, made of a woman, made under the law so that He might redeem those who were under the law that we might receive the adoption of sons.* (Gal. 4:4–5)[1]

That is, when the redemption promised to the first man was to be accomplished by the second, the eternal Father sent His only begotten and eternal Son, who, for that reason, was true God, consubstantial with His Father. He was made of a woman alone, without the seed of man, for which reason He was also true man but without sin. He was, moreover, the true Christ who was made under the law and for that reason was also circumcised, in order to fulfill the law by His most perfect obedience in the name of us all (Gal. 4:4).

He became obedient to the Father for our sake, even unto death. He did this on our behalf, for He did not deserve to die, since He was without sin. He did it so that, by His obedience, His death, and the outpouring of His blood, which is to say, by an infinitely valuable sacrifice

---

1. Zanchi arranged this section in a very complex manner, integrating the text of Galatians 4:4–5 with a running commentary on the economy of redemption. Unfortunately, however clear this format might have been to the original readers, it breeds confusion in translation. For the sake of clarity and readability, I have chosen to separate the biblical text from the running commentary.

(for it was the blood of God; Acts 20:28) and by a fully efficacious ransom,[2] He might redeem all the elect.

That is to say, He did this in order to redeem them from their sins unto the pristine image of God and, therefore, unto perfect righteousness and, what is more, from death unto eternal life, and from the kingdom of Satan unto the kingdom of God. And He did it so that we might receive the adoption of sons and, therefore, that we might ultimately also be received as sons and legitimate heirs for the full and perfect possession of the heavenly inheritance (Gal. 4:5).

Finally, He did this so that all things—both things in heaven and things on earth—might be gathered together under one head and joined to Him, to the glory of God the Father (Eph. 1:10).

2. *Christ the Redeemer is true God and true man.*

Therefore, we believe that Christ is the only begotten Son of God and, thus, that the Son is by nature consubstantial[3] and coeternal with the Father and, indeed, that He is true Jehovah God. He is also true man, from the true seed of Abraham and of David, conceived without the aid of man but solely by the power of the Holy Spirit and, therefore, in the womb of a virgin and without sin (John 1:14; Mic. 5:2; Phil. 2:6; 1 John 5:20; Matt. 1:1). He was born of her, provided with a true soul and a human mind, and was like us in all things except sin (Heb. 4:15; Matt. 26:35).[4] As true God, He was begotten of the substance of the Father before all ages, but as true man was born of the substance of His mother in the world (Athanasian Creed[, §31]).[5]

3. *The Son alone is both God and man, and He alone is the Christ.*

But we believe the Son of God to be both true God and man and, therefore, the true Christ, and we believe this in such a way that we also confess this of Him alone, since we read that neither the Father nor the

---

2. ἀντιλύτρῳ.
3. ὁμοούσιον.
4. The reference to Matthew 26:35 does not seem pertinent.
5. Athanasian Creed[, §31]: Schaff, *Creeds*, 2:68.

Holy Spirit but only the Word[6] was made flesh (John 1:14). And the apostle says that only the Son was made of a woman, and so only He suffered (Gal. 4:4).[7] Nevertheless, the Father and the Holy Spirit also acted together to create the nature assumed by the Son.

4. *The Son was made man without any change to Himself but only by assuming a human nature.*
Moreover, we believe that the Son of God was not made man by confusing His divine nature with the human in any way—neither by converting it into flesh nor by any change in the flesh—but only by assuming a human nature into the unity of His person. Just as Athanasius says, *Not by the conversion of divinity into flesh but by the assumption of humanity into God* (Athanasian Creed[, §35]).[8] Thus, what He was by no means diminished. Rather, He assumed what He was not. As the apostle says, the Son assumed *the seed of Abraham* (Heb. 2:16). Thus, he teaches that, just as the Son, in His assuming, was not changed into the thing He assumed (for God cannot be changed at all) but rather remained what He was, distinct from the thing He assumed, so the seed He assumed was not converted into the thing that was assuming. Rather, it was united with the divine nature only insofar as it relates to the unity of His person in accordance with the saying, *The Word became flesh* (John 1:14). Flesh, therefore, remains flesh and is not changed into Word.

5. *The Son of God's nature did not assume another nature, nor did His person assume another person, but rather His person assumed a human nature.*
From this we also understand that the common divine nature of the three persons—indeed, the one and the same nature of them all—did not take to itself a human nature, nor did a person [in God, that is, the Son] assume another person. Rather, He merely assumed another nature. For the Son of God did not take to Himself a specific son of

---

6. τὸν λόγον.
7. That is, only the Son, *and not the Father or the Spirit*, was incarnate and suffered.
8. Athanasian Creed[, §35]: Schaff, *Creeds*, 2:69.

Abraham. Instead, He assumed the seed of Abraham, that is, a human nature propagated from Abraham. Therefore, we do not recognize two persons in Christ but just the one person by whom all things were made and who was so perfect before He assumed to Himself the seed of Abraham that He did not become another person nor a more perfect person nor, indeed, was He made imperfect in any way by that assuming.

6. *Christ did not assume a human nature to constitute a new person or to perfect a previously existing person; rather, He merely assumed a human nature into the society and unity of that eternal and most perfect person.*

* Although we acknowledge that there are two natures in Christ, a divine one and a human one, nevertheless we do not accept that the human nature was, on that account, assumed in order to compose a new person unto Christ out of this or that (out of parts, as it were). Nor do we accept that the human nature was assumed in order to perfect the previously existing and eternal person by adding a new nature. Rather, we merely grant that, having assumed a human nature into the unity of the person that existed most perfectly from all eternity, the Son of God became what He was not while remaining what He was so that He might have something to offer the Father on our behalf.

This is why we do not approve unconditionally of someone saying that the person of Christ was composed out of the divine and human natures in the same way as the person of each man also consists of a soul and a body. But we do approve of the customary phrase used in the church: Christ clothed Himself, or was clothed, with our flesh. This is also why Augustine says, *Christ descended from heaven like a man descending naked from a mountain, but He ascended clothed with our flesh as a garment* [sermon 263A, §3].[9] For this phrase, although it does not

---

9. [sermon 263A, §3]: "After all, if someone climbs a mountain, or a wall, or any high place, with clothes on after coming down without any clothes, or goes up armed after coming down unarmed, would anybody say it wasn't only the one who came down that went up? So just as you can say about such a person, 'No one went up except the one who came down,' although he went up with something he had not come down with; in the same way, nobody has ascended into heaven except Christ, because nobody has come down from heaven except Christ, although he came down without a body, ascended with a body, and we too are going to ascend, not by our prowess, but by our and his oneness."

explain the hypostatic union perfectly, nevertheless makes a clear distinction between the person of the Son of God (who assumes) and our nature (which is assumed). For this same reason we embrace the sayings of the fathers such as *The human nature is borne by the Son of God*, and also, *It subsists in the person of the Son of God*, and similar sayings that distinguish the person of the Son of God (who assumes) from the nature that is assumed and teach that, by assuming a human nature, the person of the Son of God did not become something else, nor did it become more perfect.

[* Observation 11.6]

7. A confirmation of the previous judgment, with an explanation of the topic in Athanasius.
* Indeed, we bear witness with Athanasius that, just as a rational soul and a body is one man, so God and man is the one Christ.[10] That is, although there are two natures in Christ, He is only one person. However, if we want to speak properly, this is not true in such a way that Christ's person is constituted out of both natures (out of parts, as it were) in the same way that the coming together of the body no less than the soul (as essential parts) is necessary to constitute a complete man. This is the case since Christ's person already existed in a full and altogether perfect way before He was manifested in the flesh, but the person of a man—Adam, for instance—was nothing before soul was joined with body (1 Cor. 10:9; 1 Peter 3:19).[11]

A soul does not take to itself a body, nor does a body take to itself a soul, in the same way that the Son of God took to Himself—into the unity of His very person—the seed of Abraham. And furthermore, the

---

Augustine, *Sermons*, vol. 7, 230–272B, ed. John E. Rotelle, trans. Edmund Hill, The Works of Saint Augustine: A Translation for the 21st Century III/7 (Hyde Park, N.Y.: New City Press, 1993), 224.

10. "For just as one man is both rational soul and flesh, so too the one Christ is both God and man." Athanasian Creed, §37 (Schaff, *Creeds*, 2:69).

11. The significance of these citations appears to be that they point to the preexistence of the person of Christ before His incarnation and assumption of a human nature.

body and the soul are two subsisting things[12] as is established in the creation of Adam, but the human nature never subsists of its own except in the person of the Son of God. For these reasons, very unjustly do some people abuse that holy man's [that is, Athanasius's] pious statement in order to prove their own delusions. For it absolutely must be the case that He who manifested Himself—this, indeed, is the person of the Son of God—differs from the flesh in which He manifested Himself. And this must be true not only before but also after His resurrection and session at the right hand of the Father, which did indeed bring glory to the flesh but did not remove its nature, as Augustine says.[13]

[* Observation 11.7]

8. *How Christ can be only one eternal and immutable person but have two natures in Him, and in what sense He can be said to consist of them.*

We, therefore, acknowledge and confess the following against Nestorius: first, that there is only one person in Christ—namely, the person of the eternal Son of God—and that that person is eternal, most simple, and most perfect, and that He remains so forever. Next, to this eternal person was truly added in time not another person but rather another nature, namely, a human one. And that nature was not added as a part of His person—that is, the person that assumed the human nature. Rather, it was added as a thing distinctly different from His person, and yet assumed into the unity of the person. And thus, in the third place, we acknowledge that in the one and the same person of Christ there are even now two natures, divine and human. We do not doubt that the person subsists, lives, and works in them. This is the reason why we do not fear to speak in this way as well: Christ now consists of a divine nature and a human one assumed into the unity of the person and, moreover, in some sense, is composed of them.

---

12. ὑφιστάμενα.

13. Baschera and Moser note that this passage does not appear in any of Augustine's works. See *De religione*, 1:208n139. They refer the reader to "To Peter on the Faith" by Fulgentius of Ruspe (c. 467–532), who was influenced by Augustine. See Fulgentius of Ruspe, *Selected Works*, trans. Robert B. Eno, Fathers of the Church 95 (Washington, D.C.: Catholic University of America Press, 1997), 83, 98–99.

9. In what way the two natures are united in the one person unchanged and unconfused,[14] *with the properties and actions of each safe and distinct.*

We believe and confess that these two natures are, thus, truly and inseparably conjoined and united; nevertheless, we do not doubt that each nature remains whole, complete, and truly distinct one from the other. Nor do we doubt that each nature retains its distinct essential properties and operations, utterly free from all confusion. Thus, just as the divine nature, retaining its properties, remained uncreated, infinite, immense, simply omnipotent, and simply wise, so also the human nature, retaining its properties, remains created, finite, and bound within certain limits.

And just as the divine nature has its own will and power whereby Christ as God wills and works those things that are of God, so the human nature has its own will and power whereby the same Christ as man wills and works those things that are of man. This is the case to such an extent that, insofar as Christ is God, He neither wills nor works by human will and power. Nor does Christ will and work by divine will and power insofar as He is man.

This is just as the fathers wisely set down both against Eutyches and against Marcion. Thus, what Leo I said to Flavian when he wrote about this same matter has always pleased us. He says: *He who is true God, the same is true man, and there is no fraud in this union, since both the humility of man and the loftiness of deity are mutually present. For just as God is not changed by compassion, so man (that is, the human nature in Christ) is not consumed by the dignity. For each form does what is proper to it, in communion with the other—namely, the Word working that which is of the Word and the flesh carrying out that which is of the flesh* (Letter [to Flavian], ep. 10 [that is, 28], §4).[15] These are the words of Leo the Great. Subsequently, he illustrates his point with a few examples whereby he clearly demonstrates that, just as the natures are truly united in Christ while remaining distinct and unconfused, so too were (and are) Christ's actions. For the things that are of the Word do not pertain to the flesh

---

14. ἀτρέπτως καὶ ἀσυγχύτως.
15. Letter [to Flavian], ep. 10 [that is, 28], §4: Leo I, *Letters*, trans. Edmund Hunt, Fathers of the Church 34 (New York: Fathers of the Church, 1957), 97–98 (*NPNF2*, 12:40). This letter to Bishop Flavian is commonly known as Leo's *Tome*.

but to the Word; and the things that are proper to the flesh do not pertain to the Word but to the flesh.

Raising Lazarus from the dead was proper to the Word, and calling out, *Lazarus, come forth*, was proper to the flesh. Nevertheless, in the resurrecting of Lazarus, both actions were united because they were done by and in the one Christ and were directed toward the one work, yet they were distinguished. Likewise, to forgive sin was the proper action of the divine nature, and to say, *Your sins are forgiven you*, was of the human. To give light to the man born blind was an action of the divine nature, and to put mud on his eyes and say, *Go and wash*, was of the human nature.

Therefore, just as the hypostatic union did not confuse the natures, so neither did it confuse the actions. Instead, they remained distinct, and so neither did it confuse the properties of the natures. For these three things are in the one person of Christ: the natures, the natures' properties and faculties, and the actions of each of the natures. And Christ has in Him the properties of the natures in the same way as He has both the natures and the actions. Therefore, as it is evident that nature is not transformed into nature nor action confused with action, so also it is clear that properties work in the same way.

10. A true and real intermingling of the divine properties into Christ's human nature cannot at all be demonstrated on the basis of the union of the natures.

For we approve the axiom of the fathers against the Eutychians and the Monothelites, namely, that things that share the same essential properties also share the same natures and essences. And things in which natural properties are confused are also confused in their natures. Of itself, this is true in all things, but it is especially true in God, in whom the essential properties are actually nothing other than the essence itself. For this reason, it is necessarily true that, if the divine properties can actually and properly speaking be communicated to some other created substance in such a way that the thing becomes as God is—for example, if it were to become simply omnipotent—then the divine essence itself can be communicated to that same created substance. Thus, if the created substance is equal to God in power[16] or in any other property, then it is made equal to God in essence[17] and consequently is consubstantial[18] with God.

So, here a twofold and grave error is admitted. First, any time we truly and properly speaking communicate to a creature things that are proper to God, we make that creature equal to God. Nor does it avail to make an exception, that God has these things from Himself but that the human nature in Christ has them from the deity. For not even the Son is of Himself, nor does He have the divine essence of Himself, but rather from the Father—albeit He is still equal with the Father and has the very same nature as the Father.

Second, any time we attribute divine and thus infinite properties to the human nature (for example, infinite power), we rob it of its finite property in just the same way as the glory of the resurrection strips our ignominious bodies of their corruption when it is truly communicated to them. This happens in the same way that the immense light of the sun absorbs the light of a candle when sunlight enters a space that had been illuminated only by candlelight.* For if an infinite power acts and performs all the work, a finite power sits idle and, consequently, does nothing. Yet, since this heresy has actually been refuted by many learned men in our age in a most abundant and clear fashion, we who present our brief and simple confession of faith to the church of God and to all of posterity wish to add nothing else to what has been said.

[* Observation 11.10]

11. How great is the force of the hypostatic union.
At the same time, we believe and confess the force of the union of natures in the person of Christ to be so great that, first, whatever Christ is or does according to the divine nature, the whole Christ—the Son of Man—is said to be or do it.* Conversely, the Holy Scriptures proclaim that whatever He is, does, or suffered according to the

---

16. τῇ δυνάμει.
17. τῇ οὐσίᾳ.
18. ὁμοούσιος.

human nature, the whole Christ—the Son of God and God—is, does, and suffered.

Take the passage that says, *God (that is, Christ, man and God) redeemed the church by His blood* (Acts 20:28). The power of redemption pertains to the deity, while the effusion of blood pertains only to the humanity. Nevertheless, both of these actions are united into one, and both are simultaneously predicated of the whole Christ, although they were and are distinct actions. For although the natures are also distinct, they are nevertheless bound together in the one person of Christ. Indeed, Christ the Mediator never did anything according to His humanity without the past and present cooperation of the divinity. And He performed nothing according to His deity to which the humanity did not submit or give consent. Thus, all the works of Christ the Mediator might well be said to be performed by God and man.[19]

In the second place, just as the force of the union between the Father and the Son is so great that even the Father does nothing and never imparts any blessing upon the world except by way of the Son, so also, such is the power of the hypostatic union of the two natures that nothing of grace, salvation, or life flows unto us from the deity except by way of the humanity, which we apprehend by faith. So, if someone wants to partake of eternal life, he must be joined to the flesh of Christ. That saying of Christ pertains: *Unless you eat the flesh of the Son of Man, you will not have life in you* (John 6:53).

Finally, it follows that we cannot worship the deity in Christ unless we simultaneously also worship the humanity in Him and that we should worship Him wholly, the human nature and the divine, with only a single worship. This accords with that saying: *And when He brings the Firstborn into the world, He says, "And let all His angels worship Him"* (Heb. 1:6). It says, *Him*, meaning the whole—God and man at the same time—even though the human nature considered in and of itself alone cannot and should not be worshiped, for God alone is to be worshiped. But this [that is, the worship of the whole Christ] is the result of a specific sort of union: a hypostatic union of the divine nature with the human. Hence,

---

19. Θεανδρικαί.

although God dwells among the saints, yet they are not to be worshiped or prayed to like the man Christ.

Therefore, we bear witness to the great force of this union about which we speak, but we nevertheless say that the union is such that it excludes all confusion and transfusion. For if the union between the Father, Son, and Holy Spirit in one essence—a union than which no greater can either exist or be imagined—does not eliminate the distinction of persons, then neither can this union of natures (and, so, of properties and actions) in one person eliminate the distinction between them and produce confusion.

[* Observation 11.11]

12. *Assuredly, Christ as man was given great, but nevertheless finite, power and other gifts.*
Finally, we believe that, insofar as Christ is God, He is simply omnipotent, simply wise, and so on with regard to all the other attributes. In the same way, insofar as He is man, the Father gave Him power and knowledge far surpassing, almost by infinite degrees, the power and knowledge of all created things—both heavenly and terrestrial. Nevertheless, it was a finite power and knowledge. The same is true with regard to all other gifts and virtues: charity, prudence, fortitude, justice, grace, truth, and so forth. Concerning this, Isaiah says: *And the Spirit of the Lord shall rest upon Him* (Isa. 11:2; John 1:14). Again, as Luke says, *He advanced in wisdom and grace before God and men* (Luke 2:52). For this reason, it is also said that, as man, Christ was exalted *above all principalities and powers* (Eph. 1:21). Again, *The Spirit was given to Him without measure* (John 3:34). Again, *In Him are hid the treasures of wisdom and knowledge* (Col. 2:3).

This is why, insofar as He is man, Christ is ignorant of nothing and is incapable of nothing that pertains to His office. However, it is with the power of deity that He does those things that cannot be performed by any created substance but only by God alone. Yet the human will always consents and, as it were, offers a prayer of supplication in such a way that Christ's soul always in some sense assents with love, desire, and will to all the actions that pertain to our salvation, which He performed insofar as He is God. And in the same way, the deity always concurs with everything that He does as man, even in suffering itself and the death of Christ. This is not because the deity suffered but because the deity willed both His suffering and death and ascribed infinite significance to His suffering and death whereby our sins could be expiated.

In summary, with regard to Christ's two natures and their union and properties, we believe whatever was set down in the Nicene, Constantinopolitan, Ephesian, and Chalcedonian Councils against Arius, Apollinaris, Nestorius, Eutyches, and in the sixth synod against the Monothelites too.

13. Christ's actions are of two types, and everything we read that He did or suffered was done in actual fact and not as an empty display.
* Now, let us move on from Christ's person, His nature, and the union of the natures to His actions and office specifically. First, we believe that, just as there are two true natures in Christ, each of which had and has its own true and essential properties, so are there also two types of actions joined together in the same way as the natures are united but simultaneously unconfused. And in just the same way, we believe that there are two types of actions that we read our Lord Jesus Christ partly offered and, indeed, partly continues to offer for our salvation. Some of these flow from the deity itself, while others flow from the humanity. And thus indeed, at the same time, they partly were and partly are joined, yet were and are distinct, such that, as Leo says, *Each form always acts in cooperation with the other; the Word doing those things that are of the Word and the flesh carrying out those things that are of the flesh* [Leo's *Tome*, ep. 28.4].[20]

Second, those things that Christ did and does by virtue of the divine nature are true and unfeigned works, for He truly reconciled us to the Father, truly remitted sins, truly sanctifies and regenerates. Just so, whenever we read that He did or suffered something on our account according to His human nature, we believe He truly and really did and suffered all those things, not merely as an empty display nor (as they say) for appearance's sake.

[* Observation 11.13]

---

20. [Leo's *Tome*, ep. 28.4]: Leo I, *Letters*, 97–98 (*NPNF2*, 12:40–41).

14. An explanation of the previous judgment.
We believe, therefore, that just as Christ was truly conceived of David's seed and truly also was born true man, and truly ate, drank, and performed other human works, so He also truly kept the law for us, truly suffered and died in the flesh, and truly rose again from the dead in the same flesh (1 Peter 4:1; Luke 24:39). And with His visible, palpable, and true human flesh bounded by fixed dimensions, He ascended into the true and created heaven, which is set above all these visible heavens (Heb. 11:10; Eph. 4:10). And there He lives and abides by His own free will until, in that same visible body, He truly returns from heaven to judge the living and the dead (Acts 1:21 [that is, 3:21]). He also truly wills our salvation in heaven, cares for us, and directs the flow of spiritual and vital motion and perceptions into us as into His members. Finally, He rules over the whole church (Eph. 1:22; 4:16).

15. The fruits of Christ's obedience, suffering, death, and resurrection.
But we believe that Christ, by His perfect obedience, gained eternal life not only for Himself but also for us. He expiated our sins in His flesh by His suffering and death. He redeemed us from Satan's hands, death's tyranny, and slavery to sin. He reconciled us in Himself to God and made us beloved, so that, in Him, we might be reckoned righteous before God the Father. Truly, by His resurrection and ascension into heaven, He also obtained for us, as John says, both the first and the second resurrection (Rev. 20:5). And He also received unto Himself possession of the heavenly inheritance in our name. And He sits at the right hand of the Father, that is, He received authority over all things in heaven and on earth such that, as He is Mediator and man, He obtained from the Father the second place, being appointed Head of the whole church, both in heaven and on earth, so that, from Him—even from His own flesh—everything pertaining to our vivification and spiritual life may be conveyed by the Holy Spirit unto those who are joined to Christ as members to a head (Eph. 1:29 [that is, v. 22]).

Thus, we acknowledge, believe, and confess that the whole of salvation, redemption, righteousness, the grace of God, and eternal life is deposited in the one Christ, according to that saying, *Who became to us wisdom, righteousness, sanctification, and redemption from God* (1 Cor. 1:30). Again, *He is our peace* (Eph. 2:14). Again, *Jehovah our righteousness* (Jer. 23:6). *In Him we have redemption through His blood, the remission of sins* (Eph. 1:7). Again, *It pleased God that all fullness should dwell in Christ* (Col. 1:19). Again, *Life is in His Son* (1 John 5:11). Thus, we understand that the promise concerning redemption that had been made to the first man received its fulfillment in this other man, Jesus Christ, such that it is altogether necessary that he who desires to become a partaker of the promise must be joined to Christ as his Head and must become one of His members. For we have redemption and salvation not only by way of Him insofar as He is Mediator but also insofar as we are in Him as Head. This is our faith concerning Christ the Redeemer; concerning His person, natures, and office; and concerning the salvation of humankind completed and set forth in Him.

16. Errors.

We therefore condemn all heretics, both old and new, who taught or teach anything to the contrary: Arius, Photinus, and Servetus in particular, and all other impious men of this ilk, who deny the true deity of Christ. We also condemn Cerdonians, Marcionites, Valentinians, Manicheans, Priscillianites, Apollinarians, and others who oppose the true humanity of Christ. Some of these deny that Christ came in the flesh or had real flesh, alleging instead that He had an imaginary body from heaven or from the elements (but not one conceived of the seed of Abraham). Or, similarly, they contend that he was not born of a woman. Others, at least conceding true human flesh, nevertheless rob Him of a rational soul, substituting the deity in the place of a soul.

We also condemn Nestorians, who denied the true union of the human nature with the person of the Son and established two persons in Christ and two sons—the Son of God and the son of man. No less do we condemn Eutyches, who conversely allowed that, just as Christ is only one person, so also there is only one nature in Him, namely the divine, teaching that the human nature He assumed was either utterly converted into the divine or so mingled and confused with the divine nature that no difference remains in Him between the properties and actions of the divine and human natures.

We also condemn those who spring up from these: Macarius with his followers, who allege only one will in Christ, namely the divine one, and thus admitted no action proper to the human will in Christ. Likewise, on this point we also condemn the Cerdonians, who taught that Christ neither truly suffered nor truly died but rather that He pretended to suffer or, as other heretics said, that His suffering and death were imaginary. And with them, consequently, we condemn all those who taught or teach similar things, namely either that Christ was not truly resurrected in the same flesh that died but rather in some other flesh of a different nature, or that, if He was resurrected in that same flesh in which He died, nevertheless, He did not truly ascend into heaven and bring it into heaven or change its location.

Likewise, with Jerome, Cyril, and other fathers, we condemn the Origenists and those like them, who taught that Christ was resurrected with a body in the form of a very subtle spirit that was invisible by its nature and not liable to any senses. Likewise, we condemn the Jews and the Turks, who deny the world to have been redeemed by benefit of Christ's death.

Finally, we condemn all those who contend that salvation, either in part or the whole, is deposited in anything other than in Christ alone or who blasphemously claim that sins are expiated or remitted by any sacrifices other than Christ's alone. For we acknowledge Jesus Christ as the only Redeemer, apart from whom there is not only no true God but also no true salvation. We acknowledge Christ as the unparalleled sacrifice who, His singular oblation having been offered, not only expiated in His person all the sins of the elect once but also pardons believers daily to the end of the world, their sins having already been expiated.

Chapter Twelve

The Actual Distribution of the Redemption, Salvation, and Life Deposited in the One Christ
(and the Indispensable Union and Fellowship[1] with Christ)

1. Salvation and eternal life are deposited in Christ so that they might be imparted to us.

We believe that the sin of Adam and the death that accompanied it did not only remain in Adam but flowed and flows out of him, as from the head of all humankind, into all men who were or are born from him by ordinary generation. In the same way, we also believe that Christ's righteousness and the eternal life that it merits are not only retained by Christ but distributed to all those who are made one with Him by the regeneration of the Holy Spirit and who are joined to Him as true members, as to the Head of the whole church (Rom. 5:12). And this is why Christ came in the flesh and why the whole of salvation and life was deposited in Him as Head, namely, so that it might be distributed and imparted unto all the elect, who are united to Him.

2. Assuredly, the grace of redemption and salvation is sincerely offered to everyone; yet in fact it is imparted only to the elect, who are made one with Christ.

For we believe that the grace of redemption, salvation, and eternal life distributed by God is sincerely offered to all men through the preaching of the gospel, for it is on account of their own fault and guilt that many do not become partakers of it. Yet that grace is imparted in fact only to those who have been elected and predestined from eternity in Christ as Head of all the elect. This is that unto which they are elected: becoming

---

1. Κοινωνία.

His members and thus partakers of salvation (Mark 16:15–16). Subsequently, in due time, having been called by the proclamation of the gospel and granted faith by the Holy Spirit, the elect are grafted onto Christ and made one with Him.

3. *How indispensable is the actual union (or fellowship[2]) with Christ for truly partaking of salvation.*
Branches cannot draw vital sap from a vine, nor a bough from a tree, as a member cannot derive motion, sense, and life from a head unless the branch and bough are truly joined to the vine and the tree, and unless a member is truly joined to its head. In the same way, men cannot gain salvation and life from Christ, in whom alone those things are located, unless they are truly grafted onto Him, unless they are bound together by a true and real union, and unless they remain bound together in Him (John 15:1–7).

4. *We cannot be united to Christ unless He first makes Himself one with us.*
Our entire participation in true righteousness, salvation, and life necessarily depends upon this fellowship.[3] Hence, the preaching of the gospel, the administration of all the sacraments, and, indeed, the church's whole ministry are set forth unto that end. It is on that account, therefore, that we wish to explain and bear witness to Christ's whole church as briefly and clearly as possible what is our confession on this matter with the following trustworthy theses.

Concerning Fellowship[4] with Christ
First then, we believe that, just as we love Christ because, as John says, He first loved us [1 John 4:19], and just as we approach Him by our spirit because He first came unto us by His, and just as we embrace Him by faith because He, having first laid hold of us by the power of His Spirit, stirred up faith in us, so also we cannot cling to and become one

---

2. κοινωνία.
3. κοινωνίᾳ.
4. κοινωνίᾳ.

with Him unless He first joins and makes Himself one with us (1 John 4:10). For the one is the cause of the other; the former of the latter. This is why we must pray for Him to come to us and to make us His dwelling (John 14:23).

5. *How manifold is Christ's union with us and ours with Christ, and how they are ordered in relation to each other.*
Moreover, we acknowledge a threefold union of Christ with us and, in turn, of us with Christ. The first happened in our nature one single time. The second happens daily in each of the elect, but as pilgrims unto God. The final union shall likewise be with the Lord in our persons, but then we shall be present with the Lord—when God will be all in all to us [1 Cor. 15:28].

The first of these is, indeed, traced back to the second, and the second to the third, just as nature is ordained unto grace and grace unto glory. For the first union was actually accomplished through the assumption of our nature into the unity of the person of the Word.[5] The second is accomplished by the assumption of our persons unto grace and into one mystical body with Him and, thus, as Peter says, into the participation of His divine nature [2 Peter 1:4]. The third will be accomplished by the assumption of us all into glory with Christ forever. And since Christ chose to show us the latter from the former and the last from the latter, we doubt not but that we will be confirmed in the hope of what will be done by what has already happened.

6. *Just as the first union happened in order to expiate sins, so the second happened that we might partake of that expiation.*
Let us omit for the moment that which does not pertain to the matter at hand, so that we can focus on what does. Therefore, we believe that, having been conceived by the power of His Spirit in the womb of the virgin, the Son of God assumed our flesh—that is, our human nature—by the eternal will of the Father (and, therefore, by His own will and that of the Holy Spirit). And we believe that He assumed our flesh unto Himself

---

5. τοῦ λόγου.

in the unity of His person and, having been made truly obedient to the Father unto death, perfectly fulfilled God's law for us in that flesh. And, finally, we believe that, having offered that flesh as a sacrifice for our sins, He secured eternal salvation for us in Himself.

So, in the same way, in order that He might indeed make us partakers of this salvation acquired for us already by the sacrifice of His flesh, He chose and was disposed to assume and join unto Himself each of the elect by another kind of union, namely, by the sort of binding whereby we are made one with Him. If we are not made one person with Him, we are nevertheless made one true mystical body with Him, a body of which He is the Head and each one of us a member and whereby we are made partakers of His divine nature.

7. As the first union happens by the power of the Holy Spirit, so also does the second.

We do not doubt that, in the first union, the Son of God, our Lord Jesus Christ, bound our body and blood to Himself by the power of His Spirit (for He was conceived as a man of the Holy Spirit and, consequently, was without sin, for which reason He is also called the Man of heaven [1 Cor. 15:48]). Just so and in turn, in the second union, He likewise imparts His flesh and His blood and His whole self to us. In that communion, He connects, joins, and incorporates us into Himself by the power of His very Spirit, such that the bond whereby Christ is united to us and whereby we are in turn united to Christ is that same Spirit of Christ. That same Spirit caused the Son of God to become flesh of our flesh and bone of our bones in the womb of the virgin. Thus, by working in our hearts and incorporating us into Christ by participation in Christ's own body and blood, He also causes us in turn to become bone of Christ's bones and flesh of His flesh, especially as the Spirit also stirs up faith in us, whereby we know and embrace Christ as true God and man and, thus, as perfect Savior.

8. Our union with Christ is spiritual in such a way that it is nevertheless true and real.

* Thus, we believe that the second union—nearly as much as the first (if we may speak in this way)—is likewise so spiritual that it is yet true and real. For we really and truly are bound together by Christ's Spirit so that, while still on earth, we reign with Christ's body, blood, and soul in heaven. And His divine nature abides in us to such an extent that this mystical body, which consists of Christ as Head and the faithful as members, is sometimes simply called Christ (1 Cor. 12[:12]). The joining together of Christ with His faithful and of them with Christ is such that it seems not at all incorrect to say, in some manner, that, just as the first union made one person of two natures, so this union made one nature of many persons. This is in accordance with the following: *That you may become sharers of the divine nature* and *We are members of His body, of His bones and of His flesh* (2 Peter 1:4; Eph. 5:30).

[* Observation 12.8]

9. A confirmation of the previous judgment; how intimate is this union.
In a man, the soul—because it is one and the same and is no less entire in the head and the individual members than it is in the whole body all at once—makes a unity out of each of the individual members in a body and causes them to grow together under one head. In the same way, by the power of Christ's Spirit, this union causes each of us who are spiritually bound together as one in souls and bodies to be one and the same body with Christ as Head, for one and the same Spirit is in Christ and in each of the faithful. Indeed, this is a mystical and spiritual body because we are joined and framed by the secret binding of the same Spirit.

10. Because this union is accomplished by the power of the Holy Spirit, no physical distance can impede it.
From this it also follows that physical distance, no matter how great, cannot impede this true, real, and spiritual union of our bodies and souls with Christ's body and soul, seeing that it is accomplished by the efficacy of the sort of Spirit who extends from earth all the way up into heaven and beyond and who unites together Christ's members that exist on earth with their Head, who sits at the Father's right hand. And He does so in a way that is no less intimate than a man's soul joining his feet and legs and other members with his head in one body. And this would be the case even if the man were so large that his head reached to the ninth

sphere and his feet remained at the earth's center. Such is the power of the soul. But how great is the power of the true and omnipotent God's Holy Spirit?

11. *The Spirit who accomplishes this union at the preaching of the gospel and the administration of the sacraments is given by Christ.*
Again, we believe that this Spirit whereby Christ binds Himself to us and us to Him and by which Christ unites His flesh with ours and our flesh with His is imparted to us by this same Christ, even by His grace, when and where and how He wants. Ordinarily, however, this happens at the preaching of the gospel and the administration of the sacraments. As we read, a visible testimony of this was given when those in the newborn church—those who embraced the gospel by faith and were baptized in the name of Christ or upon whom hands were laid—received not only the invisible grace of regeneration but also various perceptible gifts of the Spirit.

12. *This union is the chief end of the gospel and the sacraments.*
From this we can also easily grasp what is the chief end of gospel preaching and administering the sacraments. It is fellowship[6] with Christ the Son of God incarnate, who suffered for us and died and now reigns in heaven, imparting salvation and life to His elect. This fellowship[7] begins here but will be perfected in heaven, so that, by this true and real binding together of us with His flesh and blood and with His whole person, we might also be made partakers of the eternal salvation that was gained by and abides in Him.

13. *This union is not imaginary, nor is it accomplished merely by the sharing of gifts but by substantial imparting.*
Furthermore, we say that our present incorporation with Christ is true, real, and substantial in order to oppose those errors whereby certain people suppose that we are forging some kind of imaginary and (hence)

---

6. κοινωνίᾳ.
7. κοινωνίᾳ.

false union, or that we establish a union that is true only insofar as it happens by the reception of spiritual gifts and Christ's grace, apart from the communication of the substance of His flesh and blood.

14. *The union happens only by means of the Holy Spirit and faith.*
Conversely, however, others should not falsely conclude from this that we imagine the sort of union that happens by means of some physical contact with Christ's flesh really existing on this earth—whether solid or subtle—in the way that all perceptible things are united with senses, some more solidly and others more subtly. Nor should they conclude that the union happens, as the philosophers say, by means of intelligible species in the mind, with the flesh remaining in heaven, in the same way that our intellect is united with all the things that we understand as it perceives them by means of certain images. Therefore, to what has already been said, we add the manner whereby this union and incorporation takes place, which is by means of Christ's Spirit imparted to us—indeed, remaining in us and binding us together with Christ and causing faith to be stirred up, that we might embrace Him.

15. *A confirmation of both points, namely, that the union is essential but is only accomplished by means of the Spirit and our faith.*
Without doubt, the Holy Scriptures abundantly and plainly declare that this union is essential and also that it takes place solely by means of the Holy Spirit and our faith. The members of the Ephesian church had been reconciled to God and to one another as Jews and Gentiles (two very different peoples) and had all been grafted onto Christ and regenerated by one and the same Spirit, the enmity having been removed by Christ and the dividing wall destroyed. This is why, when the apostle wrote to them, he did not hesitate to say that both of them were being built up. But they were not being built up into a single people, as it seems he should have said. Even better, for the sake of expressing how intimate is this union, he said they were being built up *into one new man*, in Christ Himself (Eph. 2:14–16).

Therefore, because we all live by one and the same Spirit, as though regenerated by one and the same soul, and are joined to one Head

Christ, we also are all properly called one new man (Eph. 4:15). And in that same epistle, describing this most intimate and essential incorporation, Paul likens Christ to a head and all of us to members, connected and fastened to a head by means of nerves, joints, and ligaments, which draw life and movement from it. Nothing is more common in the Holy Scriptures than this analogy, so that we might thereby easily and clearly understand of what sort and how great is the union of us all with Christ on account of His Spirit, who indwells all the regenerate.

This is the very reason why that same apostle likens Christ to a foundation and all the faithful to stones—albeit they are living stones, just as the Foundation is also living, so that they can receive growth from Him, built upon that very Foundation. On the basis of all of this, the whole building is joined together and grows into a holy temple in the Lord by means of the Holy Spirit [Eph. 2:21].

Before the apostle, Christ Himself did the same thing more than once, making Himself the Foundation and the church the building truly supported by the Foundation and joined by an inseparable bond (Matt. 16:18). Hereto also pertains the fact that Christ calls Himself the Vine but calls us the branches, we who live by drawing life and vitality from the Vine and bear good fruit (John 15:1). Again, this is demonstrated by the parable of the tree or olive tree onto which the faithful are grafted like branches from a wild olive tree, so that they might bear good olives (Rom. 11:17). Moreover, they are ingrafted by the Holy Spirit and by faith.

This is the reason why the union is described to the Philippians as the *communion of the Spirit*, and it is why Christ is said to dwell in our hearts by faith (Phil. 2:1; Eph. 3:17). Nor is the reason obscure why the apostle calls the incorporation of the church with Christ and of Christ with the church and with each one of the faithful *a union*. He does so in accordance with the convention of the prophets in which the two are made one flesh. God said, *They will be two in one flesh*, and the apostle says, *This is a great mystery, but I am speaking of Christ and the church* ([Gen. 2:24;] Eph. 5:32).[8]

---

8. On this theme, see Zanchi, *Spiritual Marriage*; John L. Farthing, "De coniugio spirituali: Jerome Zanchi on Ephesians 5:22–33," *Sixteenth Century Journal* 24, no. 3

To be sure, what John writes about this union and the Spirit who causes and makes it known always comes to mind: *By means of this*, he says, *we know that we dwell in Him and He in us, because He has given to us from His Spirit* (1 John 4:13). He, therefore, dwells in us and we in Him by means of one and the same Holy Spirit who is in Him and in us. To this also pertains that saying, *He who does not have the Spirit of Christ is not His* (Rom. 8:9). On the other hand, the apostle understands those to be *of Christ* who are Christ's true and living members.

16. *Conclusion: This union is essential and takes place only by means of Christ's Spirit and our faith.*
Therefore, with these and other similar testimonies of the Holy Scriptures adduced, we do not doubt but that Christ and His apostles intended to inform us that the communion that all the faithful have with Christ—as much the small as the great among us—and indeed with His flesh and blood, is true and real. Nevertheless, it takes place by no other means than by the bond and power of the Holy Spirit. Thus, because it takes place by means of the Spirit and faith, this communion is secret and full of mysteries and spiritual. Yet we ought not doubt that, on account of that very same Spirit, it is as true and essential as the communion between a man and wife joined into one flesh, as between the foundation and the stones built upon it, as between the tree and its boughs, as between the vine and its branches, and indeed as between members bound to a head with ligaments and nerves and with one and the same living and operating soul in such a way that this union with Christ cannot be made any greater while we exist in this perishable flesh.

17. *A confirmation of the judgment by another analogy and from philosophy itself.*
Surely, if one and the same soul were in all men, the result would be that innumerable persons were just one man. It would be just as theologians

---

(Autumn 1993): 621–52; J. V. Fesko, "Jerome Zanchi on Union with Christ and Justification," *Puritan Reformed Journal* 2, no. 2 (July 2010): 53–76; J. V. Fesko, "Girolamo Zanchi on Union with Christ and the Final Judgment," *Perichoresis* 18, no. 1 (March 2020): 41–56.

conclude that there is only one God from the fact that one and the same essence exists in three divine persons. Moreover, this would seem even more clearly to be true if those many men were to have a single head to which they were attached and by which alone they moved. What wonder, then, that it is the one and very same Holy Spirit who is in all the devout, and also in Christ, who really binds us together with Him in such a way that we are one body with Him and among ourselves—indeed, one new man, all in Christ Himself the Head. For it is by these two considerations—namely, the one Spirt *by means of whom* and the one Head *to whom* we are all attached—that Paul said all the faithful are one new man (Eph. 2:14 [that is, v. 15]).

18. Participation in the benefits of Christ's death and resurrection are transferred unto us on the basis of our union with Him.
To be sure, participation in Christ's benefits and salvation in His flesh follows from and depends upon this fellowship[9] with Christ, and salvation is imparted to and resides in us by His flesh and blood. For branches cannot draw vitality from a vine nor members from a head nor living stones from a foundation unless they are really connected to their foundation—with the head, with the tree, with the vine—and unless they abide in them. In the same way, neither can we draw from Christ our Head, Foundation, Tree, Vine, unless we are actually grafted onto Him by means of the Holy Spirit and unless we remain in Him and become flesh of His flesh and bone of His bones.

Let it be as the greatest injury to us if someone says that, because we do not admit—since we cannot—that Christ's true body really passes physically into our bodies by means of our mouths, that we on that account deny true participation in His flesh and blood or that we allege no more than a participation in His gifts and benefits. But it is not as if the communion accomplished by the Holy Spirit and by faith were not true and essential, for, as we see in the incarnation of the Son of God and in the creation of man composed of a soul and a body, nothing can more intimately unite diverse substances and natures into a single one

---

9. κοινωνία.

than the Holy Spirit. Indeed, if that sort of fellowship[10] with Christ's flesh and blood—the sort that takes place only by means of the Holy Spirit and faith—is true and saving only if it also passes physically into our bodies through our mouths, then Christ has provided poorly for His church. Hence, Christ intends to accomplish the same thing in both the reception of the gospel and in receiving baptism, just as John testified concerning the gospel and as the apostle testified concerning baptism (1 John 1:3; 1 Cor. 12:13).

19. Errors.
Therefore, we reject the errors of those who teach that the remission of sins and salvation are imparted to men, as they say, *per opera operatum* [by means of the work that is performed], apart from faith and apart from true union with Christ. Indeed, we condemn the blasphemy of those who contend that it takes place by means of a work not commanded by God but rather by one contrived by men and full of superstition and idolatry. No less do we likewise condemn the blasphemy of those who, making nothing of the ministry of the Word, teach that salvation is imparted equally with or without the hearing of the Word and the reception of the sacraments. But even more do we condemn those who contend that all infants in the wombs of their mothers—regardless of whether their parents have faith—become partakers of Christ's benefits.

---

10. κοινωνία.

Chapter Thirteen

The Gospel and the Abrogation of the Law by Means of the Gospel

First the gospel and then also the sacraments—baptism and the Supper—are the external instruments by the legitimate administration of which our Redeemer, the Lord Jesus Christ, offers and dispenses the grace of redemption and the remission of sins to the world, imparts Himself to us (the elect) by the power of His Spirit, and in turn incorporates us to Himself. By them He thus really makes us partakers of the salvation and life that we have in Him. For that reason, we also wish to explain briefly and simply to the church of God what our confession is concerning these matters.

1. What the gospel is.
In accordance with the meaning received and used in the church, we therefore believe that the gospel is nothing other than the heavenly doctrine concerning Christ, preached by Christ Himself and by the apostles and contained in the books of the New Testament, bearing to the world that best and most welcome news: that the death of Jesus Christ, the only begotten Son of God, is the means whereby humankind is redeemed, such that free remission, salvation, and eternal life are provided for all men if only they repent and believe in Jesus Christ (Matt. 3:2). On this account, the apostle calls it *the gospel of our salvation* (Eph. 1:13).

2. The gospel was promised by the prophets but proclaimed by the apostles.
For although this mystery had already been revealed to the fathers, even from the beginning of the world, and although the prophets spoke of it, nevertheless they preached the promises of the gospel, which were

preserved among the Jews, rather than the gospel itself, which was broadcast to all peoples. For prophecies speak of future things but do not announce things that are present or past, as the apostle teaches the Romans and as Peter teaches in his first epistle (Rom. 1:2; 1 Peter 1:10).

3. *The fathers were no less saved by the application of faith to the promises about Christ the Redeemer than are we who believe in the gospel.*
Yet, we do not doubt but that the fathers, believing in the evangelical promises of Christ's coming and of His crushing the Serpent's head, were no less saved than we are by the application of faith to the gospel, which announces that Christ has now come and redeemed the world. The apostle teaches this often, in Romans concerning Abraham and in Hebrews concerning all others, not to mention in other places too. So, it is the height of blasphemy to say that only earthly things—but not heavenly things, the remission of sins and eternal life—were promised to the fathers and that they understood the promises to be merely earthly. For what we receive as the gospel proper were to them evangelical promises, namely, *the power of God unto salvation of all who believe* (Rom. 1:16).

4. *As regards its substance, the doctrine of the gospel is truly ancient and eternal.*
For this we understand as well: as regards its substance, the doctrine of the gospel is hardly new but rather very ancient. It was preached already to the fathers from the creation of the world, so that it is not inappropriate for John to have called it *the eternal gospel* (Rev. 14:6).

5. *How many and what are the parts of the gospel.*
Moreover, we encounter three divisions that characterize the gospel: repentance unto God, faith in Jesus Christ, and zeal to observe everything Christ commanded (Acts 20:21; Mark 1:4; Matt. 28:20).

6. *Explanation of the previous judgment.*
For the gospel, which sets Christ before us with all of God's grace and mercy, with the expiation and remission of our sins, and, indeed,

with all salvation and eternal life placed in Him, demands only these three things.

First, it demands that we, having been moved to earnest sorrow for the whole of our wickedly spent life, might sincerely long for our mind (and thus all of our affections) to be transformed and restored by God unto obedience of the divine will. And we entreat with prayers that He might do this and that we might labor toward it.

Second, it demands that we, having embraced Christ with true faith, along with all His treasures, might firmly and without any hesitation believe that all our sins are pardoned forever by God's grace and mercy on account of Christ alone and that we are received in grace and made sons of God and heirs of eternal life.

Third, it demands that we, having been thus persuaded that we are graciously and eternally saved on account of Christ, might henceforth endeavor to observe whatsoever Christ has commanded us for God's glory and the prosperity of our neighbor. At all times and unto the end, we do this being accompanied by faith, whereby we might also believe that, on account of Christ, whatever we lack or however we sin in this new obedience, it is not imputed to us. Rather, Christ's perfect obedience, righteousness, and holiness are imputed to us—our imperfect obedience is perfected and, in the sight of God, accepted and reputed as altogether perfect.

Moreover, all of Christ's commands amount to three things: that we, having rejected impiety and worldly desires, *might live soberly* (toward ourselves), *uprightly* (toward neighbor), *and piously* (toward God) *in the present age, waiting for the blessed hope and the coming of the glory of the great God* (Titus 2:12[–13]). We believe this to be the greatest of those things that Christ requires of us by His evangelical doctrine, and so, those who are truly evangelical and truly Christian will exert themselves unto the earnest pursuit of these things.

7. In what ways the gospel principally differs from the law.
On the basis of what has been said, it is also apparent that we do not confuse the law with the gospel. For, although we bear witness that God is as much the law's author as He is the gospel's and that *the law itself is*

as holy, righteous, and good as the gospel, we nevertheless believe that the difference between the two is great (Ex. 20[:1–17]; Rom. 7:12).

This is the case not only because the law was given only to the Israelites, while the gospel is extended unto all, even the Gentiles. Nor is it only because the law was temporary, lasting only until Christ, while the gospel is eternal. Nor is it only because the law was given by Moses and was explained by the prophets, while Christ announced the gospel, and the apostles proclaimed it to the whole world. But it is also the case—and this above all—for the following reasons.

First, because the subject matter of the law is merely commands, to which are added irrevocable curses if they are violated in the smallest part. The law does hold certain promises as well, and these are not just earthly promises but also promises of eternal benediction. However, all of them are conditioned upon utterly perfect obedience, and none of them are freely given. But, properly speaking, the gospel is good news that sets forth Christ the Redeemer, freely remits sins, and also freely saves. And it requires nothing of us for the salvation that is to follow except true faith in Christ, which cannot exist without repentance and without the zeal to fulfill the divine will, that is, *to live soberly, uprightly, and piously*, as explained above [Titus 2:12].

Second, the gospel differs from the law because the law did not grant what it required. That is to say, it offered no power whereby one could be saved. So, it was ineffective and a killing letter and a minister of wrath and death, provoking greater sin rather than removing it [2 Cor. 3:7, 9]. But what the gospel requires it also grants, and thus what it offers it also really imparts to us, since the Holy Spirit is effective in the elect by the gospel at its preaching to stir up in them true faith, whereby they lay hold of Christ offered to them and, along with Him, eternal life. *For faith comes from hearing* the gospel, but obedience does not come from hearing the law (Rom. 10:17). For, at the hearing of the law, the Holy Spirit grants no one power with which to be able to keep it as He does when He stirs up faith in the elect at the hearing of the gospel. This is why, just as the law is called a killing letter, so the gospel is designated a life-giving Spirit and is thus a true and effective instrument unto the salvation of all who believe [1 Cor. 15:45].

For this reason, a third difference also follows: that the law was not written on hearts but remained written merely on tablets, and so it did not change men. But the gospel is written on the hearts of the elect by the Holy Spirit and thus transforms and restores them as well, because, of course, the gospel is the Holy Spirit's instrument to sanctify and preserve us (2 Cor. 3:18).*

[* Observation 13.7]

8. *The gospel abolished the law of Moses in part but not the whole.*
On the basis of what we have said, what we believe about the abrogation of the law by the gospel is also clearly apparent. First, the gospel teaches that the law of ceremonies, sacrifices, and the entire outward form of Mosaic worship are simply abrogated, insofar as everything in the Old Testament that pointed ahead figuratively to Christ declares itself fulfilled in Jesus (as was said in chapter eleven). This is in accordance with the apostle's statement that all these things were *until the time of correction* (Heb. 9:10). And, *The law was, indeed, given by Moses, but truth came by Jesus Christ* (John 1:17).

Second, insofar as the gospel is the instrument used by the Holy Spirit to engraft and unite us to Christ and make us partakers of redemption and salvation (as was said above in chapter twelve), to the extent that it pertains to the curse against transgressors, we confess that the law, even the moral law, has been abrogated by the gospel of Christ. This is in accordance with the apostle's statement: *There is no condemnation for those who are in Christ Jesus*, the sign of which is that they *walk not according to the flesh but according to the Spirit* (Rom. 8:1[, 4]). Notwithstanding, the doctrine of the gospel requires the repentance and sanctification of all of life and for us to live soberly, uprightly, and piously insofar as the gospel did not do away with the law as regards morals. For the whole law is agreeable with the doctrine of the gospel as regards the avoidance of vices and the pursuit of virtues.

Lastly, insofar as Christ has not abolished political laws among the nations by His gospel, so long as they are not contrary to natural law, we therefore also understand that any magistrate is free to introduce the political laws that were given to the people of Israel (than which none are more just) into his city and to rule over his people with them. For this reason, it is the greatest injury to the gospel of Christ for someone to say that the commonwealth is troubled or overturned by the gospel. This is our confession concerning the gospel of Jesus Christ.

9. Errors.

We, therefore, condemn antinomians and whoever rejects the moral law and expels it from the churches as if it were contrary to the gospel or as if it pertained not at all to Christians. And we condemn those who reject magistrates who endeavor to introduce into their cities the political precepts of Moses insofar as they are able.

Chapter Fourteen

The Sacraments of the New Testament

In order to perfect that fellowship[1] with Christ wherein consists all participation of salvation, God willed to use not only the very word of the gospel but also external signs accommodated and adjoined to the word for the same purpose. A sacrament is constituted from these two things—the word and an external sign. Therefore, following our confession about the gospel, we also add a brief summary of the sacraments, consistent with the Holy Scriptures and with the first principles of the Christian faith.

1. What we mean by the word sacraments.
We acknowledge that, properly speaking, a sacrament is a holy oath, or a promise, made between two parties, that is, between God and people. It is not established simply, but with sacred rites and ceremonies, just as manifestly appeared in the sacrament of circumcision between God and Abraham and between Christ and us in baptism, which replaced circumcision. Thus, the fathers often considered a sacrament to be the entire act (whether baptism or the Lord's Supper) preceded by a mutual promise inviolably confirmed with external rites and symbols, even with the blood of Christ. Later, others understood the word sacrament, by means of a synecdoche,[2] to mean only the rites or symbols added to the word. And this other understanding has prevailed in the church. Therefore, in accordance with its received meaning in the church, we call a sacrament

---

1. κοινωνίαν.
2. συνεκδοχή.

not only a word, nor only an element, but rather an element—water or bread and wine—joined together with the word of the gospel according to Christ's institution. As Augustine says, *The word comes to the element, and it becomes a sacrament* [Homilies on the Gospel of John, §80.3].[3]*

[* Observation 14.1]

2. *The things whereof the sacraments are sacraments.*
But since every sacrament is a sacrament of something else, we say that this *something else* is that which the word of the gospel signifies, namely, the grace of God in Christ, or rather Christ Himself with grace and salvation deposited in Him. For He is what the gospel, in summary, sets forth. And just as the word so also the sacraments were instituted that we may have fellowship[4] with Him. And, by their meaning, they direct our minds toward that fellowship. Thus, we say that what is displayed externally is the sign of that which is perceived internally, and what is done externally is a symbol of that which the Holy Spirit works internally in our souls.

3. *The parts that constitute a sacrament.*
From these things we also understand which are the parts that properly constitute a sacrament, namely, the word and an external symbol, but one with a relation to the thing signified and represented by it. For the thing of which something is a sacrament cannot be the sacrament itself (nor a part of the sacrament), since every sacrament is a sacrament of something other than itself. Nevertheless, we do not simply separate that thing from the sacrament, nor do we deny that, according to the fathers and many other learned and pious men, the word *sacrament* also expresses the very thing of which it is a sacrament, just as by the word *baptism* we understand not only the external washing of water along with the word but also the internal purification and regeneration of the conscience from sins contained in baptism. So then, according to Irenaeus's

---

3. [*Homilies on the Gospel of John*, §80.3]: Augustine, *Homilies on the Gospel of John 41–124*, 287 (NPNF1, 7:344).

4. κοινωνίαν.

statement about the Eucharist, we hold that a sacrament consists of an earthly thing and also a heavenly thing, and we are not accustomed to avoid speaking in this way when we discuss the sacraments. However, when we do so, it is not because we mean that the thing itself is properly part of the sacrament, since that is the very thing into which the sacraments draw us to participate. Rather, we speak this way because the sacrament has a mystical relationship with the thing itself, and, by the bond of that relationship, the earthly thing is bound together with the heavenly thing.

And, thus, we reconcile the sayings of many learned men as well as of the fathers, which appear to speak somewhat divergently, since they all are everywhere of the same opinion. Almost all of them simply call the sacraments signs, figures, symbols, types, antitypes, forms, images, seals, ceremonies, visible words, and other similar terms. Others say that sacraments consist of an earthly thing and a heavenly, and we just indicated how this was to be understood. But all of them frequently call the sacraments by the names of those things of which they are sacraments, according to the custom of the Holy Scriptures. Yet everyone has understood and professed these three things to be in the sacraments: the word, a symbol added to the word, and that whereof they are symbols.

4. The reasons why God determined to add the word of the gospel to external signs, and why they are called visible words.
We also believe and openly confess that, by the institution of God, visible signs were added and should be added to the word for the fuller and firmer confirmation of the word in our souls, since that is, moreover, the purpose for which seals are usually applied to written letters and wills everywhere and by all people. This is also the reason why Augustine refers to external symbols and those things perceived by our senses as *visible words*, because they were created and added to the word for this reason: in order to accomplish what the word does, that is, in order that the signs might exhibit to the other senses the same thing that the word makes known to the ears and, thus, confirm God's word and promises. They were also added because, just as faith is stirred up in our souls by the word, so also is it sealed, more powerfully confirmed, and increased

by external symbols or seals (Rom. 10:17). And, finally, they were added so that, just as the word, so also the holy symbols might be instruments of the Holy Spirit whereby we are brought into fellowship[5] with Christ and grow together in it. Moreover, we do not doubt in the least that all this was put into place by God on account of our weakness and ignorance and the feebleness of our faith, so as to support it not only by the word but also by visible signs. This faith is that whereby we embrace Christ and grow together in Him.

5. *Where the Words of Institution are not recited, there is no sacrament, and, thus, outside of that usage, they are nothing more than what they are by nature.*
But just as we believe that the sign is added to the word not for the sake of superstition but for the greater confirmation of our faith, so we also confess that the word is necessary in the administration of the sacraments, not as an incantation but to stir up faith. Thus, we deny that there is a true sacrament where the Words of Institution are not recited in such a way that they may be heard and understood, that faith might thereby be stirred up. And, so, we affirm that the symbols are not sacraments outside of their legitimate use but merely that which they are by their own nature and nothing else. For a symbol is transferred from profane to holy use only by the word. Many call this *consecrating* or *sanctifying*, and thereby things are made sacraments. As Augustine says, *The word comes to the element, and it becomes a sacrament* [Homilies on the Gospel of John, §80.3].[6] Indeed, it comes so that it might be understood and believed.

6. *Sacraments are not bare tokens or naked signs.*
Thus, we do not believe that the sacramental signs are merely bare tokens that distinguish us from everyone else, those who are foreigners to the true church. Nor do we believe that they are merely symbols to us of a Christian society, nor even that we publicly profess our faith thereby and give thanks for the benefit of redemption. Rather, we believe that they

---

5. κοινωνίαν.

6. [Homilies on the Gospel of John, §80.3]: Augustine, *Homilies on the Gospel of John 41–124*, 287 (*NPNF*1, 7:344).

are instruments whereby, as they are displayed to us, Christ's actions and benefits are recalled to our minds, promises are sealed, and faith is stirred up. We believe that by them the Holy Spirit grafts us onto Christ, preserves those who are engrafted, and daily causes us more and more to grow into unity with Him. And we believe that having thereby been granted a greater faith in God, a more passionate love for our neighbor, and mortification of our own selves, we might live a life as much like Christ's life as possible, in spiritual joy and delight, until, at last, we dwell eternally with Him in heaven, altogether holy and happy.

7. What the sacraments of the New Covenant are like.
Along with Augustine in *On Christian Belief* (bk. 3, ch. 9),[7] we also confess that the sacraments given to us by Christ are few in number, very easy to perform, and to be understood in a most solemn way. They are few in number because there are only two: baptism and the Supper. They are easily performed because there is nothing either in baptism or the Supper that cannot easily be given and received, nothing bothersome, nothing unpleasant or averse to the customs of mankind. Finally, they are to be understood in a most solemn way because, although the things that are seen are common, nevertheless, the things signified—the things displayed for consideration and to be reflected upon and understood with the power of the mind—are most solemn, heavenly, and divine, pertaining to eternal salvation.

8. Understanding and faith are necessary to receive the sacraments in a worthy manner.
Whence also we understand that the worthy reception of the sacraments requires action and attention of mind and a faith in us whereby we come

---

7. bk. 3, ch. 9: Augustine wrote, "But at the present time, when a brilliant demonstration of our freedom has been revealed in the resurrection of our Lord, we are not oppressed by the tiresome necessity of attending to signs, even the signs which we now understand. Instead of many signs there are now but a few signs, simple when performed, inspiring when understood, and holy when practiced, given to us by the teaching of our Lord himself and the apostles, such as the sacrament of baptism and the celebration of the Lord's body and blood." *De Doctrina Christiana*, ed. and trans. R. P. H. Green (Oxford: Clarendon Press, 1995), 75 (*NPNF*1, 2:560).

to know that which is signified and displayed by the sacrament and whereby, with a mind moved by faith, we lay hold of it. And this is just as Christ teaches when He says of the Supper: *Do this in remembrance of Me* (Luke 22:19). And the apostle, carefully weighing these words of Christ, explains them more than sufficiently (1 Cor. 11:24). The *sursum corda* also pertains to this.[8] For those holy, celestial, and divine matters are set forth for the mind to understand and for faith to receive.

9. The substance of the sacrament is offered to all in earnest; however, not all truly receive it but only the elect faithful.
While not everyone who comes to receive the sacraments does so with faith and true understanding, nevertheless, just as the symbols are held forth to all those who profess Christ, so we also believe that the things signified by the sacraments are offered in earnest to all by Christ. Therefore, we believe that the sacraments' soundness, which naturally depends solely upon Christ's institution and the truth of His words, is not diminished in any way merely on account of the unfaithfulness of those receiving the symbols.

10. When the sacraments are administered, the Spirit of Christ is effectual in the faithful, and therefore, they not only receive the symbols but also participate in the thing signified.
Yet, although Christ's Spirit is not effectual in all men to whom the sacraments are distributed (just as Christ's Spirit is not effectual when the Word is preached to them—and this is their own fault, because they do not bring to it understanding and faith), nevertheless, we believe that it is effectual for those who are the faithful elect. This is the case insofar as the Spirit leads those granted faith by the hearing of the word and as

---

8. The *sursum corda* is an ancient liturgical element that urges worshipers to "lift up your hearts." Various versions were incorporated into liturgical forms throughout the course of church history. Beginning at least with Guillaume Farel's 1533 liturgy for the service of the Lord's Supper, a version of the *sursum corda* was frequently included in Reformed worship services in which the Lord's Supper was served. See Jonathan Gibson and Mark Earngey, eds., *Reformation Worship: Liturgies from the Past for the Present* (Greensboro, N.C.: New Growth Press, 2018), 206, 231, 244, 328, 373, 427, 536.

they are established in it more and more by the reception of the sacraments unto the fellowship[9] of Christ, or rather as the Spirit causes them to grow together in Him. Therefore, we confess that such people are truly washed of their sins in baptism and feed on Christ's true flesh and drink His true blood in the Supper.

11. Christ is both the Institutor and the true Dispenser of the sacraments.
But just as we acknowledge one Institutor of the sacraments, so we also acknowledge one true Dispenser, our Lord Jesus Christ. He does, indeed, dispense the symbols by men who are His ministers, but He is the one who properly and truly communicates the substance of the sacraments in an effectual manner on His own, or by His Spirit. He does so just as John the Baptist said that, while he truly baptized with water, Christ would baptize with the Spirit (Matt. 3:11). And so, just as no one can institute new sacraments, neither can anyone boast that he truly and properly cleanses consciences of sin or that he causes others to eat Christ's true body and blood—except (as they say) in a ministerial sense.

12. The sacraments are not defiled by the ministers' defects.
But if Christ alone is not merely the true Institutor of the sacraments but also their Dispenser, then we easily understand that, to the faithful, the sacraments are not defiled by the defects of those whose works He uses. This is the case since they are able to receive them worthily and, by means of the sacraments, become participants of the thing signified and offered. For, to the pure, all things are pure. And Christ dwells by faith in the hearts of the faithful, with all His treasures (Titus 1:15; Eph. 3:17).

13. Grace is not bound to the sacraments.
Based on the same foundations, we are confirmed in the judgment that the pious have received: the grace of God is not to be bound to the sacraments, such that he who receives them also necessarily secures grace (that is, the substance signified and offered by the sacrament), even if he is devoid of faith. It is not as if one were able to obtain the substance

---

9. κοινωνίαν.

of the sacrament *ex opere operato* [on the basis of the work that is performed], as they say. For Christ does not simply say, *Whoever will be baptized will be saved*, but first says, *Whoever will believe* (Mark 16:16). And Simon Magus received the sacrament of baptism, yet he did not gain the substance of the sacrament, since, according to Peter, he was still caught in the bitterest gall of sins and the bond of iniquity and of the Devil as well (Acts 8:13[, 23]). Thus, he had no share in Christ's kingdom. As Augustine says, many also eat the Lord's bread but do not eat the Lord who is the bread [*Homilies on the Gospel of John*, hom. 59.1].[10] For just as it is not the case that all who hear the gospel preached are made to partake of the remission of sins—but only if they repent from the evil of their wickedly conducted life and believe in Christ—so neither are all made to share the substances that are displayed and offered by the sacraments just because they receive the elements—unless true repentance and faith are added.

14. *The power of the sacraments is not removed or impaired by the unworthiness of those receiving them.*
Yet nor do we, for that reason, remove or impair the power of the sacraments and the efficacy attached to them, which we confess depends not at all upon the unworthiness of those administering or receiving but rather upon faith and the strength of Christ, who established the sacraments. For just as the gospel by itself always preserves both its meaning (which, granted, not everyone understands) and the power of holding forth those things which it offers, so also the sacraments, the visible words, maintain themselves in the same way. That is, just as the gospel is by itself always the power of God unto salvation (but, in fact, only to those who believe), so also the sacraments are always the efficacious instruments of the Holy Spirit unto salvation (however, only those who believe take possession of this efficaciousness).

---

10. [*Homilies on the Gospel of John*, hom. 59.1]: "The former [that is, Peter] ate the bread, the Lord; [Judas ate] the Lord's bread against the Lord; they [were eating] life, he [was eating] punishment." Augustine, *Homilies on the Gospel of John 41–124*, 197 (*NPNF*1, 7:308). See also 135 (hom. 50.10; *NPNF*1, 7:281).

This is why the apostles did not hesitate to call all those who have been baptized saints, regenerated, and justified, even though they knew that many among them were hypocrites. For, with words of this sort, they were expressing the efficaciousness God has imparted to the sacraments and what we should believe that they accomplish, unless perhaps our hypocrisy hinders them. In this sense, if one were also to say that whoever eats the Lord's bread also becomes a partaker of the Lord's very body (that is, that there is no resistance by the power of the sacrament, or rather by its Institutor and Distributor, such that those participating in the sacrament do not also really become partakers of that which it signifies and offers), we could not condemn such a saying. But this is only the case if some explanations were also added to instruct the people and immediately banish any spurious notions about *ex opere operato* that their minds might conceive.

15. Between the sign and the substance is a sacramental union, and what exactly that is.
Granted, we also say that the substance of the sacraments is bound to the sacraments, but it is not confined to them physically, locally, or corporeally, nor by a debt of obligation, as if God had simply promised the substances themselves to all those who lay hold of the sacraments without regard to their lack of faith, such that He was obliged to impart them to those who are unrepentant and even unbelieving. Nevertheless, we do not for that reason entirely decouple the thing signified from the signs. For we acknowledge and confess a sacramental union, that is, the sort of union that is suitable between sacraments and their substance.[11]

---

11. The language of "sacramental union" was criticized by some of Zanchi's successors, including his student Franciscus Gomarus. See "Disputationes theologicae," in *Opera theologica omnia* (Amsterdam, 1644), 2:125 (disputation 31.36, De sacramentis). Some retained the language of sacramental union. See, for example, Harm Goris, ed., *Synopsis Purioris Theologiae / Synopsis of a Purer Theology: Latin Text and English Translation*, vol. 3, *Disputations 43–52*, trans. Riemer A. Faber, Studies in Medieval and Reformation Traditions 222/9 (Leiden: Brill, 2020), 117–19, 150–51 (disputations 43.24 and 44.24). Others used it to refer to the union of believers' souls with Christ by means of the "spiritual food and drink obtained by true faith" rather than to the union

Moreover, this sacramental union consists in a certain mystical and holy relation, insofar as the signs signify the thing and offer it to be received. And the things that are signified by the signs are held forth to be received, just as a union also exists between the word that signifies and displays and the things signified and displayed by the word. But that union—both of the sacraments and of the word joined together with the things themselves—depends upon the will and counsel of God who established them. For when He established the preaching of the gospel and the administration of the sacraments, He did so for the purpose that we have just now explained and so that we, hearing the word and seeing and partaking of the signs, might immediately lift up our mind's eye to the things signified by them and, with the hands of faith, lay hold of what is offered and be truly united to Christ, whom the word and the signs proclaim and to whom, by their meaning, they point with their finger, as it were. Thus, just as our union with Christ is chalk full of mystery (as the apostle teaches in Ephesians 5[:22–33]), so we also understand that the union of both the word and the sacraments with the substances of which they are the signs and sacraments is a mystical and spiritual union.

16. *Definition of the sacraments.*

Therefore, to summarize many things with a few words, we conclude that the sacraments are external signs inflected toward the senses that are, by the institution of Christ, added to the word of the gospel on account of our ignorance and weakness for the more ardent building up and confirming of our faith by grace. Indeed, all men are in earnest called by the sacraments toward trust in and real fellowship[12] with Christ—even with His flesh and blood—and, hence, they are called to share in the blessings of those who are in Christ, and the blessings that are signified and offered by word and symbols. Only those who are elect and faithful, however, are actually persuaded by the Holy Spirit, who draws them internally in their souls so that, having been incorporated into Christ,

---

of the sign and the thing signified. See Johann Heinrich Heidegger, *Corpus theologiae Christianae* (Zurich, 1700), 2:480 (locus 25, §113).

12. κοινωνία.

they might ultimately constitute the body of the whole church, which was appointed beforehand by the Father unto the praise of His glorious grace and their eternal joy.

17. *What the sacraments of the Old Testament generally had in common with ours.*
We do not say much about the Old Testament's sacraments, since they have been abrogated. Only this one thing: since the same God was with the patriarchs, however much their ceremonies differed from ours, they received the same promises, the same Mediator, the same regenerating Spirit, the same faith and hope, and the same substance as we receive, which is Christ. This is particularly the case because theirs were given to them for the same purpose for which ours were given to us, namely, that we might be confirmed in faith in Christ and grow together in fellowship[13] with Him. This is what *the Lamb of God who was slain from the beginning of the world* means (Rev. 13:8). So also: *They all drank from the same Rock, and that Rock was Christ* (1 Cor. 10:4). And, *Christ yesterday, today, and forever* (Heb. 13:8).

18. *There are only two sacraments of the Christian church.*
Moreover, we acknowledge two sacraments that ought properly to be reckoned by that name and that have always been common to the universal Christian church: baptism and the Lord's Supper. Of these, the first pertains properly to the beginning of fellowship[14] with Christ and the second to its increase. It is also for this reason that the first is called the laver of regeneration and the other is called the holy banquet and supper.

19. *Errors.*
We cannot, therefore, approve of those who wish there to be a sacrament where the element of the sacrament is seen but the word is not heard. Nor can we approve of those who do not distinguish the substance of the

---

13. κοινωνία.
14. κοινωνία.

sacrament from the sacrament but instead want the substance to come into their mouths in the same way as the sacramental sign, although the substance of the sacrament is that which causes the sign (being perceived by the senses) to enter our thoughts but not what is sensed by the hand or mouth. Nor can we approve of those who observe that there is nothing in the sacraments except what is exposed to the eyes or who want them to be mere tokens whereby we are distinguished from other people or bare signs rather than the instruments of the Holy Spirit by which He efficaciously works in us and confirms us in communion with Christ. To be sure, we condemn those who establish new sacraments, besides those which Christ established, as well as those who bind the grace of God and the things signified by the sacraments to the sacraments in such a way that it is truly said that all who receive the signs also always receive the substance itself.

Chapter Fifteen

Baptism

In addition to what we have said in the chapter on the sacraments in general, we also believe and confess these things in particular about baptism.

1. *What baptism is and what are its effects.*
Baptism is the first sacrament of the new covenant (Matt. 28:19).[1] It not only seals to Christ all those who, having professed repentance for their sins, profess faith in Christ as well—and, indeed, faith in God the Father, Son, and Holy Spirit—but it also seals those who (minimally) are reckoned to belong to the covenant on account of their parents' piety but especially those who truly do belong to the covenant (Acts 19:5; 1 Cor. 7:14). Those who are sealed in this way—having already been incorporated, as it were, into Christ by the Holy Spirit so that they might no longer be their own but His (1 Cor. 6:19)—are said to have been adopted into covenantal fellowship and, therefore, into one body with Him and with all the saints, and they are adopted unto sharing in every spiritual and heavenly blessing.

---

1. Zanchi explores the covenant motif more explicitly in his exegetical labors than in his systematic theological writings, and in this confession, the word "covenant" has appeared only very occasionally up to this point. Nevertheless, as John Farthing notes, "Zanchi appropriates the language and conceptuality of covenant in ways that both reinforce the central affirmations of his orthodox system and offer occasions for elaborating a number of typically Zanchian emphases," including God's sovereignty and freedom, salvation by grace alone, and the election and perseverance of the saints. See John L. Farthing, "*Foedus Evangelicum*: Jerome Zanchi on the Covenant," *Calvin Theological Journal* 29 (April–November 1994): 164.

By means of this baptism, as if it were a laver of regeneration, they are cleansed of their sins by the power of Christ's blood and buried together with Christ in death, so that *we might also walk in newness of life*, just as He rose again from the dead by the Father's grace (Rom. 6:4). For this reason, baptism has often also been called the sacrament of penance for the remission of sins, the sacrament of faith, the symbol of faith, the laver of regeneration, the washing of sins, and the sacrament of new life (Eph. 1:12[?]; 5:26; Rev. 5[:9?]; Titus 3:5; Mark 1:4).

2. Baptism's power has its effect only in the elect, and they alone are baptized not merely with water but also with the Spirit.
All these things are declared of baptism, and their accomplishment is truly attributed to baptism, as the Holy Spirit's instrument, as it were, and all who undergo baptism are thus truly said to be and are baptized sacramentally. Nevertheless, we believe that all of this is actually fulfilled only in the elect, who are granted Christ's Spirit. For they are the only ones who also believe, and they alone belong to Christ and to His mystical body. And so, all are baptized with water, but only the elect are baptized by the Spirit. And while all receive the sign, not all receive the substance signified and offered by baptism; only the elect become participants thereof.

3. The parts whereof the entire sacrament of baptism consists.
We believe, moreover, that the two components instituted by Christ suffice for constituting the entire sacrament of baptism. These are: the simple element of water that makes men wet—either by immersing or sprinkling them—and the form of words whereby Christ taught that we are to be baptized in the name of the Father, and of the Son, and of the Holy Spirit. And we are not persuaded that the apostles added any other form of words or anything other than water.*

[* Observation 15.3]

4. Whether infants should also be baptized.
With the whole of the ancient church, we also believe that adults who, having professed repentance from their sins, profess faith in Christ

should be admitted to the sacrament of baptism and that their infants should be admitted as well. For they are universally reckoned to belong to the covenant—as the apostle says, the children of the faithful are holy (1 Cor. 7:14). This is especially the case because Christ never altered God's command to Abraham concerning the sealing of the children of the faithful with the sign of the covenant.* On the contrary, Christ said, *Allow the little ones to come unto Me, for of such is the kingdom of heaven* (Matt. 19:14).

[* Observation 15.4]

5. *The extent to which baptism is necessary in the church, and the extent to which it is necessary for anyone's salvation.*
We believe that baptism is altogether necessary in the church as a sacrament established by Christ and that the church cannot be bereft of it. Hence, we do not recognize the church of Christ to exist where baptism is absent when it could be present. However, we consider baptism to be only so necessary for each person's salvation that we do not believe that, if one were to fall short and remain unbaptized because of a minister's failure (albeit not out of contempt), that person would be condemned or enveloped in eternal ruin on that account.*² For the children of the faithful are saved because they are in the covenant of God and are holy, but adults are saved because they believe in Christ with true faith, which certainly must not result in contempt for Christ's commands.

6. *Baptism, having been rightly administered once, is not to be repeated.*
Furthermore, we believe that, just as circumcision in the flesh was only done once, so water baptism, which has succeeded circumcision, is not to be repeated after having been rightly and legitimately administered once (Col. 2[:11–12]). Furthermore, we understand that baptism is rightly and legitimately administered when, first, it is preceded by the teaching of the gospel concerning the true God and Christ and His office in accordance with Christ's institution. Next, baptism is rightly administered

---

2. Although an asterisk is inserted here in the 1586 and 1601 Latin editions, there is no discussion of the fifth aphorism in the appended observations.

when men are baptized with water and by a legitimate minister in the name of the Father and of the Son and of the Holy Spirit. For Christ also died and was buried but once, and we are *baptized into His death* and *buried with Him through baptism* (Rom. 6:4). Nor do we read of the apostles having rebaptized anybody at any time, except Paul, who baptized those who had not been rightly baptized (Acts 19:5).*

[* Observation 15.6]

7. *The force of baptism is ongoing.*

Although the sacrament of baptism should only be undertaken once, nevertheless, we believe that the substance and power of this sacrament is ongoing: being grafted onto Christ Himself and, consequently, participating in His benefits: the washing away of sins and regeneration, which are accomplished daily more and more by the Holy Spirit. For the apostle says that Christ cleanses the church *by the washing of water in the word, so that she might be presented to Him glorious and without stain* (Eph. 5:26–27). And *His blood purifies her* (daily) *from all sin* (1 John 1:7).

Thus, we think that the faithful, content with having received the sacrament once, should sincerely stir up the memory of their baptism every day. For example, we should consider into whom we were baptized or what we have gained from God through baptism or, alternatively, what we have promised to God Himself. We should do this so that we might thereby be confirmed more and more in faith and together be drawn into fellowship[3] with Christ and made all the more diligent about carrying out our duty. For baptism does not confer merely the remission of original sin or past offenses. Rather, it confers the remission of all sins for the whole of life, just as drawing a person out of the waters is the sign of new life not for one day but for all of life. As the apostle says, *We were buried* (forever) *with Him by baptism into death, so that, just as Christ rose again from the dead by the glory of the Father, so also might we walk* (ongoingly) *in newness of life* (Rom. 6:4). We were cleansed once externally with water, but the blood of Christ is an ever-flowing river, daily cleansing us and washing us of our sins.

---

3. κοινωνία.

8. By whom baptism should be administered.

Additionally, we believe that holy baptism should be administered by those who are also preaching the gospel. For to those whom Christ had told, *Going into all the world, preach the gospel,* He also said, *Baptizing them in the name of the Father, and of the Son, and of the Holy Spirit, teaching them to observe whatsoever I commanded you* (Matt. 28:19–20).

9. Errors.

Therefore, we condemn both ancient and modern heresies that have at any time been strewn about contrary to sound teaching on baptism — Seleucus and Hermias, who baptized with fire; the Cerdonians and the Marcionites, who used another form of words than that which was given by Christ and in the name of another god rather than in the name of the Father, Son, and Holy Spirit; those who baptized in the name of John or another man; the Cataphrygians [that is, the Montanists], who also baptized the dead; both the Anabaptists and the Donatists, who rebaptized those who were added to them; those who deny that infants are to be baptized; as well as those who deny that there is any true baptism without the addition of exorcisms, spittle, salt, and other ceremonies contrived by men.

Chapter Sixteen

The Lord's Supper

Based on what we have said both about fellowship[1] with Christ as well as about the word of the gospel, the sacraments in general, and baptism, one can also easily grasp what we believe regarding the Lord's Supper.

1. The sacrament of the Supper is the instrument whereby the Holy Spirit increases fellowship[2] with Christ and with the church.

Consequently, we believe that the sacrament of the Supper does not merely attest to our communion with Christ (and, thus, with His flesh and blood) and the whole church but also that the Supper is the Holy Spirit's instrument for confirming and increasing that communion. As the apostle says, *The bread that we break, is it not a communion with the Lord's body?* (1 Cor. 10:61 [that is, v. 16]). He calls the breaking and taking of the blessed bread a *communion with the Lord's body* because the one who eats it with active faith in the Lord Himself grows in fellowship[3] together with that same Lord and with His flesh and blood in the same way that the one who embraces the word of the apostles by faith also partakes of communion with the apostles, and that communion is *with the Father and His Son Jesus Christ* (1 John 1:3).

---

1. κοινωνία.
2. κοινωνία.
3. κοινωνία.

2. A confirmation of the previous judgment.

For just as baptism is an instrument whereby this fellowship[4] is established—for thereby we are reborn in Christ—so the Supper was instituted to increase that fellowship, because we are nourished in it by Christ's flesh and blood so that we might grow to maturity in Him. As the apostle says, *We have all been baptized into one body and become drunk with one drink into one Spirit* (1 Cor. 12:13).

3. The particular purpose of the Lord's Supper is to increase our fellowship[5] with Christ.

There are additional reasons why the Lord's Supper was instituted, namely, so that as we are admonished by both words and symbols that display Christ's death and His blood poured out for us, we might recall the benefits of our redemption. As the apostle says, *As often as you eat this bread, you make known the Lord's death* (1 Cor. 11:20 [that is, v. 26]). Therefore, the purpose is for us to be confirmed in our faith with regard to the remission of our sins, to be nourished in the hope of our blessed resurrection, to give thanks to Him for so great a benefit, to be stirred up to repentance, and, finally, to publicly renew the covenant we have entered into with God in the presence of the whole church.

All of these things incline toward this goal: that we might more and more be united to Christ and be made one with Him and that He might live in us efficaciously and we in Him, having now become flesh of His flesh and bones of His bones. For that reason, let us not doubt that the Supper has chiefly been instituted to promote our union and communion with Christ in which our salvation is brought to completion and made perfect (Gal. 2:20; Eph. 5:30). This is the goal toward which the bread and the wine, which are provisions for the body, aim: that we might have absolute certainty that Christ's flesh and blood nourish our souls and preserve them in life in the same way that bread and wine do for our bodies.

---

4. κοινωνία.
5. κοινωνία.

4. Why the bread is called Christ's body.
From this we also understand why Christ called this bread His body. That is to say, properly speaking, He did not call it His body because it is His actual body or because such a body is concealed in the bread, or even because the bread is a bare sign of His body, which was broken and died for us. Rather, He called the bread His body because it is the sacrament of His body. (For, according to Augustine, sacraments take upon themselves the names of those things of which they are the sacraments [*Letters*, ep. 98.9].[6]) And thus, the bread is the instrument whereby the Spirit imparts Christ's actual body to us and whereby He confirms us in His fellowship. For the same reason, the apostle did not refer to baptism as the sign of regeneration but instead called it the very washing of regeneration. He did this, obviously, because Christ efficaciously washes, cleanses, and regenerates us internally by His Spirit through this washing of water in the word—using a suitable instrument, as it were (Eph. 5:26).

5. The actual and substantial body of Christ is predicated of the bread only in an improper[7] and figurative manner.
No doubt this is why Christ's actual and natural body is predicated of the bread at the same moment when a reason for that description is also imparted.[8] Therefore, what you receive is Christ's body, just as it is most

---

6. [*Letters*, ep. 98.9]: "For, if the sacraments did not have some likeness to those events of which they are sacraments, they would not be sacraments at all. But because of this likeness they generally receive the name of the realities themselves." Augustine, *Letters*, 1:431 (*NPNF*1, 1:410).

7. To predicate improperly (*improprie*) is to attribute something to a subject by "a figure of speech or by relation to some other attribute with which it is connected, while the subject lacks that perfection as such." Bernard J. Wuellner, *A Dictionary of Scholastic Philosophy*, 2nd ed. (Milwaukee, Wis.: Bruce, 1966), 240. As Muller comments, this "virtually never means 'improper' in the colloquial sense of inappropriate, incorrect, or unseemly." To predicate *proprie*, by contrast, is to speak in a "strictly conceived and specific" way. *Dictionary*, 296.

8. The point here is that, in the Words of Institution, the predication of the bread as Christ's body in the Supper is tied to the reason why the bread is being offered to communicants, namely, because Christ's body was broken for them. In this sense, they take place "at the same moment" liturgically.

truly said to be. To be sure, what we receive plainly is Christ's body, but this is meant in an improper and figurative way, since it was not really the bread that was given for us. Rather, Christ's actual body was given; the bread is the sacrament of that body.

6. In a real and proper sense, Christ's body is not in the bread.
This also strengthens our claim that, just as the bread is not the very body of Christ (properly speaking) but rather its sacrament, so, too, Christ's body is not really and properly in the bread. For although sacraments take on the names of the substances of which they are sacraments, they do not actually include their substances within them. Take baptism, about which there is no controversy: no one includes the blood of Christ (which washes away our sins) or regeneration itself in baptism. Similarly, those things that the gospel proclaims are not really contained within the word of the gospel. Rather, sacraments are visible words.

Nor did Christ say, *My body is in this*, that is, in the bread. Rather, He said something very different: *This*, that is, this bread, *is My body*. For if someone argues that those statements mean the same thing, it follows that if Christ's body is really in the bread, then the bread really, properly, and substantially is Christ's body. But we think that if it is irreverent to say the one thing, then it cannot be pious to say the other. Nevertheless, we do not deny that His body is sacramentally present in the same sense in which we also say that the remission of sins and salvation and life, which the gospel announces and offers, are present in the word of the gospel. But since language of this sort often draws the common man toward superstition, we find that we should refrain altogether from such words and instead make use of the Holy Scriptures' simple language.

7. Both the symbols and the very things signified are distributed in the Supper.
For us, however, the following is beyond the bounds of controversy: although the Lord's body and blood are not actually and properly in the bread and wine (that is, they are not present according to their substance) but rather are in heaven, nevertheless, when the bread and wine are actually distributed, the true eating of Christ's own body and

the true drinking of His own blood are truly offered to all. We do not, indeed, assert this in a simplistic way but rather insofar as the former was given for us in death and the latter was poured out for the remission of our sins. For Christ's words in the gospel of John about eating His body and drinking His blood if one wishes to have life in Him are plain (John 6:53). And the apostle's words are consistent with Christ's: *He who eats the bread and drinks the cup of the Lord unworthily becomes guilty of the Lord's* (true!) *body and blood* (1 Cor. 11:27). Neither do we doubt that, just as Christ expressly ordered the bread to be eaten, He also then tacitly ordered His body to be eaten no less than the bread when He added, *This is My body*—but each of them [that is, the Lord's body and the bread] is eaten in its own way.

8. Only the faithful truly eat Christ's true flesh.
But although Christ's flesh is offered up to be eaten in the Supper, we nevertheless believe it is truly eaten only by those who are truly faithful. This is not only the case because the faithful alone presently have communion with Christ (and, consequently, with His flesh and blood), while the rest neither have fellowship nor partake of Him when they take up the bread, but also because the faithful alone have Christ's Spirit, by whose power alone Christ's flesh is truly communicated. And it is furthermore the case because they alone bring true faith to the sacrament, without which it cannot be received or eaten. For Christ really and actually delivers His true body to be eaten, but only to those who equally believe that He was given for them in death and that His blood flowed unto the remission of their sins and who also believe the truth of His words: *This is My body.*

9. Hypocrites eat Christ's body sacramentally.
At the same time, we do not deny that hypocrites, who lack true and justifying faith, also receive and eat the bread as the sacrament of the Lord's body. We do not even deny that they could be said to eat the true body of Christ—sacramentally, of course, but not truly and actually. In the same way, the apostle also said that all the Corinthians who had been baptized were sanctified and justified—sacramentally, of course, as we

previously stated—although not everyone was truly sanctified and justified (1 Cor. 6:11).*

[* Observation 16.9]

10. *There are three different types of men who eat and, so, three different ways for them to eat.*
We have also learned from this that there are three types of men about whom we can pose the question: Did they eat Christ's flesh? The first type is the one who takes the bread merely as a common meal but not as a sacrament. In no way do such ones eat Christ's true body. Rather, they are true Capernaeans, and theirs is merely a carnal consumption.[9] Conversely, some men do believe in the gospel but do not take the bread (albeit not out of contempt). Their eating is only spiritual. Finally, there are those who, dissatisfied with just having faith in the gospel, also take the bread, not simply or as though it were chiefly bare bread but rather as a sacrament of the Lord's body. Hence, they are also said to take and eat sacramentally. However, this last way of eating may be done either by the pious or by wicked hypocrites (but in different ways—the ones by faith, the others without true faith). For this reason, we also say that wicked hypocrites eat in a merely sacramental fashion but that the pious eat sacramentally as well as truly and spiritually, and thus they eat unto salvation.*

[* Observation 16.10]

11. *Christ's true body is eaten by faith alone.*
But while we say that only the faithful take Christ's true body not just sacramentally but also truly, we understand that it is eaten not by the bodily mouth but by the mental and spiritual mouth—by faith, as we previously said. And this happens by the work of the Holy Spirit, who works efficaciously in us and applies the whole Christ to us. For, as

---

9. John 6:22–59 records Jesus's encounter with the inhabitants of Capernaum who responded to Jesus's claim that He is "the bread of life" (v. 35) by asking, "How can this Man give us His flesh to eat?" (v. 52). Thus, according to Zanchi, they asserted that bread could be nothing more than bread.

Cyprian says, it is *food of the mind, not of the belly*.¹⁰ And *the flesh profits nothing*, as Christ says (and as Augustine expounds), *but it is the Spirit who makes alive* (John 6:63[; Augustine, *Homilies on the Gospel of John*, hom. 27.5]).¹¹

The apostle teaches us that we were all baptized into one body and that we are also made to drink one drink in one Spirit (1 Cor. 12:13). And if the entirety of our truly being united with Christ is done by the Holy Spirit, and if Christ even now abides bodily in heaven (although we remain on earth), then the eating must also take place in that same way. For what does it mean to eat? To take and unite to yourself food for the nourishing of that part toward which it is directed. But Christ's flesh, as was said, is food of the mind, not of the belly. Certainly, Christ's body is eaten in no other way than as the One who died and was drained of blood for us. This is exactly what the Words of Institution express and what the breaking of the bread displays; it is also the same way in which the paschal lamb and all sacrifices were eaten. But now the body is alive and cannot be drained of blood, just as Christ's body was neither drained of blood nor dead at the first Supper. We therefore cannot properly say that Christ's body passes into us or that, in fact, it does so by way of the mouth without committing sacrilege.

Likewise, why is it that, just as the sacrament of the bread is distributed without the wine and the wine without the bread, so the body is

---

10. Although this work was attributed to Cyprian (d. 258) in Zanchi's time, its author was in fact the twelfth-century Benedictine Arnold Bonaevall, who included it in his *Liber de cardinalibus operibus Christi* (1156). See Nicholas Thompson, *Eucharistic Sacrifice and Patristic Tradition in the Theology of Martin Bucer 1534–1546*, Studies in the History of Christian Traditions 119 (Leiden: Brill, 2005), 76n14. The phrase "food of the mind, not of the belly [*mentis non ventris*]" is, however, found in Augustine's writings, for example in *Homilies on the Gospel of John 41–124*, 370 (hom. 98.7; *NPNF*1, 7:379).

11. [; Augustine, *Homilies on the Gospel of John*, hom. 27.5]: "So, what is this then, 'the flesh is no use at all?' It is no use at all, but in the way those people understood it; they understood flesh as that which is torn off a cadaver or sold at the butcher's, not as that which is animated by the spirit.... So too here: 'The flesh is no use at all,' but that means flesh by itself; let spirit be joined to flesh, in the way charity is attached to knowledge, and flesh is very useful." Augustine, *Homilies on the Gospel of John 1–40*, ed. Allan Fitzgerald, trans. Edmund Hill, The Works of Saint Augustine: A Translation for the 21st Century III/12 (Hyde Park, N.Y.: New City Press, 2009), 469 (*NPNF*1, 7:175).

given in the Supper without the blood and the blood is given separately from the body? It must be so that we might understand that, according to their substances, the body and blood, insofar as they are in heaven, do not pass through our mouths but are received only by a faithful remembrance efficaciously stirred up by the Holy Spirit. For this is also what the Lord Himself aimed at when He said, *Do this in remembrance of Me*, and also, *This is My body, which is given for you* [Luke 22:19]. For by speaking in this way, He was requiring faith whereby they might believe this and, believing, might eat, that is, that they might apply it to themselves as the soul's food and life.

This is why we consider it a settled matter that they truly feed on Christ's flesh—and not only in their imagination—who, believing that it was given unto death for the expiation of their sins, embrace Christ's flesh with a faithful mind and apply it to themselves as a sacrifice of that sort. And we do not doubt that those who thus eat Christ's body as having died are more and more united to that same body, which now lives and makes alive, according to the promise of Christ, who first said, *He who eats My flesh*, and then added, *remains in Me and I in him* (John 6:56).

12. The opinion should be rejected that physical eating is, as it were, empty and useless.
Again, this way of eating Christ's flesh (namely, by faith) is both sure and beneficial, but the other way (whereby one imagines His flesh to be eaten by the bodily mouth) cannot be demonstrated from the Holy Scriptures. And even if, perhaps, something probable could be said with regard to it, nevertheless, it is neither necessary nor actually profitable for the soul. Instead, it brings with it many evils into the church and occasions abundant heresies, idol manias, idolatries, tumults, divisions, the scattering of churches, and finally, the mocking of Christians by infidels. This being the case, we believe that piety requires that, in the Supper, everyone should be content with eating that is by Spirit and faith and that we should not concern ourselves with that other manner of eating.

Instead, bidding it farewell, let us cultivate the brotherly love and peace for which purpose the Supper was established. For, ultimately, we cannot concede to that expression any meaning other than what we understand by the word that we hear with our ears—as we often say, what we have drunk in with our ears. But, indeed, we judge that expressions foreign to the Holy Scriptures should not be introduced into the Christian religion, especially those which are dangerous and altogether useless.

13. Christ's true flesh is present in the Supper, but spiritually.
But based on these things which we have said, both about the true union and the true eating, one can easily understand what we ought to believe about the true presence as well. We believe, therefore, that if we are truly and really united with Christ (and, so, with His flesh and blood), and if, in fact, we eat His flesh and drink His blood, then the very same Christ must be present—not only by His deity but also by His flesh and blood—to those who are united with Him and who eat His flesh and drink His blood. For what can be more present to you than that which you truly eat and drink and with which your substance is united and the substance of which, in turn, is bound together with you and from which, as if from a head, life flows and moves into you, as if into a member.

14. As is the union and the eating, so is the presence—namely, spiritual.
But just as both the union and the eating are by the Spirit and by faith, so we also believe and have learned that the presence is only spiritual, and it takes places only in men granted God's Spirit and faith. Thus, geography does not hinder that union at all, no matter how great the distance.

15. A certain thing becomes present or absent insofar as it is received or not received.
For, in other regards, neither geographical proximity nor distance determine whether a thing is present or absent. Surely, although we are separated from the sun by a greatest distance, nevertheless, it is said to be present and is rightly said to be *in our eyes* when we become partakers of it. On the other hand, it is said to be absent if we do not perceive it when it is hidden by clouds or has departed for the other hemisphere. Its

light is certainly never present to a blind man, even if it strikes intensely and directly against his eyes, just as is also the case when loud music is played for a deaf man or a skillful oration is delivered to an ignorant man (Augustine to Volusian, ep. 3, col. 10 [that is, ep. 137, §2.7]).[12] God is likewise said to be far off from the wicked because they do not perceive Him by faith, yet in His substance, *He is not far off from any one of us, for in Him we live and move and are* [Acts 17:27–28]. Therefore, insofar as something is perceived or not perceived—whether by nourishment[13] or by senses or by the mind or in some other way—to that extent it is said to be present or absent.

16. What sort of presence we deny and what sort we grant.

We deny that the substance of the bread is changed or that it is reduced to nothing, to be replaced in the bread by Christ's true flesh, which, accordingly, is made present in order for the true substance of Christ's body to be hidden under the accidents of the bread. We also deny that Christ's flesh is really and substantially present in the bread, which actually has only a sacramental union with Christ's flesh, established by a mystical relation. And we deny that the substance of Christ's flesh is present to the wicked who do not have spiritual fellowship[14] with Christ and who cannot truly be said to consume His flesh. Likewise, we do not accept that Christ's body is present to the faithful who are now on earth (albeit invisibly and imperceptibly) in the same way that it was visibly present at the first Supper to the apostles at the table.

---

12. Augustine to Volusian, ep. 3, col. 10 [that is, ep. 137, §2.7]: "Understand the Word of God through whom all things were made, not so that you think that something of him passes and from the future becomes the past. He remains as he is, and he is whole everywhere. But he comes when he is revealed, and he withdraws where he is hidden. He is nonetheless there, whether hidden or revealed, just as the light is there for the eyes of one with sight and of one who is blind. Yet the light is there for the one with sight as present, but it is there as absent for the one who is blind. A spoken word too is there for ears that hear; it is also there for those that are deaf, but is disclosed to the former and hidden for the latter." Augustine, *Letters*, vol. 2, 100–155, ed. Boniface Ramsey, trans. Roland J. Teske, The Works of Saint Augustine: A Translation for the 21st Century II/2 (Hyde Park, N.Y.: New City Press, 2003), 216 (*NPNF*1, 1:475–76).

13. τῷ θρεπτικῷ.

14. κοινωνίαν.

The reason why we reject these things is because they conflict not only with the nature of Christ's body but manifestly with the Scriptures as well. And, finally, although we loathe that presence whereby some imagine that Christ's flesh really exists everywhere according to its substance, nevertheless, we do believe in and acknowledge the sort of presence that is no less essential than it is spiritual—the former on account of the things truly present to us (of which we obviously partake) and the latter on account of the manner whereby they are made present and actually communicated.[15] Moreover, we hardly reject the presence of Christ's flesh in the bread or of His blood in the wine. Rather, they are present, but they are present in the same way that we are accustomed to say that the very thing proclaimed and presented by the word of the gospel is present and contained in the presentation. For the sacraments are also visible words, and everything that is signified is in some way present in its own sign and is customarily offered along with it.

17. The presence of Christ's body in the Supper does not depend on ubiquity but on Christ's words.
From this it is also evident that Christ's presence in the Supper does not depend, as some imagine, upon ubiquity but rather upon the very speech of Christ working in us whereby He is present by the Holy Spirit. For if the apostles consumed the bread that they received from Christ's hand, then they surely neither received nor ate anything other than bread unless they heard His words and received them with faith, namely, *This is My body*. For the only thing that could aid them in establishing Christ's real presence in the bread is the monstrous dogma of ubiquity, which is detested by God and His church and derived from certain scholastic distinctions, albeit even against the opinion of the scholastics themselves. And this is our faith and confession regarding the true fellowship,[16] the true eating, and the true presence of Christ's body.

---

15. In both the 1586 and 1601 Latin editions of the text, this already complex sentence contains a printing error. A significant portion of the sentence's main clause (following "nevertheless") appears twice.
16. κοινωνία.

18. Which rites ought to be used in the celebration of the Supper.
With regard to rites and ceremonies, we say only this: those who come as near as possible to apostolic simplicity in the celebration of the Lord's Supper ought especially to be approved.

Chapter Seventeen

Faith, Hope, and Love

1. Faith is altogether necessary for fellowship[1] *and, therefore, for partaking in salvation.*

We confess that, without doubt, the Holy Spirit uses external instruments—the word of the gospel and the sacraments—to graft us onto Christ. But unless the Spirit stirs up faith within us with which to embrace Christ (who is offered to us along with His treasures), no instrument is of any use for salvation. And so we do not doubt that faith is necessary for union with Christ and to participate in His blessings.*

[* Observation 17.1]

2. What we mean by the word faith.

By the word *faith* we do not mean some human opinion or belief about God and Christ but rather a gift of divine wisdom and prudence stirred up in our hearts by the Holy Spirit from the hearing of the Word (Eph. 1:8). We assent by faith with a sincere, steady, and steadfast soul to the whole of God's Word in the Holy Scriptures (on account of the authority of God speaking) and especially to the gospel (which conveys the joyous news of the redemption accomplished by Christ). When we do, then we truly understand, surely know, and very lovingly embrace God and His will, Christ the Mediator, and His benefits in that Word. What is more, we call upon God with firm faith in His immense mercy and love toward us. In return, we are kindled to love Him and unceasingly

---

1. κοινωνίαν.

driven to offer Him faithful compliance and to glorify Him with good works and loving service toward our neighbor until the end of our lives.*
[* Observation 17.2]

3. *A confirmation of the previous judgment.*
For true faith is not a result of a natural human disposition but is a gift of God (Phil. 1:29) and is not given to everyone but only to the elect (Titus 1:1; Acts 13:48). Nor is it an uncertain and hesitant opinion about things that have been promised but rather their substance,[2] a firm and steady certainty of the things promised and a fully settled apprehension of things unseen (Heb. 11:1). Nor is it born from the hearing of human arguments but is received from hearing the Word of God and depends entirely upon the authority of God, who speaks and promises (Rom. 10:17). Nor is it a hypocritical or feigned assent but rather is sincere (1 Tim. 1:5). Nor is it a temporary conviction but rather stable and continuous, although we do undermine it by our sins (Matt. 13:21). Nor is it a blind or reckless matter but rather the highest wisdom whereby we come to know God and Christ and divine things, and it is Christian prudence whereby it happens that we do not squander that knowledge of God but rather devote ourselves to its proper use (Eph. 1:8). Nor, finally, is it dead but rather living and powerful through love (Gal. 5:6; James 2:20).

4. *Faith must increase.*
To be sure, we confess that while the faith of the elect never wholly perishes but rather always lives on, yet we know that it is never so perfect or complete but that it must grow daily. This is something for which the apostles asked God, and for which we should ask likewise (Luke 17:5; Eph. 1:17–18).

5. *Confession of the truth cannot be separated from true faith.*
We also believe that true faith cannot be separated from the frank confession of the truth when it is necessary, since the apostle says, *With the*

---

2. ὑπόστασις.

heart, one believes unto righteousness, but with the mouth, confession is made unto salvation (Rom. 10:10). And thus, we condemn Libertines and other men of like stuff who reckon themselves free to hide the truth anywhere and before all and to adjust religion in whatever way suits them.

6. *Hope is born of faith.*

We also believe that hope is born of faith and that hope is faith's foundation; as the apostle says, *Faith is the substance[3] of those things that are hoped for* (Heb. 11:1). For that reason, we hope for and (through patience) firmly anticipate future blessings, for we trust the divine promises.

7. *What hope is.*

Moreover, hope is a gift of God whereby, as we are firmly confident of the promised blessings (through patience, on the basis of God's mercy and on account of Christ's merits alone), we firmly anticipate those blessings that, as yet, we neither possess nor see (Rom. 8:24).

8. *Whence arises the certainty of hope.*

Indeed, as the hope of Christians is not born of human promises, so neither is it nursed by or dependent upon human deserts but solely upon the truth of divine promises, which are confirmed and sealed in our hearts in various ways. Likewise, hope is also announced to all who believe solely on the basis of the effective omnipotence of that same God, the one who makes the promises. But that hope was particularly and openly revealed in Christ when God *raised Him from the dead and made Him to sit in the high heavenly places at His right hand* (Eph. 1:20). Finally, hope (which is supported and sustained by the obedience and merits of Christ alone, in whom we believe and in whom we hope) firmly and continuously looks toward the fulfillment of our salvation, our resurrection from the dead, the coming of the glory of our great God and Savior Jesus Christ [Titus 2:13], and, indeed, toward the full possession of the heavenly inheritance [1 Peter 1:4].

---

3. *hypostasin*. The Greek ὑπόστασιν is transliterated here.

9. Love itself is likewise born of faith.
We also believe that true love is likewise born of true faith by means of which it works and, indeed, makes known the extent of its effectiveness. As the apostle says, the sort of faith that works through love avails much in Christ (Gal. 5:6). And John affirms this: *He who does not love does not yet know God* (1 John 4:8). Thus, we do not acknowledge as brothers those who disregard faith, since none of them are endowed with love (James 2:15–16).

10. Love is the gift of God.
Moreover, we believe that love itself is also a special gift of God whereby we are moved to return the love of God the Father and Christ the Redeemer and to glorify them with our whole heart, that we might be inclined and favorably disposed with benevolence and kindness toward all men (including even our enemies) but especially toward the saints (1 John 4:18 [that is, v. 8]). Thus, we condemn those who say that man can love God supremely by his own natural powers. *For love is from God,* as John says (1 John 4:7).

11. The witness of true love.
To be sure, we do not believe true Christian love to be the sort that does not correspond to its nature. The apostle described true Christian love of this kind in 1 Corinthians 13:4–7 as being *patient, kind, not envying, not doing wrong, not puffed up, not behaving shamefully, not seeking its own, not provoked, not thinking evil, not rejoicing in injustice but rejoicing in truth, suffering all things,* and so on.

12. Love fosters fellowship[4] with Christ and the church.
We believe that fellowship[5] with Christ and with the church is very much fostered, promoted, and maintained by true love insofar as love unites the one who loves and the one who is loved, since, as John says, *He who remains in love remains in God, and God is love* (1 John 4:16).

---

4. κοινωνίαν.
5. κοινωνίαν.

Chapter Eighteen

Repentance

Although we know that none of these—faith, along with hope and love, repentance, justification, the duty of good works, and a holy life—can really be separated from one another, nevertheless, insofar as one depends upon another, so ought each one also to be distinguished from the rest and considered separately with regard to what they are and do. Thus, we reckon that we should briefly explain what we think about each one, beginning with repentance, faith's constant and inseparable companion. For although, in the wake of justification, repentance daily becomes more perfect, yet because no one is justified without repentance and because its commencement precedes justification, we have for that reason decided first to explain what we believe about repentance.

1. Repentance is necessary for justification and, therefore, for fellowship[1] with Christ.
We believe that repentance is necessary in order for us to partake of Christ's righteousness (and, so, for fellowship[2] with Christ). By repentance we are turned from our sins and from the world, having been diverted by an alteration of the soul and will unto Christ and joined unto Him. That is how we lay hold of the remission of our sins in Him and on the basis of Him and are clothed in His righteousness and holiness. For the first thing that John the Baptist preached—and, likewise, Christ Himself—was repentance unto remission of sins. And, as Christ says, *Unless you repent, you will likewise perish* (Mark 1:4, 15; Luke 13:3, 5).

---

1. κοινωνίαν.
2. κοινωνίαν.

2. What we mean by the word repentance.

Furthermore, by the word *repentance* we chiefly mean two things. First, we mean serious sorrow and true sadness for the sins committed against God, not so much on account of the punishment deserved or the sin for which we are indebted as on account of having offended God Himself, the highest Good, who is our Creator and Father. Second, we mean a true change of mind and heart, of intention and will, and thus of the whole life. Indeed, the apostle teaches that the latter (which, properly speaking, Christ calls *a change of mind* and which the prophets call *turning to God* and the *circumcision of the heart*) arises from the former part when, joining both together, he says that godly sorrow *produces in us a change of mind unto salvation* (2 Cor. 7:10).

3. Repentance is the gift of God.

We believe that repentance is the gift of God arising out of His mere grace but is not owed on the basis of any of our own merits or preparations. As the apostle says, *If at some time God might grant to them repentance unto knowledge of the truth, that they might recover from the Devil's snare* (2 Tim. 2:25[–26]), and, as the prophet says, *Turn me, O Lord, and I will be turned* (Jer. 31:18).

4. Ordinarily, God uses the word of the law and the gospel to stir up repentance in us, and, thus, both need to be heard in the church.

Furthermore, as is evident to any pious man who reads the Holy Scriptures, God ordinarily uses the expounding of the law (which exposes our sins and discloses God's wrath) as well as the preaching of the gospel (which makes known the remission of sins and God's grace in Christ). And thus, we judge it necessary for both to be expounded and read in the church.

5. The summary of the doctrine of repentance, which is necessary for the salvation of all adults everywhere and always.

Therefore, the summary of our faith concerning the repentance necessary for salvation for all adults everywhere and always is this: repentance is a change of mind and heart that the Holy Spirit stirs up in us by the word of the law and the gospel. By that change, we sincerely grieve, hate, deplore, and with indignation detest all our sins (as the law teaches), and even the very corruption of our nature (which things fight, as it were, against the will of God), the expiation of which (as the gospel proclaims) required the death of the Son of God. And we confess them to God, and we humbly ask pardon and forgiveness for them. Moreover, we zealously seek an amended life, ongoing integrity, and pursuit of Christian virtue, and we ourselves diligently practice repentance every day of our lives for God's glory and the edification of the church.

6. *The parts of repentance commonly called contrition, confession of sins, and satisfaction should not simply be condemned.*
Being convinced from the Holy Scriptures that repentance consists summarily in the earnest mortification of the old man and vivification of the new man (the former being empowered by Christ's death and the latter by His resurrection, and both being imparted to us by the Holy Spirit), we have little to say regarding the various parts of repentance beyond what has already been explained. Nevertheless, we do not simply reject the distinction, long since received and preserved in the schools, of dividing repentance into contrition, the confession of sins, and satisfaction, so long as the distinctions are considered according to the rule of the Holy Scriptures and do not deviate from the pious customs and practices of the ancient church.

Moreover, we do not deny that, if one who is oppressed by a mass of sins and entangled by temptations seeks private counsel, instruction, and consolation, he should ask it of either a minister of the church or from some other brother well versed in the law of God. Similarly, we cannot condemn ecclesiastical satisfactions (in Tertullian, Cyprian, and others) that consist merely in providing a trustworthy attestation of true repentance to the whole church, or what they called *doing penance*. We do, however, condemn additional superstitions, the torturing of consciences, and wicked opinions whereby the benefit of the death and the satisfaction of Jesus Christ, the sole Expiator of our sins and our perfect Redeemer from every guilt and punishment, are so thoroughly ruined.

Chapter Nineteen

Justification

1. The recipients of true repentance also receive living faith, are grafted onto Christ, and are justified in Him.
We believe that the man who is justified is the contrite man who hates his sin with heart and soul (Isa. 66:2), who truly repents of all his life's wicked deeds, who furthermore sighs unto God for the remission of his sins (Ps. 32:6), and who hungers and thirsts after Christ's righteousness (Matt. 5:6). We believe that, just as the Holy Spirit has granted to that man this true repentance unto God, so also does the Holy Spirit grant life in Christ by faith. Accordingly, this is likewise the reason he is joined to Christ from eternity as a member to its Head. And it is on that account, before all else, that he assuredly obtains the remission of sins in Christ and is granted His perfect righteousness. Thus, he is accounted truly righteous on account of Christ, onto whom he is grafted and absolved of all guilt. As the apostle says, *There is no condemnation for those who are in Christ Jesus* (Rom. 8:1), and *Christ became righteousness to us* (1 Cor. 1:30).

2. He who is reckoned righteous on account of Christ, onto whom he is grafted, also receives inhering righteousness.
Moreover, we believe that whoever is now reckoned righteous on account of Christ, onto whom he is grafted by the Holy Spirit, and who truly is righteous, having already obtained the remission of sins in Christ and the imputation of His righteousness—he is also and immediately furnished with the gift of inherent righteousness. This happens in such a way that he not only is completely and fully righteous in Christ his

Head but also has true righteousness in himself whereby he might really become like Christ.

Nevertheless, while we are in this flesh, we never possess that righteousness fully. Rather, by our own fault, it is always contaminated with the filth of many sins. John says regarding this righteousness, *He who does righteousness*, that is, who does righteous works, *he is righteous* (1 John 3:7). For both in the letter to the Romans and in other epistles, the apostle always links the one righteousness with the other, and he teaches that each one is given to the faithful by Christ, just as he likewise declared to the Philippians (Phil. 1:11).

And we also say that inherent righteousness, the fruits of which are evident to men, is thus clear testimony of imputed righteousness, such that we profess with the holy apostles that, where the latter is lacking, there the former is also absent (James 2:21 and following). Far be it that we loosen the restraint upon wicked men with the doctrine of justification in which, by faith alone, we lay hold of the remission of sins and the imputation of Christ's righteousness.

3. Because of our sin, inhering righteousness is always very imperfect, and, for that reason, we are truly righteous before God only on account of Christ's righteousness.

At the same time, we confess that, because of our sin, this inhering righteousness is so imperfect that we are made truly righteous before God only by Christ's own righteousness, whereby our sins are not imputed to us, and only thereby can we be regarded as righteous. And this is the case not only at the beginning of our conversion (when we who were wicked are made pious) but also subsequently, all the way to the end of our life. As David says (and as the apostle quoted), *Blessed are they whose iniquities are forgiven* (Ps. 32:1; Rom. 4:7), and again, *In Your sight no one living will be justified* (Ps. 143:2). Therefore, we conclude that our true justification before God consists only in the remission of our sins and the imputation of Christ's righteousness.

4. Being justified in Christ is something one receives by faith, and, hence, such a one is therefore said to be justified by faith.

Moreover, knowledge and feeling accompany justification, and so no one is justified apart from his consent (I speak of adults), and, further, this perception is the perception of faith. Therefore, we say that a man is justified by faith only when he who is grafted onto Christ, perceiving that engrafting, is persuaded that he is engrafted solely on the basis of God's mercy toward him and that his sins are forgiven (solely on the basis of the obedience, satisfaction, and sacrifice of Christ, onto whom he is grafted) in such a way that he is straightforwardly released from all guilt and punishment owed for sins. Moreover, we say that such a man is justified when he is persuaded that Christ's perfect righteousness is imputed to him such that he, therefore, in fact perceives that eternal life is owed to him no less than it was owed to Christ and, thus, truly understands that it is owed to him on the basis not of his own works but of grace.

5. *A confirmation of the previous judgment, and what it is for a man to be justified.*

Indeed, in the Holy Scriptures—both in the Old Testament and in the New, especially in the writings of the apostle when he pursues this matter (Rom. 4:8; 5:19)—*to justify* chiefly means to remit sins and, thus, to absolve from all guilt and punishment. It also means for one to be received into grace as well as to pronounce and consider as righteous not one who is simply unrighteous but rather one who is no longer unrighteous because he has obtained the remission of sins.

God has always acknowledged as His own all those who are in Christ, whom He elected from all eternity as sons in Christ, as members under a Head, and He has freely made them acceptable in the Beloved, albeit we are not yet really in Christ except insofar as we are grafted and incorporated onto Him by the Holy Spirit. This is no longer the situation that we adults are in when we are given to know Christ by faith as our righteousness and embrace Him as such. It is for that reason that the Scriptures teach that we are only justified (and only justified by faith in Christ and apart from our own works) when we believe all of this with true faith. That is, we are justified only when we are persuaded that our sins, as they have once been expiated in Christ, are no longer imputed to us but are pardoned on the basis of God's grace and on account of

Christ alone and, conversely, that Christ's righteousness is imputed to us as our own and that we are adorned with it in God's sight, truly reckoned as righteous and truly righteous. The effect and, consequently, the clear testimony of this is, as we said before, that very righteousness begun and inhering in us, which consists in the hatred of sin, the love of righteousness, and the pursuit of good works (James 2:12).

6. A confirmation of what it is for us to be justified.
Thus, when we say that man is justified by faith (or by means of faith), we do not mean that we are justified by the virtue of faith—as if by *formed faith* (as they say) or true righteousness.[1] Nor is faith that whereby we earn the remission of our sins and our justification. Nor is it that which, as the first of all the other virtues and the cause and source of all good works, brings with it other virtues, charity, cleanliness of heart, internal righteousness, and good works whereby we are justified.

Rather, we say that man is justified by faith because faith is (as it were) a light whereby, peering into the mirror of the gospel, we see that it is on the basis of God's goodness and will and on account of the merits of Christ Himself that we are in Christ. And, moreover, because faith is the hand (as it were) with which we lay hold of and embrace this grace of God and the benefit of Christ extended to us in the gospel and given in the person of Christ. Or, to describe faith yet more concisely, we are said to be justified by faith (that is, by the remission of sins and the imputation of Christ's righteousness apprehended by means of faith) in such a way that faith (or that which is apprehended by faith) is taken for the thing believed in. This is just as we read concerning Abraham: *Abraham believed God, and it*—that is, what he believed regarding the Seed promised to him, namely, concerning Christ—*was imputed to him as righteousness*

---

1. According to Aquinas, "The act of faith will be perfect, if the will is perfected by the habit of charity and the intellect by the habit of faith, but not if the habit of charity is lacking. Consequently, faith formed by charity is a virtue; but not unformed faith." Thomas Aquinas, *Commentary on the Letter of Saint Paul to the Romans*, ed. J. Mortensen and E. Alarcón, trans. Fabian R. Larcher, Latin/English Edition of the Works of St. Thomas Aquinas 37 (Lander, WY: Aquinas Institute, 2012), 37–38 (§106). See also Aquinas, *Summa theologiae* II–II, q. 4, art. 4. For the Council of Trent's appropriation of the concept, see Schaff, *Creeds*, 2:96, 112–13.

(Gen. 15:6).* For He is the righteousness of all the elect, those who truly believe, and as the Scriptures say, the sons of promise [Rom. 4:3; 9:8].
[* Observation 19.6]

7. *People are justified by faith alone.*
There follows another thing easily understood: with the Holy Scriptures and the holy fathers, we have always confessed and resolutely do confess that we are justified by faith alone. For when we are justified by faith before God, this is nothing other than to be reckoned righteous by the remission of sins and the righteousness of Christ laid hold of by faith. Furthermore, this alone is true righteousness, since whatever righteousness inheres in us and whatever good works we do are such that they cannot stand upright before the judgment of God. It is splendidly clear on the basis of passages like *Do not enter into judgment with Your servant, O Lord, for in Your sight no one living will be justified* (Ps. 142:2 [that is, 143:2]) and *If you, Lord, were to attend to iniquities, O Lord, who could endure it?* (Ps. 130:3). Hence, it is clear that our confession of justification by faith alone is altogether certain and true.

8. *We are justified by faith alone not only at the beginning of our conversion but throughout the whole course of our life, all the way to death.*
For this reason, we cannot avoid believing and resolutely confessing that we are justified by faith alone in Christ not only when we first are righteous, having previously been unrighteous, but also at every moment of our lives thereafter all the way to the end. Thus, our righteousness is always from faith to faith. For there is no one who does not sin daily, so we always have to say, *Forgive us our sins* (Matt. 6:12), and David says, *Let everyone pray unto You* for the forgiveness of their sins (Ps. 32:6). And Christ, not just once but always, is *our righteousness, sanctification, and redemption* (1 Cor. 1:30), and *the propitiation for our sins* (1 John 2:2).

9. *Justification by faith alone is not an imaginary or fictitious thing.*
We repeat, however, let no one suppose that we contrive some imaginary righteousness that has no foundation or power in us. For we have also previously declared, first, that we say that the faith whereby we are justified is certainly living faith and that it works through love. Next, we say

that God does not justify us by the remission of sins and the imputation of Christ's righteousness without also making us partakers of His divine nature, without regenerating, remaking, and sanctifying us, giving us inherent righteousness, and conforming us to the image of His Son.

And we say that this begun-but-not-completed righteousness bears witness to that other true and perfect righteousness, which we have in Christ alone, and that they are both joined together—the one with the other—by the bond of that same Holy Spirit. As the apostle says, *Not only God's grace but also the gift in the grace, which is of the one Man, Jesus Christ, overflowed unto many* (Rom. 5:15). For just as Adam's disobedience was imputed to us, and his corrupt nature was transferred to us, so also Christ's obedience and righteousness are imputed to those grafted onto Him, and His righteous nature really is communicated to them, so that we might be made new creatures, righteous and holy in ourselves as well, pursuing good works (2 Cor. 5:17; Eph. 2:10; Titus 2:14).

10. Inherent righteousness increases by good works.
But just as we do not say that that first righteousness is based on our good works or that it is begun but not complete or that it increases, so we confess that, although this second righteousness leads the way to good works, it is neither based on nor initiated by them (for they are all sins, since good works do not go before being justified but rather follow from justification). Nevertheless, this second righteousness is preserved, promoted, and increased by subsequent works and pious exercises. According to the saying of the apostle, the gifts of God in us are stirred up, fostered, and fed like a fire by exercises of this sort (2 Tim. 1:6). And regarding that increase in righteousness, John says, *He who is righteous, let him be justified* (Rev. 22:11). And hence, if one is speaking merely about this inherent righteousness, we do not deny that a man may be justified (that is, he may become more and more righteous) on the basis of good works and not merely from faith.

11. Properly speaking, a man is justified by righteousness that rests upon the remission of sins and the imputation of Christ's righteousness and not on the basis of works, but he is shown to be justified and righteous by them.

But if we are asked about the former type of righteousness, we respond that man is never properly justified on the basis of his own works but always on the basis of faith alone. Nevertheless, it is on the basis of works that one is shown to be righteous or not. This is as true for the one type of righteousness as for the other, since no one is justified by the first [that is, imputed] righteousness without also being granted the latter [that is, inherent righteousness], and both are revealed by good works. We do not doubt that it was in this sense that James spoke [James 2:24].

12. Errors.

We condemn all Pelagians, who imagined that infants were conceived without sin and, thus, did not need the remission of sins or the benefit of Christ for salvation. Likewise, we condemn those who teach that, even if they do need the remission of sins, they can obtain it apart from faith in Christ. Likewise, we condemn those who think that, even if faith in Christ is necessary, it is nevertheless insufficient and that our works are also necessary to obtain the remission of sins. Above all, however, we condemn those who taught that this was to be done by way of irreverent worship and superstitions.

Nor do we approve of those who have taught that we are not justified by an alien righteousness but rather but by an internal and inherent righteousness. Conversely, however, we also disapprove of those who imagine that the remission of sins can be established apart from internal renewal and righteousness. We also condemn those who suppose that they can be justified and saved by historical faith about Christ, which James also called dead, that is, no faith at all. Likewise, we do not approve of the opinion of those who teach that man is justified, not by the remission of sins and the imputation of Christ's righteousness, but rather by (as they call it) the very essential righteousness of Christ really communicated to us.[*][2]

[* Observation 19.12]

---

2. While no asterisk is included in this aphorism, nevertheless, an observation about it exists.

Chapter Twenty

The Regenerate Man's Free Will and His Power to Do Good

1. Those who are justified in Christ are also regenerated in Him and receive power to do good.
We believe that, just as those who are grafted onto Christ are justified in Him, so also are they regenerated in Him and made new creations by participation in the divine nature [2 Peter 1:4]. Thus, they become children and receive power from Christ Himself to turn from evil and pursue good, as members receive from the head and as branches from the vine. As the Lord said, *You will be truly free if the Son of Man sets you free* (John 8:36). Indeed, when we are grafted onto Christ and regenerated by His Spirit, then we are free, since the apostle also says, *Where the Spirit of the Lord is, there is freedom* (2 Cor. 3:17).

2. Christ lives and works in the regenerate.
Indeed, we confess with the apostle that Christ lives in us who are born again from His Spirit (Gal. 2:20). And He does not live idly; rather, He works both that *we might will and that we might accomplish according to His good will for us* (Phil. 2:13). And, *His Spirit helps us in our weaknesses* (Rom. 8:26).

3. Even in activities related to animal and human life, the one who is regenerate conducts himself more excellently than he who is not and, therefore, is freer.
Thus, the regenerate man conducts himself much better and more excellently in all activities than one who is not regenerate. This is not only because he always retains a will that is free of compulsion (unlike the

man who is not regenerate) but also because the Holy Spirit leads him even in those actions that have to do with animal and human life (which any unregenerate man can also do). The Holy Spirit does this by illuminating his mind, governing his will and judgment, and, finally, drawing forth his actions from a good source (that is, from a good heart) and directing him unto the very best end (that is, God's glory). The apostle also teaches this to us: *Whether you eat or drink, or whatever else you do, do everything unto God's glory* (1 Cor. 10:31).

Hence, the regenerate man is also freer in these sorts of actions than is the unregenerate, but, of course, not insofar as he is carried unto these activities by his carnal desires in the same way as the unregenerate man. Rather, driven by the Holy Spirit, the regenerate man considers, wills, and undertakes all things with greater care, prudence, and devotion, and is always closely attentive to do all things to God's glory, for his own salvation, and to his neighbor's benefit. For he always holds on to that apostolic saying: *None of us lives only to himself or dies only to himself; but if we live, we live to the Lord, and if we die, we die to the Lord, for we are always the Lord's* (Rom. 14:7–8). And thus, he entrusts all his activities to divine providence and, with James, says (or at least thinks), *If the Lord wills, I will do this or that; I will set out for this place or that place* (James 4:15).[1]

4. *The regenerate man is also freer and more vigorous in gaining moral virtues than he who is unregenerate.*

Let us also confess that, while the unregenerate man can gain for himself moral virtues when aided by God's special help, we nevertheless believe that this special help is more preeminent in the regenerate man on account of the presence of the Holy Spirit by whom he is illuminated, governed, and led. Contrary to the empty boasts of the Gentiles, the fathers rightly proved that even what the Gentiles call moral virtues are far different in Christians than they were or could be in those without faith, since they merely had in them the likeness of virtues, while true

---

1. With reference to "this place or that place," Zanchi seems to be drawing upon material from James 4:13.

virtues were in true Christians (Tertullian, *Apology*, ch. 45; Augustine, *Against Julian the Pelagian*, bk. 4, ch. 3[, §14] and *City of God*, bk. 19, ch. 25; Origen, *Against Celsus*[, §1.4]).[2]

5. Only[3] the one whom the Holy Spirit has regenerated is truly enlightened, turned toward God, and driven to understand, choose, and fulfill those things that are of God and that pertain to His kingdom.

However, we believe that only the regenerate are ruled by the Holy Spirit in such a way as truly to understand, desire, and do that which pertains to the true kingdom of God, since the apostle says, *The natural man does not perceive the things that are of God, nor can he perceive them*. And he adds this concerning the one who is born again: *But the spiritual man judges all things* (1 Cor. 2:14[–15]). And again, *God works in us that we might desire and that we might accomplish* (Phil. 2:13).

6. *Not only is the regenerate man acted upon by the Holy Spirit, but he also acts by the Holy Spirit.*

On the basis of what is taught both in apostolic sayings and in other testimonies of the Holy Scriptures, we confess that the regenerate are acted upon by the Holy Spirit in such a way that they also act. And, thus, God works in them to will and to accomplish in such a way that they themselves are the ones who are willing and accomplishing. For they are neither posts nor beasts but men, gifted with minds whereby they understand and wills whereby they desire. And thereby they rule

---

2. Tertullian, *Apology*, ch. 45: Tertullian, "Apology," 109–10 (*ANF*, 3:50).

Augustine, *Against Julian the Pelagian*, bk. 4, ch. 3[, §14]: Augustine, "Answer to Julian," 386–87 (*FOTC*, 35:176–78)

…and *City of God*, bk. 19, ch. 25: Augustine, *The City of God: Books VIII–XVI*, trans. Gerald G. Walsh and Grace Monahan, Fathers of the Church 14 (Washington, D.C.: Catholic University of America Press, 1952), 244–45 (*NPNF*1, 2:418–19).

Origen, *Against Celsus*[, §1.4]: Origen, *Contra Celsum*, trans. Henry Chadwick (Cambridge: Cambridge University Press, 1980), 8–9 (*ANF*, 4:398).

3. In both the 1586 and 1601 editions, the word "not" (*non*) precedes "only" (*solum*) in this section heading. This appears to be a printing error in light of what is confessed subsequently, and, indeed, in the *OOT*, *non* has been removed.

over all the other powers of the body and soul, that they might order the performance of good things.

7. *The power of free will is still weak, even in the regenerate, so that we might always have need of God's help and might not accomplish everything that we want.*
Again, the regeneration in us is hardly begun and is not yet perfect. This is the case such that, while we were previously all flesh, we now consist partly of Spirit and partly of flesh. These struggle mutually against each other such that we cannot achieve the good things we desire. Instead, with the mind we serve the law of God, but with the flesh we serve the law of sin (Gal. 5:17).

This, then, is why we believe that, in the regenerate, a great deal of enslavement remains—many mists in the mind, perversities in the heart, and weaknesses in all the faculties of the soul and body—as our experience also confirms. This happens so that we might at every moment have fresh need of God's help and grace (which more and more enlightens our minds and ever more agreeably reforms our wills) and so that they might increase and perfect our power to do good. And so, as long as we are in this flesh, our free will is never truly and perfectly free, that is, sufficiently able to avoid evil and do good on its own power, especially since the outcomes of all things are indeed placed not in our power but are in God's hands. And so, it is necessary that all things happen—not what we imagined but whatever His hand and counsel have determined to be done (Acts 4:28).

8. *God so rules the minds and wills of the pious that, in the very conflict of temptations and of the flesh, He does not permit them altogether to fall away from Him.*
At the same time, we maintain that those who are grafted onto Christ, their souls and wills now having the Holy Spirit bestowed upon them, are so ruled and sustained by God on account of Christ that, although they may be permitted to be shaken in many ways and by many temptations, nevertheless, they are not permitted to succumb to them in the end or ultimately to perish (Jer. 32:40; Luke 22:32; Rom. 8:35).

9. Errors.

We condemn those who, either denying or diminishing the new birth of the regenerate man, claim that he is just as incapable of doing good and just as much the servant of sin as he was before he was regenerated. This is contrary to all the many and manifest testimonies of the Holy Scriptures about the deliverance of the regenerate from enslavement to sin and their freedom to do good, to say nothing of the affront it causes to the Holy Spirt, who is dwelling and working in us.

On the other hand, we also disapprove of those who claim that the regenerate man is so free from all enslavement to sin that it is no longer possible for him to commit sins of any kind, which generally contradicts the entirety of Holy Scripture as well as daily experience. For although we are not allowed to sin unto death, nevertheless, it is well known that we commit many sins that are by their own nature worthy of death. Therefore, we also disapprove of the opinions of those who so diminish the Spirit's power in the regenerate and so magnify the vestiges of the flesh as to say that the Spirit's work is frequently altogether quenched by the power of the old man and to teach that the regenerate man himself may fall away entirely from God's grace and perish eternally. This contradicts what God said through the prophet: *I will put My fear in their hearts so that they will not depart from Me* (Jer. 32:40). And this is affirmed by the apostle: *The sure foundation stands* (2 Tim. 2:19) and *He who began a good work in you will complete it until the end* (Phil. 1:6).

Chapter Twenty-One

Good Works

1. As a result of their engrafting, the very ones who are grafted onto Christ have life and bring forth the works of life for others, and this is the principal purpose of the engrafting.

A branch not only draws vital sap from the vine out of which it lives but also has it from itself, whence it bears good fruit for us. We believe that, in the same way, saints not only receive the life whereby they live from Christ, onto whom they have been grafted, but also have power with which to bear the fruit of good works unto God's glory and the church's edification. This accords with the Lord's saying, *I am the vine, and you are the branches. He who remains in Me and in whom I remain, he will bear much fruit* (John 15:1 [that is, v. 5], etc.). The following also pertains to this point: *We are His workmanship, created in Christ Jesus for good works, which He has prepared that we might walk in them* (Eph. 2:10).

2. What we mean by the words good works.

Moreover, when we say *good works*, we mean any action or work done by the regenerate on account of a precept of the divine will revealed in the Word and from a living faith in Christ and, hence, from a pure heart through the Holy Spirit (1 Peter [that is, 2 Peter] 1:5, etc.; 1 Tim. 1:5). For just as anything that is not from faith is sin, so anything done from faith (and thus from a pure heart and a good conscience) must be a good work (Rom. 14:23). It is for this reason that we think it impossible for the deeds of the wicked (who lack faith, stand apart from God's Word, and disregard the Holy Spirit's guidance) to be counted among good works and things pleasing to God. This is the case despite whatever appearance they might have of great piety and divine worship (Col. 2:18, 23; Matt. 15:8–9).

3. *We are able to do good works on account of the power of Christ's Spirit.*
But the shoots of a vine (or wild olive branches that have been grafted onto a good olive tree) do not produce fruit on their own but rather on account of the power of the vine (or the olive tree onto which they have been grafted). In the same way, we do not perform good works from ourselves but on account of the power of Christ's Spirit, by whom we are incorporated into Christ Himself. He works in us by His Spirit, and from Him we also draw the life whereby we ourselves live—that we might first will the good and then do it (Phil. 2:13). *For without Me*, He said, *you can do nothing* (John 15:5).

4. *Good works are not the cause but the effect of our being united with Christ and of our justification and life.*
Likewise, shoots and branches do not bear good fruit in order to be grafted onto the vine and the olive tree or in order for life to be given on their account. Accordingly, their good fruits are not the causes but rather the consequences and the conspicuous evidences of their engrafting and life. We believe that the situation is the same with regard to Christ in us, just as Augustine also frequently taught. Indeed, he said, *Good works do not precede being justified but follow justification* [Faith and Works, 14.21].[1] And, therefore, we consistently confess that man is not justified on the basis of works (properly speaking and with regard to justification to life) but is declared to be righteous.

5. *Although we are not justified on the basis of our works, nevertheless, others are frequently built up and preserved by them.*
At the same time, we say this as well: although trees themselves do not live off of their own fruits, they nevertheless nourish and sustain others—animals and men—in life. Just so, although we are not justified

---

1. [*Faith and Works*, 14.21]: In *On Christian Belief*, ed. Boniface Ramsey, trans. Edmund Hill et al., The Works of Saint Augustine: A Translation for the 21st Century I/8 (Hyde Park, N.Y.: New City Press, 2005), 241 (*FOTC*, 27:247).

on the basis of our works, nevertheless, others are amply edified by them and stirred up by our example, first unto the glorifying of God and then unto pursuing true righteousness and life in Christ, and thus they are preserved (Matt. 5:16). The apostle likewise said that it was for that reason that he adorned his ministry (with diligence and holiness of life) among the Gentiles, in order to provoke his kinsmen to jealousy and save some of them (Rom. 11:13[–14]). And elsewhere he says that, sometimes, an unbelieving spouse is saved by a believing spouse, referring here to one who lives in a godly and holy way and does his or her duty (1 Cor. 7:16). And he writes to Timothy that, if he takes care of himself (that is, if he fulfills the duty of a bishop), he will save both himself and others (1 Tim. 4:16).

6. Although we deny that man is justified by works, nevertheless, we do not for that reason condemn works.
That is why, although we deny that good works should be done in order to justify us (for this would overthrow the free righteousness of God and the whole benefit of Christ), yet we do not for that reason disapprove of pursuing a holy life and good works. No indeed, we continually commend and urge people toward them to the utmost of their ability.

7. There are many and very significant reasons why the doing of good works should be pursued.
Indeed, the Holy Scriptures set forth many and very significant reasons why we still ought to diligently press forward in pursuit of good works, despite not being justified by them. Of these reasons, some pertain directly to God's glory, others to the salvation of our neighbors and the advantage of the church, and yet others relate to our gratitude toward God and, of course, our own salvation too.

God commands that we do this, and we should simply obey God. God is glorified by these things, and we should be driven by God's glory (Matt. 5:16). This is why God elected, created, redeemed, and grafted us onto Christ: so that we might live soberly, righteously, and piously in this age, for God should not be cheated of what is due Him (Titus 2:12). Good works please God, for He hates wickedness and loves righteousness, and we should do what pleases God even if neither we nor our neighbors reap any kind of advantage (Acts 10:35; Col. 1:10).

But there are many benefits that accrue from our good works—both to our neighbor and especially to the church itself. This is the case not only with regard to our bodies and external advantages but also with regard to eternal salvation, while at the same time the elect are stirred up by our example (to say nothing of other things) to the pursuit of that same piety (1 Thess. 4:7; 2 Cor. 1:4, etc.; Heb. 10:24).

To be sure, good works profit us, first, because we thereby prove our election and calling to ourselves and others, which is to say, we do so by the effects of our election and calling (2 Peter 1:10). Second, they profit us because faith not only reveals and exposes itself by its own fruits but is also cultivated, kindled, strengthened, and increased by being practiced. All moral virtues undergo growth and are established in this same way (2 Tim. 1:6). Third, they profit us because, just as we grieve the Holy Spirit dwelling in us by our sins, so we gladden Him with good works, and thus we shape our hearts and consciences with spiritual joy, and, moreover, we withstand the Devil's temptations (Eph. 4:30). Fourth, they profit us because, just as we avoid much hardship when we avoid sins, so we also gain many blessings from God, both in this life and especially in the next, by doing good works (Deuteronomy 28). And finally, they profit us because they are the ways whereby God ordinarily leads His elect unto eternal life, and unless the branch bears fruit, it will be cut off and cast into the fire (Eph. 2:10; John 15:6).

8. A reward is promised and given for our good works, but on the basis of grace and because of Christ.

On the basis of these things, we understand that we cannot (properly speaking) gain possession of the heavenly inheritance for ourselves by our good works (for eternal life is by God's favor). Yet, we can gain that reward, as it were, albeit only by God's free mercy and on account of the merits of Christ (Luke 10:17 [that is, 17:10]; Rom. 6:23; Jer. 31:34; Matt. 5:7).

9. Errors.

We therefore condemn all those who teach that, on the basis of their good works, they deserve either forgiveness of sins or eternal life or any blessing whatsoever. For even if we were to keep God's commands perfectly, we would still be unprofitable servants (Luke 17:10). However, even after having been grafted onto Christ and justified, no one keeps God's commands as they really ought to be kept. At the same time, we do not disapprove of the fathers when they use the word *merit*, since, by that word, they certainly meant nothing other than that a good work done from faith is recompensed with a reward on the basis of grace and merely on account of Christ's merit.

On the other hand, we cannot approve of those who discuss good works as if they were things indifferent and who, therefore, say that they are not only unnecessary but even that they have nothing to do with our salvation. For how can someone be saved without faith (Heb. 11:6)? But how can faith be alive unless it is pursuing good works (James 2:20)? Again, how can someone hold on to faith unless he also holds on to a good conscience (1 Tim. [1:]19)? But how can someone hold on to a good conscience unless he holds on to the avoidance of sin and the doing of good works and the construction of his whole life according to God's will?

To be sure, we simply condemn the Libertines, for whom keeping God's commands is no different than not keeping them and for whom doing good is no different than doing evil.

We also condemn those who teach that our good works benefit even the very souls of the dead who are gathered in a certain burning fire, which they call purgatory. For Scripture says that each one will be judged according to the works that he himself did in his body. And it follows that the dead themselves will be judged not by the works of others but by their own works (2 Cor. 3:10 [that is, 5:10]; Rev. 14:13).

Chapter Twenty-Two

Prayer and Oaths

Prayer is not the least among the good works commanded by God, such that, in the Holy Scriptures, it is often even received as the whole worship of God. To this swearing is also added as a part of sacred worship. For this reason, we also think that it is necessary to briefly explain what we believe about these two matters, especially since a certain amount of controversy about both prayer and oaths exists among those who profess Christ.

1. God alone—and, thus, Jesus Christ—should be invoked.
We believe that, when we engage in religious invocations, we should call upon the true God—He, indeed, is Father, Son, and Holy Spirit—and, thus, upon Jesus Christ our advocate, and no one else. For clear commands exist that we are to invoke no one but God, because He, indeed, is the only one who is to be worshiped and adored (Ps. 50:16).[1] Likewise, we do not lack testimonies or examples of Christ being invoked as our mediator and advocate in the Acts of the Apostles, the epistles, and Revelation [for example, Acts 7:59; 1 Thess. 3:11; 2 Thess. 2:16–17; Rev. 5:9]. But just as we are clearly warned not to adore or worship any mere

---

1. This citation, as given in the 1586 edition, is clearly wrong. The 1601 edition gives Psalm 15:16 (which does not exist), and the *OOT* suggests Psalm 10:16. None of these (nor any of the immediately neighboring psalms) seem to be a good fit. Baschera and Moser suggest that Psalm 50:15 may be in view, which is possible but hardly the most obvious text to prove the point. Baschera and Moser, *De religione*, 1:372.

creatures,[2] no matter what they are, whether in heaven or on the earth, so we are likewise forbidden to call upon them (Deut. 10:12; Matt. 4:10; Col. 2:18).

However, anything that is not of faith is sin [Rom. 14:23]. So then, how much more sinful is it to allow that which opposes God's clear Word, since not even the Gentiles had imagined that anyone ought to be invoked other than the one whom they regarded as God (John 1:6).[3] And how, the apostle asks, *shall they call upon Him in whom they have not believed?* (Rom. 10:14). Moreover, all of Holy Scripture and the whole catholic church plainly teaches—even in the Creed itself, which is recited on a daily basis—that we are to believe only in God and in Jesus Christ.[4]

2. It is permissible for a Christian man to swear legitimately.
We also believe that a Christian man is permitted to swear in a legitimate way, namely, as the prophet teaches, *in truth, in judgment, and in righteousness* (Jer. 4:2). That is, he is permitted to swear in such a way that the oath is neither false nor rash nor wicked. In fact, it is not the taking of the name of the Lord that is condemned but rather the taking of it in vain and for a lie. And according to everyone since the creation of the world, an oath has been kept when it glorifies God and benefits our neighbor.

Indeed, since oath-taking is a part of divine worship, it has been sanctioned by the example not only of God Himself but also of Christ and the apostles, so we need not even mention the uninterrupted consensus of the whole church. Hence, Christ's teaching in Matthew or the epistle of James cannot conflict with this (Matt. 5:34[–37]; James 5:12). For they were speaking against the abuses of swearing and wished to explain the true meaning of the command about swearing.

---

2. *Puram creaturam*. That is, as opposed to the God-man Jesus Christ, who is worshiped and adored because His one person is the person of the eternal Son of God who assumed a created body as well as "a true soul and a human mind." (See above, CCR, 9.2.)

3. Another incorrect citation without an obvious alternative. The 1601 edition repeats John 1:6; OOT has simply removed the reference. Baschera and Moser suggest 2 John 6, which seems unlikely. Baschera and Moser, *De religione*, 1:373.

4. Zanchi refers here to the Apostles' Creed, which confesses belief "in God the Father Almighty…and in Jesus Christ," as well as "in the Holy Spirit."

3. We should not swear except by God.

We believe that, when one must swear, none other than God should be called upon or appealed to as a witness to our conscience, for God alone is the examiner of our hearts, and He alone has authority over our souls. And thus, He alone is to have this honor and worship, so that we might appeal to Him as witness to and punisher of our souls if we fail to keep what we promise when we swear.

4. Righteous and legitimately made oaths should be kept.

Hence, we confess that all legitimately made oaths should be kept on account of the honor of God, in whose name the oath is made, as if He were pledged as surety. This is the same thing that the law also commands, that God's name should not be taken in vain or falsely [Ex. 20:7].

5. Oaths regarding wicked or unjust matters—that is, matters opposed to God's law—should not be taken, and having been taken, they should not be kept.

On the other hand, we judge that, since nothing should ever be promised that is wicked or unjust (which is to say, in opposition to God's law) much less should it be sworn or confirmed by oath in God's name. But we affirm that, if such an oath is taken, which of itself is forbidden, it should not be kept. For to do so is to take upon oneself double the sin, just as we read in the Gospels concerning Herod (Matt. 14:7).

6. Oaths that cannot be kept without transgressing divine law should not be kept, even if nothing about them is in and of itself unjust.

To this we also add that any oaths that cannot be kept without transgressing a divine command should not be kept, even if they are not unjust in and of themselves. Thus, for example, we think that, if one were to swear an oath of perpetual celibacy, which subsequently cannot be kept without openly transgressing God's law, such an oath absolutely ought not to be kept (Gratian, *Decretum* causa 22, q. 4[, ch. 16]).[5]

---

5. Gratian, Decretum causa 22, q. 4[, ch. 16]: "An oath whereby evil is incautiously promised should not be kept." Gratian, *Corpus Iuris Canonici*, ed. Aemilius Friedberg (Graz: Akademische Druck- und Verlagsanstalt, 1959), 1:879.

7. Errors.

We therefore reject those who invoke or worship idols, dead men, or inanimate objects. We also reject the Anabaptists, who unconditionally condemn all oaths, which they argue are not permissible to the Christian man. We also reject those who call upon any but God to stand as witness to their souls. Finally, we reject those who argue that vows and oaths should be kept no matter what, even if they are wicked in and of themselves or cannot be kept without sin.

Chapter Twenty-Three

Christ's Church in General

It is well known that those who are joined to Christ as members to a head by the bond of the Holy Spirit do, on that basis, constitute Christ's church, which is His body. And it is also well known that the word of the gospel and the sacraments (the instruments, so to speak, whereby men are united to Christ) are only administered in the church and that everyone who has been endowed with true faith in Christ, with hope, love, repentance, and zeal for good works, belongs to the church. For these reasons, we consider it a very worthwhile labor to explain what our confession is concerning the church, particularly since the greatest controversies have chiefly to do with this article of the faith. And thus, let us first confess our faith concerning Christ's church in general along with the whole of that same church. Subsequently, we will address the church militant in particular and the things pertaining to it.

1. *The article of faith concerning the church from the Apostles' Creed. We believe…the holy catholic church, the communion of saints.*[1]

---

1. The received text of the Apostles' Creed does not repeat the preposition "in" with reference to the church. See Wolfram Kinzig, ed., *Faith in Formulae: A Collection of Early Christian Creeds and Creed-related Texts*, Oxford Early Christian Texts (Oxford: Oxford University Press, 2017), 2:351–52. Elsewhere, Zanchi asserts that, while Christians place their believing faith *in* the Father, Son, and Holy Spirit, they merely *believe* (or perhaps, *believe about*) the church. See *In d. Pauli Apostoli epistolas ad Philippenses ad Colossenses ad Thessalonicenses, commentarij* (Neustadt, 1595), 65 (OOT, 2/6:67).

2. What we mean by the word church, and a description of it.

When we say *the church of Christ*, we do not only mean a fixed number and assembly of angels and men known by God, elected and predestined to have unending fellowship with Christ and one another, to the unending worship of the true God according to His will and command, and to love one another with mutually sincere and unending love. We also mean those who, in time, are efficaciously summoned by the Holy Spirit out of the number of the rest and who are joined to Christ as their Head and thus made truly holy.

From the foundation of the world to today, and continuing until the world's end—in fact, into all eternity—this assembly has been gathered and joined together in an unbroken line and by the bond of the Holy Spirit. Part of the church is triumphant even now, with Christ in the heavens; part remains on earth, waging war against various enemies for Christ's sake, proclaiming and hearing the word of the gospel, administering and receiving the sacraments, and attending both publicly and privately to the keeping of Christ's commands.

3. The church is an assembly consisting of many.

The Holy Scriptures indeed teach that the church is an assembly consisting of many and, as it were, a body composed of many members, since the Scriptures call her Christ's body distinguished by many members (Eph. 1:23). They call her as well a flock of sheep, the kingdom of God, a city comprising many citizens, and other similar phrases (John 10:3, etc.; Heb. 11:10).

4. The church consists only of the elect who are already incorporated to Christ.

Yet, those same Holy Scriptures frequently teach that the many who constitute the church are none other than the elect who are already grafted onto Christ and granted His holiness. For, although the apostle also discusses the church and her members elsewhere, it is in the epistle to the Ephesians in particular where he says that all of us who were elected in Christ have redemption in Him, that we are sealed with the Holy Spirit of promise, that Christ is given as Head to the church herself, and that the church is His very body (Eph. 1[:13–14, 22–23]).

Therefore, the church is the sort of body wherein each member is joined together by that one and the same Spirit both to Christ as Head and to one another, and in which each and every member is made alive by the Head and granted His holiness such that the whole body is truly holy and is called the holy church.

5. *The holy angels are not excluded from the body of the church.*
We certainly do not exclude angels from Christ's body, which is the holy church, not only because, when the apostle discusses the church, he clearly also includes the angels in her but also because they are united with us into one body under one and the same Head, Christ, and the apostle plainly called Christ the Head of the angels [Heb. 12:22; Eph. 1:10; cf. 1 Tim. 5:21]. Furthermore, we do not exclude them because they call themselves our fellow servants, and they share with us the same Father and worship the same God, and we will all be together forever in the same heavenly city, Jerusalem. Finally, we do not exclude them because they, too, are holy, and the church is the fellowship of all those who are holy.[2]

6. *Although base hypocrites might be in the church, they are not of the church.*
Thus, we believe and profess with good reason that, while base hypocrites might dwell in the church and go about amongst the saints, they

---

2. Zanchi briefly discusses the inclusion of the angels in the church in *Spiritual Marriage*, 48–49. While this understanding of the relationship between Christ, His church, and the angels may seem idiosyncratic, it has a long history. Something like it was articulated by patristic authors such as Augustine and Chrysostom, and it was relatively common among early modern Reformed theologians such as Calvin, Bucer, Junius, John Davenant, Antonius Walaeus, and others. Zanchi also addresses the topic of Christ's mediatorial relationship to the angels in Girolamo Zanchi, *De operibus Dei intra spacium sex dierum creatis* (Neustadt, 1591), cols. 159–64 (*OOT*, 2/3:159–64; pt. 1, bk. 3, ch. 21). See also Michael Lynch, "Weird Reformation: Christ the Mediator of Angels?," Davenant Institute, May 25, 2018, https://davenantinstitute.org/weird-reformation-christ-mediator-angels/ and Benjamin Morgan Palmer, "The Relation between the Work of Christ and the Condition of the Angelic World," *Southern Presbyterian Review* 1, no. 1 (June 1847): 34–63. I am grateful to Michael J. Lynch and Richard C. Barcellos for shedding light on this issue.

are nevertheless not of the church. Nor are they members of the church, since they are not actually joined to Christ as Head. Nor are they given His Spirit. And, thus, they are not truly holy. Likewise, with regard to certain hypocrites, the apostle John says, *They went out from us*, like feces from the body, *but they were not of us. For if they were of us, they would certainly have remained with us* (1 John 2:19). Therefore, none of those who ultimately turn away from Christ and do maintain ongoing fellowship with Christ and with all the saints are of the church, no matter how great and admirable such men might appear to be for a time in the church, even if they steer the ship of state for a Christian republic or are in charge of the whole church. For whoever does not have the Spirit of *Christ* but of Antichrist is a member of Satan, not of Christ.[3]

7. *There only ever was and is one church of Christ.*
Furthermore, we confess that there only ever was and is one church of Christ, because there only ever was and is one body to which Christ was given by the Father as Head, only one Spirit by whom all the members are linked together with their Head, only one God whom all we who are elected and called ought to worship and glorify eternally, one single faith of all believers and salvation, and finally, one heavenly inheritance of all (Eph. 4:4–6). For this reason, Christ always called His church *one* and *one flock* [John 10:16; 17:21–23]. We do not, therefore, bring another church into existence different from that one that already is, which was from the foundation of the world and before Christ's advent and which will remain until the world's end. Rather, we say that there is one church for all times and all places and for all people who are joined to Christ, and, therefore, we say that there is one fellowship of all the saints. And, convinced by the Holy Scriptures, we hold that those who permanently break from that church have nothing to do with this one body.

8. *There is only one Head of the Christian church, Jesus Christ.*
Hence, we assert in faith that, since there is only Christ's one church, which is His body, there also is and always will be only one Head of her.

---

3. The emphasis on the word "Christ" in this sentence is in the original.

Moreover, by the word *Head* we mean Him whom, already from the foundation of the world, God gave to the church to become the same nature as her in order to redeem her, in order to join Himself to her, in order to make her alive, in order to illuminate her with the brilliance of His wisdom. This He did so that He might set her aflame with the fire of divine love and, having endowed her with every blessing, effectually provoke her unto good works and continuously direct her and protect her. For, in addition to what we experience daily from nature, we say from the Holy Scriptures that this is the usual duty of the head with respect to the whole body.

Moreover, we acknowledge that no one besides Jesus Christ could have or has or does play this role for the church. At the same time, we do not deny that there might actually be one head of all the hypocrites who are in the church and, thus, one head of the hypocritical church itself, since the prophets predicted this for the future, and the apostles confirmed it [e.g., Jer. 23:1–2; Ezek. 34:1–10; Acts 20:29–30]. But with the holy Apostles we believe and confess that there is only one Head of the holy church, Jesus Christ (Eph. 1:22; 4:15; 5:23; Col. 1:18).

9. This church is truly holy.
From this, therefore, it follows as well that this church is truly holy, because her Head is most holy and makes her holy, because He imputes no sins to her, because she draws from Him the Spirit of sanctification, and because every bit of holiness that is in her Head, the whole of it is imputed to each one of His members.

10. This church is also truly catholic.
We also confess that this church is truly catholic (that is, universal), because her Head is indeed catholic and eternal. At all times, already from the establishment of the world until its end, that Head joins to Himself members from every type of men and every nation and every place and directs and preserves them unto eternal blessedness for Himself.

11. This one church is partly in heaven triumphant and partly on earth militant.
We acknowledge, however, that, although this church is one and always

has been, yet she is one in such a way that one part is already in the heavenly places, having been raised with Christ, and is sitting at the right hand of the Father, triumphant. The other part is on earth in a continuing battle with flesh and blood, the world, and the Devil. For this reason, all the pious accept a distinction between the church triumphant and militant.

Chapter Twenty-Four

The Church Militant

Although it would be easy for anyone to imagine what we believe specifically about the church militant on the basis of what we have confessed with regard to the church in general, we nevertheless have resolved to explain our judgment concerning this church separately so that our faith might be more plainly and easily understood. We will do this partly by referring to what has already been said about the whole by brief repetition and partly by adding those things that pertain specifically to the church militant.

1. A description of the church militant.
Accordingly, we believe that the church militant is an assembly of men from every people and nation elected before the creation of the world to eternal life in Christ. In time, these are summoned out of the world unto Christ and out of the kingdom of the Devil unto the kingdom of God by the preaching of the gospel and by the Holy Spirit. They are gathered into one body under one Head, Christ, and so are made truly righteous and holy, wherever they are and however many or few they may be (Eph. 1:4; Matt. 28:19; Mark 16:15; Rom. 10:14; Eph. 1:22).

They sincerely profess faith in the same God and in Christ, they have the same hope of heavenly inheritance solely on account of Christ's merits, and they keep the same commands of Christ (and, thus, maintain brotherly love among themselves and, indeed, charity toward all) with the greatest harmony (Matt. 18:20). They proclaim and hear the word of the gospel; they administer and receive the sacraments according to Christ's instructions; and they give their diligent attention to seeing that everyone lives soberly, righteously, and piously in this age (John 10:27; 13:4 [that is, 13:34][; Titus 2:12]). Meanwhile, while they are in this flesh, they continually fight for Christ's kingdom and struggle—against sin dwelling in the flesh; against the world, which either draws them toward sin or persecutes them on account of Christ; and finally, against the Devil. And they patiently await Christ's coming and eternal happiness (Rom. 7[:23]; Eph. 6:12).

Indeed, many reprobates and wicked hypocrites who profess the same Christ dwell among them even now (Matthew 13), but in no sense are they truly *of the church*, so their wickedness has nothing to do with the church and cannot mar the church's name (1 John 2:19). For we do not deny that the hypocrites in her are, in fact, also included in the word *church*. As the Lord said, the church is like a threshing floor in which are grain and husk, a field in which are wheat and tares, a net in which are good and bad fish, an assembly of ten virgins in which some are wise and others foolish (Matthew 13; 25:1). But those others are not *of the church* [1 John 2:19]. This is what the Lord taught when He said that He was building the sort of church against which the gates of hell would never prevail (Matt. 16:18). And John developed this in his epistle when he said, *They went out from us, but they were not of us* (1 John 2:19). We believe this to be the true definition of the church militant, for it is based on clear evidence from the Holy Scriptures.

2. *The differences between the church triumphant and militant.*
Thus, although the church triumphant and the church militant are one and the same, we can nevertheless easily grasp how great are the differences between the two. For instance, we understand that the militant church is comprised only of mankind, while the triumphant church also has blessed angels joined to it and present with it. Likewise, here below we attend to the preaching of the Word, the administration of the sacraments, the discipline of morals, none of which have a place in heaven. All wicked people and hypocrites are excluded from the triumphant church; in the militant church, however, the evil are always going to be mixed in with the good.

And certainly, those heavenly brethren triumph over their enemies and rejoice—as if they had received an honorable discharge—being present with the Lord, whom they see face-to-face. As for us, however, we must yet strive with flesh and blood, with the world, with sin, and with Satan, the prince of this world. We, being pilgrims to the Lord, see through a darkened mirror [1 Cor. 13:12]. Finally, the church triumphant is always one and the same in such a way that it is neither divided into factions nor subject to any bothersome changes; the same certainly cannot be said of the church militant.

3. *The church militant is one and the same and is also catholic, yet in such a way that she does not always conduct herself identically, and she is divided into many particular churches.*
We therefore acknowledge that this militant church was always and is one church, and a catholic one at that. For, even from the foundation of the world, it has always and everywhere had one and the same Head, Christ, who joins all the elect to Himself in one body out of every nation. Nevertheless, she has not always conducted herself identically—nor does she do so now—and she is distinguished into many particular churches, just as there are many different members depending on differences of times, places, and peoples. For she conducted herself one way in the earthly paradise before sin and differently after sin but before the flood or among the patriarchs. She conducted herself differently under the law than she did under grace and differently at the time of Christ only among the Jews than after Christ's glorification among those gathered by the apostles out of the Jews and the Gentiles. And they were gathered not just in one place but in various places, nor out of just one people but out of many different peoples.

Nor has she always and everywhere held onto the same ceremonies, with respect to which we are accustomed to say that some ceremonies were before and others after Christ, of which the former correspond to the church of the Old Testament and the latter to the church of the New Testament. Likewise, we read that the one was customarily called the old people and the other the new people. Likewise, there was one church that was at Rome and another that was at Corinth and another that was at Ephesus, and so on for the others.

4. The one catholic church is composed of the many particular churches.
On the other hand, while there are and have always been many particular churches—even ones with dissimilarities—on account of the many different considerations already set forth, we nevertheless acknowledge that, as regards substance, all of them together have always composed the one and only church, the catholic, apostolic, and holy one. She is one because she has always been (and is) gathered into one body under one Head, Christ, by one and the same Spirit, and because there is one faith and one confession of faith for all (Eph. 2:15, 18; 4:5). She is catholic because she extends into all times and places and is composed of all types of persons and peoples. She is apostolic because she has been established upon the foundation laid by the apostles, namely Jesus Christ, and because she advances the apostolic teaching, which, of course, is the same as was the teaching of the prophets since the foundation of the world (Eph. 2:20). Finally, she is holy not because she is without sin but because, having been grafted onto Christ and granted continuous repentance and faith, no sins are imputed to her. Instead, she has obtained forgiveness for all of them. Likewise, she is holy because she became a partaker of the Spirit of Christ and of regeneration and, finally, because Christ's righteousness and holiness are imputed to her. For this reason, she is also said to be without any wrinkle, meaning in Christ, her Head and Bridegroom (Eph. 5:27).

5. How it can be known whether particular churches are true churches.
This indeed is why we believe it is possible to discern whether a specific particular church is a true church gathered in the Lord on the basis that the Lord Jesus wanted churches to be founded, namely, the preaching of the gospel, the administration of the sacraments as established by Christ, and the observance of His commands (Matt. 28:19–20). Thus, we acknowledge those churches as true churches of Christ in which, first and foremost, the pure gospel teaching is indeed preached, heard, and received, and where it alone is received such that no place or hearing is given to anything that is opposed to the gospel. For it is characteristic of Christ's flock (or sheep) both to hear its Shepherd's voice and to reject the voice of strangers (John 10:4–5).

Second, the true churches of Christ are those in which the sacraments instituted by Christ are—as much as is possible for them—administered and obtained in a legitimate way, that is, according to Christ's institution (1 Cor. 11:20 and following). Thus, true churches are those in which sacraments contrived by men are rejected.

Finally, true churches of Christ are those in which the discipline of Christ has its place, that is, where care is taken both publicly and privately for love's sake by means of admonitions, corrections, and ultimately, even excommunications when necessary, to see that Christ's commands are kept. And this is thus done so that all may live soberly, righteously and piously unto the glory of God and the edification of their neighbors (Matt. 18:[15–]17; Titus 1:8 [that is, 2:12]). For we believe that, however many good and pious men might be in a place where wickedness and every impurity of life openly prevail and where open scandals are not silenced according to the discipline of Christ, we do not believe that assembly is a pious and Christian one. As the Lord said, *By this shall men know that you are my disciples: if you love your enemies* (John 13:35).[1] But how can there be love where no care is taken to see that sinning brothers are corrected, recovered, gained for the Lord, and saved, according to Christ's teaching?

6. The succession of bishops whereby a specific church can be demonstrated to be apostolic.

Thus, we acknowledge that a specific church can be shown to be properly apostolic by a perpetual succession of bishops, but not just any kind of succession. Rather, proper apostolic succession is the kind that is accompanied by a continuation of apostolic doctrine, as was the case for the Roman Church and her bishops once upon a time.

Even in the days of Irenaeus, Tertullian, Cyprian, and several of their successors, those fathers were accustomed to appeal to Rome and other similar churches to cite the heretics of their age, and for good reason. In fact, with Tertullian and the other fathers, we say that we do (and

---

1. Zanchi conflates John 13:35, which ends with Jesus urging his disciples to "love one another," with Jesus's command to "Love your enemies" (Matt. 5:44; Luke 6:27, 35).

should) acknowledge as apostolic those churches in which apostolic teaching, Christian discipline, and the right administration of the sacraments are kept pure, whether or not they were planted by apostles or lack an unbroken succession of bishops all the way back to the apostolic age [Tertullian, *Prescription against Heretics*, §20].[2] Conversely, however, again with the fathers, we certainly cannot acknowledge as Christian and apostolic those churches that were planted and watered by the apostles if they cannot now show, along with their succession of bishops, a continuation of Christian and apostolic teaching. This is the case even if they can demonstrate the longest continuous and least interrupted succession of pontiffs. We do, however, affirm that they certainly once were Christian and apostolic churches, for as the old saying goes, it's not the habit that makes the monk but piety and holiness of life. So, neither do bishops make a Christian church but rather Christ's teachings and Christian religion.

7. Only by their concord with Christ's teachings can specific churches be shown to be true and Christian.

Thus, we also understand that churches cannot be demonstrated to be true churches of God merely by the presence among them of interecclesial concord, since complete concord also exists among the Jewish synagogues and among the assembly of the Turks, and it formerly existed among the conventicles of the Arians and the Donatists. Rather, we

---

2. [Tertullian, *Prescription against Heretics*, §20]: The apostles "set up churches in every city, from which the other churches afterwards borrowed the transmission of the faith and the seeds of doctrine and continue to borrow them every day, in order to become churches. By this they are themselves reckoned apostolic as being the offspring of apostolic churches. Things of every kind must be classed according to their origin. These churches, then, numerous as they are, are identical with the one primitive apostolic Church from which they all come. All are primitive and all apostolic. Their common unity is proved by fellowship in communion, by the name of brother and the mutual pledge of hospitality—rights which are governed by no other principle than the single tradition of a common creed." S. L. Greenslade, ed., *Early Latin Theology: Selections from Tertullian, Cyprian, Ambrose, and Jerome*, The Library of Christian Classics 5 (Philadelphia: Westminster Press, 1956), 43–44 (*ANF*, 3:252). See *Early Latin Theology*, 52–53 (§32; *ANF*, 3:258), in which Tertullian also emphasizes the significance of apostolic succession.

judge that it can only be demonstrated when there is concord in the pure doctrine of Christ and in true piety. For when the apostle says, *I beseech you, brothers, in the name of our Lord Jesus Christ, that you all speak the same thing and that there not be any schisms among you but that you be joined together in the same mind and judgment*, he means in that Lord Jesus Christ in whose name he was entreating them (1 Cor. 1:10).

8. *Churches are not themselves destroyed merely because some disagreements arise in them.*
At the same time, however, we are not so unfair as to claim that those churches that lack total agreement on every issue are, for that reason, not Christian churches. For just as not every type of agreement establishes churches, so neither are they destroyed by every type of disagreement. Only let the firm foundation be preserved that Christ is true God and true man, the true and perfect Savior, and consequently, let there be agreement in the essence of the apostolic teaching handed down in the Creed.

9. *A confirmation of the previous judgment.*
For, just as the presence of base hypocrites in churches does not prevent them from remaining true churches, so neither can they be snuffed out by the differences stirred up by the wicked, or even those that are begun by and between the saints out of the flesh or out of ignorance. Likewise, when speaking about the ministers of true churches, the apostle teaches that, upon the same foundation, *some build gold, silver, precious stones but others wood, stubble, hay* [1 Cor. 3:12]. And to the Philippians, having explained the essence of Christian doctrine and exhorted all to abide therein whatever else they may do, he subsequently adds, *If in anything you have a different understanding, God will also reveal this to you, nevertheless, let us endure in that to which we have attained* [Phil. 3:15–16].

Otherwise, if differences arise somewhere concerning religion, it must not be denied that true churches are there. For, if this were the case, then Christ's church was not at Corinth in Paul's time, where schisms thrived (with one saying, *I am of Paul*, and another, *I am of Cephas*, and another, *I am of Apollos*) but also where there arose extraordinary controversies about religion. Nor, then, was there a church in Galatia, because in those churches, shortly after having been established in good style by Paul, seducers sprung up, and heresies were stirred up. Nor, finally, could one say that any true church ever existed either in the East or the West. For they were never free of controversies, not only controversies between catholics and heretics (who, for all that, arose out of the catholics) but even controversies stirred up among the pious fathers themselves, as history teaches in spades. To such an extent is this the case that Christians were habitually mocked in theaters by unbelieving Gentiles on account of those quarrels and sects. And the same thing happens even now as we are ridiculed among the Turks and the Jews for the same reason.

But in the ancient church, it did not follow from those quarrels between Christians that they were therefore not the people of God. In the same way, neither can one rightly demonstrate this from our quarrels. Might not one even rather say instead that the opposite can be concluded? For it is characteristic that, in the same field where good wheat (that is, the gospel) is sown whereby the churches are gathered by Christ, the Enemy, Satan, immediately sows tares as well. Certainly, at no time in the history of the church were the Simons, the Menandroses, the Ebionites, the Cerinthuses, the Valentinians, and other such plagues heard from so quickly than immediately after the gospel of Christ was first proclaimed. In fact, however, the church of this present age could not truly be called the church militant unless it has—both at home and abroad—those with whom it ought to be engaged in ongoing conflict.

10. The peace of the churches should not be disturbed, nor should schisms be created on account of every little difference in doctrine or ceremonies.
Thus, we do not approve when someone breaks from his church and disturbs the peace of the churches and violates fraternal love. All the more, we disapprove of one church condemning another on account of every little difference in doctrine or ceremonies while the foundation is yet preserved. In this we are like Irenaeus, Bishop of Lyon, who once rebuked the Roman Bishop Victor, who had excommunicated the churches of Asia because they disagreed with him about certain rites [Eusebius,

Ecclesiastical History, bk. 5].³ For the apostle did not want schisms to be created in the church or for churches to be condemned on account of the stubble or hay built on top of the foundation, since the church is not the one who determines that it is the church or, indeed, that it is holy and Christ's beautiful bride, even though she is dark and wrinkled as well and has any number of moles (Song 1:5; 2:10; Eph. 5:27).

In summary, although errors and defects must never be ignored, nevertheless, we think that peace and fellowship should be cultivated (as with true churches of Christ) among those assemblies—whichever ones they are—where the foundation, the essence of apostolic doctrine, is preserved and in which (as a consequence) no open idolatry is allowed. Such is the value we should place upon the churches' unity.

11. The unity of the catholic church ought to be pursued.
Therefore, since the one whole catholic church consists of many particular churches, like parts of the whole, which as yet struggle on earth, we are not ignorant of, nor do we deny that if union in the Lord should be cultivated with any particular church, then we ought all the more to pursue the unity of the whole catholic church.

12. What we mean by the phrase the unity of the catholic church.
Moreover, by the phrase *the unity of the catholic church* we mean the conjunction into one body accomplished by the Holy Spirit of all the elect and regenerate, wherever they are on earth, with Christ their Head and

---

3. [Eusebius, *Ecclesiastical History*, bk. 5]: In his *Ecclesiastical History*, Eusebius of Caesarea describes the incident referenced here and provides extracts of Irenaeus's (otherwise lost) letter to Victor. Discussing traditional practices surrounding the dating of Easter and the proper number of fast days, Eusebius quotes the following from Irenaeus's rebuke of Victor: "And such a variation on the part of those observing the feast did not originate now in our time, but much earlier in the days of our predecessors, who, as is likely, without maintaining it strictly, established a practice for the future which is simple and permits personal preference, and all these nevertheless lived in peace, and we also lived in peace with one another, and the disagreement respecting the fast confirms our unanimity in the faith." Eusebius, *Ecclesiastical History, Books 1–5*, trans. Roy J. Deferrari, Fathers of the Church 19 (Washington, D.C.: Catholic University of America Press, 1965), 337 (*NPNF*2, 1:243).

among themselves. In the Creed we call this *the communion of the saints*. For when the apostle describes this unity, he also teaches that the church is a body consisting of various members, the Head of which is Christ, who by His Holy Spirit is restoring, vivifying, advancing, and saving all believers into one new man (Eph 1:23; 1 Cor. 12:12; Col. 1:18; Eph. 4:12; 2:15; Rom. 8:11). Therefore, the unity of the church is the unity of the body and of every single member thereof with her Head and with one another, just as Augustine also defined church unity against the Donatists (*On the Unity of the Church*, vol. 7, ch. 2).[4]

13. Generally speaking, the church's unity consists of like faith in Christ and love toward the brethren.

To be sure, God uses both our faith in Christ, which is stirred up in our hearts by means of the word of the gospel and also by the sacraments, as well as our love and its obligations toward our neighbor. (Indeed, to put it even more correctly, these are the true and unmistakable evidences of the communion of the saints and of union with Christ.) For this reason, we confess in short that the unity of the catholic church consists in the unity of faith and in the bond of brotherly love. That is, it consists in us embracing and (briefly put) publicly professing the same doctrine that the prophets and apostles left for us in their writings. It consists in us sincerely holding fast only to those same sacraments that Christ instituted. It consists in us not neglecting the discipline instituted and commanded by Christ wherein brotherly love is put into practice. And finally, it consists in us mutually loving one another and exercising the duties of charity.

---

4. <u>On the Unity of the Church</u>, vol. 7, ch. 2: Augustine writes, "Hence it is clear indeed that anyone who is not among the members of Christ cannot have Christian salvation. But the members of Christ are joined to one another through the charity of unity, and through that same [charity] they cling to its head, which is Christ Jesus. Everything that is proclaimed about Christ, therefore, has to do with the head and the body." The work cited here as *On the Unity of the Church* is *Letter to Catholics on the Sect of the Donatists*, in *The Donatist Controversy*, vol. 1, by Augustine, ed. Boniface Ramsey and David G. Hunter, trans. Maureen Tilley and Boniface Ramsey, The Works of Saint Augustine: A Translation for the 21st Century I/21 (Hyde Park, N.Y.: New City Press, 2019), 607.

14. A confirmation of the previous judgment.

For we believe that whatever unites diverse people into a single body also preserves their unity and joins them together more and more into one body. Thus, since the gathering of the church does not result in and (properly speaking) is not preserved by ceremonies but rather by the Holy Spirit, by the Word, by faith, by charity, and by keeping God's commands, we doubt not but that her unity is upheld and increased by those same things. Hence, when the apostle addresses the unity of the church in the letter to the Ephesians, he teaches that it consists in these very things but makes no mention of any ceremonies (Eph. 4:3[–6]).

15. Although it is not always expedient for there to be unity in ceremonies everywhere, nevertheless, where and when that unity exists, it should not be disturbed.

At the same time, we do not deny that one should also preserve and foster unity in the ceremonies and rites of one's church, if this can be done in accordance with one's conscience. For a church's unity can consist of two categories of things: those that have been given in God's Word and those that are not defined in the Word, which include many of a church's external rites and ceremonies.

In the former category, we believe that unity is everywhere and always necessary. In the latter, however, unity is not necessary per se, and it is useful to have a diversity of rituals on account of the diversity of locations and times. Nevertheless, where some of these reliable rituals have been instituted and established for the church's edification, we think that unity should also be maintained there in such matters and that ecclesiastical settlements should not be disturbed. This accords with the rule established by the apostle: *All things ought to be done in the church orderly, decently, and for the purpose of edification* (1 Cor. 14:40). We also strongly approve and embrace what Augustine writes regarding these matters in his two letters to Januarius [eps. 54 and 55].[5]

---

5. [eps. 54 and 55]: The entirety of Augustine's first letter to Januarius speaks to the distinction confessed here by Zanchi, namely, that licit rites and ceremonies can be divided into those given in Scripture and those that are consequent to a given time and place. Augustine adds to the former category those traditions that "are observed

16. *Conclusion concerning the unity of the church.*
The unity of the church is twofold. The first is essential and, consequently, is always necessary everywhere on its own and, thus, is characteristic of the catholic church. The other kind of unity is accidental and can be altered depending on places and times and, thus, is characteristic of particular churches. Consequently, we therefore believe that no one is ever permitted to withdraw from the first kind of unity for any reason, for this would be nothing less than to desert Christ and God and to renounce the Holy Spirit and to separate oneself from the whole body of Christ. Without doubt this would be genuine and detestable apostasy.[6]

We are, however, persuaded that to desert the latter kind of unity for the sake of returning to and preserving the former kind is not only permissible but even necessary for everyone. And all the more if those rituals and ceremonies whereof unity consisted were also perverted by superstitions. Furthermore, this is particularly the case if the sacraments instituted by Christ have also been corrupted from their ancient state such that you cannot partake of them with a good conscience. Yes, what if the heavenly truth were banished from them too, and in its place the doctrines of demons were preached and defended? What if, indeed, you were not able even to remain silent there, but instead were compelled

---

throughout the whole world…[and that are understood to have been] taught and established by the apostles themselves or by plenary councils, which have authority in the Church most conducive to salvation." Augustine, *Letters*, 1:210 (*NPNF*1 1:300). Compare with *CCR*, 1.12.

Augustine returns to this theme near the end of his second letter to Januarius (§§32–39), where he grounds the celebration of Easter (*Pasch*) and Pentecost "most firmly on the basis of Scripture" but describes "the singing of the Alleluia only during these fifty days" as a regional variation, albeit a legitimate one (§32). Similarly, Augustine points out that, as regards "practices that are different in different places the thing to know is that wherever we see that there are being instituted or know that there have been instituted practices that are not against the faith and not contrary to good morals and have some value for encouraging a better life, we not only do not find fault with them, but we also follow them by praising and imitating them" as long as they do not cause weaker brothers to stumble (§34). For the pertinent sections, see Augustine, *Letters*, 1:210–14 and 233–36 (*NPNF*1, 1:300–3 and 314–16).

6. ἀποστασία.

either to deny the truth of God and subscribe to the Devil's lies or pour out your life and blood?

17. He who flees from the Roman church has not for that reason broken the unity of the church or withdrawn from the body of Christ.
We are accused of apostasy[7] from Christ's catholic and apostolic church and are said to have broken its unity because we refuse any longer to share in wicked superstitions and idolatrous worship with the Roman Church's assemblies but prefer instead to follow the ancient doctrine, worship, and discipline that has been revived by Christ's true servants thanks to God's kindness. To that extent, therefore, we testify before God and His angels and the church to the ends of the earth that a notorious injury is being done not only to us but also to the Holy Spirit and to the whole of the ancient church. For we neither have done nor are doing anything on this score other than what the Holy Spirit commanded us to do, what the fathers taught us to do, and even what the pontiffs themselves advised us to do.

18. A confirmation of the previous judgment.
For the Lord particularly warns us not to have any fellowship with idolaters and obstinate apostates and heretics in their idolatries and heresies [Matt. 18:17; 1 Cor. 5:11; 2 John 10]. The fathers also taught (even as they are summoned as witnesses in Gratian's *Decretum* itself) that if any man, or even any church, rejects the faith, does not hold to the foundation of apostolic preaching, and does not continue in Christ's teachings, then that man or church should be abandoned (1 Cor. 5:11; 2 Cor. 6:14–17; Titus 3:10; Rom. 16:17; Gratian's *Decretum*, causa 24, q. 1, chs. 24 and 26 and q. 3, ch. 9).[8] Nor was there any other reason why the ancient fathers always honored the Roman Church, which was flourishing back

---

7. ἀποστασίας.

8. Gratian's *Decretum*, causa 24, q. 1, chs. 24 and 26: "He who does not have faith in Christ should also be withdrawn from that body" and "Catholics should flee the close fellowship of heretics." Gratian, *Corpus iuris canonici*, 1:975–76.

...and q. 3, ch. 9: "We divide from God those whom we show to be wicked." Gratian, *Corpus iuris canonici*, 1:992.

then, and called her holy and the mother of churches than because she resolutely preserved the doctrine received from the apostles while many others were falling away from it (causa 24, q. 1, ch. 9).[9] Now, however, it is sufficiently well known what her doctrine and worship are and how far she has fallen in many matters from her former ways.

Thus, we bear witness anew that we have not separated from the present Roman Church except as we have been compelled to do so by God's Word and insofar as we were submissive to God who commanded it. And, so, we have judged that, in order for us to continue no longer in apostasy[10] from the catholic and apostolic church but to return to it at length, we must withdraw from the idolatries of this utterly corrupt Roman Church.

19. We did not withdraw from the Roman Church wholesale but in a certain sense.[11]

For we did not withdraw from the Roman Church wholesale and in all things but rather only in those things wherein she falters from the apostolic, ancient, and pure church—indeed, from her true self. Nor have we withdrawn for any other purpose than that we might also go back to her and have fellowship with her in her assemblies again if, having been corrected, she returns to the former beauty of the church. We beg the Lord Jesus with all our soul that this might ultimately happen. For what could any pious person wish for more than to live out our lives to the end in that place where we were also reborn by baptism? But we prefer this only in the Lord.

---

9. causa 24, q. 1, ch. 9: "This is the living tradition of the Apostles; this is the true love that must be proclaimed and must especially be esteemed and nourished and faithfully held by all; this is the holy and apostolic mother of all the churches of Christ, which has been shown, by God's grace, never to have wandered from the path of the apostolic tradition nor has yielded to being corrupted by novel heresies but remains inviolately faithful to the foundations of Christ's apostles as it received the pattern of the Christian faith at the first by their authorities." Gratian, *Corpus iuris canonici*, 1:975–76.

10. ἀποστασία.

11. κατά τὶ.

I, Girolamo Zanchi, along with my entire family, desire to bear witness of this to the whole of Christ's church for all eternity.

20. Certainly, the whole catholic church is not allowed to err, but individual parts of her can err.
Indeed, we believe and acknowledge that the catholic church we described above is ruled by Christ's Spirit in such a way that He never allows the whole of her to err, because He always maintains the light of truth among some of the pious and preserves it by the purity of their ministries to the end of the world and extends it to those who come after. We do not doubt that what Paul said pertains to this: *The church is the pillar and prop of the truth* (1 Tim. 3:15), for outside of the church there is no truth. Inside the church, however, the truth is continually preserved, since some assembly, no matter how great or small it might be, always exists in which the word of truth resounds.

But as for individual churches, in each of which the good always mingles with the bad, we have said that there is an altogether different account. That is to say, first of all, either the pure Word of God is preached in these assemblies or else lies are also taught alongside the truth. For where there is clearly no ministry of the Word, we acknowledge no church there. So, if churches teach false dogma alongside the truth, how should it be said that that assembly cannot err, when it obviously does err? But if the pure Word of God is taught, then reprobate hypocrites (who do not believe and who always are in the majority nearly everywhere) err constantly, since they reject the light of truth and walk in darkness [John 3:19–21; 11:10].

The pious, however, are never allowed to wander from Christ to such an extent that they persevere and perish in their errors. As Christ Himself said, the elect cannot be deceived even by the miracles and wonders of the Antichrist (Matt. 24:24), that is, they cannot ultimately be deceived to their destruction. Nevertheless, sacred and ecclesiastical histories as well as what has happened to pious and holy bishops and their churches in the East and the West have shown us very clearly that they can wander not only in morals but also in the doctrine of faith as individuals on their own and when gathered together as a group (Gal. 2:11–21; 1 Cor. 1:11–13; Gal. 1:6–9).

21. A confirmation of the previous judgment.

Certainly, Peter erred at Antioch [Gal. 2:11–14]. And many erred shamefully in the Corinthian church and even more in the Galatian, having been deceived by the pseudo-apostles, although, not long afterward, they were summoned back from their errors by the apostle. David also teaches that even the very sheep of Christ can wander when he said, *I have gone astray like a sheep that has been lost* (Ps. 119:176).

If, however, the pious are incapable of erring, why do they all need the ministry of the Word in the church? As individuals, pious people in certain true and pure particular churches have also frequently erred and continue to err repeatedly. (But hypocrites never receive true faith whereby they might rightly understand.) Since this is the case, how can it be said of any particular church that it cannot err? And how much less might you be able to affirm this about those churches for which the truth is a stranger and in which actual lies, iniquities, and Cimmerian darkness prevail?[12]

To be sure, if the church is *the pillar and prop of the truth* (1 Tim. 3:15), then Christ's true churches cannot look like that. And thus, we conclude that, insofar as every particular flock and each of its sheep led by the Holy Spirit listen only to the voice of their shepherd Christ, it is not possible for them to wander. But as soon as they stop listening to Him and give ear to the voices of others, immediately they can do nothing but wander (John 10:5, 27). To be sure, even in the greatest scattering of the whole of the church, God preserves for Himself some whom He upholds in the truth and by whose ministries He chooses to propagate the truth anew, to the end of the world. This is why we confess that the whole catholic church is never simultaneously permitted to wander.

22. Outside of the catholic church, there is no salvation.

Hence, we also think and believe that this catholic church alone is holy and preserved in such a way that, outside of her, there is no holiness or salvation. This is the case since the truth (without which none receives

---

12. In book 11 of Homer's *Odyssey*, the Cimmerians lived in a land of mist, cloud, and darkness at the world's edge, near the entrance to Hades.

salvation) shines forth in her alone in such a way that there is no truth outside of her and, indeed, since none but Christ's body can be saved. *For no one has ascended into heaven except He who descended from heaven, the Son of Man who is in heaven* (John 3:13), that is, the whole Son of Man with His whole body, which is the church. Thus, Peter was not wrong to compare the church with Noah's ark, in which alone humankind was saved, and we read that everything found outside of it perished in the flood waters (2 Peter 2:5; Gen. 7:23).

However, what we confess about the whole church with, as it were, the greatest certainty, we cannot grant to each and every particular church. We cannot grant it in such a way as to say, *Only in this* or *that church*—the Roman or Constantinopolitan Church—*does truth and salvation flourish in such a way that, outside of her, there is no salvation, and, so, we cannot withdraw from her without withdrawing from truth, salvation, and Christ.* For any church might become such that, unless you withdraw, you cannot partake of and have fellowship with the catholic church and with her Head.

23. *The catholic church is not bound to specific persons or places.*
We additionally confess that, because this catholic church is catholic, for that reason she is bound to no specific places or persons and nations, as if anyone who wanted to be part of this church had to go either to Rome or Wittenberg or as if catholicity depended on the authority of those churches, pontiffs, and ministers. This is not the case, for Christ is everywhere, and the Word can be heard, the sign of baptism can be sealed, Christ's commands can be kept, and fellowship with all the saints can be had everywhere. Furthermore, wherever these things are, that is where the church is.

This is the reason why the Donatists were appropriately condemned. For they concluded that the church of Christ was only in Africa—and, indeed, not even in all of Africa but apparently only in the part where the Donatists lived. And they taught that it was only there. No less appropriately should they be condemned who do not accept the churches of foreigners as true churches but only those consisting of men of their own nation.

24. *The catholic church is partly visible and partly invisible.*

Finally, we believe that this church is, in fact, partly visible and partly invisible, but in different respects. Indeed, it is *visible* insofar as it consists of men visibly handling and hearing the Word of God, administering and receiving the sacraments, calling upon God not only privately but also publicly, and, finally, performing love's duty toward neighbor and glorifying God with their whole life. None of these can be done without the experience of the senses. And if the church were completely invisible, how could she be distinguished from the synagogues of the wicked?

Conversely, we also say that the church is *invisible*. We say this, first, because she has many hypocrites mingled in, who perform all the same activities as the elect in an external way. And although the church consists only of the elect, we cannot know with certainty exactly who they are; only God can know. This accords with that saying, only *the Lord knows those who are His* (2 Tim. 2:19). The apostle's statement pertains to this as well: *He is not a Jew who is one outwardly but who is one inwardly* (Rom. 2:28–29).

Next, we also say that the church is invisible because of her external appearance, since the church is constantly hard-pressed with troubles in this world. Sometimes the number of those professing the faith of Christ is so diminished and all the Christian churches so reduced in those difficulties that she seems no longer to survive. For public assemblies are no longer found in which God's name is invoked, just as both sacred and church history very clearly and abundantly teach has frequently happened.

Nevertheless, it is certain that God always preserves for Himself some church on earth. As the Lord said, *And the gates of hell will not prevail against her* (Matt. 16:18). And again, *Behold, I am with you, even to the end of the age* (Matt. 28:20). This is also what we confess with the whole church in the Creed when we say, *I believe...the holy catholic church*, namely, that she was from the beginning, is now, and will continue to exist upon the earth itself until the end of the world. For, properly speaking, what we believe is always something that we do not always see (Heb. 11:1).

This is our confession concerning the church militant—what it is; how it differs from the church triumphant; how it often differs within itself; how the one catholic church consists of many particular churches; by which marks a true church can be distinguished from a false one; what succession of bishops and what kind of consensus indicates a true church; that the church's unity should not be torn asunder on account of every little difference, even differences in doctrine; what should be understood by the phrase *ecclesiastical unity*, wherein that unity consists, and also how much should be done to maintain it; also, to what extent is it possible for the church to wander and to what extent is it not possible; that outside of the church there is no salvation; and, finally, to what extent is the church visible and to what extent invisible.

Now, it remains for us to discuss the governance of the church.

Chapter Twenty-Five

The Governance of the Church Militant and Ecclesiastical Ministry

1. *The church is governed by Christ.*

We believe that, just as all things were made, are held together, and are ruled by Christ,[1] just so the church, which is His kingdom and body, is governed by Him as the Founder, King, and Head of the church in a way that is distinct from everything else. As the angel said concerning Christ, *And He will reign over the house of Jacob forever* (Luke 1:33; Col. 1:17; Eph. 1:13 [that is, v. 23]). And, as the apostle said, *He, as Son, has pre-eminence in His house,* and we (that is, the church) are that house (Heb. 3:6). And elsewhere, *He is the Head of the church, and He gave salvation to the body* (Eph. 5:13 [that is, v. 23]).

2. *Christ guides the church partly on His own and partly by those chosen to work together with Him.*

Moreover, we recognize Christ's rule over His church to be a twofold governance. The first is that whereby He on His own and by His Spirit, without the service of any men, rules and works inwardly in the souls of believers, even to the point of willing and accomplishing everything in everyone and moving us toward the good and protecting us from evil in opposition to Satan, the world, and all enemies (Phil. 2:13; Eph. 1:23).

---

1. *Per Christum.* That is, Christ does not simply do these things, full stop, but all things were made through or by means of Christ, just as they are held together and ruled over by Him. He was the agent of the Father's creative work. As the gospel of John puts it, "All things were made through Him [God's Word], and without Him nothing was made that was made" (John 1:3).

The second is that whereby He also guides the church in such a way that He does not spurn to use the works and service of angels or especially of men for the church's salvation. As the apostle says concerning angels, *They are ministering spirits, sent to minister for those who will inherit salvation* (Heb. 1:14). But with regard to men, he says, *We are God's ministers through whom you have believed* (1 Cor. 3:5, 9). For, in a man, the head rules over the whole body on its own by the mental powers that are especially active and at work in him in such a way that the works of each and every one of its members nevertheless contribute to the health of the whole body. When Christ, as the church's Head, governs the church, this is how He conducts Himself, not for His own sake or because He has need of our service but rather on account of our need and for our manifold benefit, even our honor.

3. *The difference between the ministry of angels and of men.*
We nevertheless acknowledge that there is a difference between the ministry of angels and of men. Angels are not sent to teach in the church nor to administer sacraments; instead, they carry out other services. Typically, these are not visible, and they do not happen all the time or even ordinarily, nor are these services for everyone. Rather, they happen when it has seemed good and unto those for whom it has seemed good to the Lord. The ministry of men, however, is visible and continuous and concerns all people.

4. *It is very intentional that men rather than angels teach in the church.*
Furthermore, we understand that God very intentionally and wisely established that Christ does not teach in the church through angels but rather men. He did this, first, because we are more amenable to being instructed by those who are familiar to and like us than we are to being taught by spirits of a very different nature with an unaccustomed majesty. Second, because it would then be easier for Satan to deceive us, telling us falsely that he had been sent from God, transforming himself into an angel of light. These are two of the reasons—and, in our judgment, they are hardly the least significant ones—why the Son of God, when He was appointed to the office of Teacher in the church, was

willing to become man and our brother and intimate friend, and like us in every way with the exception of sin (Heb. 4:15). Hereto pertains that verse: *I will declare Your name to My brothers; in the midst of the church, I will praise You* (Heb. 2:22 [that is, v. 12]). And this one: *In these days He has spoken to us in the Son*, that is, the Son who was made man and who labors intimately in the church (Heb. 1:2).

5. *Principally, there are two types of men whose ministry Christ uses to govern and defend the church.*
As Paul teaches, there is no member in the whole great body of the church that Christ does not use for the benefit of the other members and, thus, of the entire body. Nevertheless, we bear witness that He usually uses the labor and service of two particular types of men for the governance and preservation of the church. These are, first, teachers and other ministers of the Word and sacraments as well as of other ecclesiastical matters; and second, pious princes and magistrates. Nevertheless, we do not confuse the ministry of these two kinds of men; rather, we acknowledge that they are not only distinct but also very different. Indeed, not the least among the differences is that the church has a continual need of the ministry of teachers. The ministry of political magistrates, however, is not so necessary, since the church could never exist without the former but has often existed and can exist without the latter.

6. *The business wherein church ministry is principally involved.*
However, just as the substance of Christian piety consists in three things—faith in Christ; continual repentance, that is, putting to death our flesh and our sins, and living unto the Spirit; and, finally, in love toward our neighbor—accordingly we recognize that there are three specific elements of ecclesiastical ministry.[2] These are, first, teaching and preaching the word of the gospel together with the administration of the sacraments and offering a public sacrifice of praise to God through Jesus

---

2. Zanchi discusses the ministers of the church at length in various writings. See, for example, *De primi hominis lapsu*, in *OOT*, 2/4:716–87 (tome 4, bk. 1, ch. 19, locus 4) and *In d. Pauli Apostoli epistolas ad Philippenses*, 21–22 (*OOT*, 2/6:22–23).

Christ. The second is: the minister watching over the flock diligently, observing their habits, pressing them to reform their vices, and (like a true priest) taking care to *offer himself to God as a living sacrifice, holy and pleasing to God* (Rom. 12:1). Finally, the third element is: undertaking the care of the poor and diligently seeing to it that no one lacks anything.

7. *Three ranks[3] of ecclesiastical ministers are established corresponding to the three parts of ecclesiastical ministry.*

Thus, in accordance with the three parts of ecclesiastical ministries that we have just mentioned, we also observe in the Holy Scriptures that the Lord particularly established three ranks of ecclesiastical ministers. The first of these is engaged chiefly with those things that pertain to stirring up and nourishing faith in Christ. These are the teachers and shepherds who administer the Word and the sacraments in the assembly of the faithful.

The second rank engages in those things established specifically for stirring up repentance among the brothers. These are the elders, the censors of morals who undertake the responsibility of discipline and who see to it that everyone lives as diligently as possible in a Christian and holy manner to God's glory and the edification of the church. Concerning these, the apostle wrote especially in the letter to Timothy but elsewhere as well (1 Tim. 5:17–19). This is how Ambrose [that is, Ambrosiaster] and others of the best interpreters have explained this passage.[4]

The third sort handles those things that seem particularly characteristic of love, such as undertaking the care of the poor and the ill.[5] These

---

3. *Ordines*, a word sometimes used to distinguish between different sorts of elders/overseers and sometimes between elders/overseers and deacons—albeit Zanchi recognizes a sharper distinction between the latter than the former.

4. "Old age is honored in every society, which is why the synagogue, and later on the church, had elders, without whose advice nothing was done in the church. I do not know why the custom has faded out. Perhaps it is because of the laziness of the teachers, or more likely because of their pride, since they want to be seen as the only ones who do anything." Ambrosiaster, *Commentaries on Galatians–Philemon*, 133. See also, Calvin, *Institutes*, 4.11.6.

5. Elsewhere, Zanchi elaborates upon this distinction within the diaconate between those focused on serving the poor and those focused on caring for the ill. See *De primi*

are the deacons who are discussed in Acts 6:3 and elsewhere, especially in Paul's writings (Rom. 16:1[6]; 1 Tim. 3:8–12; Phil. 1:1).

8. Some ministers are called to be ordinary and perpetual; other are called to be extraordinary and temporary.
Furthermore, we recognize two particular kinds of ecclesiastical ministers, especially of those who are to preach the Word and undertake the care of the whole church. The first are those whom the Lord Jesus ordinarily claims for Himself as co-laborers to gather, teach, and rule His church. These, then, are the ministers whom He also wills to be perpetual, and they are typically called ordinary ministers. In the church of the Old Testament, they were priests and Levites, and in the New Testament, they are teachers and shepherds.

The second kind of ministers are those whom the same Lord raises up, calls to, and sends out for extraordinary ministry in the church so as to restore ordinary ministers who have neglected their responsibilities to their proper order and to call the church that they have ruined back to its former condition and preserve her. In the Old Testament, these were the prophets, who were raised up even from non-Levitical tribes. In the New Testament, these were the apostles, prophets, and evangelists whom the Lord specifically chose for Himself, so that, everything having already been lost in a whole region—whether among the Israelites or among the Gentiles—He might gather, establish, and preserve churches for Himself by means of these ministers.

We doubt not that, in our own age, He has assembled many heroic and brave men among the number of those called to extraordinary ministry, true servants of God. They were stirred up by Christ's Spirit over the then-desperate state of affairs in order to set themselves against

---

hominis lapsu, in *OOT*, 2/4:765–68 (bk. 1, ch. 19, locus 4). See also Calvin, *Institutes*, 4.3.9.

    6. As implied in his use of the reference to Phoebe, Zanchi holds that the diaconate, in at least some of its functions, was open to women. In the apostolic church, he contends, "this office [that is, caring for refugees, the poor, and the afflicted] was entrusted to the elderly, both men and women." *De primi hominis lapsu*, in *OOT*, 2/4:767 (bk. 1, ch. 19, locus 4).

the catholic apostasy and revive the church's original teaching, worship, and discipline, as if returning her to her home. And this they did despite the reluctance, teeth-gnashing, and striving—all in vain—of the ordinary bishops, kings, and most powerful princes, not to mention the whole world.

9. Christ established only five ranks of ministers of the Word.
Moreover, we only acknowledge the ranks of the ministers of the Word that the apostle described in the letter to the Ephesians as having been established in the church by Christ: *apostles, prophets, evangelists, shepherds, teachers* (Eph. 4:11). Of these, Christ willed the first three to be bound to no specific place but rather to be sometimes here and sometimes there, either to gather to Himself and establish churches, like the apostles, or to water, foster, and build up those churches established by apostles, as did the prophets and evangelists. For this reason, it was not proper for them also to be perpetual.

However, He wanted the latter two ranks—shepherds and teachers—to be devoted to the ruling and preserving of particular churches until the world's end, for which reason we also usually call them ordinary and perpetual ministers. For, insofar as the apostles often refer to bishops, elders, and catechists, that does not constitute them as additional ranks of ministers of the Word, since those who are pastors are invariably called bishops as well and, in fact, are often called elders. Indeed, even the apostle Peter calls himself an elder (1 Peter 5:1). Moreover, not only did shepherds and teachers often fulfill the duty of catechists but so too did the apostles themselves and the evangelists (Acts 20:28; Phil. 1:1; 1 Tim. 3:2; Titus 1:7; 1 Peter 2:25; 5:1; Acts 14:23 [that is, v. 22]; Titus 2:15; James 5:14; Heb. 6:1[?]).

10. We do not condemn the fathers who have added additional ranks of ministers.
But setting aside those whom He has obliged to be part of temporary ministries and whom we have said are sometimes called extraordinary, let us discuss those who are responsible only for the ordinary and perpetual ministry of the Word. As we said already, and as we read in the

apostle's writings, Christ gave the church only two ranks of these type of ministers, namely, shepherds and teachers. Of these the latter only taught, while the former also administered the sacraments, took the lead in discipline, and ruled over the church (Eph. 4:11). At the same time, however, we do not condemn the fathers for having increased the various ranks of ministers in order to distribute the Word and rule the church in accordance with each situation. For they were free to do so, just as we also are, and since everyone agrees that they did so at the time for credible reasons related to ordering the church rightly, to her dignity, and to her edification.

11. A confirmation of that same judgment, along with an explanation of some of the ecclesiastical ranks in the early church.
For we know that our God is a God of order and not of confusion and that the church is preserved by order but is lost by a lack of discipline[7] (1 Cor. 14:33). This is why He established multiple and, indeed, distinct ranks of ministers—not only formerly in Israel but also later in the church, gathered from both the Jews and the Gentiles. And for the same reason He also gave freedom to the churches to add more ranks (or not), so long as it is done for the sake of edification.

Therefore, although all the ministers of the Word were at first equally called shepherds, bishops, and elders since they were also of equal authority, later, one began to be placed in authority over all his companions. He was not, however, placed over them as lord but more like a rector in an academy is over the rest of the faculty. And the care of the whole church was given over to him, and, thus, by way of a certain preeminence,[8] it became customary for him alone to be called overseer and shepherd, while the rest of his colleagues in ministry were content with the title of elder. As a result, in each and every city, only one minister came to be the overseer, while the many were the elders.

Our judgment is that we cannot disapprove of this. On this matter, we approve of Jerome's (and others') account and opinion, both in his

---

7. ἀταξία.
8. κατ' ἐξοχήν.

letter to Evagrius[9] and in the tenth chapter of his commentary on the epistle to Titus. There he says that all this happened *more on the basis of custom than on the basis of the truth of an arrangement by the Lord*, in order to uproot schismatic and quarrelsome seedlings ([Gratian's *Decretum*,] dist. 93, ch. 23 [that is, ch. 24]).[10] For this reason we judge that what was set up with regard to archbishops (and, indeed, with regard to the four patriarchs instituted even before the Nicene Council itself) can be reasonably excused and defended.[11] Although later, over the course of time, it led to the highest tyranny and ambition. This is the reason why

---

9. Jerome's letter to Evangelus, or Evagrius (as Luther and Erasmus called him), became an important touchstone during the Reformation because it was the first patristic source cited by Luther to support the repudiation of papal supremacy in his *Resolutio Luthernana super propositione sua decima tertia de potestate papae* (1519). The letter also showed Jerome's reluctance to divide the office of presbyter from that of bishop. Less heavy-handedly, it also emphasized the role of custom in relations between overseers, elders, and deacons by noting, for example, that an elder (or "presbyter") was ordained in Rome only on the recommendation of a deacon but that this was not the case elsewhere. NPNF2, 6:288–89 (ep. 146.2).

Luther subsequently published this letter (with annotations and a preface) as *Epistola Sancti Hieronymi ad Evagrium de potestate papae* (1538). See Hilmar Pabel, *Herculean Labours: Erasmus and the Editing of St. Jerome's Letters in the Renaissance*, Library of the Written Word - The Handpress World 5 (Leiden: Brill, 2008), 91.

10. [Gratian's *Decretum*,] dist. 93, ch. 23 [that is, ch. 24]: Gratian, *Corpus iuris canonici*, 2:327–39, which quotes large sections of Jerome's letter to Evagrius to argue that deacons are subordinate to elders. It was by way of this quotation in Gratian that Luther first accessed Jerome's letter. Pabel, *Herculean Labours*, 91.

A longer quotation of Jerome's comments sheds light on Zanchi's use of this source. "These things [have been said] in order to show that to the men of old the same men who were the priests were also the bishops; but gradually, as the seed beds of dissensions were eradicated, all solicitude was conferred on one man. Therefore, just as the priests know that by the custom of the church they are subject to the one who was previously appointed over them, so the bishops know that they, more by custom than by the truth of the Lord's arrangement, are greater than the priests. And they ought to rule the Church commonly, in imitation of Moses who, when he had under his authority to preside alone over the people of Israel, he chose the seventy by whom he could judge the people." Jerome, *St. Jerome's Commentaries on Galatians, Titus, and Philemon*, trans. Thomas P. Scheck (Notre Dame, Ind.: University of Notre Dame Press, 2010), 290 (*PL*, 26:563C).

11. Zanchi elaborates upon the patriarchs in *CCR*, obs. 25.10–11. Briefly, according to Bucer, whom Zanchi quotes, the "four patriarchs" were the ancient overseers (or "bishops") of Rome, Constantinople, Antioch, and Alexandria (to which were later added the bishops of Caesarea, Cappadocia, and others) into whose care entire provinces

the closer we move toward apostolic simplicity, even in the ordering of ministers, the more we approve of it. And we conclude that we should take care in every place to move toward apostolic simplicity.[*][12]

[* Observation 25.10–11]

12. *In no way can anyone be put in charge as head of the whole church.*
Moreover, not only must we ultimately disapprove of the notion that one man ought to be put in charge as head over all the churches throughout the whole earth and have authority and fullness of power, as they say, but on the contrary, we cannot help but curse it—and all the more if one argues that he is owed it according to divine law.

And let us embrace Gregory I's remark to Emperor Maurice, *He who calls himself or desires to be called universal priest usurps for himself the name of and anticipates Antichrist,* in opposition to the evangelical statutes and against the decrees of the canons (*Letters*, bk. 4, ep. 21 and bk. 6, ep. 30 [that is, bk. 5, ep. 37 and bk. 7, ep. 30]).*[13]

[* Observation 25.12]

13. *Not just anyone should be admitted to ministry but only he whom Christ sends.*
We also believe that it pertains to the true and healthy governance of the church that no one—whether he puts himself forward or is sent by others—should be admitted to ministry unless it is first known whether

---

of churches were entrusted. Although Bucer recognizes that Constantinople was also a later addition, Jerusalem is curiously omitted altogether.

12. No asterisk is inserted in the tenth or eleventh aphorisms; however, there is a corresponding combined observation.

13. *Letters*, bk. 4, ep. 21 and bk. 6, ep. 30 [that is, bk. 5, ep. 37 and bk. 7, ep. 30]: Zanchi quotes from Gregory's letter to Emperor Maurice (bk. 7, ep. 30). The modern translation renders it as follows: "But I say confidently that, whoever calls himself a 'universal' priest, and desires to be called so, anticipates Antichrist in his pride. For he puts himself above all others by being arrogant, and he is not being led into error by a different sort of pride." Gregory the Great, *The Letters of Gregory the Great*, trans. John R. C. Martyn, Mediaeval Sources in Translation 40 (Toronto: Pontifical Institute of Mediaeval Studies, 2004), 2:487 (*NPNF*2, 12:226b, where it is numbered bk. 7, ep. 33).

See Gregory the Great, 2:348–51 (bk. 5, ep. 37) for the other letter that Zanchi cites.

he who is to be engaged in ministry is called to ecclesiastical service by God (or by Christ, the church's Head). So, let him be chosen and ordained by the church herself in a legitimate manner; as the apostle says, *No one takes to himself this honor but only he who is called by God, as Aaron was* (Heb. 5:4[–5]).

14. Who is called by Christ to ministry.

Furthermore, we believe that those whom Christ calls to ministry, He makes suitable for attending to it. And those are made suitable for it to whom, alongside a desire to promote God's kingdom and glorify Him with a holy life, He has also given knowledge of sound doctrine along with the ability to display it before the people for their salvation, just as the apostle taught not only in his letters to Timothy and Titus but elsewhere as well (1 Tim. 3:2[–7]; Titus 1:6[–9]). For those whom God chooses and calls to carry out a particular task, He also equips with the gifts necessary to accomplish it, since He calls us to the thing itself rather than merely to words.

Thus, we deny that they are ministers who do not hold to the sound teaching of the gospel and do not teach it to the people but instead teach what is opposed to it, regardless of whether they come of their own volition or have been sent by men (even if sent by one who has authority to do so). And consequently, we do not think we should even listen to such men. As John says, *If someone comes to you*, whether he does so of his own volition or having been sent by some men, *but does not bear this doctrine, then do not receive him or say to him, "Be well"* (2 John 10). In Jeremiah also, God describes the prophets who are and are not sent by Him with these words: *They ran, and I did not send them; they prophesied, and I did not speak to them* (Jer. 23:21). For, explaining the earlier words by way of the later, Jeremiah teaches that they are not sent by God who do not speak from God's mouth and, conversely, that they who bear God's Word are sent by Him. Nor are we ignorant of the reason why this is the case. For, since ministers are sent by God for the building up of the church, but human doctrines tear the church down instead, and only God's Word builds her up, therefore God does not send those who do not bear His Word (Eph. 4:12).

15. Christ calls men to ministry in two ways.
Certainly, we believe that, while all ministers are truly called by Christ, He calls men to ministry in a twofold manner: either He calls them directly on His own or He calls them indirectly through men, that is, through the church. Thus, we should listen to the one no less than the other and consider both to be true ministers of God (Gal. 1:1).

16. How Christ reveals to the church those whom He sends on His own.
In fact, Christ reveals that He sent those whom He calls by making them suitable. Thus, He especially supplies this in those whom He directly calls and sends by His Spirit and apart from the normal process.[14] For He usually gives them specific and distinguishing gifts in a liberal way—chiefly the gift of the Holy Spirit in great abundance, a burning zeal for God's glory, a remarkable knowledge of the Word of God that they announce, a useful and clear teaching style, and even a happy success in their labors. With these gifts they may more quickly and effectively call churches back to their former (that is, their apostolic) beauty, and Christ also uses them to make known these ministers' legitimate and divine call to the churches more readily and definitively. For all those whom Christ gives as ministers to the churches, He gives for their edification. Thus, one may easily conclude from this that the works of those whom we see building up the churches are the works of those who have been called by Christ and that their ministries are divine and legitimate (Eph. 4:12).

17. The calling of those ministers whom Christ sends outside of the normal process and on His own is not always confirmed by miracles, nor are miracles necessary to confirm a calling.
For we do not confess that miracles are always necessary for confirming the call and ministry of this kind of minister, since we do not read of all the prophets who were sent having been confirmed by miracles. Instead, true prophets were confirmed by God's Spirit, by the zeal for His glory

---

14. Here and in the following two sections (*CCR*, 25.17–18), Zanchi has in view those ministers whom he previously identified as "extraordinary and temporary" (*CCR*, 25.8).

that enflamed them, and, above all, by the truth of the divine Word, which, when they preached it, was always accompanied by the renewal of the saints, that is, of the elect in the church. Conversely, many false prophets displayed signs and portents. The apostle, and Christ before him, predicted that the same would also be true of Antichrist (2 Thess. 2:9; Matt. 24:24). Yet the Lord did not (and does not) want His people to listen to false prophets, because they bore lies rather than God's Word and exhorted the people to go after foreign gods. No indeed, the Lord even commanded that they should be stoned (Deut. 3:2–10 [that is, 13:1–10]).

18. Those churches which Christ establishes through ministers called in an extraordinary way are true churches, and thus, a legitimate ministry and authority exists in those churches to call and ordain ministers.
In fact, in light of what has been said above concerning those ministers called by Christ in an extraordinary way, we also believe that the churches established and successfully reformed by the labor and ministry of these men are true churches of Christ. That is, they are a true church of Christ having been restored to the preaching of true doctrine and the legitimate administration of the sacraments, having their worship purified of idolatries and superstitions, and having also been called back as much as possible to the true method of discipline and, thus, to fellowship with the apostles. Hence, we also believe that they, in turn, have legitimate authority to call and ordain ministers and, so, to continue in them the succession of ministers. Consequently, no one can doubt but that those ministers legitimately succeed to the position of minister in those churches and are the church's true and ordinary ministers as long as they also follow and abide in the preaching of sound doctrine along with what they call personal succession.

19. Just as a true church exists where there is true doctrine, so also, where true doctrine is absent, neither a true church nor legitimate ministry exists.
We know that, even without an unbroken succession of bishops going back to the beginning, we can identify a true church wherever we find nothing but [apostolic] doctrine. We can identify a church that also has a

true and legitimate ministry in the same way. Thus, conversely, there is no legitimate ministry anywhere that lacks the purity of Christian doctrine but boasts merely personal succession. For, as is the case with the church, ecclesiastical ministry has been bound to God's Word and not to persons.

20. *The authority of ministers should extend only to those things unto which Christ also called them.*
We also believe that Christ gives great authority to legitimate ministers. Namely, they have authority to carry out that which they have also been called to do: preach the gospel, interpret the Holy Scriptures according to the analogy of faith, catechize, teach the people what is God's will, accuse and rebuke both the great and the small, remit and retain sins (ministerially), bind (the impenitent) and loose (the repentant), administer the sacraments that Christ established and in the way that He gave, exercise discipline on the basis of Christ's rule as it was also explained by the apostle, and, finally, do everything else that concerns order and dignity and that builds up rather than tears down, even if it is not expressly stated in the Holy Scriptures (Matt. 28:19; 1 Cor. 12:10; Heb. 6:1; Gal. 6:6; 1 Tim. 5:20; 2 Tim. 4:2; John 20:23; Matt. 18:18; Matt. 28:19 [sic]; 1 Cor. 11:23[–29]; Matt. 18:15; 1 Cor. 5:4[–5]). This accords with the general rule given by the apostle: *Everything in the church should be done orderly, decently, and for building up* (1 Cor. 14:40[, 26]).

Indeed, we do not believe that any authority is given to ministers to go beyond the limits of God's Word or to pursue any end other than the building up of the church. Hence, we categorically deny that any of the overseers (or even all of them together) has authority to establish anything contrary to the Scriptures, to add anything to or take anything away from them, or to change anything in them, to dispense with God's commands, to compose new articles of the faith, to establish new sacraments, to introduce new forms of worship to the church, to propose laws that bind consciences or that are regarded as equal to divine laws, to domineer in the church and in the consciences of the faithful, to prohibit that which God permitted and wished to be free, or, finally, to command anything as necessary to salvation apart from God's Word. For not even the entire church can be truly said to have this authority.

21. The political authority of overseers who are also princes is not denied.
* At the same time, we do not deny that overseers who are simultaneously princes also have their political rights and secular powers besides ecclesiastical authority. Nor do we deny that, like other princes, they have the right of secular rule and the right of the sword. Some have the right of electing and confirming kings and emperors and of establishing and administering other political matters and of compelling their subjects to fulfill their obedience to them. Hence, we acknowledge that their subjects should comply with any of their political commands that can be kept without transgressing divine law. They should do this not only out of fear but also for conscience's sake (Rom. 13:5). For we know that all power is from God and that whoever withstands those in power stands against God's decree (Rom. 13:1–2). Likewise, kings should be honored, and we should submit ourselves to princes and lords in all fear, not only when they are kind and gentle but even when they are perverse and cruel (1 Peter 3:17).

[* Observation 25.21]

Marriage

22. Marriage ought to be free, both for the church's ministers and for others.
We truly believe that, for the respectability and welfare of ministers, for the honor of the ministry itself, and for the proper governance of the church, it is absolutely necessary that marriage be permitted to all ministers. It should be as unrestricted for them as it is for the laity (as they are called), since Christ did not prohibit marriage to any types of men. No indeed, with regard to celibacy, He said, *Not everyone receives this*, namely, entry into the celibate life (Matt. 19:11). By this He meant what the apostle later explained with more polished words: *he who cannot contain himself ought to marry a woman* (1 Cor. 7:9). For we confess with the apostle that marriage is honorable among all and that the bed is pure (Heb. 13:4).

23. It is good and laudable if someone who has been given the gift of continence abstains from marriage.
We do not, however, deny that there are those to whom God has given the gift of a pure life of singleness. They are more conveniently available

for divine matters and can serve the church more easily than those who are joined in matrimony, because of the many heavy cares and distractions that accompany marriage and that often pull us away to domestic matters, even against our will, from the pursuit of divine matters and by which we are distracted by the business of this life. This also accords with the apostle's saying: *He who is single cares for the things of the Lord, how he might please the Lord, and he who has a wife cares for the things of the world, how he might please his wife, and he is divided* (1 Cor. 7:32[–33]).

Hence, just as they who marry a wife are not, for that reason, to be stripped of their esteem in order to be able to live with clean and pure consciences to God, so it seems to us that they should altogether be praised who delight themselves in a chaste single life (with which they are able to serve the church zealously with fewer encumbrances) and live in it for as long as they can.

24. Marriages should be contracted in the Lord and cultivated in a holy manner.

Furthermore, we know and confess on the basis of natural law and divine precept that all matrimony should be contracted in the Lord and should be cultivated according to honorable customs in a holy way. Likewise, no one may divorce a legitimate wife except on account of fornication (1 Cor. 7:39; Matt. 19:9). If, however, an unbelieving wife refuses to dwell with a believing husband because of hatred for his religion, she should not be forcibly compelled to stay. In such matters, the believer is not subject to servitude, but the Lord has called him to peace (1 Cor. 7:15).

25. And he who has put away an adulteress and who has been forsaken by an unbelieving spouse is permitted to contract a new marriage no less than he whose wife has died.

In addition, we believe that he who has in a legitimate manner put away an adulteress or has been forsaken by an unbelieving spouse is permitted to remarry no less than he whose previous wife has died. For such is the true and wholesome word of the apostle concerning the unmarried and perpetual widows: *Good for them if they remain as I am, albeit if they are not content, let them marry. For it is better to marry than to burn* (1 Cor. 7:8[–9]).

26. *Judges of matrimonial disputes should be appointed in the church.*
On the other hand, however, we do not approve of anyone in the church doing any of these things without a proper inquiry, judgment, and pronouncement by the church and the Christian magistrate (if there is one). Hence, we think that pious, experienced, and prudent men who understand cases pertaining to marriage should by all means be appointed in the church to offer judgment on such matters. This should be done lest anything happen in a thoughtless or imprudent manner and so that no one is permitted to do whatever he wants. Rather, it should be done so that everything happens properly, for edification, and without injury to anyone, lest God's name be blasphemed among unbelievers on our account (1 Cor. 14:26; Rom. 2:24).

27. *Those who lead churches should see to it that the children of the faithful are trained up and either given a formal education or taught an honorable trade.*
The care of children is tied to these matters. Therefore, we believe it is necessary for the ongoing preservation of the church that an individual provide for the training up of each of his children in true piety, Christian morals, and either a formal education or an honorable trade. However, we also believe that the church herself must assume oversight of this matter, in order that each child might eventually render himself useful both to the church and to the republic. Public grammar schools and training in honorable professions as well as catechizing in the churches are suitable to this purpose.

Incomes and Goods Belonging to the Church

28. *Ministers and their families should be supported by honorable and generous incomes.*
We likewise believe that the church cannot be rightly governed unless ministers are generously supplied with whatever they and their families need to lead an honorable life. For no one can do his duty unless he has what he needs to live. And Christ says, *The laborer deserves his wages* [Luke 10:7], and in several places the apostle writes about this matter at length. He frequently explains that whatever ministers who serve the church need in this present life is owed to them by that same church,

and they have the right to request it (1 Cor. 9:7[–10]; 1 Tim. 1:17 [that is, 5:17–18]). It is hardly the case that they sin if they receive, as some falsely claim. Yet, with the apostle, we utterly condemn greed in all people, especially ministers, just as we disapprove of extravagance and teach that neither of these vices should be fostered or tolerated (1 Tim. 3:3–8).

29. *The goods of the churches should not be squandered but rather distributed in support of ministers and for other pious uses.*
Out of the generosity of princes and other pious people, many gifts have previously been made and even now are sometimes still made to the churches. We judge that, if churches have goods of that sort, they should be carefully stewarded and neither squandered nor given over to worldly uses, much less to sacrilegious ones. Nor, having been converted to coin, should the proceeds be kept secret but rather apportioned unto those things for which they were given in the first place, namely, for pious uses.

Moreover, we approve of the ancient division of church goods, namely that one part should go to pious overseers (that is, to the teachers and ministers of the Word and their families); a second part to other clergy (that is, students, those assigned to the church's ministry, and all those who take care of the church); a third part to the poor and to pilgrims; a fourth part to the repair of churches and schools, to which part pertains not only the dwellings of ministers, teachers, and students, the library and its books, and all the instruments and other things necessary for church buildings and schools, but also hospitals and guest houses and other similar places (where they exist) in which the churches ought to take a special interest (Deut. 14[:22–29]).

Church Buildings and Ceremonies
30. *What kind of church building ought Christians to use; what languages should be employed in them; with what ornaments and coverings; what holy days should be kept; to whom prayers should be offered; and, finally, what ceremonies (not having been appointed by Christ or His apostles) should be permitted.*
To be sure, among the reasons why the faithful usually dwell together in the same cities, towns, and districts whenever they can—as they

should—are the following: not only for the fostering of a common faith among themselves on a daily basis through godly conversations and cultivation of mutual love for one another with Christian kindnesses but also so that all may assemble as one in designated places at specific times for public worship and call upon God, hear His Word, receive the sacraments, and perform public works of charity for the poor. Indeed, none of these things can be done without language or apart from rituals and ceremonies. Seeing that these are not insignificant matters, we shall briefly explain our judgments about them as follows.

1. Church Buildings
It is beyond dispute that everything should be done for the sake of edification in the church, having eliminated every kind of superstition. Therefore, we conclude in the first place that true piety and the edification of churches certainly requires that, if one assents to the use of ancient church buildings that have been desecrated, then they should be purged of every idol and all superstitious relics and monuments of idolatry. *For what complicity does God's temple have with images* (2 Cor. 6:16)?

2. Language
Second, a language should be used only if the whole church is familiar with it. For what does an unknown language contribute to the edification of the church? At any rate, the apostle commands those who speak an unknown language to be silent in the church unless the interpretation is also given (1 Cor. 14:28).

3. Ornaments
Third, every extravagance of apparel, every vanity, and, indeed, all ornaments that are more fitting for the worldly theaters of the nations than the holy churches of Christians and more useful for delighting in the flesh than building up in the Spirit should be eliminated. Instead, everything should be managed with the greatest reverence and modesty in the churches in the presence of God and of the angels.[15]

---

15. The Second Helvetic Confession, ch. 22 is likely in the background of this statement. See James T. Dennison Jr., comp., *Reformed Confessions of the 16th and 17th*

However, as regards the forms of vestments that ministers should wear publicly, whether during the service or outside of it, we reckon that this matter should not be disputed in such a way as to disturb the churches' peace. Nevertheless, we declare those churches that more nearly approach apostolic simplicity are more commendable.[16]

4. Holy Days
Fourth, the church should assemble every Lord's Day, since, even from apostolic times, we see this day having been set apart and made holy for this holy rest. Beyond the Lord's Day, we cannot but also approve of sanctifying those days celebrated by the ancient church that remind us of the nativity, circumcision, passion, resurrection, and ascension into heaven of our Lord Jesus Christ and the sending of the Holy Spirit upon the apostles. In accordance with how each church has judged it expedient, so let the holy assembly gather for the Word, the sacraments, the prayers, and the collection on other days as well (Col. 2:16). But always avoid any superstitious observance of days.

5. Prayers
Fifth, prayers should be poured out to God alone and to Jesus Christ without any invocation of angels or departed saints, just as the prophets and the apostles and the whole of the early church did (as can clearly be seen in the ancient collects), to say nothing of the command of God, who desires that we offer this sacrifice of worshiping mouths to Him alone (Heb. 13:5 [that is, v. 15]).

6. Rites
Sixth, regarding the keeping of rites and ceremonies in the church, the same piety and edification of the churches demand that they not be disputed too fiercely, as if they were struggles for hearth and home, as they say. Rather, let each church be left free, as was the case for the ancient

---

Centuries in English Translation, vol. 2, 1552–1566 (Grand Rapids: Reformation Heritage Press, 2010), 570 (Schaff, *Creeds*, 3:296).
    16. This statement regarding clerical vestments contrasts with Zanchi's 1571 advice to Queen Elizabeth. See Hastings Robinson, ed., *The Zurich Letters (Second Series)* (Cambridge: Cambridge University Press, 1845), 368–80 (*OOT*, 3/8:111–14).

church, as we read in Socrates[17] and other ecclesiastical writers. With regard to these matters in general, we approve of and embrace both of Augustine's letters to Januarius (vol. 2, eps. 118 and 119 [that is, eps. 54 and 55]), for these things contribute to the church's edification.[18]

Fasts
31. *Public fasts, which are eminently useful and praiseworthy, should be proclaimed at times, but no one should be forced to observe them.*
Similarly, it pertains to the church's healthy governance that, in the same way as private fasts are free, so also should everyone be welcomed to participate in public fasts but not compelled to do so. The usefulness of fasts can hardly be commended enough. And often, it turns out that they are necessary, such that pious magistrates and the church's ministers are driven to proclaim public fasts for the whole church to appease God's intense fury, just as was customarily done in the Old Testament and in the early church. The purpose of fasts was not to earn the remission of their sins or relief from divine wrath but so that, the flesh having been tamed, the Spirit might be stirred up to call upon God more passionately and to appease Him by faithful supplication. At the same time, it matters for the edification of the church that no one's conscience be bound and constrained unto these types of fasts, since they ought to proceed from a free, voluntary, and truly humble Spirit. As the apostle wrote concerning the giving of alms to the poor, this should not be done bitterly or out of necessity, but each person should do as he determines in his heart [2 Cor. 9:7].

The Restricting of Foods
32. *At no time, not even during public fasts, should any type of food be forbidden to the faithful.*
From this it also follows that at no time—whether during a fast or

---

17. Socrates of Constantinople (or, Socrates Scholasticus), who died in the mid-fifth century, wrote *The Ecclesiastical History* (NPNF2, 2:v–153), which covered the period from the early fourth century to the year 439.

18. vol. 2, eps. 118 and 119 [that is, eps. 54 and 55]: Augustine, *Letters*, 1:210–14, 233–36 (NPNF1, 1:300–303, 324–26).

not—should anyone be forbidden to eat any type of food, since none of them are able to pollute man (Matt. 15:11). Rather, *To the pure all things are pure* (Titus 1:15). And the apostle calls the teaching of those who command one to abstain from foods for the sake of religion *the teaching of demons* (1 Tim. 4:1, 3). How, then, could this teaching contribute to the church's edification?

The Sick and Burial
33. *The sick should be visited; they should be furnished with consolations and confirmed in their faith. The dying should be accompanied by prayers and entrusted to Christ; and the bodies of the dead should be buried with honor.* The church's sick should not be cared for any less than those who are well, nor the dead any less than the living, since all are Christ's members, and their bodies are the temples of the Holy Spirit. Thus, we acknowledge that it pertains to the true governance of the churches that pious and prudent men be organized to visit the sick and comfort them from God's Word and confirm them in their faith. But if it happens that the Lord calls the sick whom they visit from this world, let the visitors inspire them for the departure from this life. For as soon as the souls of the faithful have left the body, they immediately depart to be with Christ in heaven and are conveyed there by Christ's Spirit and escorted by His angels. Blessed are those who die in the Lord.

To this let the visitors also add prayers with which to accompany those who are dying until they arrive at their refuge, and let them entrust the dying to Christ. We doubt not that the bodies themselves should be buried with honor, just as our churches teach by their words and deeds, making public testimony to their bodies having been the temples of the Holy Spirit. To be sure, for right now they have been torn down, but in God's time they must again be restored and raised to life, even eternal life. Meanwhile, the graves themselves and cemeteries should be cared for religiously and reverently, as is the case among us.

Moreover, the children of the deceased (or their parents, relations, and neighbors) should be comforted with every human kindness that can be afforded to them. We endeavor to give those kindnesses, and we teach that we should give them.

And if a portion of the Psalms about the resurrection of the dead is sung somewhere during the burial, or if people come together after the body is committed to the earth for a gathering in which others who have died are called to mind in a decent manner, we by no means disapprove. For this is not done for the salvation of the dead person (or persons) but for the consolation and benefit of the living and the edification of the whole church, for we believe that the unbound souls of the faithful immediately depart from their bodies for Christ in heaven and thus have no need of our aid. But the church's edification should always be promoted whenever the opportunity arises.

Synods

34. *The church cannot be rightly governed without legitimate, free, and Christian assemblies and synods.*

Having been taught both by the Holy Scriptures and repeated experience, we are also persuaded of the following: the church cannot be rightly governed unless assemblies of ministers are convened at certain times. Individual assemblies should meet in each church, in which case it is usually called a consistory or a council. Public and common assemblies should meet in each province or kingdom, for which reason they are customarily termed provincial synods. And as often as possible, joint assemblies of all people in the whole Christian world should meet. These are known as ecumenical councils.

In these assemblies, let everything pertaining to the health, preservation, and edification of the churches be discussed. Let everyone's free opinion be heard. And by common consent, let the council be constrained by God's Word and the best of the other councils, just as we read that the apostles and the whole ancient church did.

Discipline

35. *A confirmation of the previous judgment as regards ecclesiastical discipline.*

For the church is guided by discipline, and without discipline it cannot be rightly governed. Moreover, discipline is the method and the manner whereby we, as Christ's disciples, learn to live in His school and to do everything according to gospel teaching both publicly and privately, for the church's edification and our salvation. For that reason, it embraces every element of piety—beginning, middle, and end.

36. *Discipline is twofold.*
Moreover, this discipline in the church is twofold. One kind is common to all Christian people, which many call popular discipline. The other kind is specific to ministers and men intended for ecclesiastical offices. For that reason, it is also customarily known as clerical discipline.

37. *The components of common discipline.*
Common or popular discipline consists most particularly in the following. First, as regards the beginning, when someone is received into the church, let him learn to know God and Christ, call upon Him, and understand what He wills. Let this be done by means of catechism, by which the summary of Christian piety is taught as well. But let him who is instructed profess his faith before the whole church and promise his obedience to Christ and His church in accordance with the teaching of the gospel (Rom. 10:10; Matt. 28:20).

Second, not to progress in God's way is to regress. For this reason—so that the pious might make true progress in piety—they should gather frequently in holy assemblies at the appointed times and places and give themselves over to the hearing of God's Word, offering prayers along with others, and having generously gathered their offerings, practicing charity toward the poor.

However, because we all slip and fall repeatedly in this progress—some more seriously and with greater scandal to the church, others less seriously—a third part of popular discipline is established for the oversight of behavior. This entails each one submitting himself to oversight during the entire course of his life and receiving brotherly correction. And if a person has fallen into a deeply disgraceful act that is known to the church and, having been rebuked, has not truly repented, he may consequently render himself deserving of temporary separation from the Supper and of being bound to true penitence until he gives public indication of genuine repentance to the church. Let such a brother be separated from things that are holy and be bound. Let him, however, be loosed when he repents and is received in grace and accepted back into his former fellowship (Matt. 18:15[–18]; 1 Tim. 5:20).

This is the first kind of discipline, the goal of which is that everyone might live to God and, at length, also die in the Lord Jesus.

38. *The components of clerical discipline.*

However, although all Christians—both ministers as well as (so called) laypeople—are subject to this kind of discipline, the fathers also added to it a distinct type of discipline in the case of the clergy, to whom it is given to lead others not only in word but also by the example of their lives and the diligent performance of their duties. These are the specific components of clerical discipline:

First, they are to abstain from many things that might otherwise be tolerable in some way among the laity. These include things such as: lots of gourmet feasts, sumptuous displays, dazzling banquets, extravagant furnishings, ungodly servants, and things of this sort.

Second, they are to refuse any of life's activities that hold them back from being able to execute their duty, which consists especially in attending regularly to holy matters, preaching the Word, and exercising discipline over behavior. The sorts of activities that they must refuse include military service, trade, legal occupations, shopkeeping, running a tavern, and all disgraceful practices.

Third, they are to promise singular obedience to their bishop and the bishop's metropolitan in honorable matters.

Fourth, they are to apply themselves more diligently to the reading and study of the Holy Scriptures than the laity, to the skills and languages whereby they can better understand the Holy Scriptures, and, indeed, to prayer and holy meditation.

Fifth, they are to also apply themselves more diligently to care not only for the specific office entrusted to them but for everything that might seem to pertain to the building up of the whole church.

39. *The necessity of a synod is deduced from the necessity of discipline.*

We do not see how any church can be rightly administered and preserved without these three parts of discipline.[19] But how can there be any room for this kind of discipline if ministers never gather together in order to discern the needs of the church or her missteps, to assess behaviors, to render judgment about doctrines when new ones are spread abroad, and, finally, to discuss everything that pertains to the health of the churches? For this reason, we judge that assemblies of ministers and ecclesiastical synods are very necessary for the true and wholesome administration and preservation of churches. For no polity—whether a republic or a kingdom—can exist without its senates, councils, parliaments (as they are called), and assemblies.

Thus, we would find it extremely pleasing for the ancient custom of the churches to be revived, which Emperor Justinian himself confirmed by a new decree, namely, that synods be celebrated twice a year in each province and that a general synod also gather occasionally from the whole province's most learned, modest, and prudent gospel-professing ministers, along with the princes' ambassadors. If ever this was a pressing need, it seems to us that it is in this truly calamitous age, when heresies—so many and so great—are being recalled far and wide from hell.

We pray God the Father through our Lord Jesus Christ with our whole heart that He might stir up pious and powerful Constantines, Valentinians, and Theodosiuses who, by their authority, might convene such a synod in which, they themselves being present as well and acting as moderators, there may be friendly fraternal discussions about pious harmony and the peace and health of all the churches based on the Holy Scripture and God's Spirit, to the glory of God and Christ's name and for the salvation of all the elect.

40. *Errors.*

We therefore disapprove of everything opposed to the aforesaid doctrine, which is confirmed by the Holy Scriptures, and especially these particulars: (1) that the church consists only of men and that angels have

---

19. The "three parts of discipline" referenced here are likely those described above in CCR, 25.37.

nothing to do with her; (2) that the true church, which is Christ's body, consists not merely of the elect but also of base hypocrites, and that they are true members of the church; (3) conversely, that the church consists of the elect and the truly holy in such a way that no hypocrites are contained in her and that at no time do the Holy Scriptures include them in the word *church*; (4) that the church that existed before Christ's coming was not Christ's true church but merely the type of the church, which was to be gathered by Christ and the apostles; (5) that Christ's church has two heads, one invisible and existing in heaven (namely, Christ) and the other visible and ruling on earth (the Roman pontiff) and that he who disagrees with the latter in anything pertaining to religion and does not obey him in all things does not belong to the church and cannot be saved.

We disapprove of those who (6) affirm that some specific church cannot err in faith; (7) bind the church to certain places or persons in such a way that they say the church is limited only to them; (8) refuse to acknowledge those churches to be Christ's churches that maintain the foundations of the faith while not agreeing with us on every point with regard to ceremonies or even certain elements of doctrine; (9) separate from churches because of some kind of error or on account of the wicked life of others; (10) assert that the place from which true doctrine, true worship, and the pure administration of the sacraments is banished is nevertheless a true, apostolic, and pure church because it can show an unbroken succession of bishops from the age of the apostles but that, conversely, those which cannot demonstrate an uninterrupted personal succession and continuation of bishops are not true churches, despite maintaining pure doctrine, sacraments, and genuine discipline.

We disapprove of any who assert (11) that the authority of some bishop, just because he is a bishop, extends beyond the church to which he has been called by Christ; (12) or that any church has authority to alter the Holy Scriptures or do away with God's commands or compose new laws binding the conscience. We disapprove of any who (13) forbid ministers of the Word to enter into marriage, or even marry a second time; (14) forbid ministers to receive a settled income; (15) permit a language to be used in church buildings that is unknown to the church without a translation being provided; (16) allow departed saints to be called upon in addition to God and Jesus Christ the Mediator and direct prayers and the sacrifice of thanksgiving unto them; (17) or forbid Christians from eating any type of food during Lent or on other fixed days. Finally, we disapprove of any who assert (18) that the church does well if it prays for the souls of the dead in order to free them from the fires of purgatory.

Chapter Twenty-Six

The Magistrate

We have now stated what we believe concerning the first type of men whose labors God uses to govern the church (namely, ecclesiastical ministers) and their offices and other matters pertaining to them. It thus remains for us now also to explain something of what we believe about the other type of men, that is, the political magistrate. For the Lord often uses the magistrate's ministry to protect and preserve His church, especially if he is a Christian.

1. Whether or not he is pious, every magistrate is from God, and so no magistrate should simply be opposed.
Therefore, we believe that every magistrate, not only the pious but also the wicked, is from the Lord God and is God's minister to take vengeance upon the wicked and to commend those who behave rightly (Rom. 13:1; 1 Peter 2:13). Accordingly, he should be both feared and honored, and we should be submissive to commands that can be kept with a good conscience and without violating the divine law (Rom. 13:7). And we should do this not only out of fear but also on account of conscience, for this is what the Lord commands (Rom. 13:5). Thus, insofar as the magistrate is God's minister, he should not be resisted, because whoever stands opposed to God's arrangement stands opposed to God Himself (Rom. 13:1).

2. A magistrate should not be obeyed when he commands anything contrary to God.
Nevertheless, if a magistrate commands us to do something that is

contrary to the will of Him by whom he was sent and whose minister he declares himself to be, then, with the apostles, we doubt not but that we must refuse to obey him and instead must say, *It is better to obey God than man* (Acts 5:29). For, to that extent, such a magistrate is not a true minister of God. This is why we conclude that, if we are to be subject to and obey the magistrate for conscience's sake and not merely out of fear, then, when it is wrong to obey for conscience's sake, we should not obey merely out of fear (Rom. 13:5). Otherwise, we say that whoever stands against authority stands against God and brings judgment upon himself (Rom. 13:2).

3. All magistrates should be prayed for to actually fulfill their duty, and what the duty of each magistrate is.

Moreover, it is the duty of every unconstrained magistrate to take the greatest of care—by establishing just laws, making judgments, and punishing the wicked—to see to it that those under him live according to God's laws on account of both power and nature. The sum total of those laws is for us to live soberly (and thus virtuously and decently), justly (and thus peacefully with our neighbor) and piously (toward God) in this age (Titus 2:12). However, princes cannot fulfill this duty on their own unless God grants them knowledge of their duty and stirs them up to will and to perform that duty (Phil. 2:13). This is why we instruct others to do the same thing we do on behalf of magistrates in accordance with the apostle's command: pray that they have the desire and ability to fulfill their duty, no matter what sort they are. And thus, we pray for them so that we can live quiet and peaceful lives in all honor and piety. That is, we pray that we may live together agreeably and in peace with everyone, that public honor may be preserved as well, and that true piety and religion may be protected and propagated (1 Tim. 2:2).

4. It is the particular purview of the Christian prince to care for the Christian religion.

We believe, however, that if the magistrate also happens to be Christian and pious, then caring personally for the Christian religion belongs especially to him. This comes even before the pursuit of public and political good or convenience or of public and political peace and reputation. For the Lord made the magistrate the guardian of both tables and commands him as prince always to hold God's law in his hands and to punish idolaters, blasphemers, false prophets, and deceivers, just as he punishes murderers and adulterers. This is demonstratively confirmed by the examples of Israel's pious kings and of Christian princes such as Constantine, Valentinian, Theodosius, Justinian, and others. Obviously, they served the Lord according to God's command, not only as private men but also as kings. Blessed Augustine also observed and explained this same point, with great prudence from Psalm 2, when he wrote to Count Boniface about the duty of magistrates (vol. 2, ep. 50 [that is, ep. 185.19]).[1]

5. *The duty of the pious princes in religious matters is twofold, and the place wherein it primarily consists.*
Moreover, the pious prince (that is, the sort of magistrate who has an unconstrained legal right among a certain people and has within his power the authority to establish or reform religion) has a twofold duty. His first duty is to occupy himself with those matters that particularly

---

1. vol. 2, ep. 50 [that is, ep. 185.19]: "Those who do not want just laws to be established against their wickedness say that the apostles did not seek anything of the sort from the rulers of the earth. They do not take into account that it was a different time and that all things are done at their proper times. For what emperor then believed in Christ and would serve him by issuing laws in favor of piety and against impiety when those words of the prophet were still being fulfilled, 'Why have the nations raged and the peoples planned folly? The kings of the earth rose up, and the princes came together against the Lord and against his anointed.' (Ps 2:1–2) There was as yet no realization of what it says a little later in the same psalm, 'And now, O kings, understand; receive instruction, you who judge the world. Serve the Lord with fear, and exult before him with trembling.' (Ps 2:10–11) How, then, do kings serve the Lord with fear except by forbidding and punishing with religious severity actions done against the Lord's commandments? For he serves in one way because he is a man, and he serves in another way because he is king. For, because he is a man, he serves him by living a life of faith, but, because he is also a king, he serves him by upholding with appropriate force laws that command what is just and forbid what is unjust." Augustine, *Letters*, vol. 3, 156–210, ed. Boniface Ramsey, trans. Roland J. Teske, The Works of Saint Augustine: A Translation for the 21st Century II/3 (Hyde Park, N.Y.: New City Press, 2004), 190 (*FOTC*, 30:159–60).

have to do with religion, and the second is truly to care for the men whom he has in his power, who are subject to him. For this reason, we believe that his primary duty is, first, diligently to see that religion is established in his principality or kingdom—or that, having been established, it is preserved; or, having been corrupted, that it is restored and reformed—according to the pure Word of God by means of the Word of God itself. And he must see that it is understood according to the first foundation of the faith—what is often called the analogy of faith—unto God's glory and the salvation of his people. For we read that this was commanded by God and by Moses and that all pious princes observed it.

6. *A step-by-step explanation of the previous judgment.*
Thus, we believe that the first duty of every pious magistrate is to know from God's Word what the true and Christian religion (or apostolic teaching) is, both in general and with regard to the chief articles of the faith, according to which the church must be reformed. This is necessary lest he do or consider doing anything merely on the basis of the judgment of others rather than on the basis of his own settled knowledge.

The next duty of the pious magistrate is, with this knowledge in hand, to make certain that suitable men are chosen, called, and ordained to the office of minister, not on the basis of his own judgment but in accordance with the rule of God's word and apostolic examples.

His third duty is to cause the doctrine of salvation delivered in the Holy Scriptures to be declared, explained, and impressed through these ministers; the sacraments administered according to Christ's instruction; and the discipline instituted by Christ exercised.

Fourth, he is also to take responsibility for seeing schools established that teach good arts and languages. But even more and especially, these schools should faithfully explain the Holy Scriptures and teach students the principal elements of Christian wisdom.

Fifth, a magistrate should see to it that, in addition to regular and private consistories, the previously mentioned provincial synods are convened at least twice a year so that ministers and teachers hold fast to that duty and, consequently, preserve true religion in the church.

Sixth and finally, he should see to the care of ecclesiastical goods, assuring that they are faithfully distributed unto their proper (that is, unto truly pious) uses and that whatever is necessary for the church and her ministers is available as required.

7. Pious princes should not treat every type of religious men identically.
Furthermore, to speak briefly about the pious prince's other duty[2] as regards religion, it may be that he exercises authority over various kinds of men. There are those who simply are unbelievers. Others at least profess faith in Christ but are clear idolaters at the same time and apostate from the apostolic church in many matters. Others may be manifest heretics on some article of the faith or may simply be going astray. Finally, others may hold correct opinions about everything. For this reason, we are altogether convinced that a prince should not treat everyone identically. For some should be considered precious, nourished, and treated with honor; others should be tolerated; others should not be put up with; and yet others should even suffer capital punishment. None, however, should be permitted to blaspheme Christ or worship idols and maintain ungodly ceremonies.

8. All men ought to be subject to those who have power over them, but all who are in power—even the higher ones—are subject to Christ Himself and to His Word.
Finally, we believe that every soul (that is, every man without exception and, thus, every inferior power) ought to be subject to the power that is superior and higher (Rom. 13:1). However, the superior power ought to be subject to Christ Himself, the King of Kings and Lord of all Lords, no less than inferior powers and all other men are subject to Him (Rev. 17:14; 1 Tim. 6:15). For God wants all of them to *kiss the Son* and place themselves under His yoke and discipline (Ps. 2:12). And thus, we believe it has bearing upon the church's true governance and edification for princes to be the first to submit themselves to being taught, admonished, and corrected by God's Word, so that everyone else, seeing their example, might more eagerly do likewise. And besides, princes will then

---

2. That is, the second part of the twofold duty mentioned above in *CCR*, 26.5.

be able more boldly to punish those who refuse to do so, and to hold everyone to their duty.

9. Errors.

Therefore, we condemn all despisers of magistrates, rebels, the seditious, the enemies of their own republic, and anyone who either openly refuses or cunningly declines to make good on the duty owed to the magistrate. We condemn by name the error of the Anabaptists, who say that a Christian man is not permitted to hold the office of magistrate and, even less, make use of his authority to support the cause of religion, for everyone is free to follow whichever religion he wishes, and, consequently, no one should be compelled unto faith. We also disapprove of those who grant magistrates authority in religion only for appearance's sake while denying they have the authority to convoke synods, resolve religious issues, reform the churches, and make decisions on the basis of the Holy Scriptures about things pertaining to their people's salvation.

Yet, neither do we approve of those magistrates who, lacking a proper understanding of matters, alter religion according to their fancy or who condemn people without a hearing, despoil them, and deprive them of their property. We disapprove of those who do not establish rules about religion on the basis of the Holy Scriptures but in opposition to God's Word instead—and likewise, those who do not behave like God's servants but like the lords of the churches in *Christ's* church, refusing to subject their necks to the yoke of God's Son. For these, we pray to God the Father and the Lord Jesus Christ for a greater knowledge of God and a better mind.

Chapter Twenty-Seven

The Ongoing Remission of Sins in Christ's Church

1. *There is ongoing provision for the remission of sins in the church, and the ongoing ministry of the Word is ordained unto this end.*
Previously, we confessed that, as soon as one is grafted onto Christ by the Holy Spirit, he immediately obtains remission of all the sins he had committed and draws in new life from Christ his Head. Consequently, he became a living member of the church. To be sure, however, until the end of their lives, even the most holy members in this church militant sin daily. Thus, their need for the remission of sins is constantly renewed, just as is their ongoing need for a repentance and faith that lays hold of the remission of their sins in Christ. Moreover, faith and repentance are ordinarily stirred up by the ministry of Word and sacrament. For this reason, we believe that, in the church, the remission of sins is continually provided for by means of the ministry of Word and sacraments. And the whole ecclesiastical ministry, which is perpetual in the church, is ordained unto this.

2. *What we mean by the phrase* the remission of sins.
Furthermore, there are three things in sin: the transgressing act, the iniquity of the action (and, thus, the abiding guilt of the ones who sinned), and the obligation to pay the penalty owed corresponding to the guilt. Likewise, we understand that our sins are forgiven both when guilt and iniquity are not imputed as well as when the obligation is removed and the penalty owed is pardoned. For, strictly speaking, debts are forgiven. And when we ask in prayer for our debts to be forgiven us, we are not only asking to be absolved from guilt and that iniquity not be imputed

to us. We are also asking that the penalty and condemnation we deserve on account of our iniquity be pardoned, and pardoned in such a way that we are released from our obligation and debt [Matt. 6:12]. For we do not say that we have forgiven our brothers' debts unless we release them from the payment and the penalty they owe us. And it is certain that God would not tell us to ask for something other than what He Himself is willing to give. And Christ blotted out the handwriting of our entire debt by the perfect payment and penalty He made for us [Col. 2:14].

3. Afflictions that oppress the saints subsequent to their sins having been pardoned are not penalties or satisfactions for past sins but fatherly chastisements for the future.

God often afflicts and strikes His sons with various scourges subsequent to their sins being remitted. We do not, however, believe that God does this in order thereby to satisfy His justice for the sins that have been committed, either in whole or in part. For the singular and complete satisfaction of Christ imputed to us is sufficient and more than sufficient. We do, however, believe He does this in order that, by them, (as by the rod of fatherly discipline that surely leads to the mortification of sin dwelling in us) we might become more circumspect in the future and not give ourselves over so easily to sin. For this reason, with Augustine, we call them and teach that they ought to be called *the challenge of faith* and *the exercises of the saints* but not *the punishment of sins* (*The Punishment and Forgiveness of Sins*, vol. 7, bk. 2, chs. 33–34[, §53–54]).[1]

---

1. *The Punishment and Forgiveness of Sins*, vol. 7, bk. 2, chs. 33–34[, §53–54]: Augustine writes: "But there are such people, and we answer them, once the question has been raised, by saying that before the forgiveness of sins those things were punishments, but after the forgiveness of sins they provide challenges and exercise for the righteous. And so, we must say to the people who are similarly disturbed over the death of the body that we admit that it came about as a result of sin and that we do not deny that after the forgiveness of sins it was left as a challenge for us so that, as we grow in strength, we might conquer our great fear of it." Augustine, *Answer to the Pelagians*, vol. 1, ed. John E. Rotelle, trans. Roland J. Teske, The Works of Saint Augustine: A Translation for the 21st Century I/23 (Hyde Park, N.Y.: New City Press, 1997), 114–15 (*NPNF*1, 5:65–66).

4. Properly speaking, sins are forgiven freely by God alone and on account of Christ the Mediator.
We also believe that, properly speaking, sins are forgiven by God alone on the basis of grace and on account of Christ the Mediator. Properly speaking, He Himself is the only one who is sinned against, whether immediately or mediately. Consequently, when we transgress His law, it is given into the power of the Creditor alone to show kindness to His debtors and to forgive debts. This is why Christ, as a man, asked the Father on behalf of those who were crucifying Him that He pardon them and forgive their sin (Luke 23:34). And He confirmed what the Jews had said—*Who can forgive sins but God alone?*—partly by remaining silent and partly by the miracle He performed (Luke 5:21–25). Christ forgave sins on His own authority, and it is for this reason that we, along with the fathers, believe that it is justly demonstrated that He is true God, since a mere man could not have done this, unless he did so ministerially (as they say) and in God's name and on the basis of His authority. We know this was given not only to one of the apostles but to all of them equally, and so to all legitimate ministers of the gospel (Matt. 18:18; John 20:23).

5. Christ the God-man does, indeed, forgive sins, but He does so in a different way as God than He does as man.
From this also follows what we confess: that Christ the God-man, together with the Father and the Holy Spirit, forgives sins, but that He does so in a different way as God than He does as man. For as God, properly speaking, He accomplished this by His own authority and in a truly efficient manner.[2] As He is man, however, He does it (and previously also did it) in His mortal body, cooperating,[3] as it were, with His deity. Thus, consenting to His divine will, His human will pronounced these words: *Your sins are forgiven you* [Luke 5:20].

Leo I also explained it this way in his letter to Flavian and said that each form—that is, of God and of man—*does what is proper to it, in*

---

2. Vere efficienter.
3. συνεργός.

communion with the other: namely, the Word working that which is of the Word and the flesh carrying out that which is of the flesh (ep. 10.4, [that is, 28.4]).[4] To forgive sins was properly an action of the divine nature, but to say, *Your sins are forgiven you* was an action of the human nature. Thus says Leo.

6. *Forgiveness of sins is offered only in Christ and is received only by the elect, who have been given faith.*

Moreover, just as we have redemption—the remission of sins—by the blood of Christ, who, as the Head of the whole church, is the only Mediator and Redeemer to such an extent that there is no redemption outside of Christ, so we also believe that only the elect (by the true repentance and true faith given to them) are grafted onto Christ by the Holy Spirit as members to their Head and made partakers of Him. And thus, although the remission of sins is proclaimed to all men through the gospel, nevertheless, the sins of the reprobate are never forgiven, since they are unrepentant and unbelieving. Rather their corruption and guilt are always retained.

7. *The faithful are forgiven all their sins simultaneously.*

We also believe that, just as Christ's one sacrifice sufficed for all our sins and not just some of them, so all our sins (and not just some of them) are simultaneously forgiven to us who truly repent. They are forgiven by Christ and in Christ, who is offered through the gospel, partaken of by the Holy Spirit, and received by faith, since God declared—having set it forth with a parable—that He forgives our whole debt and not just part of it (Matt. 18:23[–35]).

8. *The forgiveness of sins is disbursed only in the church, is only received by faith, and only happens in this life.*

Finally, that we might bring this to a conclusion, we believe that, just as the forgiveness of sins is found only in Christ, so also is it disbursed only in His church. And just as it was procured for us only by Christ's merit

---

4. ep. 10.4, [that is, 28.4]: Leo I, *Letters*, 97–98 (*NPNF2*, 12:40).

and blood, so also is it received only by true faith in Christ, apart from our own merits. And just as the gospel is proclaimed only in this life, and the forgiveness of sins is announced through it to those who repent and believe, so, likewise, we can become partakers of it only in this life, since no opportunity exists for faith and repentance after this life.

And thus, the church with her ministry can offer no additional service toward obtaining forgiveness for those who have quit this life. Cyprian said this as well: *When one has withdrawn from here, there is no longer any opportunity for repentance; there is no accomplishment of satisfaction. Life is either lost or kept here; provision is made here for eternal life with the worship of God and the performance of faith* (To Demetrian[, ch. 25]).[5]

9. *Confirmation of the same doctrine based on the arrangement of the Creed.* We interpret the article concerning the remission of sins in the Creed in terms of the following three points: first, that this article follows the article concerning the church and is appended to the article concerning the communion of the saints so that we may understand that there is no disbursing of or opportunity for the remission of sins outside the church. Second, that article follows the confession of our faith in God the Father, in the Son, and in the Holy Spirit and our confession of faith that we believe Christ's church to be holy and to consist in the fellowship and communion of the saints. This is so that we might bear witness that it is not based on our own merits that we are in the church and have communion with all the saints. Rather, it is on account of our faith in God the Father, in the Son, and in the Holy Spirit, and that is also the reason why we daily obtain the remission of our sins. Finally, on the basis of the arrangement of the articles of faith, we believe and confess that, as far as the dead are concerned, after the remission of sins is obtained in this church militant, nothing more remains but the resurrection of the flesh and eternal life.

---

5. To Demetrian[, ch. 25]: Cyprian, *Treatises*, trans. and ed. Roy J. Deferrari, Fathers of the Church 36 (Washington, D.C.: Catholic University of America Press, 1958), 190 (*ANF*, 5:465).

10. Errors.

Thus, we condemn that error whereby some teach that there remains a debt of punishment to be paid after guilt has been forgiven since eternal death is commuted by the sacrament of penance into temporal punishment. They teach that that debt must be discharged either in this life or after death in purgatory, unless we are set free from that place by masses, indulgences, or other kinds of intercession. Second, we also condemn the blasphemy of those who seek the remission of sins or teach that the remission of sins should be sought elsewhere than in Christ. Likewise, we condemn those who assert that the remission of sins can actually be applied to and received by them in any way other than by true faith and by the Holy Spirit. Likewise, we condemn the sacrilegious doctrine of those who teach that it is not always the case that God forgives all the sins of those who believe but that certain sins are in fact frequently retained and must subsequently be atoned for with our fasts, almsgiving, prayers, and other works, or even by the offerings of others and the sacrifices of priests.

Chapter Twenty-Eight

The State of Souls after Death and the Resurrection of the Dead

1. *Souls neither die with their bodies, nor, having been released from their bodies, do they sleep, nor are they idle somewhere outside of heaven or Tartarus,[1] nor are they tormented by the fires of purgatory.*

We do not believe that our souls die with our bodies, nor that, having been released from their bodies, they sleep or are idle in some secret places outside of heaven or Tartarus. Nor do we believe that they are tormented by the fires of purgatory. On the contrary, even apart from the body, the souls of all men live, think, and will. However, the souls of the pious rule in heaven with Christ, and the souls of the wicked suffer in hell with the devils.

With regard to the former, the Lord said that when the pious and merciful die—that is, when they depart from this life—they (that is, their souls) are received to an eternal home (Luke 16:9). And elsewhere He taught that they would be with Him in paradise (Luke 23:43). But by telling the parable of the rich man,[2] He taught that the souls of the

---

1. Here and elsewhere, the confession uses the transliterated Greek word *Tartarus* (see CCR, 5.3). This word appears in the New Testament only in 2 Peter 2:4, where it is often translated into English as "hell." Subsequently in this section and elsewhere in the confession, *Tartarus* is used interchangeably with *infernus*, which might be translated as "lower" or "infernal region," that is, the place where demonic spirits are chained until the day of judgment (Jude 6). By the end of this section (and in CCR, 28.7 and 29.6), it is clear that Zanchi also understands *infernus* to be a place of eternal fire (namely, "hell") where the wicked suffer after their deaths and then, body and soul, after the final judgment. I translate *infernus* as "hell" and leave *Tartarus* untranslated.

2. *Epulonis*, literally "carouser" or "banquet guest." In the parable of Lazarus and the

latter were destined to go to hell, that is, to the place of eternal fire, to suffer there (Luke 16:23), just as we also read of Judas (Acts 1:25).

2. After death, the souls of believers and unbelievers abide in different places. However, since the condition of the souls of believers and unbelievers are so different, we believe that the places to which they go are also different. That is, there is an eternal home or heaven, a paradise destined for the pious, and there is Tartarus, a hellish place prepared for the wicked inasmuch as the Holy Scriptures assign an immeasurable light to the one place and the greatest darkness to the other, which Christ calls *outer darkness* (2 Peter 2:4; Matt. 8:12). And again, this is the case inasmuch as the Lord said that it was His desire for those who believe in Him to be where He is (John 17:24). By this He was clearly indicating that believers will also be in that place where He now is, body and soul. But first, they will be there with their souls, and then subsequently, at the appropriate time, with their bodies as well. Unbelievers, however, will never be in that place with either their souls or their bodies.

Thus, we judge it to be the height of wickedness to say that heaven is everywhere, since it is never allotted to the wicked but, throughout the Holy Scriptures, is allotted solely to the pious as their proper and eternal habitation. In fact, not only is it necessary for bodies to be circumscribed within a determined area of space, even after the resurrection, but souls also, at least in a definitive sense (as they say), must be contained.

3. The end of this world is certain, and all things will be renewed, although the specific timing is unknown.[3]
Moreover, although we do not know when the end of this age will be (in the sense that it cannot even be known), we nevertheless believe that it

---

rich man (Luke 16:19–31), the latter, who is unnamed in the parable, was often referred to as *dives epulo*, the "rich carouser" or "wealthy glutton."

3. Zanchi's eschatology has been addressed in John L. Farthing, "Christ and the Eschaton: The Reformed Eschatology of Jerome Zanchi," in *Later Calvinism: International Perspectives*, ed. W. Fred Graham, Sixteenth Century Essays and Studies 22 (Kirksville, Mo.: Sixteenth Century Journal, 1994), 333–54; and Fesko, "Girolamo Zanchi on Union with Christ and the Final Judgment."

certainly will happen and that not only the earth but the heavens too will be changed and that there will be a new heaven and a new earth (Matt. 24:36; Acts 1:7; Isa. 24:23; 65:17; 66:22; Ps. 102:27 [that is, vv. 25–26]; 2 Peter 3:13; Rev. 21:1). And we believe that all the dead, even the wicked, will be resurrected when Christ calls them unto universal judgment with the archangel's voice and trumpet (Dan. 12:2; Mal. 4:1; Jude 14–15). It pertains to the certainty of these things that, when the Lord Jesus predicted the destruction of Jerusalem, He then immediately went on also to discuss these matters. He did this so that, knowing what happened to Jerusalem, we might also believe that what He predicted about the end of the age would certainly happen as well (Matt. 24[:1–44]; Luke 21:5[–36]).

4. In the end, all those who are dead will be made alive and resurrected from their graves.

Thus, we believe that, just as through Adam all died, so also through Christ all will be made alive. Even the wicked (as regards their bodies) will be made alive, the soul of each one taking up again its body—albeit we confess that some will rise again unto eternal happiness and others unto everlasting damnation (1 Cor. 15:22). As Christ said, *And they who have done good will come forth unto the resurrection of life, but those who have done evil unto a resurrection of judgment* (John 5:29). This passage also indicates the order of the resurrection as well. The apostle taught the same thing saying, *First, those will rise again who are Christ's, then the rest* (1 Thess. 4[:15–16]).

5. New bodies will not be created for our souls; rather, the same bodies that died will be resurrected.

Moreover, we do not believe that a new body will be formed for each soul but rather that each one that died will be resurrected according to its substance, albeit different in certain qualities. This is as the apostle teaches (by way of an analogy of a single seed) with regard to the bodies of the pious: they are sowed one thing and raised another; they are sowed liable to corruption and raised incorruptible, and so on (1 Cor. 15:36, 42, and so forth). And according to the Vulgate version, Job testifies of his hope in this way: *I know that my Redeemer lives, and on the last day I will be raised up again from the earth, and in my flesh I will see God my Savior, whom I myself will see and my eyes, not those of another, will behold* (Job 19:25[, 27]).[4] For with our bodily eyes we will see Christ bodily returning unto us in the clouds and reigning in heaven as well.

6. *The example of our bodies after the resurrection demonstrates that Christ's body is not everywhere.*
The apostle says that Christ will transform our humble bodies, that they might be conformed to His glorious body. Therefore, we believe that, if Christ's body received the power to be everywhere according to its substance on account of the glory that it received at its resurrection, then our bodies would also be everywhere on account of that same glory (Phil. 3:21). But since this is not going to happen, we also do not believe that Christ's body—however abounding in glory and majesty it is—is now everywhere according to its substance, since it is finite, and its glory is finite. This is particularly the case because He said that He wants us to also be in that place where He is, but our bodies will not be everywhere (John 17:24).

7. *Errors.*
We condemn the wicked madness of those philosophers who have taught that the human soul is mortal. We also condemn those heretics who have imagined that the souls of all men either sleep separated from their bodies in some secret places (that is, that they are deprived of all feeling and mental operations) or that they do indeed remain awake but are at peace until they take up their bodies, and only then will they enter heaven or be driven to hell. And we likewise condemn those who have dreamt that the multitude of pious souls are in purgatory somehow being purged by fire from the remnants of their sins and suffering temporal punishments. We also disapprove of those who do not distinguish heaven (where we read that the pious shall be) from hell or Tartarus

---

4. The reference to the Vulgate is absent in the Legat (1599) and Winterton (1659) translations.

(where the wicked shall be) but locate the difference between them only in this: that some are made blessed and others wretched, although all are in one and the same place. Neither, however, can we approve of those who say that it is possible to determine and know the specific time—the month or the year, if not the day or the hour—in which the Lord will return and will bring this age to an end. Christ, however, said, *It is not for you to know the times* (Acts 1:7).

We, indeed, detest those who imagine that the world will remain like this forever and who deny and deride any idea of future life. These are those whom Peter called *scoffers* (2 Peter 3:3[–4]). We also condemn all those who deny the resurrection of the dead, not to mention those who dream that we will not have these same bodies but some other new ones instead. Likewise, we condemn those who taught that, after the resurrection, bodies will be so spiritual that, like spirit or air, they will not be able to be seen or touched. Some even falsely claimed that sort of body for Christ after the resurrection, and others imagine and shamelessly pretend that His body was, as it were, transformed into the divine nature, so that it can no longer be said to be a created thing.

Chapter Twenty-Nine

The Glorious Advent of Our Lord Jesus to Judge the Living and the Dead

1. Once the resurrection of the dead and the transformation of the living has taken place at the coming from heaven of the Lord Jesus, Christ will then present Himself to be seen by all in the clouds, and all the faithful shall go to meet Him in the air.

We believe that, once the resurrection of the dead by the ministry of the angels has taken place at the coming of the Lord Jesus, those who remain alive shall not actually die but shall nevertheless be transformed immediately into the same condition as those who have been raised up. And then Christ, having returned from heaven as far as the clouds to judge everyone from there and to render His decision about each one, will present Himself, that He might be observed by all men.

All the pious, however, having been transferred from the earth into the clouds of heaven, will rise to meet Him in the air, surrounded by His angels and appearing in His majesty and glory. This is what Christ Himself and the apostles taught and left in their writings (1 Thess. 5:1 [that is, 4:14–16]; Matt. 24:3 [that is, vv. 29–31]; 25:31[–33]).

2. Christ will return visibly—coming from one place to another place—and so with a visible, localized, and finite body.

Therefore, we believe that Christ will visibly return in the same way that He also previously ascended from earth into heaven while the apostles watched. And He will indeed return from that heaven where He now is, which must stand at a distance from the clouds into which He will descend and from the earth. Thus, we also believe that He will descend with His natural body in such a way that it must be both local and finite.

Consequently, it does not exist everywhere inasmuch as the kind of descent that the Holy Spirit describes to simple people is the sort that cannot happen without a change of location.

3. *Faithless reprobates will not come unto Christ as He is seated in the clouds but will hear the sentence of the Judge while remaining on the earth.*
However, since Scripture declares that only the pious will be caught up in clouds to meet Christ in the air, we believe that the wicked will not come unto Christ. Instead, remaining under His feet on the earth, they will hear the sentence of the Judge: *Depart, cursed ones, into eternal fire* [Matt. 25:41]. And all the saints who will be in the air with Christ will endorse the Judge's sentence, in accordance with the apostle's statement that the saints will judge the world and the angels (1 Cor. 6:2–3).

4. *The reasons why the universal judgment was established.*
Moreover, we believe that there are principally two reasons for the establishment of that judgment wherein Christ will judge everyone in full view of all. The first is, indeed, so that what is now hidden from men—as much the innocence, faith, and good conscience of the pious as the hypocrisy and sins of the wicked—might be made manifest to the whole world, and just how righteous God's judgments have always been might ultimately thereby be made marvelously obvious. This is why the apostle calls that day *the day of revelation* (Rom. 2:5). The second reason is so that the reward promised to the good for their good works and to the wicked for their wicked works might then be fully rendered to each one according to the saying of the apostle, *We must all be laid bare before Christ's tribunal, that each one may receive according to his conduct in the body, whether good or evil* (2 Cor. 5:10). Hence, that same apostle calls it *the day of righteous judgment* (Rom. 2:5).

5. *The eternal life that will be given to the elect is called a reward, which is what it is—but it is an altogether free reward and not in any way owed to us, except for Christ's sake.*
For although what the elect will receive is purely the gift of God acquired by Christ's merits alone, nevertheless, we do not doubt that it is (and

truly is called) a reward, since the Lord Jesus saw fit to describe it in that way, namely, as a free reward. For even the good works of the pious and the motives from which they proceed are God's free gifts: free election, free redemption, free calling, faith, justification, regeneration, the remission of sins, and, finally, free pardon of the weakness and imperfections with which our good works themselves are stained. And conversely, the free imputation of the perfect obedience of Christ with which our imperfection is adorned and made altogether pleasing to God is God's free gift. And so, if we want to speak properly, the reward is not owed to us on account of our works considered in themselves but only on account of Christ's imputed merits.

6. *Immediately after the judgment, the pious will be in heaven with Christ, but the wicked will be in hell with the Devil and his angels.*
Further, we believe that, immediately after that judgment, the pious will follow Christ into heaven, but the wicked will be thrust down into hell with the devils. This is according to what Christ said to the former: *Come, blessed of My Father* [Matt. 25:34]. But unto the latter: *Depart, cursed ones, into eternal fire* [Matt. 25:41].

7. *That day will be fully pleasing to the pious and so should be desired; it will be altogether sorrowful for the wicked, and so even hearing about it is intolerable to them.*
Thus, we believe that, for those who have been grafted onto Christ, that last day will be the happiest and most pleasing of all days and so is loved and longed for by them—and should be loved and longed for by us (2 Tim. 4:8). For the wicked, however, it will be the unhappiest and most sorrowful of all days, and so it is no wonder that they hate that day and cannot bear mention of it.

8. *Errors.*
We condemn anyone who denies that Christ will truly and really descend in His human body out of heaven into the clouds or that He will then return to heaven with the elect but instead contends that all this will happen without any change of location—by means, as they say, merely

of some external appearance and disappearance. By saying this, they contradict what the angels told the apostles: *Just as you saw Him ascending into heaven, so He will come* (Acts. 1:11).

We also disapprove of those who teach that pious works considered in and of themselves are the true reason on the basis of which eternal life is given and are the true merits of it. This is contrary to what the apostle wrote, saying, *The gift of God is eternal life* (Rom. 6:23). Furthermore, neither do we approve of the opinion of the chiliasts regarding the millennium.[1] According to them, Christ will dwell in this world after the judgment with His elect, and they will enjoy fleshly (but honorable) delights and will as yet bear children (albeit holy ones), and only then will they be conveyed into heaven.

Moreover, we condemn and detest the error of those who argue that the fire into which the wicked are sent will at length finally be extinguished such that everyone—even the devils—will live happily in the kingdom of God. This goes against Christ's clear words: *Depart into eternal fire* (Matt. 25:41).

---

1. Chiliasts (Gr. *chilioi*, meaning "thousand") held that Christ would return to earth to reign for a thousand-year reign before the consummation. The view existed in the early church but was opposed by Augustine and others. It reappeared during the Reformation era among some of the radicals (such as Thomas Müntzer, Melchior Hoffman, and the Anabaptists of Münster) but was regarded as heretical by confessional Protestants.

Chapter Thirty

Eternal Life

1. Eternal life will be given to all who bear witness with good works that they truly were grafted onto Christ and believed in Christ.
We therefore believe that, ultimately, eternal life—that is, the full and perfect possession of eternal life—will be given on that last day to all those who have been truly grafted onto Christ by the Holy Spirit and who, thus, have believed in God the Father, in His Son Jesus Christ, and in the Holy Spirit, who have been living members of the holy church and had fellowship with all the saints, and who have obtained remission of their sins. This will be plainly declared by their unmistakable works of true faith and piety; it will be shown with absolute clarity before the eyes of every angel and man; and it will be pronounced by Christ's sentence of judgment. The Lord taught this very thing when He said that He would say to those who were on His right, *Come, blessed of My Father; inherit the kingdom prepared for you from the foundation of the world, for I was hungry, and you gave Me food to eat*, and so on (Matt. 25:34[–36]).

2. Confirmation of the previous judgment; and that, properly speaking, eternal life is not given on account of our works but on account of Christ, in whom we are freely elected, blessed, and made sons of God.
For with these words, the Lord appears to have declared to us that our good works testify to our election, blessing, and sonship in Christ and, thus, to our right of inheritance. However, the reason why we obtain eternal life and possession of the heavenly kingdom is twofold. In part, it is because, already before the foundation of the world (that is, before we did anything good), that kingdom was freely prepared for us in Christ

[Rom. 9:11]. And in part, it is because we have been blessed by the Father with every spiritual blessing in Christ and (consequently) were called by grace, justified, obtained remission of sins, sanctification, and adoption as sons of God in that same Christ and were reborn by means of His Spirit and so were made coheirs of His kingdom (Eph. 1:3). That is plainly what is meant by the word κληρονομήσατε, meaning *possess as sons*, that is, by right of inheritance [Matt. 25:34].

Therefore, because the Lord will recall pious works, we do not doubt that He does so in order to reveal to the whole world on the basis of them that we truly were blessed, elect, righteous, sons of God to whom the inheritance was owed. The apostle likewise said this: *If we are sons, we are heirs as well* (Rom. 8:17). But that we are God's sons is revealed by regeneration, and regeneration is revealed by the effects of regeneration, which are called works of faith and piety.

3. Just as the life of the pious will be eternal, so also the punishment and fire of the wicked will be eternal.
Moreover, just as we believe that eternal life will be obtained by the sons of God, so we also confess that all hypocrites and wicked people will depart into fire that will never be extinguished and that they will suffer agony for eternity in that place. Christ clearly said, *Depart into eternal fire* (Matt. 25:41).

4. How happy that eternal life will be can neither be said nor imagined.
With regard to the nature of the life indicated by the phrase *kingdom of heaven* and what it will be like and how great the happiness will be, we frankly admit with the apostle that neither has eye seen nor ear heard, nor has it entered into man's heart (1 Cor. 2:9). For it is a greater and more excellent thing than can be comprehended by the human mind and of such happiness that we can long for nothing happier.

Thus, we who are Christ's—who are ruled by His Spirit, who listen carefully to His Word, and who place all our trust of salvation in Him—we simply believe that all of us will be utterly happy (Phil. 1:23). We will all shine just like the sun in God's sight (Matt. 13:43). We will all see God as He is. We will all live a heavenly and divine life with Christ and with His angels. We will be freed from all sin, all misery, all evil. We will no longer experience suffering, anxiety, need, or desire for anything else, because God will be all in all (1 Cor. 15:28). And we ourselves will see His face (1 Cor. 13:12). And there will be no more night in that city, nor will there be need for a lantern or sunlight, for the Lord God will enlighten us, and we will reign, world without end, with Christ Jesus, our Head, Husband, Savior, and Lord, to whom be praise, honor, and glory forever (Rev. 22:3–4 [that is, vv. 4–5]). Amen.

Zanchi's Own Observations on His Confession

The reasons why I have preferred to add these observations to my confession as a separate section rather than altering anything therein are neither few nor inconsequential. Many people are aware on what occasion, at which time, at whose request, in whose name, and for which purposes—admittedly, against my will and under constraint—I wrote this summary of Christian doctrine.[1] But although everyone can see that this confession was never published according to plan on behalf of those for whose sake it had been drafted, they do not fully grasp who did what or why it happened. Many people are astonished at what occurred, but they have no idea about the actual reasons behind it. Who could be ignorant of just how much suspicion is likely to arise as a result, not to mention the various assumptions that churches (let alone individuals) might make, either about me or about the confession itself? Lastly, who doesn't see how malicious rumors of many sorts might well be spread among the general public as a result? Hence, before I die, I had finally better respond to the malicious and depraved suspicions, judgments, and rumors about my doctrine.

I decided that I could do nothing more useful than undertake to publish the confession on its own, exactly as it had been composed, along with but separate from some observations on the confession that would explain anything unclear and develop anything dubious. Then I would

---

1. On the circumstances surrounding the composition of Zanchi's confession and the reasons why it did not serve its intended purpose, see the introduction to this book as well as Baschera and Moser, "Introduction," in *De religione*, 1:14–19.

leave the whole business to the judgment of the whole and truly catholic church. Besides this, I reckoned that it might well be useful for the removal of false suspicions conceived in the minds of men if I were to make known to all the pious the judgments of certain learned men about the confession on the basis of their own letters. This might be especially useful because they clearly explain the reasons why the confession was not brought out publicly in the way that had been planned.

One notable man wrote to me about the matter in these words:

> With respect to the confession that you are writing, it was read through with great pleasure by myself [that is, Lambert Daneau],[2] [Theodore Beza], and others, and it was written in both an extremely learned and a meticulous fashion. And it altogether satisfied me, if only you would remove what you insert at the end regarding archbishops and the hierarchy. But while we were consulting with the [French] brothers who are here about the way and means of obtaining unity among all the churches of our confession, they unanimously recommended that the only completely safe and wholly convenient option is for the confessions of faith that have already been accepted and promulgated by the individual provinces to be bound together and compiled into a single harmony, since they are all so similar with respect to the essence of the faith[3] and so that none of the churches might refuse to accept it as their own. When they had commended this suggestion of theirs to us with various arguments, we wrote to you all[4] about it and to the venerable [Zurichers] and to other of our neighboring churches. It was likewise strongly approved by all.[5]

---

2. Zanchi removed names and other identifying markers from this letter. They have been reinserted here in brackets.

3. πίστεως οὐσίαν.

4. That is, presumably, to the Reformed churches of the German Palatinate.

5. Lambert Daneau to Zanchi, May 11, 1580, in *OOT*, 3/8:197–98. Daneau's letter continues: "However, most eminent man, you whose extraordinarily learned writings testify to conspicuous piety and to the loftiest of doctrine and whose reputation is highly renown in the churches, I will not convince you in this way, that a great many things—and how great is the number—are not done by us. Truly, we all esteem you as a father and all the most significant territories reckon you altogether worthy. Therefore, may you be content with what is right and good, which we take up at the insistence of

Thus far the letter of that notable man. We could also bring forward from the letters of many others written about the same matter that are firmly of the same opinion, but since doing so is not necessary, we lay them aside for the sake of brevity.

Therefore, on to the matter at hand.

---

the French ministers and which was first investigated in accordance with your judgment, and understand that we scorn neither you nor your confession." In addition to having been written by Daneau (1535–1590), the letter included salutations from Daniel Tossanus (1541–1602), Zacharias Ursinus (1534–1583), Franciscus Junius (1545–1602), and Theodore Beza (1519–1605).

Zanchi replied to Daneau the following month, noting that, before having been asked to draft a new confession, he himself had preferred and indeed proposed the idea of harmonizing existing confessions (Zanchi to Daneau, June 11, 1580, in OOT, 3/8:198).

An Observation on the Confession as a Whole
When we use the word *condemn*, we do not mean anything other than that we condemn the heresies that the catholic church has condemned. And the things that she has not approved are also disapproved of by us. And we wish this to be our testimony to all posterity.

On Chapter One
Aphorism 4
Insofar as we have assigned the apocryphal books the first place alongside the holy books, after the canonical books, we did this having been led to it by the authority of the Greek and Latin church, which has always considered those books (and only them) to be worthy of the honor of being associated with the canonical books.[6] Furthermore, the discussion was specifically about books, not about writings of every sort. In any case, we prefer the ecumenical creeds to the apocryphal books.

On Chapter Two: God
Aphorism 1
Although the particular characteristic of a subsisting one[7] is to subsist in an essence,[8] nevertheless, when speaking about God, we have inclined for certain reason toward different speech than is commonly used. Principally we do this in order to demonstrate, against the accusations and taunts of the Arians of our times, that the divine essence is not to be found except in the persons. Therefore, we do not teach that the essence is constituted separately from the persons in which the three persons in turn subsist, as if the catholic church imagined four subsisting ones[9] in God.

Aphorism 3
We have ourselves also written a treatise about the real communication of God's essential properties in a book on the words in Philippians 2[:6],

---

6. See the citations of Jerome, Cyprian, and the Council of Laodicea (CCR, 1.5).
7. ὑφιστάμενων.
8. ὑφιστάναι ἐν τῇ οὐσίᾳ.
9. ὑφιστάμενα.

Who although He was in the form of God, that will bear the title *On the Incarnation of the Son of God*.[10] Anyone who wishes for a fuller explication of this doctrine may read that treatise at his leisure. In any event, when the Lord Jesus said that no one knew the Son except the Father and that no one knew the Father except the Son and those to whom the Son chose to reveal Him, He obviously exempted the whole of His created mind from that essential knowledge whereby the Father knew—or, as the scholastics say, *comprehended*—the Son and whereby the Son knew the Father [Matt. 11:27]. He was teaching that whatever knowledge of God creatures have is revealed to them in some fashion. Thus, it is not knowledge about God of the essential and infinite sort but rather of the created and finite sort.[11]

On Chapter Five: The Creation of the World, etc.
Aphorism 2

The heaven of the blessed in which the Lord Jesus is now bodily present differs from the earth and from the rest of the heavens and is beyond all the regular visible heavens. In addition to what has been said already, the following handful of passages also confirm this. Christ is said to have *ascended beyond all the heavens* (Eph. 4[:10]). Elsewhere we read that He has ascended not *beyond* but *into* heaven and that He is seated at the Father's right hand *in* heaven [Eph. 1:20]. So, this heaven is beyond the others and is distinct from them. Thus, the apostle distinguishes the place where Christ is at the right hand of God the Father from the earth. And he calls it *up*: *Seek the things that are up above; set your mind on things that are above, where*[12] *Christ is* (Col. 3[:1–2]). And in 1 Thessalonians 4[:17], he says that the Lord will descend from heaven, that is, into the lower parts, and that all the pious will be caught up into the clouds to meet Christ in the air. Therefore, the

---

10. This work appeared posthumously as *De incarnatione Filii Dei libri duo* (Heidelberg, 1593).

11. Both the 1586 and 1601 Latin editions read "created and infinite [*sic*]," but this is corrected in OOT 3/7:563 to read "created and finite," which is certainly the intended meaning.

12. τὰ ἄνω ζητεῖτε; τὰ ἄνω φρονεῖτε οὗ.

heaven where He resides is elevated. It is not on the earth nor in the air, much less is it everywhere. For He will descend out of the high heaven with the form of a visible body into other regions, so that He might judge the living and the dead in this place. We particularly gave our attention to this heaven in the book *On God's Works Created in Six Days*.[13] Therefore, we reject the contrary doctrine, which does not distinguish heaven from earth or the heaven of the blessed from the other heavens but argues instead that heaven is everywhere.

On Chapter Seven
Aphorism 11
When Augustine asserted and defended original sin, among the things about which Julian the Pelagian taunted him were these: original sin either made God the author of sin, or it made the Devil man's creator, the latter because the Pelagians supposed that, for Augustine, original sin constituted man's very essence. Augustine refuted all these objections in *Against Julian the Pelagian* with these words: *Nor do we ascribe iniquity to God but rather equity because it is not unjust even for infants to suffer punishment with so many and such great evils as we discern all the time. Nor do we ascribe to the Devil the creation of man but rather the corruption of the human race. Nor do we regard sin as the substance but rather as an action in the first men, indeed as a contagion in their posterity. Nor do we regard infants in whom there is neither knowledge nor conscience as having a conscience without knowledge. But he in whom all have sinned knew what he was doing, and everyone draws in evil from there…* (vol. 7, bk. 5, ch. 1[, §3]).[14]

On Chapter Nine
Aphorism 5
We do not see how they who deny that the fathers ate Christ's true flesh can plead an exception for themselves from this error. As if Christ did not appear in God's trustworthy promise because He did not yet actually exist in nature and, hence, could not be laid hold of and eaten by

---

13. This third work of Zanchi's so-called *summa* was published posthumously as *De operibus Dei intra spacium sex dierum creatis* (Neustadt, 1591).
14. vol. 7, bk. 5, ch. 1[, §3]: Augustine, "Answer to Julian," 433 (*FOTC*, 35:242–43).

faith. For it is a general proposition that pertains to all people and all times that *unless you eat the flesh of the Son of Man, you will not have life in you* [John 6:53]. For life is not communicated to any but those who are joined by faith to Christ's flesh, as members to a head, and who are joined by His flesh to the Spirit—or to the Word,[15] which is life.

On Chapter Ten
Aphorism 3
God willed.... What I said about the first, second, third, and fourth estate would have been clearer if I had said: what man was before sin, what he was after sin, what he is under grace, and what he will be in glory.

On Chapter Eleven: Christ the Redeemer
Aphorism 6
To state it carefully, with the scholastics we rightly deny that the person of Christ is truly and properly speaking composed, as it were, of two parts—the immense and most simple divine nature on the one hand and the finite human nature, which is infinitely less than a mere point in comparison to the divine (Aquinas, *Summa theologiae*, III, q. 2, art. 4). For what symmetry is there between the finite and the infinite or the creature and the Creator? Nevertheless, we confess with the ancient fathers that Christ's person can be called composite[16] in that sense in which Scripture says that *the Word*[17] *became flesh* and that *He who was in the form of God* now was *made in the likeness of man* [John 1:14; Phil. 2:6–7]. But this is nothing other than the eternal hypostasis[18] that presently subsists in two natures, such that, even now, Christ is no less true man than He is true God.

What we said earlier about the analogy of the soul and body pertains to this point—namely, that it does not square up at every point. For the human person consists of body and soul as true and essential parts. However, we still approve of this analogy in the same way as

---
15. τῷ λόγῳ.
16. σύνθετον.
17. τὸν λόγον.
18. ὑπόστασις.

Athanasius[19] and other fathers did, who were accustomed to use it to demonstrate the true and hypostatic union of the different natures even if it does not correspond to this mystery in every particular, even as Justin frankly admitted in his *Exposition of the Faith*, as have other fathers.[20]

The ancient fathers, especially Athanasius, often use the analogy of a garment, and it is in harmony with the Scriptures.[21] For the apostle calls Christ's flesh, which concealed His deity, a veil (Heb. 10:20). And most beautifully of all, this garment analogy utterly overthrows the dogma of the real effusion or communication of the divine properties, which some people attempt to demonstrate by way of the analogy of the fiery iron, or even the ensouled body, although they cannot do it.

Aphorism 7
We said that the body and the soul are two things subsisting,[22] and this is apparent in Adam, whose body first subsisted independently. Then a soulish substance also subsisting on its own was added to it. The same thing is also apparent in the separation of the soul from the body, both of which subsist on their own. Again, since they are the essential parts of a man, they are indeed both things subsisting,[23] but they are incomplete. However, when joined together, they constitute one complete subsisting one,[24] that is, a human person. In Christ, on the other hand, the situation is different with relation to the divine and human nature. For the human nature did not in any sense subsist on its own before it was assumed, nor does it subsist on its own after doing so. Rather, the human nature only subsists in the Word, but the Word was always a subsisting one[25] on its own and most perfectly.

---

19. "For as the reasonable soul and flesh is one man: so God and Man is one Christ;" Athanasian Creed, §37 (Schaff, *Creeds*, 2:69).
20. That is, Pseudo-Justin. *PG*, 6:1228C.
21. Athanasius, *De Incarnatione*, in *Contra Gentes and De Incarnatione*, ed. and trans. Robert W. Thomson, Oxford Early Christian Texts (Oxford: Clarendon Press, 1971), 247, 249 (*NPNF2*, 4:60–61).
22. ὑφιστάμενα.
23. ὑφιστάμενα.
24. ὑφιστάμενον.
25. ὑφιστάμενον.

Aphorism 10
Indeed, the image of the sun does not square nearly so well with the image of the glory that will exert its influence upon our bodies, because this glory utterly removes the disgrace of our flesh, but the sun merely obscures the light of a candle without extinguishing it wholly. Nevertheless, the image of the sun emphasizes the particular element that we want, namely, that the light of the candle is rendered utterly useless by its real communication with the air and, hence, is either extinguished or becomes insignificant. However, on account of the hypostatic union, it is certain that the essential properties of Christ's flesh are never altogether removed or diminished in such a way that they serve no use. Yet that would be unavoidable if the human nature really were to partake of divine omnipotence such that it could do whatever God can do. For the Word,[26] the Son of God, has neither assumed nor retained, nor does He now retain, anything in vain. Therefore, the image of the sun effectively confirms what is proved by the image of glory, which removed all disgrace from our bodies.

Aphorism 11
The whole Christ is said to be or do it… Here in the first part is added to Christ's name *the Son of Man*, and in the other part is added *the Son of God* and *God*, in order for us to signify that divine things are predicated of the human Christ and human things of the divine Christ, since it is the very person of Christ that is signified in both cases. For Christ—one and the same person—is the whole God and the whole man, albeit not wholly (as John of Damascus says) inasmuch as He subsists as one and the same person in two distinct natures. The Damascene explains it thus: *And so the whole of Him* (holos[27]) *is perfect God, but He is not entirely* (holon[28]) *God (for He is not only God but also man), and the whole of Him is perfect man, but He is not entirely man (for He is not only man but also God).* The word "entirely" is indicative of nature, whereas "the whole" is

---

26. λόγος.
27. ὅλος. Zanchi gives both the Greek and the transliteration of the Greek in roman script.
28. ὅλον.

indicative of hypostasis ([*On the Orthodox Faith*], bk. 3, ch. 7[, §51]).²⁹ He says *whole*³⁰ against Nestorius; he says *but not entirely*³¹ against Eutyches. However, what we said about Christ's actions—that they are displayed according to either the human or the divine nature, although the one and the same whole Christ is responsible for them—depends upon the previous point because, as the scholastics put it, they are the actions of self-subsisting things³² (or subsisting ones³³). However, the diversity of actions proceeds from the diversity of natures (or forms) by means of which they happen. Thus, since there are two natures in Christ but only one person, it thence also arises that there is only one who acts, two that have capacity for activity, and two activities,³⁴ as that same John of Damascus explains (bk. 3, ch. 15[, §59]).³⁵ Indeed, they are called

---

29. [*On the Orthodox Faith*], bk. 3, ch. 7[, §51]: Zanchi quotes the Greek text: Ὅλος μὲν οὖν ἐστι Θεὸς τέλειος, οὐχ ὅλον δὲ Θεόςρ́ οὐ γὰρ μόνον Θεός, ἀλλὰ καὶ ἄνθρωπόςρ καὶ ὅλος ἄνθρωπος τέλειος, οὐχ ὅλον δὲ ἄνθρωπόςρ οὐ μόνον γὰρ ἄνθρωπος, ἀλλὰ καὶ Θεός. Τὸ μὲν γὰρ ὅλον φύσεως ἐστι παραστατικόν, τὸ ὅλος δὲ ὑποστάσεως, ὥσπερ τὸ μὲν ἄλλο φύσεως, τὸ ἄλλος δὲ ὑποστάσεως. The translation is from John of Damascus, *The Orthodox Faith*, 180 (*NPNF2*, 9:52; *FOTC*, 37:283).

30. ὅλος.

31. οὐχ ὅλον δὲ.

32. Here Zanchi introduces the word *suppositum* for the first time, which is "a substance that is complete in itself and uncommunicated; an ultimate complete subject of its own being." The term conveys essentially the same meaning as hypostasis or subsistence, although hypostasis is sometimes restricted to refer to persons. See Bernard J. Wuellner, *A Dictionary of Scholastic Philosophy*, 1st ed. (Milwaukee, Wis.: Bruce, 1956), 55, 118–19. I take the term "self-subsisting thing" from Muller, *Dictionary*, 348.

Drawing from Nicholas Wolterstorff, O. D. Crisp notes that "medieval ontology was a 'constituent' ontology, according to which objects are composed of various parts (God excepted), which constitute a concrete particular, or given object. A fundamental object in this ontology is a *suppositum*. Yet in the incarnation, we have one entity—the second person of the Trinity—that assumes a human nature that is not a *suppositum* independent of the Word. Unlike other human beings who are also human persons (you and I included), the relevant '*suppositum*' in the case of the incarnation is the Son of God. He is a divine person with a human nature." Martin Davie et al., eds., *New Dictionary of Theology: Historical and Systematic*, 2nd ed. (Downers Grove, Ill.: IVP Academic, 2016), 111.

33. ὑφισταμένων.

34. ἐνεργῶν, δύο ἐνεργετικὰ, καὶ δύο ἐνέργειαι.

35. bk. 3, ch. 15[, §59]: Zanchi distinguishes here between the *actor* (the person of Christ), that which has the capacity for activity (Christ's two natures), and the activities

theandric energies[36] not so much because they are performed by the same agent (who is both God and man[37]) as because both Christ's deity and His humanity concur in the work of our salvation, uniting the actions of each one of His natures with those of the other.[38] And this is the first and primary power of the hypostatic union, namely, that the two natures and their properties and actions are thereby so united in one and the same person that He is God (on account of the form of God in which He has subsisted from eternity) and man (on account of the form of a servant in which He now subsists). He, the whole God, is the whole man, and the whole man is the whole God, and so, the whole is omnipotent and everywhere present, and the whole is powerless and exists in a specific place, and that same whole died, and the whole destroyed death by dying.[39] And, finally, it is as a result of the hypostatic union that not only does

---

(the dual energies or operations that proceed distinctly from the two natures as the work of the one person).

John of Damascus offers the following: "And one should note that activity (*energeia*) is one thing and having a capacity for activity (*energetikon*) is another, and an accomplished act (*energema*) is another, and one who acts (*energon*) is another. Activity, then, is the efficacious and essential movement of nature; that which has a capacity for activity is the nature from which the activity derives; an accomplished act is the result of the activity; one who acts is one who carries out the activity, namely, a hypostasis." *The Orthodox Faith*, 198–99 (NPNF2, 9:60; FOTC, 37:304).

36. θεανδρικά ἐνέργειαι.

37. θεὸς καὶ ἀνήρ.

38. Zanchi continues to follow John of Damascus in *On the Orthodox Faith* (bk. 3, ch. 19, §63): "When we speak of a single theandric activity of Christ, we understand by this the two activities of his two natures, the divine activity of his divinity and the human activity of his humanity." *The Orthodox Faith*, 217 (NPNF2, 9:68; FOTC, 37:323). Muller defines *actiones theandrikai* as "actions or works of Christ that are the common works of both natures or, more precisely, the conjoint work of the divine-human person." *Dictionary*, 7.

39. This is a challenging section to translate, but John of Damascus (bk. 3, ch. 6, §50) again provides some context for Zanchi's statements: "For by no reckoning did the Father and the Holy Spirit participate in the incarnation of God the Word except by good pleasure and will. And we say that the whole of the essence of the Godhead was united with the whole of human nature. For God the Word lacked nothing of what he implanted in our nature when he created us. On the contrary, he assumed all of it, body, intelligent and rational soul, and their properties (for the animal that lacks one of these is not human). For the whole of him assumed the whole of me, and the whole of him was united with the whole of me, that salvation may be granted to the whole, 'for what

the divine nature work to secure, impart, and apply to us salvation, but the human nature cooperates as well.

The second power of the hypostatic union follows from the first: namely, that the hypostatically[40] united human nature became the instrument of the deity (and thus became altogether effectual) for conferring all blessings upon us.

Third, that, on account of this union whereby this lump has been exalted to dignity, we cannot—nor should we—focus the action of our adoration, faith, invocation, and love only on the Son's deity, as was explained in the confession. For the Son Himself is the very person whom we are commanded to adore (Heb. 1[:6]), and we are to believe in Him.

The fourth power of the hypostatic union is that, because this human nature is hypostatically[41] united to the divine nature, therefore, the gifts of God are gathered in Him without measure, as the following aphorism explains [John 3:34].

Aphorism 13[42]
Although, when I was writing this confession, it seemed to me that everything that pertained to this article concerning Christ's person had been covered, nevertheless, I resolved also to add the things that follow to what I previously said, for the sake of further explanation.

1. There is and always was only one person of Christ. For there is only one only begotten Son of God, one and the same Christ.

2. This person, who, from all eternity, by natural generation from the Father, is particularly the person of the Word, but in time, by the grace of the hypostatic union, that person became common to the human nature that was assumed.

---

has not been assumed cannot be healed.'" John of Damascus, *The Orthodox Faith*, 175 (*NPNF2*, 9:50; *FOTC*, 37:280).
   40. καθ' ὑπόστασιν.
   41. καθ' ὑπόστασιν.
   42. This is incorrectly designated "Aphorism 12" in the various early modern editions and translations.

For the essence[43] in the Word,[44] which indeed is held in common with the Father and the Holy Spirit, must be distinguished from the particular mode of subsisting, which distinguishes the Word from the Father and the Holy Spirit as a specific hypostasis[45] (or person). And thus, properly, the Word is called and is the hypostasis[46] and person of the Word.[47]

But as we said, by the grace of the union, the particular eternal hypostasis that was by nature characteristic of the Word[48] was made common to an assumed human nature along with the divine, so that the Word[49] really subsists in this human form[50] no less than in that divine. And for that reason, that thing [that is, the hypostasis of the Word] is no less true and perfect man than true and perfect God. Nevertheless, the natures, properties, and actions of each are preserved and remain distinct.

3. Accordingly, a finite, compound, and very necessary human nature—that is, the mass that consisted of a rational soul and a human body—was assumed into the unity of that immense, utterly simple, most perfect person.

But how? Not in such a way that, for example, it included that infinite person within the limits of its own finite substance or penetrated into the person's infinite expansiveness—expanding itself, as it were. And the same thing as we have said regarding this property ought also to be accepted and believed for all the properties because they all remain unchangeable and unconfounded. Well then, how was the human nature assumed? Indeed, it was assumed in such a way into the unity of that same person that it nevertheless did not become the person itself but

---

43. οὐσία.
44. λόγῳ.
45. ὑπόστασις.
46. ὑπόστασις.
47. τοῦ λόγου.
48. τοῦ λόγου.
49. λόγος.
50. μορφῇ.

rather exists in the person, is born and sustained by the person, and always depends entirely upon the person.

For this union[51] of natures in a hypostatic manner[52] (or the uniting of the hypostasis[53]) happened without alteration, without confusion, and without division.[54]

4. On the basis of these things, it also follows that the assumed nature is not, strictly speaking, a part of this person, as was said above.

For just as no third nature was brought about as a result of the union of the two natures, so neither is a new person—one that would be Christ's own and would differ from the person of the Word,[55] which is the very Word[56]—composed, as it were, as a result of the assumption of the human nature into the unity of the divine person. For the person is altogether the same and does not differ from itself except in this: that which was subsisting only in the form of God[57] and was only God now also subsists in the form of a servant and is man. And previously, the person was, as it were, an unveiled king, but it is now clothed with our flesh, as with a purple robe. For this reason, the fathers were not wrong

---

51. ἕνωσις.
52. καθ' ὑπόστασιν.
53. εἰς ἑνότητα τῆς ὑποστάσεως.
54. ἀτρέπτως, ἀσυγχύτως, ἀδιαιρέτως. These adverbs were part of the classic description of the unity of the divine and human natures in Christ as confessed in the Chalcedonian Formula, which stated that the two natures in Christ are united "without confusion, without change, without division, without separation." They first appear in Cyril of Alexandria's letter to Succensus (ep. 45.6): "We unite the Word from God the Father without confusion, without change, and without alteration to holy flesh owning mental life in a manner inexpressible and surpassing understanding, and confess one Son, Christ and Lord, the self-same God and man, not a diverse pair but one and the same being and being seen to be both things…. [We] do not damage the concurrence into unity by declaring it was effected out of two natures; however, after the union we do not divide the natures from each other and do not sever the one and indivisible into two sons but say 'one Son' and, as the fathers have put it, 'one incarnate nature of the Word.'" Cyril of Alexandria, *Select Letters*, trans. Lionel R. Wickham, Oxford Early Christian Texts (Oxford: Clarendon Press, 1983), 75–77 (FOTC, 76:192). See Aaron Riches, *Ecce Homo: On the Divine Unity of Christ*, Interventions (Grand Rapids: Eerdmans, 2016), 60–61.
55. τοῦ λόγου.
56. λόγος.
57. μορφῇ τοῦ θεοῦ.

to say that the person is now (in a certain manner) composite. But above all, note this difference: a robe does not pertain to a king's essence, but the human nature in Christ is so constituted that what Christ is cannot now be asserted without it.

5. This is the reason on account of which the assumed human nature is to be considered and acknowledged as part of Christ's person, as it were. Namely, because it was assumed into the unity of His person, that, just as the Word[58] with this human flesh is called and is man, so also this flesh in the Word[59] and with God the Word[60] is called and is God, as Athanasius, Gregory of Nazianzus, John of Damascus, and other fathers teach on the basis of the Holy Scriptures. For that flesh is not God by nature but rather by hypostasis,[61] and in that sense the flesh is also omnipotent and ubiquitous. This is the reason why the honor that is owed to the Word[62] by faith ought to be paid also to the flesh in the Word[63] and on account of the Word,[64] because the hypostasis[65] of both natures is one and the same.

6. Moreover, for the sake of further explanation, add to this that, wherever the Word[66] is—which is everywhere—He is there not only as God but also as man, because the Word has united the human nature to Himself hypostatically.[67] Nevertheless, it is not the case that the Word exhibits Himself as a hypostasis[68] in all circumstances. Rather, the Word does so only where the human nature is present, such that the human nature is sustained, born up, and directed by the divine nature.

---

58. λόγος.
59. λόγῳ.
60. λόγῳ.
61. ὑπόστασις.
62. λόγῳ.
63. λόγῳ.
64. λόγον.
65. ὑπόστασις.
66. λόγος.
67. καθ' ὑπόστασιν.
68. ὑπόστασιν.

For how can we say that the human nature is sustained somewhere that it is not present? Feet are not sustained by a mind where the mind is, since the mind is in the head, but only where the feet are. When the flesh was in the virgin's womb, the Word[69] united to that flesh hypostatically[70] was not sustaining it outside of Mary's womb. Rather, only in the womb was there a hypostasis[71] for it [that is, for the flesh] of the sort that sustained the flesh there but nowhere else. The same thing must be said about Christ's whole subsequent life, since He dwelt in various places. After death also, the hypostasis[72] was with the dead and buried flesh, sustaining it in itself—but where? Certainly, it was not sustaining the flesh in heaven, where it was not. Rather, the hypostasis was sustaining it in the grave, just as, by contrast, the hypostasis was also with the soul, being separate from the body, similarly sustaining it not in but outside of the grave. And now it sustains both together—body and soul—in heaven, not on earth, and much less everywhere.

7. It does not follow from this doctrine that the personal union is weakened. Nor does it follow that the personal union becomes such that, with regard to the flesh, the hypostasis[73] is not the whole person but only part of it.[74] The reason is because, just as the person of the Word[75] is infinite, so it is also most simple. And thus, the whole person is the hypostasis[76] with regard to the flesh itself, wherever it exists. And elsewhere, where the flesh does not exist, the whole person is the hypostasis[77] as well, existing in the form of God. Certainly, as was said previously, with regard to the head, the whole mind is the hypostasis[78]—making it alive

---

69. λόγος.
70. καθ' ὑπόστασιν.
71. ὑπόστασις.
72. ὑπόστασις.
73. ὑπόστασις.
74. For some of the patristic context from which Zanchi is drawing this language, see John of Damascus, *The Orthodox Faith*, 233 (bk. 4, ch. 5, §78; NPNF2, 9:76; FOTC, 37:339–40).
75. λόγου.
76. ὑπόστασις.
77. ὑπόστασις.
78. ὑπόστασις.

and sustaining it. But where specifically? Not in every part of the body but only in the part where the head itself is. And with regard to the feet, the head is altogether beyond the hypostasis,[79] which also sustains them—indeed, not where the head is but rather where the feet themselves are. So, is the union of the mind with the head weakened as a consequence of the fact that the whole hypostasis is in the feet, which is beyond the head?

8. Finally, I add to this once again everything that has been discussed concerning the personal union, that they might be explained more clearly.

The soul is the hypostasis[80] to the eyes, but what sort of eyes? This sort: the kind, as it were, that are accommodated to seeing and not to hearing. Conversely, the soul is the hypostasis to the sort of ears that are for hearing and not for seeing. So, the Word[81] was the hypostasis[82] to the human nature not for destroying death, which is characteristic of the Word,[83] but for fully enduring death, which is characteristic of the flesh.

In short, the Word is not the hypostasis[84] to the flesh so that the flesh might be what the Word is or so that it might be the same sort of thing as the Word. Rather, the Word is the hypostasis to the flesh so that the flesh might be what it is and so that it might be the sort of thing as it is itself, whether that happens by nature or by the real introduction of a grace (which they call infused or habitual) to the flesh. For the grace of this union is that the flesh is assumed into this unity of the person.

This same doctrine of ours is confirmed on the basis of what both the Holy Scriptures and the fathers taught concerning the office of the Mediator, that is, concerning the purpose of the incarnation.

Many purposes for this incarnation are noted by the fathers in the Scriptures, especially by Anselm in the book he entitled *Why the God-Man?* But the principle and most immediate purpose was not simply so

---

79. ὑπόστασις.
80. ὑπόστασις.
81. λόγος.
82. ὑπόστασις.
83. λόγου.
84. ὑπόστασις.

that God the Word[85] might save us (for He could have accomplished that by His omnipotence and simply by decree without taking on flesh) but so that, in a very specific way, He would save us from death by the particular death of His person and call us back to life by its particular resurrection. This accords with what the apostle says to the Hebrews, *That by means of death He might destroy him* (Heb. 2:14). And, *who destroyed death and brought life and light* (2 Tim. 1:10).

The ancient church agrees with these things, saying that He destroyed death by dying and restored life by rising again.[86] Leo I expressed this purpose, saying that the Son of God took on our flesh in order that He might die in the one nature and not die in the other [Leo's *Tome*, ep. 28.3].[87] Therefore, this is the principal purpose for which He took on flesh: in order to do by means of His flesh what He could not furnish of Himself in the form of God—suffering and dying, for example—for the sake of accomplishing so great a salvation for us. For, on His own, He could have simply killed death, but He could not have killed death by means of death without having assumed mortal flesh into the unity of His person. Therefore, the Word[88] did not take on flesh in order that, by the flesh, He might perform actions characteristic of it but so that He might be effectual toward the completion of the work:[89] our salvation, specifically accomplished by His characteristic actions conjoined with the actions of our flesh.[90]

---

85. λόγος.

86. From the liturgy of the early church as transmitted through the sacramentary of Gregory I (*PL*, 78:92B). In the Reformation era, it was incorporated into the 1560 English *Book of Common Prayer* by Thomas Cranmer as part of the Easter liturgy.

87. [Leo's *Tome*, ep. 28.3]: The context in which Leo makes this comment is worth quoting: "In this preservation, then, of the real quality of both natures, both being united in one person, lowliness was taken on by majesty, weakness by strength, mortality by the immortal. And in order to pay the debt of our fallen state, inviolable nature was united to one capable of suffering so that (and this is the sort of reparation we needed) one and the same mediator between God and men, the man Jesus Christ, could die in the one nature and not die in the other." *Letters*, 95–96 (*NPNF2*, 12:40).

88. λόγος.

89. ἀποτέλεσμα.

90. Muller notes that the term ἀποτέλεσμα was "used by the fathers with reference to the hypostatic union...and the cooperation of the two natures. It figures...generally in

On Chapter Twelve
Aphorism 8
With regard to our true and essential union and the union of our flesh with Christ's flesh, the most notable passage is that of Cyril of Alexandria's *Commentary on John* (bk. 10, ch. 13 [that is, bk. 2], col. 500):[91]

> Nor do we deny that we are directly united to Christ spiritually by faith, and by sincere love. Certainly, however, we flatly deny that there is no way in which we are united to Him according to the flesh, and we say that that is altogether foreign to the divine Scriptures. For who has doubted even that Christ is the vine and we the branches in such a way that we obtain life for ourselves from Him? Listen to what Paul says: *For we are all one body with Christ. For although we are many, nevertheless we are one in Him, for we all participate in one bread* [Rom. 12:5; 1 Cor. 10:17]. Or perhaps someone supposes that we are ignorant of the power of that mystical blessing?[92] When we do it, does it not also cause Christ to dwell in us corporeally by the communication of His flesh? For why are the members of the faithful Christ's members? *Do you not know,* he writes, *that your members are Christ's members? Shall I then make Christ's members the members of a prostitute? Far be it* [1 Cor. 6:15]. The Savior likewise said, *He who eats My flesh and drinks My blood remains in Me, and I in Him* [John 6:56]. For this reason, we should take into consideration not only the disposition—whereby Christ is understood to be in us by means of love—but also

---

both the Lutheran and Reformed doctrines of Christ's work, which is viewed as brought to completion through the cooperation of the natures: in the case of the Reformed, by special gifts of divine grace." *Dictionary*, 35.

91. bk. 10, ch. 13 [that is, bk. 2], col. 500: Zanchi quotes without error from George of Trebizond's fifteenth-century Latin translation of Cyril's *Commentary on John* as published in *Operum divi Cyrilli Alexandrini tomi quatuor* (Basil, 1546), cols. 500–501. The modern translation of the commentary, which is based on the critical edition of the text prepared by P. E. Pusey in 1872, includes some additional material that was not in the edition used by Zanchi. However, the additional material does not meaningfully alter Cyril's message as conveyed by George of Trebizond through Zanchi. See Cyril of Alexandria, *Commentary on John*, ed. Joel C. Elowsky, trans. David R. Maxwell, Ancient Christian Texts (Downers Grove, Ill.: IVP Academic, 2015), 2:xxi.

92. Elowsky notes that "blessing" here refers to the Eucharist. Cyril of Alexandria, *Commentary on John*, 2:214n92.

natural participation. For just as if someone were to mix together wax melted by fire with other similarly molten wax so thoroughly that one thing seemed to have been made out of the two, in the same way Christ is in us, and we are in Him, by communication of His body and blood. For there was no other way for this corruptible natural body to be transferred to incorruptibility and life than for a body of natural life to be united to it.

If you will not take my word for it, I beseech you to put your faith in Christ: *Truly, truly,* He said, *I tell you that unless you eat the flesh of the Son of Man and drink His blood, you will not have life in yourselves. He who eats My flesh and drinks My blood has eternal life, and I will raise him up at the last day* [John 6:53–54]. You hear Him declaring clearly that we shall not have life unless we have drunk His blood and eaten His flesh. Moreover, He says *in yourselves*, that is, in your body. But life can be rightly understood to be this flesh of life, for this revives us on the last day, and I will not hesitate to explain how.[93] The flesh of life, having become the flesh of the Only Begotten, was transferred unto the power of life; thus, He could not be overcome by death.[94] Wherefore, life having been made in us, He expels destruction from us. For the only begotten Son of God is not absent from the flesh. Hence, it is because He is one with His flesh that He said, *I will raise Him up* [John 6:54].

Why deny then that it is according to the flesh that we are called branches?[95] Is it not more consistent to say that the vine is

---

93. This cryptic sentence is somewhat clarified by the modern translation of the sentence in Cyril's *Commentary*. Maxwell renders it, "And 'eternal life' is quite rightly understood to be the flesh of life, that is, of the Only Begotten. How or in what way this raises us on the last day, you must surely hear…" Cyril of Alexandria, *Commentary on John*, 2:214.

94. Here the modern translation of Cyril suggests a slightly different idea: "Since flesh came to belong to life, that is, to the Word who shines forth from God the Father, *the flesh was transformed with the power of life*, and it is impossible that life should be conquered by death" [emphasis added]. Cyril of Alexandria, *Commentary on John*, 2:214.

95. Cyril here challenges those (Nestorians) who claimed that, when Jesus called Himself "the vine" in John 6, He did so specifically and only with reference to His divinity. The modern translation provides additional detail: "Why, then, does the heretic utter such vain foolishness, claiming that we have been united in fellowship with him not corporeally but by faith and by a disposition of love according to the law, and that Christ

His humanity and that we are the branches on account of having the same nature? For a vine and its branches are of the same nature. Thus, both spiritually and corporeally, we are the branches, and Christ is the vine.[96]

In this whole sequence, Cyril's objective was to demonstrate that Christ is the vine, not only according to His deity (as his Nestorian adversaries preferred) but also according to His flesh, from whom life flows into us as branches. And thus, he also intended to demonstrate that, as branches, we are grafted not only onto His deity but also onto His humanity and, indeed, onto His flesh. And thus, we derive all spiritual life and vitality not only from His deity but also from His flesh. And the reason behind this derives from the hypostatic union, which causes the Word,[97] having assumed the flesh into His unity, to be nothing other than one person, one and the same Christ, and one and the same vine. Therefore, since we are also united to His flesh, we cannot be joined to Christ's deity, nor can we derive life from it, unless we derive life from His flesh as well.

In order to explain this real and intimate binding of our flesh with Christ's flesh, Cyril turns to the analogy of the wax, not, of course, because it is a perfect analogy but because it aptly depicts our fellowship[98] with Christ not as incidental[99] but as real and substantial. And in his conclusion, Cyril indicates this when he says we are united to Christ not merely spiritually but also corporeally—that is, not only with respect to the Spirit but also with respect to the body.[100] And Christ is the vine, and we are the branches. Therefore, Cyril is not arguing about the manner whereby we are joined to Christ—whether that be spiritually or corporeally; rather, he is arguing about the things that are joined, namely,

---

did not call his flesh the 'vine' but his divine nature?" Cyril of Alexandria, *Commentary on John*, 2:215.

96. Cyril of Alexandria, *Commentary on John*, 2:214–15.
97. λόγος.
98. κοινωνίαν.
99. σχετικὴν.
100. Referencing the end of the lengthy passage previously quoted. Cyril of Alexandria, *Commentary on John*, 2:215.

that not only are our souls (or spirits) united in the most intimate way possible with Christ's Spirit and soul but so too our flesh with His flesh. This is clear from the opponents' case, against which Cyril argues that we are united with Christ by the flesh (col. 500B [that is, 501B]).[101]

Therefore, for Cyril, the adverbs *spiritually* and *corporeally* did not indicate the manner whereby we are united to Christ the Branch but the things that are united, as was said and explained. However, it is that same Cyril's fixed determination that the manner is also spiritual, that is, by means of our faith and by means of Christ's Spirit. For everywhere in his commentary—and especially in John 6—he teaches that we eat Christ's flesh by faith, and it is on the basis of this eating that Cyril demonstrates our incorporation.

On Chapter Thirteen
Aphorism 7
Someone might take an exception on this point with regard to the law and ask whether, in the Old Testament, the elect were granted grace to keep the law just as, in the New Testament, we are granted grace to believe the gospel. I respond: They were granted grace, but when they heard the law, they were not granted grace in the same way as we are granted grace when we hear the gospel with faith. Rather, they were granted grace because they had first believed the gospel promises regarding Christ. Thus, they received the gift of keeping the law (albeit incompletely and only in part) not because they had heard the law but because they had believed in Christ who was to come, in order that obedience to the law might always follow upon faith in Christ as an effect following upon its cause.

On Chapter Fourteen
Aphorism 1
We say that the received meaning of a sacrament is that neither word nor element on its own is called a sacrament but rather that a sacrament is an element together with the word. When we say that, we only mean that, just as the word alone, without the element or sign, cannot be called

---

101. col. 500B [that is, 501B]: The reference is again to *Operum divi Cyrilli Alexandrini tomi quatuor*, col. 501.

a sacrament, so neither can the sign be called a sacrament without the word. For, according to the church's usual definition, the sacrament is a visible sign of invisible grace (and moreover) from the word. That is, it is consecrated to that purpose on the basis of Christ's institution—transferred from a profane use unto this holy purpose.

Thus, Augustine: *Therefore, a visible sacrifice is a sacrament or sacred sign of an invisible sacrifice* (*The City of God*, vol. 5, bk. 10, ch. 5).[102] And in Gratian's *Decretum* "On Consecration," he says, *A sacrament is an invisible grace in visible form* (dist. 2, case 32, "Sacrifice").[103]

And again, with regard to the word of the gospel, Augustine says, *The word comes to the element, and it becomes the sacrament itself, even a visible word, as it were* (*Homilies on the Gospel of John*, vol. 9[, §80.3]).[104] And for what purpose? Invisible grace. But whence does it happen that it signifies such a thing? From the word of Christ the Institutor. For if Christ's word is eliminated, the thing would not be a sacrament. Augustine says, *Remove the word, and what will the water be but water?*[105] This is the meaning of our words: not that the word is the sacrament or, properly speaking, part of the sacrament (given that a sacrament is defined as a visible sign of invisible grace) but that, without the word, the visible element cannot be the visible sign of an invisible thing. This is the reason why it is the visible sign of an invisible thing: because the word of the Lord established it for this.

Irenaeus also, without mentioning the word *sacrament* (but always presupposing it), wrote that the Eucharist—meaning, the sacrament of the Eucharist—consists of two things: *an earthly thing* (that is, the sign) *and a heavenly thing* (that is, the thing signified).[106] Yet, neither the thing signified nor the sign is the sacrament. But because there can be no sign

---

102. *The City of God, vol. 5, bk. 10, ch. 5*: Augustine, *The City of God: Books VIII–XVI*, 123 (*NPNF2*, 2:183).

103. (dist. 2, case 32, "Sacrifice"): Gratian, *Corpus iuris canonici*, 2:1324.

104. *Homilies on the Gospel of John, vol. 9[, §80.3]*: Augustine, *Homilies on the Gospel of John 41–124*, 287 (*NPNF1*, 7:344).

105. Augustine, *Homilies on the Gospel of John 41–124*, 287 (*NPNF1*, 7:344).

106. Irenaeus, *Against Heresies*, in *ANF*, 1:486 (bk. 4, ch. 18.5): "Bread, which is produced from the earth, when it receives the invocation of God, is no longer common bread, but the Eucharist, consisting of two realities, earthly and heavenly."

without the thing signified (for, otherwise, of what would it be a sign?), Irenaeus therefore says that the sacrament of the Eucharist consists of both an earthly thing (that is, the sign) and a heavenly thing (that is, the thing signified). These are pertinent to the corroboration of what we said about the word and the element.

On Chapter Fifteen: Baptism
Aphorism 3
The point about the water is evident from Acts, where it is manifestly apparent that nothing was ever added to the water by the apostles. Christ instituted no specific mode of baptizing other than the one that we have from Matthew 28. Moreover, it is beyond controversy that the apostles simply obeyed Christ. Therefore, insofar as we read in Acts that some were baptized by the apostles *in the name* or *into the name* of Christ, that has no bearing at all upon the Christian form of baptism [Acts 2:38; 8:12–16; 19:5].

Indeed, it is understood that John the Baptist was baptizing into the name of the Christ.[107] As Ambrose explains, however, John was tacitly indicating the Trinity by using that name: the person anointed (that is, the Son according to His assumed nature), the person anointing (that is, the Father), and the Anointing (that is, the person of the Holy Spirit) [*On the Holy Spirit*, bk. 1, ch. 3, §44].[108] Yet, it was Christ who expressed

---

107. During the Reformation and post-Reformation era, Reformed theologians generally agreed that John's baptism was essentially identical to Christian baptism, in opposition to Rome, Anabaptists, Arminians, and others. See, for example, Calvin, *Institutes*, 4.15.7–8; Johannes Wollebius, *Compendium theologiae christianae*, Editio nova prioribus correctior (London, 1760), 115 (bk. 1, ch. 23, §21); Turretin, *Institutes of Elenctic Theology*, 3:398–403 (topic 19, q. 16); Mastricht, *Theoretico-practica theologia*, 921–22 (bk. 7, ch. 4, §17); and Campegius Vitringa, *Doctrina christianae religionis, per aphorismos summatim descripta*, 6th ed. (Arnheim, 1761), 7:52–63 (ch. 24, §21).

108. [*On the Holy Spirit*, bk. 1, ch. 3, §44]: Ambrose, *Theological and Dogmatic Works*, trans. Roy J. Deferrari, Fathers of the Church 44 (Washington, D.C.: Catholic University of America Press, 2002), 50–51 (NPNF2, 10:99). The title "Christ" is, of course, the Greek translation of the Old Testament "messiah," that is, "anointed one."

The passage in *On the Holy Spirit* that precedes the one cited here helps to clarify Zanchi's point. Ambrose argues as follows regarding the Ephesian men in Acts 19 who told the apostle Paul that they had been baptized by John the Baptist: "And those who denied that they knew the Holy Spirit, although they said that they were baptized in the

the proper form of baptism when He said, *in the name of the Father, of the Son, and of the Holy Spirit* [Matt. 28:19]. For this reason, it is obvious that this expression—being baptized *in the name of Christ*—has absolutely nothing to do with the form of Christian baptism. This is also confirmed by the fact that, when you read about the apostles baptizing some particular person, you never read that they baptized, saying that they were baptizing him *into Christ's name*. Instead, we just read of many having been baptized *in the name* or *into the name* of Christ.[109]

So, what does the Holy Spirit mean by this expression? In my opinion, He certainly meant to indicate the following things in a brief way: first, those who had professed faith in Christ were enjoined to be baptized, and this was to be done in the name and authority and by the command of Jesus Christ. Indeed, it was even on the basis of Christ's command that they were baptized according to this form (that is, in the name of the Father, of the Son, and of the Holy Spirit). Thus, let them be baptized in the name of Christ, according to the command and form that Christ ordered.

Second, those who were thus baptized were already incorporated into Christ by faith and received into the fellowship of the new covenant in God's sight. They were, then, set apart by this new covenant sign unto Christ in the sight of the whole church and sealed for the preservation

---

baptism of John, were baptized afterwards, because John baptized unto the remission of sins in the name of the coming Jesus, not in his own name. And so they did not know the Spirit, because they had not received baptism in the name of Christ, as John was accustomed to baptize. For John, although he did not baptize in the Spirit, nevertheless preached both Christ and the Spirit. Then when he was asked whether perchance he himself was the Christ, he replied: 'I baptize you in water, but He will come stronger than I, whose shoes I am not worthy to carry; He will baptize you in the Holy Spirit and in fire.' These, therefore, because they had not been baptized in the name of Christ nor with the faith of the Holy Spirit, were not able to receive the sacrament of baptism. And so they were baptized in the name of Jesus Christ, and baptism was not repeated among these, but was received for the first time; for there is one baptism." Ambrose, *Theological and Dogmatic Works*, 49 (*NPNF2*, 10:98).

109. The distinction that Zanchi appears to be drawing here is that between describing a person as having been baptized in (or into) the name of Jesus (which we do find in the New Testament) versus a description of someone saying, "I baptize you in the name of Jesus (only)," which we do not find in the New Testament.

of their faith in Him and the fulfillment of their obedience to His commands. And by it they were grafted onto the body of His church and thus were received into the communion of the saints and unto perpetual repentance and uninterrupted faith in Jesus Christ to the end of their life. For the whole church and each of the faithful have been baptized into Christ's death and buried with Him, the symbol of which is that same plunging into water [Rom. 6:3–4]. From this we are to understand that, throughout our entire life, we are to die to sin and live to righteousness [1 Peter 2:24; Rom. 6:11]. This is what it is truly to be baptized in the name of Christ, the one who died and was buried for our sake.

Aphorism 4
Also, the substance of the law—even the ceremonial law—is perpetual and so must always be retained. For Christ did not come in order to destroy the law or the prophets with respect to the substance of their teaching. Moreover, it pertains to the substance of the law with regard to circumcision that they who are in the covenant are also sealed to God by the sign of the covenant. But the sign of the new covenant is baptism, which takes the place of circumcision (Col. 2[:11–12]).

Add to this Acts 2:38[–39] where Peter says, *Repent and be baptized each one of you in the name of Jesus Christ for the remission of your sins, and you shall receive the gift of the Holy Spirit. For the promise was made to you and to your children and to all who are far off, namely, to whomsoever the Lord our God shall call.* Therefore, the promise of salvation through Christ pertains to *whomsoever*. Baptism likewise pertains to them. Yet Peter teaches that the promise also pertains to the children of the faithful. Infants, therefore, are to be baptized.

Aphorism 6
When we said that Paul baptized anew those in Acts 19 as though they had not been properly baptized, we said it without prejudice to other interpreters, for we condemn no one. Only we beg the reader to understand the word *rebaptizing* in a favorable way. For we do not take it to mean that those who had been properly baptized were later rebaptized. Rather, Paul later taught the true and sound doctrine of Christ as God to those who had not been baptized with a true baptism—namely, one preceded

by true teaching about God the Father, Son, and Holy Spirit. Only then did they also receive true baptism. And after baptism, they received, by the laying on of hands, the Holy Spirit Himself and His gifts. Properly speaking, this was not rebaptism; rather, it was being truly baptized.

But the reason why I saw it in that way and why I continue to understand it in the same way is that I was persuaded by the authority of the fathers—especially Ambrose and Jerome—who interpreted this passage thus. I was also persuaded by a consideration derived from the text itself.

As far as authority goes: first, none of the fathers ever taught that the words *having heard these things, they were baptized*[110] were the words of Paul referring to those who had heard John the Baptist [Acts 19:5]. Rather, all of them interpreted these as Luke's comments about those who heard Paul. Thus: Chrysostom's *Homilies on the Acts of the Apostles* (vol. 3, hom. 40);[111] Oecumenius's *On Acts* (ch. 19);[112] Augustine's *Against Petilian* (ch. 7 [that is, bk. 2, §37, 85–86]);[113] Gregory's *Forty Gospel Homilies* (vol. 1, hom. 20 [that is, hom. 6]);[114] Bede's *Commentary on the Acts of the Apostles* (ch. 19);[115] and all the others.

---

110. ἀκούσαντες δὲ ἐβαπτίσθεσαν.

111. vol. 3, hom. 40: *NPNF1*, 11:247.

112. ch. 19: *PG*, 118:199–204. In the sixteenth century, the work that Zanchi cites here was widely regarded as having been written by one Oecumenius, who was probably an early sixth-century layman of high imperial rank and the author of an extant commentary on the book of Revelation. However, the name Oecumenius does not appear in any of the manuscripts of the catena-style commentary on Acts referenced here. Although the work cited here incorporates many explanatory comments (or *scholia*) from patristic commentators, it was more likely composed by a much later author. See William C. Weinrich, "Translator's Introduction," in *Greek Commentaries on Revelation*, by Oecumenius and Andrew of Caesarea, ed. Thomas C. Oden, trans. William C. Weinrich, Ancient Christian Texts (Downers Grove, Ill.: IVP Academic, 2011), xxiii–xxiv and Emanuele Scieri, "The Catena Manuscripts on Acts: A Revised Classification," *Vigiliae Christianae* 76, no. 3 (June 2022): 281–305, doi: 10.1163/15700720-bja10042.

113. ch. 7 [that is, bk. 2, §37, 85–86]: Augustine, *The Donatist Controversy*, 1:117 (*NPNF1*, 4:552).

114. vol. 1, hom. 20 [that is, hom. 6]: Gregory the Great, *Forty Gospel Homilies*, trans. David Hurst, Cistercian Studies Series 123 (Kalamazoo, Mich.: Cistercian Publications, 1990), 36–37.

115. ch. 19: Bede, *Commentary on the Acts of the Apostles*, trans. Lawrence T. Martin, Cistercian Studies Series 117 (Kalamazoo, Mich.: Cistercian Publications, 1989), 153–54.

Second, most of these authors wrote expressly that those twelve disciples were either baptized by Paul or at least baptized at his command because, previously, they had not been baptized in a proper way inasmuch as they had not heard about the doctrine of the Holy Spirit nor been baptized in His name. In his *On the Holy Spirit*, Ambrose wrote to Emperor Theodosius:

> Finally, the very ones who had said, *We have not heard whether there is a Holy Spirit*, were afterward baptized in the name of the Lord Jesus Christ. And this abounded unto grace, for by Paul's preaching they now knew the Holy Spirit. Nor should it seem contradictory. Because, although the Spirit subsequently goes unmentioned, He was nevertheless believed in, and what had gone unmentioned in word was expressed by faith. For when he said, *In the name of our Lord Jesus Christ*, the mystery is fulfilled by the unity of the name. Nor is the Spirit separated from Christ's baptism, for John baptized unto repentance; Christ baptized in the Spirit (vol. 2, ch. 3 [that is, bk. 1, ch. 3.42–43]).[116]

In his *Commentary on Joel*, Jerome wrote:

> Therefore, the salvation of God cannot appear unless the Holy Spirit is poured out. And everyone who says he believes in Christ but does not believe in the Holy Spirit does not have the eyes of perfect faith. Hence, also, in the Acts of the Apostles, those who had been baptized with John's baptism into Him who was to come (that is, in the name of the Lord Jesus) are baptized again because they responded to Paul's questioning by saying, *But we do not know whether there even is a Holy Spirit*. Or rather, they now received true baptism because, without the Holy Spirit and the mystery of the Trinity, whatever is received into one person or another is incomplete (vol. 6, ch. 2, p. 66 [that is, ch. 2, §28–32a]).[117]

---

116. vol. 2, ch. 3 [that is, bk. 1, ch. 3.42–43]: Ambrose, *Theological and Dogmatic Works*, 50 (*NPNF2*, 10:98).

117. vol. 6, ch. 2, p. 66 [that is, ch. 2, §28–32a]: Jerome, *Commentaries on the Twelve Prophets*, trans. Thomas P. Scheck, Ancient Christian Texts (Downers Grove, Ill.: IVP Academic, 2017), 2:288.

In *Against Petilian*, Augustine concludes that those twelve men must have been baptized by Paul either because they had lied about having received John's baptism or because, if they had received John's baptism, they nevertheless had not received Christ's baptism (ch. 7[, §9], col. 498).[118] For, along with Cyprian, Tertullian, and other fathers, Augustine thinks that John's baptism differs from Christ's baptism. More will be said about this later.

Furthermore, from our own ranks, the very learned Wolfgang Musculus agrees with Ambrose's opinion on Acts 19 in his *Common Places*, in the section on baptism.[119] We will not quote his words here because he discusses this topic at some length.

And before Musculus, Bucer wrote on both Matthew 3 and Ephesians 4. In his commentary on Matthew, we read these words:

> We read in Acts 19 what Paul said to the Ephesians who had been baptized in John's baptism but who did not understand what it was (for as yet they were ignorant of the Holy Spirit). At that time, he had proclaimed that Christ must baptize them: *John indeed baptized with a baptism of repentance,* telling the people that *they should believe in Him who was to come after him, that is, in Christ Jesus.*
>
> Now, do we—or should we—do anything else when we perform a baptism? Certainly, our baptism is one of repentance, provided that we bury in Christ's death those whom we baptize, that is, that we reckon them among that number which must die unto sin and live unto righteousness for the whole of their lives. Nevertheless, they do not receive even that except as Christ's gift. This is why we require faith in Christ from the adults whom we baptize, and it is why we commend the infants who are being brought up in the faith to the church. Therefore, Paul would never have rebaptized those Ephesians if they had been baptized by John's baptism into repentance and the faith of Christ (that is, the baptism with which it was his custom to baptize). Paul, however, baptized them after explaining what John's baptism was and how John had baptized

---

118. ch. 7[, §9], col. 498: CSEL 53:10; PL 43:599–600.

119. Wolfgang Musculus, *Loci communes in usus sacrae theologiae candidatorum parati* (Basil, 1560), 420–21. For an English translation, see *Common places of Christian religion* (London, 1563), fols. 283v–84r.

into Christ, since, as Luke recalled, they had only been baptized in John's baptism, but, for all that, they had misunderstood what it was, being wholly ignorant of Christ's baptism (that is, the baptism of the Spirit). Paul did not baptize them into a baptism of his own, as if that could save anyone.

Hence, Paul baptized them in Christ's name with John's own baptism (that is, the baptism with which it was John's custom to baptize). And thereupon, with hands laid on them, he also baptized them with Christ's baptism, that is, with the Holy Spirit. For the Holy Spirit immediately came upon them as we read in that passage.[120]

And in his commentary on the fourth chapter of the letter to the Ephesians, that same Bucer wrote these words:

Here and elsewhere, it is evident that those twelve Ephesian men (who did not know whether there was a Holy Spirit and whom Paul baptized) had not been baptized with John's baptism—that is, with the baptism that John administered. Rather, as they themselves testified concerning it, they had been baptized in John's baptism. For John preached to everyone whom he baptized that Christ would baptize them with the Holy Spirit, and he urged them unto this that they might believe and receive the Holy Spirit from Him. On account of this, these Ephesians could not have been ignorant of the Holy Spirit if they had been baptized by John with the baptism that truly can be called John's baptism.

The apostle's words to those men also adequately indicate this. Certainly, John baptized with a baptism of repentance, telling the people that they should believe in the One who would come after him, that is, in Christ. For with these words, he intended to teach that they who were as yet unfamiliar with John's preaching about Christ and the promise had not received John's baptism.[121]

Thus, since the fathers interpreted that passage in Acts 19 in the

---

120. Martin Bucer, *Enarrationes perpetuae in sacra quatuor Evangelia* (Strasbourg, 1530), fol. 19v.

121. Martin Bucer, *Praelectiones in epistolam ad Ephesios* (Basil, 1562), 144E.

way that we have just explained, I wonder: who am I that I would dare or that I should contradict so many learned men who held to that interpretation of this passage of Scripture, an interpretation that does no violence to the context, that opposes neither other passages of Scripture nor the analogy of faith, and that brings along with it no absurdities?

For if someone were to offer a textual objection, I respond that the words *indeed*[122] and *but*[123] in no way prevail against this patristic interpretation, since it is not unusual for the apostle to avoid the adversative *but*[124] after having used *indeed*[125] (Rom. 3:2; Col. 2:23; etc.).[126] And Luke implied another *but*[127] for this *indeed*,[128] which he left out for the sake of conciseness, as we will demonstrate shortly. For this reason, it is

---

122. μέν.
123. δέ.
124. δέ.
125. μέν.
126. Zanchi's argument is difficult to follow here, in part because it is quite elliptical and in part because he is working with a version of the Greek text that includes the particle μέν in Acts 19:4: "Then Paul said, 'John indeed [μέν] baptized with a baptism of repentance, saying to the people that they should believe on Him who would come after him, that is, on Christ Jesus'" (see Acts 1:5). The word μέν is not included in most modern editions of the Greek New Testament.

Furthermore, Zanchi argues that Acts 19:4 implies a contrast between John's baptism of repentance, which prefigured Christ, and the pseudo-baptism received by the Ephesian men. This is demonstrated, he suggests, by the presence of μέν, which indicates an adversative. But some might respond that the adversative is absent, since no δέ follows μέν in verse 4. (A μέν...δέ construction often indicates an adversative relation between two clauses. Thus, the absence of δέ potentially undermines Zanchi's claim.) To shore up his claim, Zanchi suggests, first, that it is not unusual for Paul to imply the δέ when indicating an adversative. Second, he reconstructs what the implied δέ-clause would have said—something like: John indeed [μέν] baptized with a baptism of repentance, saying to the people that they should believe on Him who would come after him, that is, on Christ Jesus (but [δέ] you were not baptized with that baptism). Third, this implied δέ-clause in verse 4 means that the δέ in verse 5 ("When [δέ] they heard this...") does not constitute the conclusion of a μέν...δέ construction (which would imply a contrast between John's true baptism on the one hand and baptism in the name of the Lord Jesus on the other).

127. δέ.
128. μέν.

not necessary to join the *but*[129] that follows in verse 5 with the *indeed*[130] in verse 4. The fathers understand verse 5 to be a continuation not of Paul's speech but of Luke's.

The fathers' interpretation is, therefore, not in conflict with the context. Nor is it in conflict with other passages of Scripture. For if someone were to say that Paul wrote to the Corinthians that he was thankful that he had not baptized anyone except the household of Stephanus [1 Cor. 1:14, 16], it could be responded that that is true specifically of Corinth but that those twelve men were of Ephesus. Besides, in 1 Corinthians, he was discussing those baptized by his own hand, but he might have baptized these twelve by the hand of another, so let us not argue about the circumstances of time.

It is certainly the case that this interpretation does not oppose the analogy of faith, nor does it bring any absurdity along with it, for the fathers were not discussing legitimately administered baptism, as if Paul repeated one of those. The interpretation of the fathers, therefore, cannot easily be rejected (in my opinion, at least).

This is the primary reason why I have and still do hold this opinion concerning Paul's action. Although, with regard to why the apostle baptized them, I do not agree with all the fathers, only with Ambrose and Jerome.

The fathers teach that John's baptism differed from Christ's in two ways. First, it differed on the basis that John said that he baptized (only) with water but that Christ would baptize with the Holy Spirit and with fire [Matt. 3:11; Mark 1:4; Luke 3:16]. Second, it differed in this: John's baptism is called a baptism of repentance, but Christ's baptism is said to be given for the remission of sins. It was for this that John had been preparing, and (as Tertullian says) *the baptism of repentance was a kind of applicant for the remission of sins and sanctification which was soon to follow in Christ* (On Baptism, p. 707[, §10]).[131]

---

129. δὲ.
130. μέν.
131. On Baptism, p. 707[, §10]: Tertullian, *Homily on Baptism*, trans. Ernest Evans (Eugene, Ore.: Wipf and Stock, 2016), 23 (*ANF*, 3:674). Some more of Tertullian's argument may be helpful in clarifying Zanchi's point. He writes, "What was intended

And Cyprian's *Sermon on Christ's Baptism and the Manifestation of the Trinity* (p. 430) has the same interpretation.[132] And so does Augustine in *Against Petilian* (vol. 7, ch. 7[, §9]).[133] But not all of us understand what the fathers meant with regard to this distinction between baptisms. For they did not mean that the one differed from the other either in the material and symbol of baptism or in the doctrine and form of baptism, only that they differed in efficacy. This is the case because, although those who were baptized with John's baptism received the remission of their sins, nevertheless, this was not as a result of John's baptism (that is, the baptism of water) but as a result of Christ's baptism, which is the baptism of the Spirit. To this pertains that statement: *I baptize with water, but He will baptize with the Holy Spirit* [Luke 3:16]. But the only ones who were baptized with this baptism of the Spirit were those who believed in Christ, whom John was saying was already coming, although not everyone knew Him. Thus, John was impressing this faith upon his own baptism, just as Paul testifies here in Acts 19. This is why they are deceived who suppose that the baptism of water was to be repeated because of this difference.

---

then was a baptism of repentance, as a kind of applicant for the remission and sanctification which in Christ was soon to follow. For that which we read, 'He preached a baptism of repentance for the remission of sins,' was an announcement made in view of a remission which was to be: for repentance comes first, and remission follows, and this is the meaning of preparing the way. But one who prepares a thing does not himself perform it, but provides for its performance by someone else. John himself admits that the heavenly things are not his but Christ's, when he says, 'He that is of the earth speaketh earthly things: he that hath come from above is above all men.' Also he said that he was baptizing solely for repentance, and that one would soon come who would baptize in the Spirit and in fire: because a true and steadfast faith is baptized with the Spirit unto salvation, but a feigned and feeble faith is baptized with fire unto judgement" (pp. 23, 25).

132. Since at least 1530 (by Erasmus), this work had been misattributed to Cyprian. In the seventeenth century, it was identified as part of the work *Liber de cardinalibus operibus Christi* by the twelfth-century Cistercian Arnold Bonaevall. See *PL*, 189:1628–33.

133. vol. 7, ch. 7[, §9]: CSEL 53:10; *PL*, 43:599–600. This work, which is distinct from Augustine's *Answer to the Letters of Petilian the Donatist*, has never been translated into English but is scheduled for inclusion in the long-anticipated second volume of the *Donatist Controversy* in the Works of Saint Augustine: A Translation for the 21st Century.

In *Against Petilian*, as we briefly mentioned a short time ago, Augustine relates that some were of the opinion that the twelve men had lied to the apostle. When asked into what they had been baptized, they responded *into John's baptism* [Acts 19:3]. Thus, on the basis of what the Ephesian men had said earlier—that they had not even heard whether there was (that is, whether there existed) a Holy Spirit, the very Giver of the gifts that were being discussed—the apostle might be said to have exposed that they were lying by the following argument: *Everyone who has been baptized has professed faith in Jesus Christ as the Son of God and, thus, in His Father and in the Spirit of Them both. For this faith was the faith that John was requiring, and by his baptizing was constantly urging that Jesus Christ was the One who baptized with the Spirit. Yet you all, according to your own confession, do not know this Spirit, etc. And so, you do not truly believe in Jesus Christ. Therefore, etc.*

But on the other hand, suggesting that those twelve men were liars to the church and the apostle seems to me very hard and cruel to men who were professing Christ. And for that reason, the opinion of Ambrose and Jerome has always pleased us more: that those twelve men spoke truly. They had been baptized in John's baptism but not by John himself. Instead, they had been baptized by some of John's disciples who did not set forth the genuine teaching about God to them and, thus, did not baptize them properly.

It is, however, beyond dispute according to the fathers that those who have not been baptized into Jesus Christ as the Son of God by nature and as Mediator and, thus, into His Father and into the Spirit of Them both have not been properly baptized. Therefore, those twelve men were not really rebaptized, having already been baptized once. Rather, because they had not been properly baptized, Paul baptized them with the true baptism, having set before them the true doctrine of the Trinity (which John also preached) in advance.

And that is what I have to say with regard to the authority of the fathers. I earnestly confess to the whole of Christ's church that, for my conscience's sake, I dare not deviate from the fathers in dogma, or even in interpreting the Scriptures, unless constrained by very good reasons, especially when there is a general consensus.

Besides the authority of the fathers, there is also a reason derived (by way of the fathers) from the context itself that has also confirmed me in the same opinion. Partly, I draw this from the response of the Ephesian men to Paul when asked whether they had received the Holy Spirit (that is, the gifts of the Holy Spirit). So far was it from them that they had received Him and His gifts that they responded by saying that they had not even heard that there was a Holy Spirit (that is, whether the Holy Spirit existed) or that the Holy Spirit to whom he referred was the subsisting one[134] whom Paul naturally thought was the Author of those gifts.

The reason for my opinion is also partly drawn from what Paul recalled about John's doctrine and baptism when he said: *John indeed baptized with a baptism of repentance, telling the people that they should believe in Him who was to come after him, that is, in Christ Jesus* [Acts 19:4]. It is as if Paul were saying, *But you all did not believe rightly in that Christ who is God the Son of God, since you did not know His Spirit.*[135]

This conclusion follows: therefore, although those men had been baptized in John's baptism—by whom I know not—they nevertheless had not been properly baptized, since they had not been established in the doctrine of the person of Christ in whom John proclaimed they ought to believe. Namely, they ought to have believed that He was not only a man and the Messiah but also God the Son of God from whom (and from the Father) the Holy Spirit proceeds. And thus, they had not been established in the doctrine of God the Father, Son, and Holy Spirit in whose name baptism is to be bestowed. And so, having received the true doctrine of God the Father, the Son, and the Spirit of Them both, and having submitted to it, it was necessary for them to receive a legitimate baptism so that they might subsequently receive the gifts of this Holy Spirit, even through hands being laid on them.

Luke teaches that this is what happened next when he says with reference to the twelve Ephesians: *upon hearing this.*[136] But *upon hearing*[137]

---

134. ὑφιστάμενον.
135. This is Zanchi's first use of the phrase *Filius Dei Deus*, which occurs several times in this observation.
136. ἀκούσαντες δέ.
137. ἀκούσαντες.

what? They heard from Paul the true faith in Christ the Son of God—and so, likewise, in His Father and Holy Spirit—which John also preached. And having submitted to it, they were baptized, and so forth. This interpretation of the fathers—namely, that the twelve men had not been properly established in the doctrine of God the Father, Son, and Holy Spirit and so had also not been properly baptized—can be supported on the basis of the twelve men's ancestry and people. It can also be supported from Paul's reason for asking these men in particular whether they had received the Holy Spirit after having professed faith in Christ despite not having asked this of anyone else.

On the basis of John's baptism in which they said that they had been baptized, one may say that they were of Jewish ancestry and that they had been baptized by a Jew. Most Jews, however, did not hold properly to the doctrine of the three persons subsisting in one essence. Thus, although these twelve men did indeed acknowledge Jesus to be the true Messiah, they nevertheless appear to have recognized only two of the persons: the person of God the Father and the person of the Messiah. (The latter they only recognized, as many people supposed, as a mere man in whom God the Father nevertheless dwelt.) But the fact that they were clearly ignorant that the Holy Spirit was a subsisting one[138] and the Author of the graces bestowed[139] is established from their own words.

Moreover, there must have been some reason why the apostle, having entered Ephesus, where there were many disciples of Christ, questioned these twelve Jewish men in particular. And, to judge from their response, it is likely that the apostle knew that these twelve did not have a proper understanding of the Holy Spirit either because of their own talk or from other brothers who gave an account of events.

In short, this was the apostle's evidence. With it, he intended to prove, based on their response, that they had not been baptized with John's true baptism.

But whoever has been baptized by John's baptism has also heard and professed the doctrine of the Father, Son, and Holy Spirit, and so that

---

138. ὑφιστάμενην.
139. χαρισμάτων.

person would know the Holy Spirit Himself as well. This proposition is left unstated, but the apostle brings the evidence of it to bear, saying, *John baptized…* [Acts 19:4], that is, *John preached not only repentance but also faith in Christ, namely, that He is not only man the Messiah but also God the Son of God from whom the Holy Spirit proceeds (just as He also proceeds from the Father), and that He baptizes in the Holy Spirit. And so, everyone who wants to be saved must believe in Him as the true Savior.*

But you all have neither heard this doctrine nor professed it. Therefore, you have not truly believed in Christ as He actually is. For you say that you did not even hear (that is, when you were baptized) whether there is a Holy Spirit or whether He exists. Therefore, etc. And so, it remains for you all, having professed this doctrine and faith, to receive legitimate baptism, and afterward the gifts of the Holy Spirit Himself by means of hands being laid on you. This is the explanation of the argument according to the interpretation of the fathers. But as is often the case with the prophets and evangelists, Luke sums up the whole thing with just a few words.

But for heaven's sake, what absurdity follows in the wake of this passage? Or, rather, what violence is done to the apostolic story? Doesn't it support the Donatist and Anabaptist heresies? Nothing could be further from the truth. For they rebaptize those who have been properly baptized, while the apostle baptized those who had not been properly baptized in order to attend to those who had neither heard nor professed the true doctrine of God. Furthermore, all the fathers teach that, when these men—for their discussion concerns adults—came to the catholic church, they needed to be baptized with true baptism, with the true doctrine of God and of Christ the Savior having been set out in advance.

As for the text, it is in no way twisted by this interpretation.

Certainly, the response, *We have not even heard that there is a Holy Spirit*[140] [Acts 19:2] cannot be understood to refer to the gifts of the Holy Spirit. This is evident from the subsequent question asked by Paul, who was completely astonished: *Into what were you baptized?*[141] [Acts 19:3], for no one is baptized into the gifts of the Holy Spirit but

---

140. ἀλλ' οὐδ' εἰ πνεῦμα ἅγιόν ἐστιν ἠκούσαμεν.
141. εἰς τί οὖν ἐβαπτίσθητε.

rather into the Holy Spirit Himself, just as also into the Father and into the Son.

Moreover, in the apostles' view, it was beyond dispute that anyone baptized either by John or by his true disciples or by Christ's disciples was baptized having been instructed about the true doctrine of the Holy Spirit, into whose name they were also baptized according to Christ's institution. This is the source of Paul's astonishment: *Into what were you baptized?*[142] [Acts 19:3]. They respond: *Into John's baptism*[143] [Acts 19:3]. To Paul it appears incoherent[144] that they might have been baptized with John's legitimate baptism and yet be ignorant—indeed, that they might never even have heard—whether such a thing as the Holy Spirit is or exists. And this despite the fact that John had been familiar with Him and was preaching Him to all who were coming to be baptized by him and was not preaching Christ apart from this Spirit. For he was saying that *he baptized with water, but Christ Jesus would baptize with the Holy Spirit* [Luke 3:16].

It is with this, in order to expose them, that Paul adduces that they had not been baptized by John nor, indeed, by any of his disciples, saying, Ἰωάννης μὲν, etc. [*John indeed...* (Acts 19:4)]. That [Ἰωάννης][145] μὲν [*John indeed*] is certainly an adversative particle whereby Paul seeks to emphasize that what they were saying—that, when they were baptized, they had not even heard whether there was a Holy Spirit—did not fit with John's legitimate baptism, since John baptized no one without mentioning Him. And Paul responds to the expression [Ἰωάννης] μὲν [*John indeed*] with an implicit *but*[146] according to the argument that we laid out previously. *John indeed baptized...* [Acts 19:4], as if to say, *John preached both repentance and faith in Jesus Christ as He truly is, namely, as the Son of God from whom the Holy Spirit proceeds just as He proceeds from*

---

142. εἰς τί οὖν ἐβαπτίσθητε.
143. εἰς τὸ Ἰωάννου βάπτισμα.
144. ἀσύστατον.
145. See the letter to the reader, which indicates that the word "John" (Ἰωάννης) was accidently omitted, and the omission discovered only when it was too late to correct.
146. δέ.

the Father and who baptizes with the Holy Spirit, and John was baptizing men into the confession of this doctrine.

The minor premise, which Luke himself merely implies, must have been appended to it because it is included in the confession of the twelve men: *Not even that there is a Holy Spirit…*[147] [Acts 19:2]. What could be clearer from the context?

Therefore, what follows in the fifth verse—*upon hearing this…*[148]— are Luke's words faithfully and briefly describing what happened following Paul's argument: *upon hearing this.*[149] What did the twelve men hear? They heard what it is truly to believe in Christ, and that Paul baptized men in accordance with the confession of that teaching (about Christ and His Father and the Spirit of Them both), and that Christ alone, as the only Savior, baptizes with the Holy Spirit. That is to say, *upon hearing*[150] not only with the ears of their bodies but also of their souls and thus believing and confessing what they heard, the twelve men *were baptized in the name of Jesus.*[151] That is, according to the language and description of Scripture, they were baptized into Jesus—not merely as a man but as God the Son of God from whom proceeds the Holy Spirit, just as He proceeds from the Father, and thus as the true and only Savior who baptizes us with His Holy Spirit, etc.

Add to this that the novel interpretation introduces a great deal of idle repetition[152] into a very short narrative.[153] Paul said of John the Baptist, *John indeed baptized with a baptism of repentance, telling the people that they should believe in Him who was to come after him, that is, Christ Jesus*[154] [Acts 19:4]. For why would the apostle then have said with regard to

---

147. ἀλλ' οὐδ' εἰ πνεῦμα ἅγιόν ἐστιν.
148. ἀκούσαντες δὲ.
149. ἀκούσαντες δὲ.
150. ἀκούσαντες.
151. ἐβαπτίσθεσαν εἰς τὸ ὄνομα τοῦ Ἰησοῦ.
152. βαττολογία.
153. The "novel interpretation" would be one that does not follow the church fathers.
154. Ἰωάννης μὲν ἐβάπτισεν βάπτισμα μετανοίας τῷ λαῷ λέγων εἰς τὸν ἐρχόμενον μετ' αὐτὸν ἵνα πιστεύσωσιν τουτ' ἔστιν εἰς τὸν Χριστὸν Ἰησοῦν.

those baptized by John, *upon hearing this*[155] (meaning the people or those men who were baptized)? For who fails to understand on the basis of the preceding words that, if John was baptizing, then those whom he baptized were those who heard and professed his doctrine of repentance and faith in Christ?

Finally, if I were willing to accept this novel interpretation, I do not see what Paul would be trying to imply with this whole account other than that the Ephesians had been properly baptized and that nothing else remained but for them to receive the Holy Spirit by hands being laid upon them. But this conclusion does not seem to me to fit with what precedes, and it is redundant.

I have explained the fathers' interpretation of this passage as well as I can. I did so humbly and without any prejudice and with no other purpose than to clarify to any brothers who may have been offended by that bit in my confession the reason why I dared to set down these words in my confession—that Paul baptized anew those twelve men as not having been properly baptized. At the same time, as we said, we do not condemn the interpretation of others.

Once again, I earnestly declare that my conscience is such that I cannot easily diverge from the dogmas of the ancient fathers or from their interpretations of Scripture unless convinced and constrained either by the manifest testimony of Holy Scripture or by necessary consequences and clear proof. In this way, my conscience is indeed made quiet, and I long to die in this peaceful conviction.

Thus, I humbly beg all the brothers not to be at all offended if I arrive at a different opinion than they do on this topic, since general concord persists among us, especially on matters that pertain to the dogmas of the Christian faith.

On Chapter Sixteen
Aphorism 9
As we also advised above in chapter 15, §14, if the passage in 1 Corinthians 6 is carefully considered, it can render a favorable judgment in the

---

155. ἀκούσαντες δὲ.

debate about the *manducatio impiorum*, that is, whether hypocrites eat sacramentally.[156]

We say that Christ's true body is not eaten by hypocrites who lack true faith, that is, it is not eaten truly, in and of itself, since, in fact, it is only eaten by means of true faith, which they lack. We say instead that, in fact, it is only eaten sacramentally, that is, the sacrament and the sign itself are eaten. Our adversaries also say that Christ's true body is merely eaten sacramentally by hypocrites. But by this statement they mean that the sacrament (that is, the sign) as well as the thing itself is received, yet not unto salvation.

They should understand this in the same way that the apostle says all the Corinthians are sanctified, justified, and so forth—namely, that, by receiving baptism, the sacrament of true regeneration and sanctification, the Corinthians are reputed as having also received the substance. For the sacrament itself did not stand in the way of them partaking of true sanctification. Yet, on account of their hypocritical faith, not all of them actually shared in that sanctification. Certainly, I do not see how that way of speaking could be rejected, provided it is understood as it ought to be, according to the apostolic meaning. In the meantime, as far as this matter is concerned, I propose that the brothers come up with a righteous plan for harmony, so that such a scandal might be removed from the church. Let everything be placed before Christ's tribunal.

Aphorism 10
Here, a distinction must be made among the pious because some receive the Supper in a worthy manner, while others receive unworthily. Indeed, the same pious person sometimes eats worthily and sometimes

---

156. Beginning in the sixteenth century, the phrase *manducatio impiorum* ("eating by the ungodly") was an important touchstone in the eucharistic debates between Lutheran and Reformed theologians. It addressed the question of whether unbelievers (who lacked faith) truly received the substance of the sacrament (that is, Christ Himself, the thing signified) when they consumed the sacramental elements (the sign). Zanchi advocates the Reformed position by arguing that unbelievers do not receive the actual and real body and blood of Christ in the Supper (which can only be laid hold of by faith). However, his position is a nuanced one that seeks to move the disagreement toward a meaningful resolution.

unworthily (1 Cor. 11[:27–32]). Likewise, the wicked, who do not truly receive the substance of the sacrament but only the element, are not all of the same sort. For hypocrites are also found among them, about whom we just spoke. For this reason, it seemed good to suggest a fuller and clearer distinction.

There are two kinds of men, the pious and the wicked, and just as they hear the Word, so also are they able to receive the Lord's Supper. Again, there are two kinds of wicked men. Some are altogether and simply wicked—such as men who are atheists,[157] Jews and Turks also, and all those who understand and believe nothing of what they hear in the preaching of the gospel or see done in the administration of the sacraments. Indeed, they would rather ridicule and scorn all of it. If they come to the Lord's table, they neither eat nor drink anything except the bread and wine. And they do not even eat the bread and wine as the sacraments they are (for they do not understand the substances whereof they are sacraments) but only what they are by their nature: bread and wine. Even when the gospel is preached, they receive nothing but mere words and the sound of words.

Others truly are wicked before God, but in a certain sense[158] (namely, by profession and before man) they are not wicked. In this sense, they are hypocrites in the church who have not been given true faith and life (which is proper to the elect) but have only temporary and hypocritical faith and life. When these people receive the Supper, they really eat and drink no more than the previous ones: just bread and wine. The reason is that they are not granted true faith, without which one cannot truly eat Christ's body. Nevertheless, there is a significant distinction between these two groups.

1. Since it is clear that the former do not believe anything they hear concerning Christ's body in the Supper, so neither do they perceive anything with the mind. Still less do they eat Christ's true body. They eat the bread as common bread merely with their mouths. To a certain extent, however, the latter do understand with their mind and do believe with

---

157. ἄθεοι.
158. κατά τὶ.

their merely historical, hypocritical, and temporary faith what is said and done. So, to that extent and on that account, they can also be said to receive Christ's body offered in the Word and sacraments with that same faith and mind. And, to that extent, they can also be said to taste, although they do not actually eat, since they swallow and retain nothing by the Holy Spirit unto the nourishment of their soul's stomach, which is properly what it means to eat. Rather, having tasted, they spit out or vomit whatever was received. For we read the same thing about temporary believers in Hebrews 6[:4–5]. They tasted the *heavenly gift* and *the good Word of God*. As it says, *they have indeed tasted*, which they do by the gift of the Holy Spirit. And in the parable of the seed, temporary believers are said to have received the seed of the Word but not to have retained it. And thus, they returned no fruit [Matt. 13:22].

These things, which can altogether truly be said of this second kind of wicked persons (namely, temporary hypocrites), cannot be said about the first kind. This, therefore, is the first distinction. A second one follows from this that distinguishes between the eating of the former and the latter.

2. The former neither know nor believe that the bread they receive with their mouths is the sacrament of Christ's body. Indeed, they accept and eat it not as a sacrament but as common bread. For this reason they also must be said not to have eaten Christ's body sacramentally. The latter, however, do not take the bread as commmon bread but as the sacrament of Christ's body, albeit without reverence, since they lack the mouth and teeth of true faith. Nevertheless, having been led (as they say) by an argument from cognates, they are said to eat sacramentally, as the sacrament they eat is [the sacrament] of Christ's body. Therefore, because they do not actually eat Christ's body but merely its sacrament, they eat Christ's body sacramentally and likewise according to the sacrament.

3. From this follows the explanation we discussed above: those who contend simply and without qualification that hypocrites themselves eat not only the sacrament but also the substance of the sacrament (that is, not merely the bread alone but also Christ's very body) do not speak wickedly. But in what way do they eat? In the same way that the apostle (who

had said that, in their previous state, all the Corinthians were impure, wicked, and so forth) subsequently said that they were not only cleansed (which someone might interpret as referring only to the waters of baptism) but also sanctified and justified [1 Cor. 6:11]. Yet, not all of them were truly thus. Rather, some among them were still hypocrites.

In this way, all who eat the sacrament of the Lord's body and who come to His supper having professed faith in Christ are likewise said to eat the Lord's true body. This is the case on account of the sacrament union, which causes him who receives the sign also to be judged by the church to have received the thing signified. For it is not the fault of the One who instituted the sacrament nor of the sacrament itself if he who receives and eats the sacrament actually receives and eats only the sacrament and not the thing signified. For Christ, through the minister, really offered both, and the sacrament's integrity and truth do not depend on our faith but on Christ's institution. So, if we do not receive the whole sacrament but merely the sign without the thing signified, the guilt abides with us who receive one part with our bodily mouth but reject the other part by our faithlessness (for hypocritical faith is a kind of faithlessness[159]) and separate what God willed to be joined together.

On the basis of these things, it is clear how great is the distinction between the eating done by those who are simply wicked and those who are hypocrites, although neither can truly be said to eat Christ's true body. For the only ones who truly eat Christ are those who are also truly grafted onto Christ by true and living faith, which is given only to the elect. Those who are phyiscally dead cannot actually eat physical food. How then could the spiritually dead feed on spiritual food? But the faithful are the only ones who live, because they have been joined by a living faith—as members to a head, as branches to a vine, as all the boughs to their tree—to *Christ who is our life* [Col. 3:4]. And if, as Cyprian said, *It is food of the mind not of the belly*, then it certainly is not eaten by bodily teeth but by the teeth of a believing soul, which only the pious possess.[160]

---

159. ἀπιστία.
160. On the quote attributed to Cyprian, see above *CCR*, 16.11.

Likewise, if Christ's body is *a heavenly thing* (as Irenaeus says), how can it be eaten by those who have nothing to do with heavenly things but are altogether earthly men, who have been provided with no faith wherewith to ascend into heaven and eat the heavenly food [*Against Heresies*, bk. 4, ch. 18.5]?[161] Thus, only the pious can do this.

But actually it is not even the case that all the pious are affected equally and in the same way. For while on many occasions they eat worthily, yet it also happens that sometimes they eat unworthily, and for that reason God chastens them in various ways.

They who examine themselves as to whether they are *in the faith* before they eat of the Lord's bread are said to eat worthily [2 Cor. 13:5]. And if they are in the faith, they also diligently consider the meaning and magnitude of this mystery. Then, they examine their conscience—whether they are bringing forth true repentance and, with ardent prayers, stirring themselves up unto faith and repentance.

But they eat unworthily who, despite having been grafted onto Christ by faith and the Spirit of regeneration, nevertheless examine themselves insufficiently, their faith having been somewhat choked by the cares of this world or by other fleshly passions. Nor do they arouse themselves to serious consideration of the mystery. Nor do they consider attentively what is being distributed at that holy table, what the Lord requires of them, and for whom and to what end the Lord established this table.

Finally, they eat unworthily who (as the apostle says) *do not discern the Lord's body*[162] [1 Cor. 11:29]. Thus, they do not come to that table with due reverence and fear of the Lord. They do not sufficiently discern—with their mind and by faith, as would be proper—the thing signified from the signs or the signs from leftover food and a regular cup. As a result, they do not open the mouth of the interior man to spiritual food in the same way as they open their external mouth to eat food that is physical (according to its nature). On account of the neglect of this duty—that is, because they do not examine themselves sufficiently

---

161. [*Against Heresies*, bk. 4, ch. 18.5]: *ANF*, 1:486.
162. οὐ διακρίνουσι τὸ σῶμα τοῦ κυρίου.

nor judge and discern the Lord's body, and because, accordingly, they eat the Lord's bread unworthily—some Christian and pious men undergo various chastisements from God. But this happens unto their salvation so that they might not be condemned with this world. The apostle addresses these people specifically in 1 Corinthians 11[:29]. Indeed, he is not speaking merely about the wicked or the true hypocrites when he says that *they eat judgment on themselves*.... This is clear from the context.

1. Note that he did not say those eating unworthily *eat condemnation*[163] *on themselves*, which would mean eternal destruction, but instead *judgment*.[164] To what extent these differ from one another in meaning is clear from the context, since the apostle says in verse 32, *But when we are judged*[165] *by the Lord, we are corrected*—or *chastened*—*so that we may not be condemned along with the world*.[166]

2. When the apostle explains the punishment that follows from eating unworthily, he does not mention anything other than temporal corrections. Clearly he makes no mention of eternal destruction: *That is why*,[167] he says, *many of you are weak*[168] [1 Cor. 11:30].

3. Add to this that he says, *If we judged*[169] *ourselves* (that is, if we tested ourselves and, having recognized our sins, corrected ourselves with penitence and separated ourselves from the world with true faith and repentance), then *we would not be judged*,[170] namely, by the Lord, who corrects us and puts us to death for this reason: because we do not put our own passions to death and do not repent of our sins [1 Cor. 11:31].

---

163. κατάκριμα.
164. κρίμα.
165. Κρινόμενοι δὲ.
166. ἵνα μὴ σὺν τῷ κόσμῳ κατακριθῶμεν. Zanchi interrupts this Greek quotation by giving part of the verse in Latin, namely, the section referencing the correction or chastening done by the Lord.
167. διὰ τοῦτο.
168. πολλοὶ ἐν ὑμῖν ἀσθενεῖς.
169. διεκρίνομεν.
170. οὐκ ἂν ἐκρινόμεθα.

4. What does this mean but that this *judgment*[171] (on account of which *we are judged*[172] for eating the Lord's bread *unworthily*[173]) summons us with eloquent words to a very profitable *disciplining*[174] [vv. 27, 29, 31–32]? For thus he says, *But when we are judged by the Lord, we are disciplined so that we might not be condemned with the world* (v. 32).[175]

5. And indeed, the apostle establishes that he and all others among the number of the truly faithful who *are judged*[176] by the Lord are being instructed unto salvation. For he establishes two orders of men. There are the wicked, who are comprehended by the word *world* and whom he teaches are awaiting *the condemnation*,[177] that is, eternal destruction. And then there are the pious, who are being instructed likewise with various punishments on account of their various missteps and outbursts so that they might not be condemned along with the wicked. These are being subjected to *judgments*[178] so that they might avoid *condemnation*.[179] Therefore, this passage should properly be understood to refer to the faithful—but ones who are imperfect and for that reason sinning gravely, because they come to the Lord's table *unworthily*.[180]

On Chapter Seventeen
Aphorism 1
This claim was made with reference to adults. There is another reason, explained elsewhere, that pertains to the infants of the faithful having been elected unto eternal life. For the Holy Spirit unites them to Christ as true members to the Head from which they draw life. Nor do we

---

171. κρίμα.
172. κρινόμεθα.
173. ἀναξίως.
174. παίδευσιν.
175. κρινόμενοι δὲ ὑπὸ τοῦ κυρίου παιδευόμεθα ἵνα μὴ σὺν τῷ κόσμῳ κατακριθῶμεν. Unlike the previous quotation of this verse (under point 2), Zanchi gives the entirety in Greek.
176. κρινόμενοι.
177. τὸ κατάκριμα.
178. κρίμασι.
179. κατάκριμα.
180. ἀναξίως.

doubt that they are given the Spirit of faith, although they cannot make use of Him because of the weakness of nature. In the same way, they are not able to exercise the power of understanding, although they do not lack a mind and its faculties.

Aphorism 2
In describing faith, I gladly used these two words: *wisdom* and *prudence*. I did so (following the very learned theologian Martin Bucer in his commentary on the epistle to the Ephesians) because, by the first word, I include the contemplative aspect[181] of the Christian religion—about God, Christ, and so forth—whereas, by the second word, I include the active aspect.[182] The whole gospel, which the Christian faith embraces and upon which it depends, is briefly distinguished in these terms.

Add to this that *wisdom* and *prudence* do indeed teach that faith is reliable knowledge of God and Christ formed on the basis of God's Word, etc. But the whole of Christian doctrine consists partly in contemplation[183] and partly in action.[184]

Likewise, the actions of faith are twofold: one is in the intellect, and the other in the will. Having been granted the light of faith, the intellect understands, assents to, and believes the things declared by the Word. Having been moved by the power of faith, the will loves, wants, and embraces them as good things. Then, it also commands the faithful and prudent performance of those things that pertain to external works by the soul's other faculties and bodily instruments as well.

---

181. τὰ θεωρητικὰ.
182. τὰ πρακτικὰ. Richard Muller writes that reference to τὰ θεωρητικὰ and τὰ πρακτικὰ "*do not* indicate a tendency toward metaphysical rationalization on the one hand and pragmatic enterprise on the other, or a statement of abstract principle on the one hand and of application on the other. To the extent that the scholastic enterprise is interpreted in terms of such a view of *theoria* and *praxis*, it is misinterpreted." PRRD, 3:340–41 [emphasis in the original]. See his larger discussion about the relationship between *theoria* and *praxis* among the Reformed orthodox at pp. 340–54 in that volume.
183. θεωρίᾳ.
184. πράξει.

On Chapter Nineteen: Justification

Aphorism 6

I explained the point about Abraham's faith from Genesis 15 and Romans 4 in such a way that I said that the very thing that was imputed to Abraham for righteousness was what he believed regarding Christ the promised Seed. I made this comment more with reference to the actual substance of faith than with a focus on the bare word of faith. I was not unaware, however, that both Moses and Paul said that it was Abraham's faith that was imputed to him for righteousness. For the apostle, clearly deducing a general doctrine from Abraham's example, adds these words: *But to him who does not work but believes in Him who justifies the wicked, his faith is imputed as righteousness* [Rom. 4:5]. That is, he is considered righteous before God on that account—because he *believes in Him who justifies the wicked*. This passage makes it absolutely clear that our works are excluded from our true justification and that, from beginning to end, the whole thing is entirely ascribed to faith alone.

Notwithstanding, when we ask what possible reason there is for why justification is attributed to faith and not to the works of faith, the usual response (well and truly) is: because faith, rather than the works of faith, lays hold of the remission of sins and Christ our righteousness. For we are not justified by faith insofar as it is a work but insofar as faith takes hold of Christ, by whose singular righteousness imputed to us we are properly reputed righteous before God. Others say it this way: faith justifies not with respect to itself but with respect to the object of which it lays hold. So, it is clear from this that what I said is true. Properly speaking, what Abraham believed was imputed to him (just as if it were his own) as righteousness because he believed God with reference to Christ, namely, that all people—and therefore Abraham himself—would be blessed in Him [Gen. 12:3].

Likewise on the last aphorism [that is, Aphorism 12]

Nor do we approve of those who imagine that our justification consists only in the remission of sins, denying the imputation of Christ's righteousness and obedience. This seems to us to conflict with the Scriptures.

Isaiah 7 [that is, 9:6]: *A Child is given unto us....* Therefore, whatever He does or has, it is all ours.

Romans 5[:19]: *Just as by the disobedience of the one man, many were made sinners, so by the obedience of the one Man many will be made righteous.* The disobedience was Adam's transgression of the divine command. Therefore, Christ's obedience consists not only in death but also in all the law-keeping that preceded it.[185] Likewise, the whole of that disobedience of Adam is imputed to us. Why, then, would not the whole of Christ's obedience be imputed to us? Again, we became sinners through Adam's twofold disobedience: through the imputation of his transgressions and through the actual overflowing of sin (that is, of concupiscence) unto us. Why then would we not think that it was the same with Christ? The power of His obedience to the commands of God the Father really are communicated to us so that we ourselves also begin to obey God's law. Therefore, what keeps us from saying that the whole of that obedience is imputed to us? First Corinthians 1[:30]: *He was made for us wisdom from God, righteousness, sanctification, and redemption.* Philippians 2[:8–9]: *Having been made obedient unto death, God exalted Him* and, on account of that humiliation and obedience unto death, He exalted us in Him, and so forth. By His obedience He earned eternal glory both for Himself and for us, as all the scholastics and the fathers teach. Therefore, His obedience to the law is also imputed to us as righteousness.

Galatians 4[:4–5]: *He was made under the law, that He might redeem those who were under the law.* Therefore, He kept the law for our sake and for

---

185. One of the first major debates among Protestants related to the doctrine of justification had to do with whether believers received only the forgiveness of sins on account of the payment rendered as the result of Christ's suffering and death (His passive righteousness) or whether His record of perfect law-keeping and sinlessness (active righteousness) was also imputed. The lightning rod in the debate was Johannes Piscator (1546–1625), whom, in 1573, Duke Frederick III attempted (unsuccessfully) to appoint to the theology faculty at Heidelberg, where Zanchi taught. See Heber Carlos de Campos Jr., *Doctrine in Development: Johannes Piscator and Debates over Christ's Active Obedience*, Reformed Historical-Theological Studies (Grand Rapids: Reformation Heritage Books, 2017).

our salvation. For the sake of brevity, we omit the testimonies of the fathers and learned men of every age as well. In sum, just as we believe that Christ descended from the heavens and was incarnate for us men and for our salvation, so we also believe that He kept the law and did all things for the same reason.

On Chapter Twenty-Five
Aphorisms 10 and 11
When I was composing this confession of faith, I wrote everything in good conscience. Likewise, I frankly said what I believed, as the Holy Scriptures teach must be done. Primarily, moreover, my faith depends simply upon God's Word. Secondarily, to some extent it depends upon the common consensus of the whole of the ancient catholic church as well, as long as that consensus does not oppose the Holy Scriptures. For I believe that what the pious fathers, having assembled in the name of the Lord, received and defined by common consensus of all and without any contradiction to the Holy Scriptures also comes from the Holy Spirit, although it is hardly of the same authority as the Holy Scriptures. From this, it arises that I neither intend nor dare to reject those things with a good conscience.

But is anything more certain from histories, councils, and the writings of all the fathers than that the ranks of ministers about whom we have spoken were established and received in the church by the common consent of the whole Christian commonwealth? Moreover, who am I to reject what the whole church has approved? Nor are all the learned men of our own time prepared to reject—indeed, they acknowledge—that the church has valued these things and that they were all effected and arranged on a pious basis for the best of purposes: the edification of the elect.

For the sake of demonstrating this, it seemed good to insert here what Martin Bucer (of pious memory), a much-celebrated man of singular godliness and erudition, wrote concerning these matters in his commentary on the epistle to the Ephesians.[186]

---

186. The work referenced, from which Zanchi extracts four extended quotations

The Seven Genuine Duties of a Teacher

But the administration of the Word ought to consist in the reading and recitation of the divine Scriptures, which are then to be interpreted and explained, after which exhortations are to be undertaken. It also consists in repetition and catechesis with back-and-forth questions and answers between the catechizer and the catechumen, as well as in holy discussions and investigations into the more difficult questions of our religion.

The duties involved in performing the task of teaching are likewise multiplied in accordance with the manifold forms of administering this saving doctrine.[187] For, anything that pertains to a wholly complete method of instruction ought to be employed with the greatest zeal in administering the doctrine of salvation, since it is a matter of teaching the most divine and difficult art of all: leading a godly life while being a man.[188]

Those who are diligently preparing to teach the arts contained in specific books—for example, those who intend to teach mathematics from Euclid—will first read and recite the proposed book.[189] Then they will explain each unfamiliar expression, as

---

below, is Bucer's *Praelectiones in epistolam ad Ephesios*. Bucer began lecturing on Ephesians in January 1550 at Cambridge University and continued in that work almost to the end of his life (in February 1551). In 1562, his lectures were edited for publication by Immanuel Tremellius, Zanchi's longtime associate and colleague at Heidelberg. See Willem van 't Spijker, *The Ecclesiastical Offices in the Thought of Martin Bucer*, trans. John Vriend and Lyle D. Bierma, Studies in Medieval and Reformation Traditions 57 (Leiden: Brill, 1996), 347–48.

187. A marginal note in the text here reads: "I propose that, strictly speaking, living unto God (or leading a godly life) is what should be taught."

188. *Scientia vivendi Deum* was an important notion in Bucer's theology that "linked" the "scientific character of theology to a survey of its practical character as well. Theology is the art of teaching people to live piously and happily. It is a difficult art indeed, the most difficult of all, because one has to learn to lead a godly life, while still being in the flesh. Nevertheless, this remains the requirement. It is not the amount of knowledge we possess which is at stake. We know enough if we know how to put into practice that which we know. In this way, scholarship and piety go hand in hand." Willem van 't Spijker, "Reformation and Scholasticism," in *Martin Bucer (1491–1551): Collected Studies on His Life, Work, Doctrine, and Influence*, ed. Christa Boerke and Jan C. Klok, Refo500 Academic Studies 44 (Göttingen: Vandenhoeck & Ruprecht, 2018), 67.

189. A marginal note in the text here reads: "What proper teaching is."

each art has its own distinct vocabulary. From there, if any summary or argument is particularly abrupt, they make it clear with an analysis,[190] illustrate it with many examples, offer particular lessons on the basis of general ones, and explain those things that are well known rather than trying to address every detail. That is what proper teaching is.

Yet, a truly faithful teacher is not content merely with providing content, however faithful. He also goes back and reviews what he has taught and makes himself available to his students so that they can ask him for a fuller explanation if they have doubts about anything. In addition, he also puts forward what he has taught to be examined in public disputations, lest doubts of any kind linger. To this he also frequently adds exhortations (as well as admonitions and reproofs and general rebukes) to encourage good progress in the doctrine that has been set forward and to discourage students from those things that might impede it. Finally, a diligent instructor of this sort observes the progress of each of his students, and if he observes that any student has stopped learning, he corrects him privately and reminds him of his duty. If he perceives one progressing laboriously in learning, he speaks to him frequently, commends him, and encourages him to pursue his studies more and more.

The Lord Christ Himself employed all seven of these methods of teaching as well. In the synagogue in Nazareth, he read from and interpreted Isaiah 61 (Luke 4[:16–30]). In the Sermon on the Mount, He explained the commands of God (Matthew 5). And here and there, He taught, exhorted, reproved, and rebuked from God's Word. He also responded to those—both good and evil—who asked Him questions, and He asked them questions in return (Matt. 22[:23–46]). He frequently catechized His disciples, and He participated in catechesis Himself (Luke 2[:41–47]).[191]

---

190. ἀναλύσει.
191. The long preceding quotation is from Bucer, *Praelectiones*, 117.

The Seven Ministerial Ranks[192] Entered the Church from the Seven Ways of Teaching the Word

1. Thus, since the ministry of teaching requires a truly complex effort, multiple ranks of ministers have likewise been allotted to this ministry—first of all, readers, whose duty it was to recite the sacred Scriptures in the pulpit, an elevated spot. But this recitation of the sacred Scriptures was established so that the language of Scripture and its way of speaking, not to mention Scripture itself, might become better known and more familiar to the people. For within the span of a year, they recited all the holy books to the people, while those who expounded the Scriptures could only finish explaining some part of the Scriptures—and not a large part either—in a year. Meanwhile, however, an acquaintance with all the dogmas of our salvation was secured for the people in a remarkable fashion simply by the public reading of the holy books. For, again and again, those things are repeated in every one of the sacred books and explained with different words in different books so that people might constantly be learning many things from a later reading that they were not yet altogether able to grasp at a previous one. This same service improved the discernment of the people as regards our entire religion and also the interpretation of the Scriptures and all doctrine that was brought to them, whether it was done by proper curates and doctors of the church or by others.

    This is why the service of simply reading the Holy Scriptures aloud to the people was a notable practice in ancient churches. Nor was anyone selected for this ministry unless he was commended by remarkable piety. Granted that this practice can be found in other ancient writings, it is most clearly observed in one or another of St. Cyprian's letters—for example, his letter about the ordination of Aurelius as reader (bk. 2, ep. 5 [that is, ep. 38.1–2]) and about Saturnus (bk. 3, ep. 22 [that is, ep.

---

192. *Ordines*, as in CCR, 25.7 and elsewhere, which could also be translated as "orders."

29]) and concerning Celerinus Coelestinus in the fourth book [ep. 39.4–5].[193]

To these readers were later added chanters, who took the lead in the singing of psalms and hymns. Thank God that, with regard to the reading of the Scriptures, it has been properly arranged in the English churches, as long as suitable readers are put in place who exhibit a gravity and religion worthy of divine services when they read the Holy Scriptures aloud. Therefore, let them carefully consider whose mouth they are representing when they read the divine books aloud to the people in holy assemblies, namely, that of almighty God. Let them also consider how serious a matter and how worthy of dignity are the words and precepts of eternal life that they are reading. And, finally, let them consider unto what sort of men and for what purpose they should devote themselves as readers of the Holy Scriptures. For they are to serve the sons of God, for whose salvation the only begotten Son of God poured out His blood, unto whom that same salvation is to be made known and more and more brought to culmination. If you consider the matter with true faith, what could be added to any action in terms of gravity, decency, and religion that such a reader would possibly overlook?

But those who perform this office ought always to have their eyes fixed on this: that what they read out should be of service for effectually building up the faith of those who hear. And that is accomplished only when they [that is, the words read] are also properly understood and received as God's words. For both of these things to happen, however, an extremely clear, eloquent, grave, and religious recitation is necessary. This reveals that they who read the Holy Scriptures aloud as if reciting them as quickly as possible were the only requirement are not Christ's ministers.

2. Now, a second duty is interpreting the teaching that has been delivered, that is, the explanation of the words and ideas more simply. Bishops and presbyters attended to this ministry, although they invited members of the diaconate and the subdiaconate, and

---

193. bk. 2, ep. 5 [that is, ep. 38.1–2]; bk. 3, ep. 22 [that is, ep. 29]; [ep. 39.4–5]: Cyprian, *Letters (1–81)*, 71–72, 97–99, 101–2 (*ANF*, 5:301, 312, 313–14).

sometimes even laypeople whom they discerned the Holy Spirit had made suitable to be charged with carrying out this task. Thus, even as a layman, Origen was admitted to this duty in the church of Caesarea in Palestine by Alexander the bishop of Jerusalem and Theoctistus the bishop of the church of Caesarea.

3. Likewise, according to Eusebius, Euelpis was admitted by Neon the bishop of Laranda, Paulinus by Celsus the bishop of Iconium, and Theodorus by Bishop Atticus of Synnada (*Ecclesiastical History*, bk. 6, ch. 20 [that is, ch. 19.16–18]).[194] Eusebius based what he wrote on the letters of those two bishops—Alexander of Jerusalem and Theoctistus of Caesarea, bishops in Palestine—to Bishop Demetrius of Alexandria, who rebuked the action of the two other bishops with regard to Origen, regarding it as something previously unheard for a layman to preach to the people in the church when the bishops were present. But those bishops distinctly denied this to be true and affirmed that holy bishops had customarily encouraged those whom they recognized as suitable among the laity to assist in being useful to the people by interpreting the Scriptures and by teaching, and they encouraged them to discharge this ministry even when the bishops themselves were present.

Thus, bishops and presbyters chiefly performed the second and third divisions of the sacred ministry—namely, the interpretation and teaching—on their own. Yet, if they recognized from among either the lower orders or the laity those who were suitable for this duty, they attached them to themselves as co-laborers.[195]

4. In the same way, bishops and presbyters performed the fourth role, delivering doctrine, as that duty to which they primarily gave themselves because it required greater authority (1 Timothy 5). On the basis of the divine books having been set forth, bishops and presbyters exhorted unto pious duties and dissuaded from sins (and everything that seeks to delay or impede

---

194. *Ecclesiastical History*, bk. 6, ch. 20 [that is, ch. 19.16–18]: Eusebius, *Ecclesiastical History, Books 6–10*, trans. Roy J. Deferrari, Fathers of the Church 29 (Washington, D.C.: Catholic University of America Press, 1969), 39–40 (*NPNF*2 1:267–68).

195. συνεργούς.

forward movement in a pious and holy life), they rebuked and reproved sinners, and they consoled the repentant.

5. The fifth role, catechizing, they entrusted sometimes to presbyters, sometimes to deacons, and sometimes to ministers of the lower orders to the degree that someone appeared more suited to this type of teaching. And thus, Origen was Alexandria's catechist (Eusebius of Caesarea, *Ecclesiastical History*, bk. 6, chs. 13 and 20 [that is, chs. 3 and 19]).[196]

6. The sixth role, holy discussions, they also bestowed upon whomever was most suitable, although, for the most part, the bishops themselves had charge of them.

7. Bishops also gave their attention to fulfilling the seventh role: private appeal or admonition. But they always encouraged individual presbyters and the graver among the lower orders to do likewise (1 Thess. 5[:12]).[197]

A Summary of the Seven Orders

Thus, readers ought to attend to the ministry of teaching by reading the Scriptures aloud. But bishops ought to do so by interpreting, teaching, exhorting, discussing, and appealing privately and by reading and catechizing (if they lack designated readers and catechists). Likewise, they entrusted catechisms to priests and deacons or even men from the lower orders selected for this purpose. In the same way also, whomever the bishops had discerned from among these as suitable for the responsibility—regardless of their order of sacred ministry, and even (as they say) from among the laity—these they employed in the duty of interpreting, teaching, and discussing.

But the thing that must be carefully observed in these matters is this: there can be no doubt that the Holy Spirit distributes these gifts of teaching to His people in such a way that He gives the gift

---

196. Eusebius of Caesarea, *Ecclesiastical History*, bk. 6, chs. 13 and 20 [that is, chs. 3 and 19]: Eusebius, *Ecclesiastical History, Books 6–10*, 16–17, 28 (*NPNF*2 1:251–52, 267).

197. The long preceding quotation is from Bucer, *Praelectiones*, 117–19.

and singular ability of interpreting and explaining the Scriptures to one person but does not equally give him the gift of skillfully and fruitfully teaching and confirming the dogmas of our religion from the Holy Scriptures, or even of defending them well. Indeed, He supplies another with the singular and remarkable ability of exhorting the brothers from Scripture, admonishing and rebuking, or, similarly, catechizing and making private appeal. Yet He does not grant him to be effective in other tasks of teaching.

We experience this variety of the Holy Spirit's gifts on a daily basis in those who publicly teach Christ's people, which are Christ's true churches, and who allow themselves wholly to be ruled by the Holy Spirit. They conscientiously observe which of the spiritual gifts are given to whom in the church, and they direct each one to the performance of his own duty to the best of his ability. On this account, if they discover among their people some whom the Lord has particularly fashioned and prepared for particular teaching duties, then they employ particular ministers in particular types of teaching. But because it is necessary for the salvation of God's people that absolutely none of the types of teaching, which I have numbered seven, be overlooked in any church, each of the ministers—or, indeed, of the laity—whatever his position in the church, ought to attend to these types of teaching as he is able: reading, interpreting, teaching, exhorting, catechizing, discussing, and appealing privately.

Each one ought also to take upon himself the administration of these roles insofar as he perceives the Holy Spirit to be directing him to each one of them. Take the example of a well-established and well-ordered house in which the father attends to certain duties, the mother to others, the sons and daughters to others, and the servants to others. So long as everyone in this place is present and healthy, each one surely attends to his duty. But if someone is absent from the family or is not completely well, the need for some service comes upon them unexpectedly. So, by necessity each one pitches in. It so happens that men often attend to the duties of women and women to those of men, masters to servants' duties, and servants to their masters."[198]

---

198. The long preceding quotation is from Bucer, *Praelectiones*, 119.

Regarding Clerical Discipline

The third part of clerical discipline is personal submission, whereby clergy and ministers of lower ranks submit themselves to those who are in a superior rank and ministry. The Lord likewise taught us this element of discipline by His own example. He established His disciples to be the teachers of God's elect throughout the whole world with special authority for this duty and a certain domestic discipline. And the apostles imitated the Lord; each one had his own disciples whom he formed to attend properly to the sacred ministry.

For all of life's more difficult tasks also require more specific and ongoing doctrine, education, and oversight, as is seen in the study of philosophy and military instruction. Lycurgus, having carefully weighed the matter, established the Republic of the Lacedemonians in such a way that there was no single order in the Republic without its own governance (as Xenophon testifies). Likewise, in his *Laws* and *Republic*, Plato also required that nothing be unguarded.[199] Our Lord also wants His own to be committed to and at harmony with one another (as members in a body have been joined together and are at harmony). For that reason, He causes each one who is His to be subject to others by whom that one is cared for, moved along, and guided. This is just as is done by bodily members that have a wider and broader range of power and effectiveness. Likewise, the Holy Spirit teaches that *we are to be subject to one another in the fear of God* (Eph. 5[:21]).

Presbyters

Thus, having considered these things, the holy fathers of the past arranged the order of clergy in such a way that all the other clergy were watched over and governed with special care by the presbytery.

Bishops

But, just as a consul among the senators of a republic, so among the presbyters the bishop bears primary responsibility and care not

---

199. ἀφρούρητον.

only over the whole church but also and especially over all those who are of clerical rank.

Suffragan Bishops
But in churches that were particularly well stocked, they ordained bishops and to each of them entrusted nearby churches of the sort that were in small towns or the countryside and, on that account, they determined presbyters and overseers from other churches. They called these suffragan bishops, and they were to heed the bishop and presbytery that was nearby them. From time to time, the superior bishops gathered them with all their clergy and refreshed them in the knowledge and industry of their duty.

But since the Lord wills for his men to embrace one another and bear one another's burdens as far and wide as possible (for all Christians are one body), the holy fathers, as bishops of each province (for all the dominions that were subject to the Romans had been divided into provinces), assembled together with the presbyters. They did so at least as often as the practice of the churches required, but certainly twice a year. And they inquired into how Christ's doctrine and discipline was being managed in each church, whether it was thriving. And wherever they discerned that sin to have been present, they corrected it; what they found to have been done well, they confirmed and approved.

Metropolitans
But so that these synods might be managed well and in an orderly way, they wanted a metropolitan—a bishop of each metropolis, as the principal city of each province was called, where a supreme governor resided—to take the lead both in calling them together and guiding them. And thus, in former times, care of and concern for all the churches throughout their province was joined to these metropolitan bishops so that, if they became aware of something having been decreed or done that was less than proper, they might swiftly warn against it. And if they were unable to correct it with their rebukes, they might convene a synod of bishops to set things right. For no judgment was granted to them to enforce anything by their own authority in churches that had their own bishops, since every judgment—both as regards the people and the clergy—was

in the hands of the bishop and presbyter of that same church. Moreover, the synod judged the bishops.

And thus, when it was necessary for a bishop to be ordained for a church, it happened that all would assemble (if it were possible for the churches to do so conveniently) at that very church. But if only some assembled, then they were not to do so with less than two or three bishops from their province to oversee the bishop's election (if it was yet to be done). And, when the election was complete, they were to assay it. And they were to scrutinize the bishop elect in an extremely severe manner and explore his life and all his skills for fulfilling the episcopal duty. And only then would they admit him to carry out the episcopal task.

The point of all this being instituted was so that as much mutual awareness and care as possible might exist between churches and their ministers to prevent and avert every cause of offense in doctrine and customs, and for the edification, sustaining, promotion, and more effective accomplishment of faith and a life worthy of Christ the Lord. Indeed, if some had been remiss in their office, the other bishops would hurry to their aid, to the point of suspending and even degrading from episcopal office those who were obstinate.

Consider what Saint Cyprian wrote to Stephen the Roman pontiff regarding Marcianus the Bishop of Arles, who transferred into the Novation sect (bk. 3, ep. 13 [that is, ep. 68]).[200] Consider, too, what he wrote about each of the bishops having received a specific flock, which was included as a preface in the Council of Carthage, as he wrote to Quirinus (bk. 1, ep. 3 [that is, ep. 59.14 to Cornelius]).[201]

Patriarchs

Moreover, there began to be so many metropolitans that not all of them had a sufficient understanding of their territories or

---

200. bk. 3, ep. 13 [that is, ep. 68]: Cyprian, *Letters (1–81)*, 239–43 (*ANF*, 5:368–69).

201. bk. 1, ep. 3 [that is, ep. 59.14 to Cornelius]: Cyprian, 186–87 (*ANF*, 5:344). For the introductory letter to the Synod of Carthage held under Cyprian in 256, see *NPNF2*, 14:517.

maintained sufficient vigilance over them. Wherever the earth was filled to bursting with churches, and the metropolitans themselves had their own need of care, then care of some provinces was entrusted to certain bishops of the principal churches, for there are always a few that are outstanding in every rank of men. These principal bishops included Rome, Constantinople, Antioch, Alexandria, and later Caesarea, Cappadocia, and certain others as necessity seemed to require for the growing churches of Christ's faithful ones.

Nevertheless, these bishops of the highest rank (which were later called patriarchs) had absolutely no authority over those bishops or churches that went beyond the authority that I said a metropolitan had over the churches and bishops of his province. Each patriarch was particularly responsible to care for and be concerned about his portion of churches. He was also responsible for admonishing bishops immediately if any of them sinned or were remiss in their duty. And if the warning accomplished nothing, he was responsible to make use of conciliar authority.

Among these, the first place was granted to the Roman patriarch, both out of respect to St. Peter and out of respect to that city's dignity. Later, following the same logic, the fathers allotted the second place to Constantinople (as the second Rome) and to the bishop of the imperial throne, although, previously, Antioch had held the second rank among the patriarchs.

However, having been spoiled by ambition, human nature always endeavors more and more to assert control as broadly as it does fully. So, in the first place, on the pretext of the general care of the churches entrusted to them, those patriarchs forcibly appropriated to themselves the ordaining of neighboring bishops and, by means of that ordination (gradually and to a certain extent), co-opted such bishops and their churches unto themselves and established jurisdiction over them. As this evil grew, a serious struggle emerged about supreme power in all churches generally. Indeed, a certain Bishop John of Constantinople[202] first tried to assume this for himself under Emperor Maurice. A great many

---

202. John IV of Constantinople (r. 582–595) was the first bishop of that see to assume the title Ecumenical Patriarch.

letters exist about this controversy in the fifth, sixth, and seventh books of the epistles of St. Gregory.[203]

It was under Phocas that the Roman patriarch eventually gained the title of universal bishop. The bishops of that see gradually began more and more to misuse that title until, first, at the division of the empire under Charlemagne, and then with the quarreling of peoples and nations that shattered the power of the Western emperors and of other kings, they exalted themselves to that anti-Christian power in which they now boast, having subdued first the power of the bishops and then that of all the kings and emperors as well.

This, then, is the way in which Satan overthrew all wholesome obedience and the management of clerical orders. For the Roman Antichrist obtained for himself direct supreme power over the whole clergy, and the laity as well, and he destroyed the care and supervision of bishops—when they were good ones—toward those given into their trust. And because it is altogether necessary for each cleric to have his own overseers and superintendents, the authority and power (but also the vigilance and attention) of bishops must be restored, and so also must that of archdeacons and of all the others (by whatever names they are known) to whom some part of the care and guidance of the clergy has been entrusted. This is necessary lest anyone in clerical orders be altogether unguarded.[204]

Thus far we have Bucer not only faithfully recounting but even praising the ancient church's custom of setting up the various orders of ecclesiastical services to which we referred above.

I should, however, also give an account of those churches that—although they have embraced the gospel—yet retained their bishops and archbishops in actuality as well as in terminology.

What? Do you mean to say that bishops and archbishops, whom they call *superintendents* and *superintendents general* (having exchanged

---

203. *The Letters of Gregory the Great*, 2:323–496.
204. ἀφρούρητος. The long preceding quotation is from Bucer, *Praelectiones*, 131–33.

good Greek words for bad Latin ones[205]), are in fact present even in Protestant churches?[206] And do you mean that even churches that maintain neither the good old Greek terms nor the bad new Latin ones are nevertheless accustomed to having a few who are of the first rank, to whom almost all the power generally belongs?

The controversy, thus, turns out to have been one of labels. But given that we agree about the actual things, why in the world are we wrangling about words? At the same time, just as I do not disapprove of the fathers in that matter being considered, so I cannot but love the zeal of those among us who, on that account, hate those names. For they are apprehensive about these labels lest the ancient ambition and tyranny also be revived, to the ruin of the churches.

Aphorism 12
For Christ did not appoint such a head, nor did the ancient fathers wish to condone one, since it was not expedient for the church. Instead, they were satisfied with the four patriarchs of Rome, Constantinople, Alexandria, and Antioch, all of whom wielded equal authority and power, and each one was content with his territory. This is how it was defined at the Council of Nicaea and confirmed at other councils. And this was done for many weighty reasons, not the least of which in my opinion is so that the gates to tyranny in the church were not opened. Rather, if anyone dared to attack the wholesome doctrine of Christ and the church's liberty, he would be opposed by no less an authority than the archbishop with his bishops. And they would be able to check his audacity and crush his tyranny. With respect to Christ, the church is a kingdom; with respect to those who are in it—who rule or are ruled—it is an aristocracy.

---

205. That is, instead of using the Latinized *episcopos* ("bishop") in place of the Greek ἐπίσκοπος, they translated the Greek directly into the target language ("superintendent").

206. Zanchi probably has in mind the Scottish Kirk, which included superintendents in the 1560 *First Book of Discipline*, but perhaps also the Lutheran churches of Germany and the Baltic, which often had both superintendents and superintendents general.

Aphorism 21

Here are two very different questions: first, whether it is permitted for bishops also to be princes and for princes to be bishops, retaining their principalities. And second, whether those who, contrary to ecclesiastical judgment, are already bishops and princes at the same time still have political authority in the cities subject to them and, therefore, whether their subjects ought to obey them as princes or not.

In my aphorism, I have not actually said anything about the first question, since it was not necessary to do so. I only address the latter. But does anyone fail to see from the testimonies I adduced that I have clearly demonstrated that, in general, princes should be obeyed whether they were made princes rightly or wrongly? For, why would those who are under the sovereignty of the prince archbishops of Mainz, Cologne, and Trier not obey them in matters that do not interfere with Christian piety? Surely it would be mere sedition to disobey. But if that is the case, then why should not those who live under Roman sovereignty not do the same thing in the same matters and for the same reason? For the same reasoning lies behind all these matters.

With regard to the first question, as I said before, I have nothing to explain. But I have also now resolved in this my short confession not to argue, since I know that not everyone is of the same opinion and that many things can be said on one side and the other. The passage in Matthew 20 — *You know that the princes of the gentiles lord it over them, and those who are greater exercise power over them. But it will not be so among you* [vv. 25–26] — has been interpreted in one way by some as referring to the apostles and ministers of the Word but in another way by others as referring to all of Christ's disciples and to all Christians.

An Appendix to Chapter Eleven:
The Redeemer, or the Person of Christ

They write that the essential properties of the divine nature are really communicated to the human nature not as they are in themselves—either essentially and formally or subjectively and habitually—but rather only and with respect to the hypostatic union. This is the obscure and, yes, ambiguous way in which they speak, although they can and should speak more clearly. If we understand these things in the same sense that Vigilius considered and taught them in his writings, then I am certainly not going to contradict.[1] (Vigilius taught that the properties of the natures become proper to Christ Himself; not reciprocally in the natures themselves but in Christ, that is, in the person that is common to both.) And I am persuaded that no one who is both good and learned should contradict this either.

For Vigilius likewise discussed and explained that what is characteristic of the human nature became common to the divine nature, in accordance with the doctrine of the catholic church speaking through the Council of Chalcedon. And that which is characteristic of the divine nature is said to be communicated to the human nature in the same way. Notwithstanding, that which is characteristic of the humanity—for instance, to suffer or to die—is communicated to the deity in such a way that the deity itself does not really become passible or mortal as a result. Vigilius offers the following as the reason why this is the case: because to suffer and to die did not become common to the deity except in the

---

1. As Zanchi noted in his letter to the reader, he is engaging with Vigilius's *Against Eutyches* in this appendix.

person. That happens in such a way that they cannot truly be predicated except with reference to the human nature per se or with reference to the person (according to and on account of the human nature).

Consequently, we should certainly understand and state the same thing with regard to the communication of the divine properties. The following are Vigilius's words from book 5, chapter 2[, §7–8]:

> Right now, we are particularly interested in those who, following the one-nature error, reject the decree of the Council of Chalcedon with pertinacious obstinacy. For that reason, I think repeating a few things and demonstrating how they are not Christian but altogether foreign to the hope of eternal life will be advantageous for crushing their foolish contradictions and shattering the glazing of their opinions about the Son of God's human nature—which they altogether deny in Him—with the hammer of truth.
>
> (A)[2] A rule of the catholic faith is that, just as one and the same Lord Jesus Christ is confessed as true God, so also is He confessed as true man—one from both, not two into each other. He was begotten of the Father apart from time and was born of a virgin at a given time such that each of these begettings might bear the one Christ in such a way that He underwent no diminishment in Himself but retained in Himself what is characteristic of each of the natures. That is to say, the nature of the Word was not changed into flesh, and the nature of the flesh was not swallowed up in the Word. Hence, the Lord Jesus Christ Himself is true God and also true man, existing in the virgin's womb according to the two natures united in the one person in an ineffable way. Because these natures were not obliterated in Him in that extraordinary union, He said and did things that pertained to both natures in order to demonstrate the existence of both in His one self. He did not distinguish the voices or divide up the appearances or separate the actions. Rather, His one self spoke and performed in Himself and from each nature that which was fitting and characteristic of each nature.

---

2. Below Zanchi indicates that this marginal notation is meant to draw the reader's attention to Vigilius's theological method.

Let us use an example to make what we are saying clear. It is I myself who discerns the colors white or black with corporeal eyes. And again, it is I myself who discerns between the evil of wickedness and the good of righteousness by mental contemplation. Nevertheless, I am not one thing and then another because these two actions are from me in different ways. For the eyes with which I discern that colors vary are not the same eyes with which I discern variance in discourse. Yet I am the one who does both; it is mine to see righteousness only with the eyes of the mind and to see colors only with the eyes of the flesh. And it is mine not to hear a voice with my eyes and mine not to see light with my ears. It is mine not to distinguish taste with my nose, and it is mine not to smell with my tongue. And while the seeing, hearing, smelling, and tasting are all mine and in me, yet it is one thing for me to see and another to hear and another to taste or smell. And while all this is in me, it is rightly diverse and distinguished in a certain way peculiar to each, although I myself cannot be divided or separated.

So then, Christ Himself is also one and the same—created and not created, having a beginning and without beginning, increasing in age and knowledge and not undergoing any increase of knowledge or age, enduring death and not subject to the laws of death, receiving honor for what was due and requiring no honor. And although all these divergent things are in Him, they are nevertheless His very own. And thus, He does not parcel out the voices, affections, and actions in Himself in a way that corresponds to each nature, because both are His own. But He has the one thing from the nature of the Word, which He did not lose, since He remained God, while He has the other from the nature of the flesh, which He received as He was made man. Yet let us speak more directly on account of those who affirm one nature because they lack understanding and who abuse or reject these words because they fail to grasp how the distinctive characteristics of and the relationship between the natures are said to be in Christ.

To have a beginning is altogether different from subsisting from the beginning, and to die is altogether different from being unable to die. Nevertheless, in the same way that both of these things are proper to Christ, so they are common—not to Him but in Him. For if we were to say, *They are common to Him*, then we would have to provide and demonstrate another person with whom the first is common. And the force of that declaration inclines toward Nestorius's wicked dogma. Therefore, we speak better and in a catholic way when we say, *They are common in Him but not to Him*, and when we say, *They are proper to Him but not in Him*.

Thus, it is proper to Him to die on account of the nature of the flesh, which is mortal. And it is proper to Him not to die on account of the nature of the Word, which cannot die. Likewise, on account of the ineffable mystery of the union of both natures, the mortality of the flesh was common in Him to the nature of the Word, which cannot die. And in Him, the immortality of the Word is common to the nature of the flesh, which succumbed to death. Consequently, just as it is proper to Him to die according to one nature and not to die according to the other, so that which is characteristic of either nature is common in Him.

For example, I might say that, on account of the nature of my flesh, it is characteristic for me to bear the mark of every blow on my body. Likewise, on account of the nature of my soul, it is characteristic for me to bear a verbal wound (that is, a harsh word) in my mind. But on account of the nature of my flesh, it is not characteristic for me to carry a verbal wound in my body. And while each of these is characteristic of me, and each is distinct on account of my body and my soul (because the body understands neither harsh nor cheering speech, nor does the soul turn black and blue when struck), nevertheless, each of them is common in me and to both my soul and my body. For neither does a soul situated outside the body feel that which was characteristic for it to feel, nor, without the partnership of its soul, does a body bear the marks of having been struck. Thus, that which is characteristic of me in one of these is also distinct from the other. What is common in me by either of them is what is characteristic of each. And yet, I myself am one and the same in either, both of which are common in me. And in each of them, I myself am one and the same, since it is me of whom they are characteristic.[3]

As I said, could anything be more appropriate for settling the

---

3. *PL*, 62:138D–40B.

present controversy about the real communication of the attributes? For as it pertains to our subject, Vigilius's entire treatise is laid open in these excellent statements. For, having first set forth a rule of the catholic faith (which, in the quotation, is marked above by the letter *A*), he then derives certain propositions whereby he plainly refutes Eutyches's heresy. The sum of that rule of faith is: one and the same Christ is God and man; in Him each nature is preserved. Vigilius assembles the following propositions based on this rule:

(1) The Lord Jesus Christ is at the same time true God and true man. The reason: He exists from the two natures (divine and human) ineffably united in one person in the virgin's belly (or womb). This opposes Nestorius, but another proposition is added against Eutyches.

(2) In this remarkable co-union, the natures are not obliterated in Him (Christ). Confirmation for this is supplied from the life of Christ, since the Lord Jesus demonstrated with words and deeds that the characteristics of each nature were preserved in Him. For that reason, Vigilius goes on.

(3) The Lord Jesus said and did things characteristic of each (of His natures) to demonstrate that both of the natures in His one self stand forth (that is, they exist; which is to say, they demonstrate that the distinct characteristics of each nature exist in Him). Just so, this is contra Eutyches.

But in what way? In such a way as to show that the things said and done were not said and done by two persons but by one. This is why Vigilius returns to add the following against Nestorius: *He did not distinguish the voices or divide up the appearances or separate the actions. Rather, His one self spoke and performed in Himself and from each nature that which was fitting and characteristic of each nature.*

Two things shine forth brighter than the noonday sun from these words. First, in Christ, there were not two who were working, willing, and doing but only one, namely, the very incarnate Word[4] who is called

---

4. λόγον.

the Christ. For this reason, Vigilius says, [*Because these natures were not obliterated in Him in that extraordinary union, He said and did things that pertained to both natures in order to demonstrate the existence of both*] *in His one self.* Likewise, Rather, *His one self spoke and performed.* This is the first point, and it is contra Nestorius.

The second point is: in the same Christ, however, there were and are two foundations of actions acting. These are distinct from each other, and, formally speaking (as they say in the schools), it is from them that the one who acted performed the actions, namely, the capacities (or powers[5]) of the two natures. And this is contra Eutyches.

And this is the reason Vigilius adds, *He spoke and acted from each* (that is, from each nature) *that which was characteristic* (namely, of each nature).

But who does not see from this that what Christ did according to one nature He did not do according to the other? For it was *from each nature* that He did the things that were characteristic of each. Thus, He did not do things characteristic of His deity according to His humanity, nor vice versa.

Indeed, by way of confirming and illustrating these things, Vigilius offers the example of a single man who does various actions according to the various faculties of his soul and performs works appropriate to each faculty.

That illustration needs no explanation: *And in order that what we are saying might be made clear…*

Only, we must pay careful attention to the details, not only to what Vigilius affirms but also to what he denies. For he denies that what a man sees with his mind's eye is seen with corporeal eyes, and vice versa. Thus, he also denies that what Christ performed according to His deity was done according to the flesh. When Vigilius applies the comparison to Christ, he clearly proposes this. The first thing he says about Him is: *He has the one thing from the nature of the Word, which He did not lose, since He remained God, while He has the other from the nature of the flesh, which He received as He was made man.*

---

5. δυνάμεις.

Likewise, we must take note that Vigilius denies that it is from the flesh (that is, according to the flesh) that Christ does those things that are characteristic of His deity. He makes this point so strongly that he even denies that Christ suffered and did things according to His deity that were characteristic of His flesh.

What is more, Vigilius adds a specific explanation of the special character and communion of the natures, and he does so in a clear and distinct fashion when he says: *Yet let us speak more directly on account of those [who affirm one nature because they lack understanding and who abuse or reject these words because they fail to grasp how the distinctive characteristics of and the relationship between the natures are said to be in Christ].* The sum is this:

(4) The characteristics of each nature are the characteristics of the very person of Christ. This, however, is mutually common to the natures, not in the natures themselves but in the person. Here is an explanation.

To die (which is a characteristic of the flesh) is characteristic of Christ. For insofar as it is said that He died, properly speaking, it is said with reference to the human nature in Him. Indeed, according to the divine nature proper, which cannot die, it is not characteristic of Him to die.

Similarly, to die is common to the Word (or to Christ's deity) but obviously not to the divine nature itself, which cannot partake of death. Rather, it was common to Him with the flesh because the person bearing the flesh could die, and Christ did die in the flesh. The same thing should be said and understood with regard to the other part, as Vigilius explains when he inserts the example of himself (that is, of a man), saying, *Let us use an example to make what we are saying clear.* Nothing in this example is difficult to understand.

But we must take careful note of the conclusion, where he says, *Thus, that which is characteristic of me in one of these is also distinct from the other. What is common in me by either of them is what is characteristic of each. And yet, I myself am one and the same in either, both of which are common in me. And in each of them, I myself am one and the same, since it is me of whom they are characteristic.*

(1) Nothing can be said more clearly to explain the question about the real communication of the characteristics.[6] For, first, it teaches that the characteristics of the one nature are characteristic of it in such a way that they are utterly foreign to the other nature. And they are so foreign that they can in no way be made common in their very essence.[7] That is, they cannot really be shared in such a way that one nature actually takes on the nature or qualities of the other—as, for example, if the humanity were to become deity or omnipotent or, conversely, if it were possible for the deity to become humanity or participate in suffering.

(2) Next, it teaches with clear words that the characteristics of each of Christ's natures are characteristic of Christ. Such is the case because it is characteristic of Him, for example, to suffer in Himself in one of His natures but to be unable to suffer in the other. In this,[8] He is unlike anything else in heaven or on earth or in Himself. For nothing else besides Christ is simultaneously God and man, and neither of the natures in Him have the characteristics of the other nature. Rather, they have only the characteristics that are in their own essence.[9] Therefore, it is for Christ alone—God and man—really to have in Himself the essential characteristics of the divine and human natures and, so, for them to be proper to Him.

This also is why what was said previously about communication is obvious. For if it is characteristic of Christ's person for these contrary things (for example, to suffer and to be unable to suffer) to be predicated of Him truly and really (albeit not simply but elsewise,[10] that is, with respect to one of Christ's two natures), then truly and really it seems impossible to say that either nature could suffer and not suffer individually in its own essence.[11]

---

6. De reali proprietatum communicatione.
7. οὐσίᾳ.
8. It is not clear what "this" refers to in this sentence, but it is probably the uniqueness of the hypostatic union between the divine and human natures in Christ.
9. οὐσίᾳ.
10. κατ' ἄλλο.
11. οὐσίᾳ.

(3) Vigilius said that the characteristics of the natures are characteristic of Christ. Indeed, he taught that these became common—not common to each of the natures but common in the person. For example, in a simple sense and of itself (in its own essence[12]), suffering is characteristic of the human nature, but elsewise[13] (that is, with respect merely to the flesh), it is characteristic of the person. I am saying that, on account of the union the flesh has with the deity itself in the same hypostasis,[14] this essentially fleshly characteristic of suffering also became common to the divine nature along with the human. In what way was it made common? In such a way that suffering is also attributed to the divine nature.

But how [is it so attributed], since the divine nature cannot suffer? Well, suffering is common to the divine nature, not in its very essence[15] (for it neither could nor can suffer) but in Christ, that is, in the person of Christ, which consists of two natures. And therefore, He merely suffered according to the flesh,[16] so that, indeed, no suffering adheres in the particular essence[17] of the deity but merely in the common person on account of the flesh. And so, God is indeed said also to have suffered, although the deity suffered nothing but only the person of God and man. That is, He who is God and man suffered according to the flesh.[18] I repeat: the characteristics of (for example) the human nature, such as being able to suffer and to die, are for that reason said to be common to the deity because it has them as well. For if the deity has them in no sense at all, then there is no way in which the deity could be said to become common with the flesh.

But this is why those characteristics are said to be common to the deity along with the humanity, not simply but in Christ Himself—because the deity does not have them in its very self (that is, in its essence[19]) in the same way that the flesh has them. But this is the case

---

12. οὐσίᾳ.
13. κατ᾽ ἄλλο.
14. ὑποστάσει.
15. οὐσίᾳ.
16. κατὰ σάρκα.
17. οὐσίᾳ.
18. κατὰ σάρκα.
19. οὐσίᾳ.

only in Christ's person, which is the one and the same hypostasis of both natures, since He subsists in both of them.

The soul also has common characteristics with its body, but it does not have them in its essence[20] in the same way as the body does. Rather, it has them with regard to the person of the man who, just as he consists of both body and soul as his essential components, so also really has characteristics of both in him. So, it can truly be said that he is visible and invisible, mortal and immortal.

But Vigilius, bishop and martyr, teaches that what is said about the characteristics of the human nature being common with the divine must be understood and asserted not of the divine nature's individual essence[21] but of the person common to both natures. The same is true with regard to the divine characteristics being common with the human.

This being the case, from this follows the sort of true expressions that can be devised with regard to these things. (1) If the characteristics of the flesh (suffering, for example) is in some way common with the deity, then suffering can be predicated of the deity in some way. (2) If suffering is common to the deity in such a way that it neither has it in itself or in its essence,[22] nor as an essential part of itself, nor in the way that an accident is in a subject, then the deity cannot be said to be to be subject to suffering in its essence.[23] (3) But if suffering is merely common to the deity in the person, then it can only be predicated of the deity concretely and not in the abstract. That is, suffering can only be predicated by the sort of word that refers to the deity in such a way as to indicate the person, as is the case with concrete words like *God*.

For insofar as the person of Christ—who is indeed God and not mere man—is signified by the word *God*, God is truly and really said to suffer and die. Yet this is not the case in a simple sense or according to the deity but only according to the flesh,[24] a characteristic of which is to suffer and die. For this reason, just as this is entirely true: *God suffered,*

---

20. οὐσία.
21. οὐσία.
22. οὐσία.
23. οὐσία.
24. κατὰ σάρκα.

so these other statements are altogether false: *the deity suffered*, or even: *Christ suffered according to His divine nature*. This is Vigilius's doctrine and the doctrine of the whole church.

However, what Vigilius teaches concerning the characteristics of the natures and their communion are said equally with regard to all the characteristics and their communion in Christ in such a way that the divine characteristics are said to become common to the humanity on account of the hypostatic union. This is the case in the same sense that human characteristics are said to become common to the divinity. That is to say, they are common not in the essences[25] of the natures themselves but only in Christ and in Christ's person. This being the case, it follows that, just as this is an irreverent statement: *The deity became a partaker of suffering in its essence*[26] *on account of the union with the flesh in the person of the Son of God*, so likewise this is a blasphemous one: *On account of its union with the divine nature, the human nature receives from the divine nature in such a way that it is really omnipotent (and so forth) in its essence*.[27]

Now, if we add to all this what that same Vigilius wrote (in accordance with the common consent of the whole of the catholic church), the doctrine that we just demonstrated from his writings will become clearer. For, while arguing against the Monophysites, he brilliantly demonstrated from the various characteristics seen in one and the same Christ, which Holy Scripture makes known, that it is impossible for there to be a single nature in Him that is both Word and flesh. This is the reason alleged by Vigilius: because one nature does not admit that which is contrary and opposite into its very self.

In addition to other words, he wrote these:

> Next, how can it be the case that there is a single nature of Word and flesh, since the Word is everywhere, but the flesh is not found everywhere? On the other hand, when the flesh was on earth, it certainly was not in heaven. And now, because it is in heaven, it is certainly not on earth. And it is absent from earth in such a way

---

25. οὐσίαις.
26. οὐσίᾳ.
27. οὐσίᾳ.

that, with respect to the flesh, we are awaiting the coming of Christ from heaven, whom we believe to be with us on earth with respect to the Word.

So, according to you, either the Word is locally restricted with its flesh, or the flesh is everywhere with the Word, since the one nature does not admit in itself that which is contrary and opposite. But to be locally circumscribed is contrary to and altogether different from being everywhere. And since the Word is everywhere, but His flesh is not everywhere, it appears that the one and the same Christ is of both natures and that He is, indeed, everywhere with respect to the nature of His divinity and locally restricted with respect to the nature of His humanity. He is created and has no beginning. He is subject to death and cannot die. He has the former on the basis of the Word's nature, whereby He is God; the latter on the basis of the fleshly nature, whereby that same God is man.

Therefore, the one Son of God who also became the Son of Man has a beginning by reason of His fleshly nature and has no beginning by reason of the nature of His divinity. He was created on account of His fleshly nature and was not created on account of the nature of His divinity. He was circumscribed on account of His fleshly nature and was not locally restricted on account of the nature of His divinity. He is even lower than the angels on account of His fleshly nature and is equal to the Father with respect to the nature of His divinity. He died by His fleshly nature and did not die by the nature of His divinity. This is the catholic faith and confession, which the apostles handed down, the martyrs confirmed, and the faithful are preserving to this very day (*Against Eutyches*, bk. 4, ch. 4[, §§14–15]).[28]

This also demonstrates what was previously demonstrated, namely, that not only is it impossible for Word and flesh to be of one single nature, as the Monophysites allege, but also that the characteristics of one nature cannot really be communicated to the other. This is to say, they cannot be communicated in such a way that the one nature has those things in its very self and becomes the same sort as the other nature. For example,

---

28. *Against Eutyches*, bk. 4, ch. 4[, §§14–15]: *PL*, 62:126.

it is not the case that the flesh, on account of its union with the Word, becomes present everywhere in its essence[29] along with the Word. The flesh does not acquire this characteristic of the Word on account of its union with the Word in such a way that it is everywhere present with the Word in its substance. From this premise, Vigilius concludes (just as all the orthodox allege in their confession) that, therefore, the flesh also does not become of the same nature as the Word. At any rate, this is Vigilius's argument and, indeed, the argument of the whole catholic church.

What's left? Only this: if the fleshly nature must be said to be everywhere present, the only way to explain how it can be said to be everywhere present is by its hypostasis,[30] which is nothing other than the Word.

For in Christ's human nature, there are only two things: [1] the particular essence[31] of its nature, with its characteristics and created gifts, and [2] the hypostasis[32] shared with the divine nature, which is nothing other than the Word. Its particular essence[33] is finite, and so it can only be in one place; the hypostasis[34] is infinite and immense and most simple. Thus, only in this way—but not in the particular essence[35]—can it be everywhere present, and only in this way is it really Christ's flesh.

But what has been said about this characteristic should similarly be understood of everything, as much the Word as the flesh. For Vigilius drew the same conclusion in the preceding argument against the Monophysites (bk. 4, ch. 4),[36] on the basis of certain characteristics of the Word—that the Word is uncreated, invisible, intangible—and he said that it is impossible for the flesh to be exposed to those conditions. He concludes from this that the flesh cannot therefore be of one nature with the Word, since it can in no way become invisible, uncreated, intangible

---

29. οὐσία.
30. ὑποστάσει.
31. οὐσία.
32. ὑπόστασις.
33. οὐσία.
34. ὑπόστασις.
35. οὐσία.
36. (bk. 4, ch. 4): *PL*, 62:120–21.

(meaning, in its essence[37]). Yet, since, in its hypostasis,[38] which is common to the flesh and the Word, the flesh actually is uncreated, invisible, and intangible, just as it is also everywhere present in view of its same hypostasis,[39] in what sense is it not also God? All these things are obvious and plain and depend upon the infallible rule Vigilius sets forth: *Therefore, we speak better and in a catholic way when we say, "They are common in Him but not to Him," and when we say, "They are proper to Him but not in Him."* (*Against Eutyches*, bk. 5, ch. 2[, §8]).[40]

By the Lord Jesus, I beg all Christians—having put aside the vain dreams of individual men as well as the influences, hatreds, and enmities characteristic of the flesh, and having instead embraced the ancient church's sure and wholesome doctrine and Christian love—all to unite in one faith and holy friendship, just as there is for us all one God, one Mediator, one baptism, one hope of our calling to God's glory, the church's edification, and our souls' salvation [Eph. 4:4–6]. Let us do this because there is no hope for pardon and no room for coming to one's senses after this life, and we will stand before Christ's judgment seat sooner than we imagine for each one of us to recount how he conducted himself in the flesh and in this life.

---

37. οὐσίᾳ.
38. ὑποστάσει.
39. ὑπόστασις.
40. *Against Eutyches*, bk. 5, ch. 2[, §8]: *PL*, 62:139.

Certain Chief Articles of the Christian Faith Debated at Various Times at Heidelberg and Neustadt against Various Heresies

Here, at the end of this confession, along with the observations and for the same reason, I have made public the following theses concerning various matters debated partly during the time of Fredrick III (of pious memory) in Heidelberg and partly here at Neustadt under Johann Casimir, founder of this school and kindest of lords. Having defended them against various heresies, I have arranged for these theses to be collected so that they might be printed along with my confession. I did this specifically so that all posterity could yet more clearly understand that I never consented to any of the heresies that have, in recent days, once more been summoned out of hell. May this be to God's glory, the church's edification, and the salvation of many, through Jesus Christ our Lord. Amen.

The One True God, Eternal Father, Son, and Holy Spirit (1572)

1. There is only one Jehovah, the Creator of the heavens and the earth and the God of Israel.

2. However, although that God is the one and only Jehovah, nevertheless, He is not one but plural Elohim, the names and number of whom the Son of God—God manifest in the flesh—has revealed to us clearly and without any ambiguity: the eternal Father, the eternal Son, and the eternal Holy Spirit.

3. Moreover, these three Elohim[1] are true subsisting ones[2]—undivided, living, understanding, and willing—and, thus, they are (as the church has always called them) true persons.

4. And thus, among themselves, the Father, Son, and Holy Spirit are distinct such that one is not the other.

5. However, each one of them is the true Jehovah.

6. For that reason, there is no more than the one and only Jehovah.

The Nature, Simplicity, and Immensity of the One True God (1573)

1. By the phrase *the nature of God* we usually mean not only His essence considered simply in itself but also all His characteristics (or attributes) whereby what He is like is made known to us and for our sake.

2. Accordingly, God is often rightly said to be kind, wise, good, and other things of this sort.

3. But although He is accustomed to describing men using many qualities that are like His own nature (whereby we are just, good, and wise), yet He shares His nature with no created thing because it cannot be shared, unless it were possible for more gods to be made.

4. Before anything else, however, God is simply simple such that there is clearly no way in which He can be said to be composed of many things, indeed, not even of being and essence.

5. For although He attributes many things to Himself in the Holy Scriptures—many qualities, as it were, with respect to which He is

---

1. In referring to three Elohim, Zanchi does not mean to suggest tritheism. In fact, he developed this language specifically as part of an extensive argument for trinitarian monotheism in *De tribus Elohim* (1572). He sees the plurality of the biblical term Elohim as properly indicating the three subsistences in the one God and the tetragrammaton as properly indicating the one divine *ousia*. See, Benjamin R. Merkle, *Defending the Trinity in the Reformed Palatinate: The Elohistae*, Oxford Theology and Religion Monographs (New York: Oxford University Press, 2016), esp. 88–117.

2. ὑφιστάμενα.

righteous, good, powerful—yet, in fact, no quality settles into God. Rather, He is whatever He is by His most simple essence, although the infinite perfection of that most simple essence is signified to us in various terms.

6. Not only does God allow no composition in Himself, He also does not enter into the materiality of any created thing in such a way that He becomes either its form or matter.

7. In addition, God is truly immense and infinite, and for that reason He is also everywhere present. And this is the case not only in His power and strength but in His whole essence, which fills heaven and earth and all things.

8. But although He is everywhere present in His essence, yet He is said to be in heaven more than on earth, and He is said to be in saints more than in the wicked, and more in one pious person than in another. But that is not said with respect to His essence. Rather, it is said with respect to the influence of His work and grace.

9. This is why, when we read in the Holy Scriptures that God either withdraws from us or draws near to us, we should believe that He does not do this by a change of location but by the internal and external influences of His presence, either projecting or withdrawing them.

10. Notwithstanding, God is in Christ's human nature in a very different way than He is in us: not only does He operate more influentially, but He also dwells bodily[3] and as part of a composite, in such a way that Christ is true God, while we cannot be.

11. Again, it is so characteristic of God to be immense and infinite, and thus also to be everywhere present, that His nature obviously cannot belong to any created thing, not even to Christ's human nature.

12. For just as a creature cannot become God in essence, so neither can

---

3. σωματικῶς.

that which is not God in its essence be made present everywhere, since it can neither be infinite nor immense.

13. Hence, just as it is demonstrated from this that Christ is everywhere by His essence, and just as He is truly proven thereby to be true God, so, if some argue that Christ's body exists everywhere by its substance, then they must either deny that Christ's deity has been proven from that argument, or they must make a new God—and a corporeal one at that.

14. Christ's body is indeed present, not only in its power but also in substance in the minds of all the pious who experience it by true faith and who are, therefore, growing together more and more with Christ Himself by means of His Spirit. To them, His body is present not less but rather more than the sun is present to all those who behold it with their eyes. But even so, since Christ's body is in heaven, it can no more exist in multiple places (let alone everywhere) at the same time than the body of the sun can exist in every particle of heaven and earth as it does in its orb.

15. Yet this does not entail (as some shamelessly accuse) a denial of Christ's true and eternal deity. On the contrary, His deity is asserted because the Word[4] is maintained as being deity of the kind that cannot be imparted to any created thing in such a way that the created thing either becomes God in essence[5] or equal to God in any divine characteristic.

16. For the Word[6] is not the true God if some creature can become exactly like Him—even a spiritual creature, let alone a human body.

17. Our opponents want divinity and essential characteristics to be imparted to Christ's humanity in such a way that His humanity is omnipotent and everywhere in just the same way as His deity. They not only swing the door wide open to the Arians but also rob Christ of His true deity.

18. And indeed, he is not the true God, whose essence and nature can be

---
4. ὁ λόγος.
5. τῇ οὐσίᾳ.
6. ὁ λόγος.

really imparted to any created thing in such a way that the created thing altogether becomes as God is—really and in itself infinitely powerful, infinitely wise, extending itself (as one might say) into infinity, and in that way actually existing everywhere in its essence.

19. For the essential characteristics of God really are nothing other than His very essence, for that is the only way that He could be most simple.

20. Therefore, to say that Christ's humanity becomes omnipotent and everywhere present in the same way as His deity is the same thing as saying that, in its essence and nature, His humanity become deity and, thus, that it becomes the true God.

21. However, that sort of deity is not true deity, and, thus, the Word[7] would not be true God, which is a terrible blasphemy.

22. Certainly, it is not merely altogether absurd but also entirely wicked to say that the characteristics of the divine nature are imparted to the human nature.

23. For at no time do we read that the Word[8] or any of its characteristics were imparted to the seed of Abraham in the same way that, conversely, we read the Son of God took on Abraham's seed. Nor could the characteristics of the Word[9] have been imparted to the human nature without imparting the Word's nature and divine essence, since those characteristics really are nothing other than the divine essence.

24. The divine nature, however, cannot be transferred into a human nature, since that would bring the union of the natures to an end and would create mixture and confusion. To be sure, things that are mixed in that way cease to be what they were.

25. Therefore, we say again that the kind of deity of which any created thing can become the equal is not true deity.

---

7. ὁ λόγος.
8. τὸν λόγον.
9. τοῦ λόγου.

26. For it is necessary either for the thing being made equal to become infinite (which is altogether impossible[10]), or else the deity to which it has been made equal is finite (since a finite thing can only become equal with something that is finite). But a finite deity is not true deity.

The Eternal Omnipotence of the One Word of God (1575)

1. When the Holy Scriptures call God powerful, our minds should not imagine that there is passive potency in God whereby He could suffer to some degree or stop being what He is or become what He is not by some change in Himself. Rather, when the Scriptures call God powerful, we should believe (and we should believe it with firm faith) that there is only active potency in God whereby He always acts and is able to act just as He truly is.

2. For God is a most simple, most perfect, truly eternal essence, free from all suffering, unchangeable, and most efficacious,[11] from whom and through whom all things are and happen.

3. But there is no active potency in God of the sort that should be imagined to be something different from His essence.

4. For in His most simple essence, God is whatever He is: just, good, omnipotent.

5. But although there really is only one potency in God, nevertheless, on account of the diverse perspectives from which it is considered, it can be said to be manifold without irreverence.

6. For there is one perspective when that potency is considered insofar as God always works in Himself (by knowing, willing, loving). And there is another perspective when we contemplate God's power insofar as He has worked outside of Himself (creating the world), and as He always works (ruling it), and as He is able to work countless things (if He wills).

---

10. ἀδύνατον.
11. ἐνεργητικωτάτη.

7. Therefore, just as it is not foolish to distinguish God's actions into immanent and transeunt, so God's power can reasonably be said to be twofold.[12] The first is that power whereby He has from all eternity always acted and does act in Himself. The second is that whereby, in time and outside of Himself, He made, rules, and works not only everything but also the infinite number of things that He could cause to happen but which He will never bring about.

8. So it is in turn that God's power is often distinguished into actual power (whereby He does whatever He wills) and absolute power (whereby He is able to do infinite things, even those that He does not will), for otherwise He could not be said to be simply omnipotent.

9. We do not agree with those who claim that the reason God can be called omnipotent is simply because He is able to bring about whatever can be said or thought—whether evil or good or contradictory by implication. And so, neither do we subscribe to the opinion of those who claim that the only reason God is omnipotent and is called omnipotent is because He can do whatever He wants, for His power extends no further than His will. Rather, we believe that He is truly omnipotent because, in addition to being able to do whatever He wants, God is also able to will and to bring about things that He will never will or bring about.

10. For since Scripture says that God did whatever He willed, it plainly teaches that He could have also done a great deal more if He had

---

12. This distinction is drawn from Aristotle's *Metaphysics* and was deployed by Aquinas in his criticism of Averroism and his defense of Chalcedonian Christology (e.g., in *De unitate contra Averroistas*, §§71–73 and *Summa theologiae*, I, q. 76, art. 1) and then developed in various ways by later scholastics. Stephen John Zylstra comments, "In the scholastic tradition, it was widely held that all actions belong to one of two kinds, typically called 'transeunt' and 'immanent'. Transeunt actions are relatively easy to describe: they are the sort of activity whereby the 'doer' of the activity, or *agent*, does something *to something else*. Throwing a ball, *burning* a piece of wood, and *building* a nest are all examples." Immanent actions are those that "really do not involve any external patient." He continues, "Certainly the clearest and least controversial examples…are mental operations like sensing, willing, and thinking." "Immanent Causation in Spinoza and Scholasticism" (PhD diss., University of Toronto, 2018), 8.

wanted. And he who says that *He has mercy on those whom He will and hardens whom He will* [Rom. 9:18] clearly demonstrates that He could just as well have mercy on and harden all as harden and have mercy on some. Consequently, He can have mercy on more people than those upon whom He wills to have mercy. And so, there is more that He can do than He wills to do.

11. For that which He can do, He can do by nature. Hence, He cannot do those things which are impossible to do while also being God. Moreover, those things that He wills outside of Himself, He wills freely, and so He is also able not to will them. Thus, it is obvious that God is able to do more than He wills to do, since it is possible for Him to will that which He does not will.

12. Moreover, we say that God can do anything except that which, if it were allowed, would conflict with His personal properties or very essence and nature, imply any contradiction, or finally, arise from a lack of power.

13. Thus, neither the Father nor the Son cease to be omnipotent on account of the fact that the Father cannot be the Son, and the Son cannot be the Father, nor because the Father cannot beget another son from Himself or the Son beget any son from Himself.

14. For the personal properties are: the Father begets and is not begotten, but the Son is begotten and does not beget. And God's essence does not tolerate the existence of multiple fathers or multiple sons.

15. Just so, neither does it fall short of God's power in any way if God can do something that is not good, just, or wise, since God cannot be anything other than what He is, which is how the Holy Scriptures describe Him.

16. Thus, we do not ruin or weaken God's power if we say that God is unable to sin or that He cannot suffer or that He cannot cause what is not to be while it yet is not, nor if we say that He cannot cause things that have been done not to have been done. The reason is partly because

these things arise from a defect of power and partly because they entail a contradiction. And therefore, they are in direct conflict with God's truthfulness and are entirely impossible.[13]

17. Moreover, it is characteristic of God to be omnipotent in a way that cannot correspond to any created thing.

18. For since omnipotence is nothing other than the very immense, infinite, and incommunicable (to any creature) essence, it cannot be appropriate for omnipotence to be in a thing in which it cannot suitably exist.

19. Nor, indeed, can a finite thing contain an infinite thing, since, as they say, everything is received according to the measure of the one receiving.

20. Indeed, it conflicts with God's nature for there to be multiple omnipotents no less that it does for there to be multiple gods. This is the reason why the Christian religion does not tolerate the three persons in God to be spoken of as three almighties.[14]

21. Thus, although the man Christ Jesus truly is omnipotent because He is not only man but also God, yet, properly speaking, His humanity cannot be or be said to be omnipotent without a charge of irreverence.

22. Christ's human nature, although it is united to the divine nature in the one person of the Word,[15] nevertheless does not become God on that account. In the same way, it does not become omnipotent, properly speaking. Rather, it retained its weakness, which could suffer and die for us.

23. Christ's human nature could not have suffered if it had also become omnipotent as God is, since being able to suffer is a weakness. For that reason, God cannot suffer—because He is omnipotent.

24. And if the human nature in Christ became omnipotent on account

---

13. ἀδύνατον.
14. Athanasian Creed, §14 (Schaff, *Creeds*, 2:67).
15. τοῦ λόγου.

of the hypostatic union, why do the Holy Scriptures attribute to His humanity rather than to His deity the fact that His body did not see corruption and that He rose again from the dead once His soul was restored to it?

25. A human body does not become an incorporeal substance gifted with intellect and will on account of its union with the mind. Nor does it receive from the mind either immortality or the power of understanding and willing. In the same way, it happens that the human nature does not become a most simple and most perfect essence subsisting of itself on account of its union with the divine nature of the Word.[16] Nor, properly speaking, does the human nature receive the gift of being omnipotent from the divine nature.

26. Indeed, we concede that the anti-Arian argument used by the fathers to prove that the Son is true God on the basis of the omnipotence accorded Him in the Holy Scriptures is altogether overthrown if omnipotence can be shared with any created thing.

27. Finally, whatever we say about religion ought to be in harmony with the Holy Scriptures and the analogy of faith. The Holy Scriptures, however, do not predicate that anything is omnipotent other than God, nor did the church ever profess otherwise in her creeds.

28. But after the resurrection, Christ said, *All authority has been given to Me* [Matt. 28:18]. Authority[17] is one thing; power[18] is another.[19] He did not say, *It is given to My humanity*, but rather He said, *to Me*. Nor did He say this with respect to His nature but with respect to His mediatorial office. Moreover, that office was and is the office of the whole person according to both natures.

---

16. τοῦ λόγου.
17. Ἐξουσία.
18. δύναμις.
19. The word translated *authority* [*potestas*] in the citation of Matthew 28:18 is ἐξουσία. Zanchi is likely emphasizing a semantic distinction here between ἐξουσία/*potestas*/authority and δύναμις/*potentia*/power.

29. Therefore, just as we believe by the Holy Spirit that God alone is truly and properly omnipotent, so we also confess and proclaim it with the whole church.

30. We have no doubt, however, that Christ's human nature was granted that power which, although finite, far surpasses the power of all created things as much on earth as in heaven. Thus, it can properly and deservedly be called the most powerful of all creatures. Furthermore, while true omnipotence is not in the human nature itself as such, we nevertheless acknowledge that, on account of the hypostatic union with the truly omnipotent Word,[20] the human nature can be called omnipotent in a certain sense, namely, insofar as it is united to the Word[21] in such a way that the things that are characteristic of the Word[22] are also predicated of the human nature. But this occurs in the concrete and in such a way that the Word[23] used and can use His soul and body as the particular instruments to perform many works of His omnipotence while nevertheless maintaining the distinction between the characteristics and actions of each nature.

God's Providence (1576)

1. On the basis of God's Word, we believe and teach that providence—called foreknowledge[24] (Rom. 13:14[25]; Luke 22[26]) or even predetermination[27] (Acts 4:28) by the Greeks—is that in God whereby things are foreknown (Ps. 139:4), foreordained (Ps. 119:91), and ruled (Dan. 4:31).

---

20. λόγῳ.
21. τῷ λόγῳ.
22. τοῦ λόγου.
23. ὁ λόγος.
24. πρόνοιαν.
25. Zanchi establishes the biblical usage of the word πρόνοιαν with an appeal to this verse, although it does not refer to God's foreknowledge (or "provision," as it is often translated in this verse).
26. This citation is curious, as neither πρόνοιαν nor προορισμὸν appear in Luke 22. Zanchi may have had Acts 24:2 in mind, which contains the New Testament's other use of πρόνοιαν.
27. προορισμὸν.

2. Moreover, God's providence is the wisest (Job 9:4; 12:13; Jer. 51:15), most just (Deut. 32:4; Ps. 145:17; Wisd. of Sol. 12:15), and unchangeable (Ps. 33:11; Isa. 14:27; 46:10) counsel by which He decreed in Himself from eternity (Prov. 8:22; Eph. 1:9) all things (Dan. 4:32), both in heaven and on earth, that would happen (Lam. 2:37 [that is, 3:37]), and the way and sequence in which it they would occur. And as a model of this (Ps. 119:91), He continually administers and rules all things (Ps. 138:8; Dan. 4:32; John 5:17) in time (Genesis 1), sometimes by settled and ordinary means (Lev. 26:4; Ps. 104:4; Hos. 2:21; Eph. 4:11) and sometimes without them (Deut. 8:3; Ps. 72:18; Jer. 32:20; 1 Kings 17:4), but always efficaciously[28] (Ps. 115:3; Rom. 9:10). And He does this for the salvation of the elect (Gen. 50:20; Rom. 81:28 [that is, 8:28]; Cor. 3:21 [that is, 2 Cor. 3:18?]) and, especially, to shine forth His own glory (Ps. 19:1; 1 Chron. 29:11–12; Rom. 9:17).

3. For it is evident that God is omnipotent (Jer. 32:17; Luke 1:37), most wise, and altogether good (1 Chron. 16:34; Matt. 19:17). For this reason, it cannot be the case that He would allow this whole wide world He created (Gen. 1:1; Heb. 11:3) and in which Christ's church endures (John 16:33) to roll around blindly according to fortune and chance. Indeed, the Holy Scriptures themselves teach with clear words that this world is governed by God's providence (Psalm 33; 147; Job 5; 9; 37; 38; 39; Wisd. of Sol. 14:3; Col. 1:16; Hebrews 3; Isa. 42:5).

4. But we do not think that there is merely a general providence in God whereby the whole world system is regulated all at once (Neh. 9:33; Acts 17:28; Heb. 1:3). Rather, we recognize and uphold that specific sort of providence whereby He directs and rules each individual thing separately (Job 37; 38; Psalm 104; 147; Matt. 6:26; 10:29; John 4; 6; 7), especially men (Ps. 8:5; Jer. 10:23), and among them His elect, along with all their actions (Isa. 43:1; Psalm 91; 139; Zech. 2:8; Matt. 6:10).

5. For we know that nothing happens or is stirred in the world apart from the will of the Father (Matt. 10:29; Luke 12:6). So, nothing could

---

28. ἐνεργητικῶς.

be more absurd than to say that anything happens in the world that God did not previously ordain and that He does not rule by His hand (Prov. 16:4; Dan. 4:32).

6. Yet we do not on this account simply deny that many things happen contingently and by chance (Ex. 21:13; Prov. 16:33), since this does not oppose God's eternal and unfailing providence when understood correctly.

7. For God, by His unchangeable providence, not only decrees that things come to pass as they do. He also ordained from eternity that all things happen in the way that they happen.

8. But because we deny that anything is permitted in the world apart from the will of the Father, we do not on that account involve God Himself, the wisest and wholly just Governor of all actions, in sin, nor do we make Him the author of sin.

9. For sin is lawlessness[29] and a turning aside from the straight line of divine law (1 John 3:4). Moreover, God cannot deviate from the uprightness of His will (Num. 23:19; Titus 1:2; Heb. 6:18; 1 John 1:5) and does not impart a defect causing deviation unto others (James 1:13; Hos. 13:9). No, indeed, He hates sin (Ps. 5:6) and is a most righteous Avenger (Deut. 32:41; Isa. 59:17; Nah. 1:2).

10. For this reason, since it pertains to God's providence for sins to be punished by God the righteous Judge, it is proven from the doctrine of providence that God should be feared and sins avoided rather than that any guilt can be shifted onto God and our misdeeds excused as a result.

11. But beyond this which we have just said, there are many other wholesome uses of this doctrine of providence. So, these two should be particularly noted: first, that by this doctrine the pious are led in every adversity to flee unto God who rules all things (2 Chron. 14:11; 20:6–12; Ps. 46:1; Matt. 10:28; Acts 27:23, 35; 1 Peter 5:6–7; James 4:10).

---

29. ἀνομία.

And second, that they might give all glory to Him alone and always be submissive under the hand of His power whereby He accomplishes all things.

Election and Predestination and the Redemption Accomplished by Christ, Based on Ephesians 1 (1579)

1. No blessing is or can be granted to us after the earth's creation unto which we were not chosen and predestined before the foundation of the world. Those blessings are not conferred by means of anything nor in any other manner than through the means and in the manner that was determined for them to be given in God's eternal counsel. This accords with what the apostle says, *We have been blessed in Christ with every spiritual blessing, even as*[30] *He chose us before the foundation of the world* (Eph. 1:3–4).

2. Just as we gain every spiritual blessing in Christ alone, so also in Him alone were we chosen and predestined to gain them, seeing that the apostle says both that we are blessed in Christ and were also chosen in Him (Eph. 1:3–4).

3. Every one of us who is chosen was chosen not only as regards the end (that is, unto eternal life) but also as regards the means ordained unto that end. For Paul says, *God chose us, that we might be holy and blameless* (Eph. 1:4).

4. Insofar as God chose us, He executes that choice on the basis of His love toward us and according to the good pleasure of His will. And so, election is altogether gracious (Eph. 1:3–4, 6).

5. The end of this gracious election is twofold: our salvation and God's glory. Concerning the first, the apostle says that we are *predestined unto adoption* as sons of God and, thus, unto a heavenly inheritance. Concerning the second, this was done *to the praise of His glorious grace* (Eph. 1:5–6).

---

30. καθὼς.

6. Therefore, the salvation of those who are elect in Christ is settled and necessary; its foundation is the eternal, gracious, and unchangeable decree of God's will.

7. The Father decreed each one who had been chosen in Christ from eternity unto eternal salvation (and as regards the means unto it). And He decreed that they alone would, in time (which is called the *fullness of time*), really be redeemed by Christ and in Christ from their sins and, so, from the consequences of those sins. This is in accordance with what the apostle says: *We have redemption in Christ, the remission of sins* (Eph. 1:7).

8. However, we are not redeemed according to our merits nor by the works of righteousness that we ourselves perform but rather by the blood of Jesus Christ according to God's mercy and the riches of His grace. Both of these are confirmed in the clearest possible way by the apostle (Titus 3:5; Eph. 1:7).

9. Moreover, although the eternal Father redeemed and saved us by the Son through whom He also created, nevertheless, it is the Son whom God's church is accustomed to call the Redeemer of humankind and our Savior with a certain preeminence.[31]

10. For the Son alone was and is simultaneously God and man, and, thus, He alone also had the right (as they say) of ownership and relationship to redeem us. And He alone shed the blood by which we were redeemed as by a ransom.[32] Finally, He alone is the One in whose person our redemption is completed and consummated (Lev. 25:48–49).

11. Moreover, we understand that the redemption[33] that we are said to have in Christ is a full and consummate redemption insofar as it embraces not only the remission of sins in this life but also those things that will be in the next age, namely, perfect redemption from all evil and freedom from enslavement to all corruption. It is such that we have no

---

31. κατ' ἐξοχὴν.
32. λύτρῳ.
33. ἀπολυτρώσεως.

redemption[34] except in Christ our most perfect Redeemer. Just as God made Him our wisdom, righteousness, and sanctification, so He also made Him our redemption (1 Cor. 1:30).

Jesus Christ's Resurrection from the Dead, His Ascension into Heaven, and His Session at the Father's Right Hand, Based on the First Chapter of Paul's Letter to the Ephesians (1581)

1. God efficaciously exercised the magnitude of His power in Christ, raising Him from the dead. Therefore, God alone in His infinite power is the efficient cause of the resurrection of Christ and of all the dead (Eph. 1:20).

2. But Christ also raised Himself from the dead by His own power, as it says: *"Destroy this temple, and in three days I will raise it up,"* but He was speaking about the temple of His body (John 2:19[, 21]). Likewise: *I lay My life down that I might take it up again* (John 10:17). Therefore, Christ is no less God than is the Father, nor is He God with less power.

3. Moreover, He cannot truly be the one who raised from the dead and the one who was raised unless He truly consists of distinct natures—a divine nature according to which He raises and a human nature according to which He is raised. Likewise, therefore, as Christ is true God, consubstantial[35] with the Father, so is He true man, consubstantial[36] with His mother and brothers.

4. Nor can just anybody be truly said to be raised and to rise again from the dead. This can only be said if one is also said to have truly died and to have been truly slain. Death, however, consists in the true separation of the soul from the body whereby it happens that the body is appropriately called a cadaver, for it falls.[37] Therefore, if Christ truly rose from the

---

34. ἀπολυτρώσις.
35. ὁμοούσιος.
36. ὁμοούσιος.
37. The English word cadaver is derived from the Latin *cadere* (to fall).

dead, it is impossible to deny that He also had truly died, that His soul was truly separated from His body.

5. But if (seeing as how Christ did truly die) His soul was not in His body at the time of His death, and if (seeing as how He was truly buried) the body on the cross was not in the tomb at the same time, and the body lying in the tomb was not hanging on the cross, and if (seeing as how God truly raised Christ from the dead) His soul did not raise His body, and His body did not raise itself from death to life, then the human nature in Christ was neither omnipotent nor everywhere present in its own substance.

6. For just as the following sequence is not sound:

> *Christ Himself died, was buried, and rose from the dead. Therefore, He died, was buried, and rose in both His natures.*

so, neither is this one:

> *Behold, I am with you until the end of the age* (Matt. 28:20). *Therefore, Christ is really present with us on earth not only in His deity but also in the substance of His humanity.*

7. But just as this is sound:

> *Christ, who is God, suffered. Therefore, He did not suffer according to His deity but according to His humanity.*

so, too, is this one:

> *Christ, who is man, is everywhere and simply omnipotent. Therefore, He is everywhere and omnipotent not according to His human nature but according to His divine nature.*

For the divine nature was united to the human in the very same person of Christ no less than the human nature was united to the divine.

8. If God Himself (and, thus, the divine nature in Christ) raised the body from the dead not by means of that body itself but rather by means of the divine nature, then it is false that the divine nature in Christ did and does everything not only in and with the human nature but also by means of it.

9. For indeed, Christ's soul does not do everything by means of His body, just as our minds do not understand or will by means of our bodies. This is the case because, as the philosophers also taught, our mind does not depend on our body. Much less, therefore, does Christ's deity do everything by means of the flesh that He assumed.

10. For, does the deity then understand according to a human intellect? Or does it will according to a human will? Or can it be that the deity sustains and preserves the human nature in the person of the Word[38] by means of that very same human nature? Or does the deity bear all things by the human flesh or by virtue of the Word itself? Finally, if the form of God does nothing unless it does so by means of the form of a servant, how is what Leo said true: *For each form does what is proper to it, in communion with the other* [Leo's *Tome*, ep. 28.4]?[39]

11. Therefore, just as the form of God is one thing, and the form of a servant is another, so the characteristics and actions of the former are one thing, and those of the latter are another, although, on many occasions, one and the same work and effect[40] belongs to both.

12. For this reason, it does not follow that whatever Christ (who is one with the Father) comes unto according to the form of God, He also comes unto it and remains in it in His substance according to the form of a servant. Much less does it follow that He is everywhere according to the form of a servant.

13. Again, in the same way that none other but that same Christ rose from the dead, so neither did He rise in any other body than the very one in which He suffered, died, and was buried.

14. For a thing is not truly said to be raised and revived from the dead unless the very thing that is revived, being made alive again, had truly died.

---

38. τοῦ λόγου.
39. [Leo's *Tome*, ep. 28.4]: Leo I, *Letters*, 97–98 (*NPNF2*, 12:40).
40. ἔργον καὶ ἀποτέλεσμα.

15. But the body with which Christ suffered, died, and was buried was a truly human body—visible, tangible, circumscribed. After the resurrection, therefore, Christ did not keep or retain any other body than the one that was circumscribed in a certain place, that could and can be seen and handled wherever it was and is.

16. Additionally, while the apostle carefully discusses the qualities of a body raised from the dead unto eternal life, He does not mention its being adorned with invisibility, absence of circumscription, or intangibility.[41] Rather, he mentions only incorruptibility, glory, and bodily strength[42]—agility,[43] as it were—and that they will rise as spiritual[44] bodies. This does not mean that their corporeal substance will be changed into an incorporeal one but that (as we say with a single Greek word) that they will be immortal[45] and filled completely by the Holy Spirit dwelling and working (1 Corinthians 15). Therefore, the apostle taught that these qualities—namely, that they are circumscribed, visible, and tangible—are never to be separated from our bodies. Hence, neither did Christ's body lay down these qualities after its resurrection.

17. Nor is it a worthy objection that, after His resurrection, Christ went in to the disciples with the doors having been closed (John 20:19). For that did not happen on account of being invisible or uncircumscribed or intangible, since, having entered, Christ then said to His disciples, *Handle* or *touch and see, for a spirit does not have flesh and blood as you see I have* (Luke 24[:39]). And thus (as the fathers teach), no change took place in Christ's body, just as there was no change when He and Peter were walking on the water. Rather, by the omnipotence of the deity who held absolute authority over all things, the doors yielded to the Son of God's true and solid body.

---

41. ἀορασίαν, ἀπεριγραψίαν, ἀψηλαφησίαν.

42. ἀφθαρσίαν, δόξαν, δύναμιν.

43. The significance of this reference to *agilitas* (nimbleness, mobility, agility) is unclear, but I take it to be a comment specifically about the nature of the "strength" attributed here to resurrected bodies. Compare with §35 below.

44. πνευματικὰ.

45. ἀθάνατα.

18. This is why the fathers condemned Marcion, the Manicheans, and others who taught that Christ did not assume a true and solid human body but rather an imaginary one and that He did everything with respect to imagination[46] and appearance.[47] And they are not the only ones; the Origenists, John of Jerusalem, Eutyches of Constantinople, bishops, and others were also condemned who said that Christ's body became so spiritual after the resurrection that it was more subtle than air and invisible and intangible (Jerome, vol. 2, "To Pammachius against John of Jerusalem," [ep. 57.9]; Gregory the Great, *On Job*, bk. 24 [that is, bk. 14, ch. 56.72]).[48]

19. Moreover, since no other body of Christ is given to us to eat in the Supper except the one that was broken for us (that is, the one that truly suffered and died), it is the case that what we eat in the Supper is the true body of Christ, which is truly circumscribed, visible, and tangible. And thus, since nothing is seen, touched, or felt in the Supper besides the bread, it is much less the case that the body—in its substance—is really contained under the appearance of bread and wine or that it lies hidden in the bread and wine itself.

20. But we know that Christ's resurrection is the cause and model of both our spiritual and corporeal resurrection. Indeed, it is the spiritual cause on account of what the apostle says to the Romans: *He rose again for our justification* (Rom. 4[:25]). And it is our model on account of this: *Therefore, we were buried together with Him through baptism unto death, in order that, just as Christ was raised from the dead by the glory of the Father, so also we might walk in newness of life* (Rom. 6[:4]).

---

46. κατὰ δόκησιν.
47. φαντασίαν.
48. Jerome, vol. 2, "To Pammachius against John of Jerusalem," [ep. 57.9]: NPNF2, 6:429.
  Gregory the Great, *On Job*, bk. 24 [that is, bk. 14, ch. 56.72]: Gregory the Great, *Moral Reflections on the Book of Job*, vol. 3, *Books 11–16*, trans. Brian Kerns, Cistercian Studies Series 258 (Collegeville, Minn.: Liturgical Press, 2016), 195–96.

21. Conversely, we have no doubt that He is the cause of our corporeal resurrection because of what the apostle says: *If Christ rose again, we also will rise again* (1 Corinthians 5 [that is, 15]).[49] And, as that same apostle says, *Christ, the firstfruits* of the resurrected [1 Cor. 15:20]. And He is our model because of what was written by the same apostle: *He will fashion our humble body after His glorious body* (Phil. 3:21).

22. From this it also follows that either Christ's body is not invisible, intangible, and uncircumscribed or our bodies will also be invisible, intangible, and uncircumscribed—thus, not spiritual bodies but rather incorporeal spirits.

The Ascension

23. For when Christ says, *Touch and see, for a Spirit does not have flesh and bones as you see I have* [Luke 24:39], He not only implied that He was not a spirit but specifically taught that invisible or intangible flesh and bones do not exist.

24. Scripture teaches and the church confesses that the Lord Jesus Christ, having demonstrated to His disciples for forty days with many proofs that He had truly been raised from the dead, was raised up from the earth and ascended into heaven while the apostles watched. Therefore, just as no other Christ rose again than the one who had died, so neither did any other Christ nor any other body ascend into heaven than the Christ who is the Son of God and the body that had truly risen from the dead, which is a truly human, visible, tangible, and circumscribed body.

25. It is also for this reason that, just as the manner of life conducted by the same Lord Jesus Christ with the apostles for forty days after the resurrection was not imaginary but real and true, so the ascension was also not only visible but (as the fathers say) truly local as well, because the apostles saw Him ascending on high from the earth.

---

49. Here, Zanchi is not quoting a single verse but is expressing the general thrust of Paul's argument.

26. Moreover, that kind of ascension and movement is not proper to the divine nature. He, therefore, ascended according to His human nature.

27. Yet, at the same time, we cannot deny that, just as Christ as God is indeed said to have descended from heaven (insofar as He emptied Himself, assumed the lowly form of a servant, and suffered in it), so also can it rightly be said in a certain sense that even the very form of God was glorified through and after the ascension, namely insofar as He was now glorified in the form of a servant (that is, He was made famous throughout the whole world).

28. But it is obvious that, just as this conclusion does not follow:

> *Christ Himself—God and man—ascended into heaven with visible and local motion. Therefore, He also ascended in the same way according to His deity.*

so, neither does this one:

> *Christ—God and man—is truly present with us by His essence until the consummation of the age. Therefore, He is present with us on earth as much by the substance of His body and soul as by the essence of His deity.*

29. Indeed, if the apostles saw Christ with their eyes ascending upward from the earth in His body by a change of location, then the heaven unto which He ascended cannot be a ubiquitous heaven but must be distinct and removed from earth.

30. Furthermore, both nature and all justice demand that everything be allotted a suitable place, just as we see that God did in the things that He created. Thus, Christ's body must exist in a specific and most blessed location, since no more excellent created thing can be found than Christ's very body—on account of its union with the Word,[50] because the most excellent of all gifts were created in it, and also on account of the utterly complete glory and blessedness in which it now resides.

---

50. λόγῳ.

31. And, unless it proceeds from true piety and true reverence for Christ, we do not believe that Christ's body dwells below the earth or in the earth or in the waters or in a little breadcrumb or in the individual leaves of trees or in the air or in the heavenly spheres. Rather, we believe that it dwells in that place that is most blessed, beautiful, and perfect—and, so, also most exalted. With Ambrose, we do not doubt that the apostle was talking about that place when he said he was caught up into the third heaven and into paradise [2 Cor. 12:2].[51]

32. What Scripture itself teaches and what the catholic faith believes and confesses agree: that same Jesus Christ will return in the clouds from that same heaven to judge the living and the dead, and we, having been raised from the dead, will be caught up from the earth in the air to meet Him in the clouds, and so we will also be with the Lord in that very same heaven forever (2 Cor. 12:2, 4; Phil. 3:20; 1 Thess. 4:16–17).

33. Moreover, Scripture, which proclaims that Christ both ascended beyond all the heavens and that He is in heaven, demonstrates that this heaven, which is called the Father's house and the heavenly city and by other names as well, is located beyond all these visible and shifting heavens (John 14:2; Eph. 4:10).

34. In fact, that heaven—the one where He is in His body and in which we will also be in both our bodies and souls—cannot be some immense and uncreated space. This is partly the case because nothing except God is uncreated and partly because Hebrews clearly proclaims that it is a work of God (Heb. 11:10).

35. Moreover, according to Philippians 2, the efficient cause of that motion whereby the body was carried off into heaven was, first and foremost, the divine nature dwelling in Him: *God exalted Him*, and He was received (by God) *into glory* [vv. 9, 11]. Secondarily, however, it was the

---

51. The reference to Ambrose is ambiguous, but Baschera and Moser suggest that perhaps Ambrosiaster's commentary on 2 Corinthians is in view (*De religione*, 2:702). See Ambrosiaster, *Commentaries on Romans and 1–2 Corinthians*, trans. and ed. Gerald L. Bray, Ancient Christian Texts (Downers Grove, Ill.: IVP Academic, 2009), 258.

gift of agility conferred by the deity upon His human nature subsequent to His glorious resurrection. It was by that gift that His flesh ascended, not carried or supported by clouds (as Elijah once was by a fiery chariot) but of His own will and without any trouble or difficulty. Hence, that motion was not caused by an external force.[52]

36. But the very ascension of Christ our Head was and is the cause and model of our future ascension into heaven. Indeed, because the Head ascended, it is therefore necessary for the members eventually to ascend as well. And just as His ascension was, so will ours be. For He will shape our bodies according to His glorious body, and we will be caught up in the clouds to meet Christ in the air, and so we will always be with the Lord (Phil. 3:21; 1 Thess. 4:17).

37. Therefore, if our ascension is to be true, and we are truly to be raised from earth into heaven, then Christ's body must also have truly—not seemingly[53] or allegedly—ascended from earth into heaven.

38. In fact, this doctrine of Christ's true ascension into that highest of heavens and His everlasting dwelling in them is altogether useful.

39. First, it is useful for confirming our faith with regard to the specific place where we are to gaze upon, touch, and lay hold of Christ's body with the eyes and hands of faith. Next, it is useful for confirming hope. For, even before the resurrection of our bodies, after our souls have been separated from our bodies, they will not descend under the earth, wander among the waters or in the air, or revolve with the heavenly spheres. Rather, they will abide above all these heavens in that most blessed house of the Father in which Christ also entered with His body, so that they might always be with Christ. Finally, it is also useful for kindling in our hearts a love of and devotion for heavenly life and conduct.

---

52. *Motus ille non fuit violentus.* Zanchi draws upon Aristotle's distinction between natural (or spontaneous) and violent (or compulsory) force. The former is the internal—we might say "natural"—inclination of body to fall downward (or, as Zanchi suggests in the case of Christ's resurrected body, to ascend upward) while the latter is the result of an external force compelling the body into motion. See Aristotle, *Physics*, 4.8.

53. κατὰ δόκησιν.

This is in accordance with that statement of the apostle: *If you have been raised with Christ, then seek those things that are above, occupy yourselves with those things that are above, where Christ is at the Father's right hand* (Col. 3:1–2).

Christ's Session at the Father's Right Hand
40. With regard to Christ's session at the Father's right hand, the apostle says this: *And He caused Christ* (now raised from the dead and carried up into heaven) *to sit in the high heavenly places, above every principality and authority and power and dominion and every name that is named, not only in this age but also in the age to come. And He subjected everything under His feet* (Eph. 1:20–22). And whatever else we read in the Holy Scriptures about this session, and whatever the church confesses in the creeds, must be consistent with these words.

41. But nowhere do we read that, on account of the session at God's right hand, Christ either selected some other body for Himself (call it whatever we might) or that some change occurred in the substance of His natural body or in any of its natural properties or essential qualities, which it retained after the resurrection. Thus, it is obvious that the body in which Christ rose again and ascended into heaven (namely, a visible, tangible, and circumscribed one) is the very same one that sits at the Father's right hand in the heavenly places. And wherever He is (or wishes to be), He always retains possession of that body for Himself.

42. The apostle also testifies, and the church confesses in its creeds, that, before Christ sat at the Father's right hand, He first died, was buried, was raised from the dead, and ascended into heaven. Thus, it is false that it was at that point that Christ's human nature really received the ability to be everywhere in its body for the first time. Or, if it is true, then Christ did not receive that ability by virtue of the hypostatic union, which happened at the incarnation itself.

43. Nor is it a valid exception to say that this was given to Him by primary actuality at the hypostatic union (so that, if He wanted to be everywhere present, then He would have been), but that, from the session at the

right hand, it was granted by secondary actuality (that is, to actually be everywhere present in fact).[54]

44. For, besides the fact that the very names of this distinction are names drawn not from the fountains of Israel but from the swamps of the sophists, Christ Himself also refuted this exception when, speaking before His death not about the first actuality but about the second (that is, about His actual presence), He said, *Where two or three gather in My name, I am there in their midst* (Matt. 18:20). And after the resurrection but before the ascension, He said, *Behold, I am with you, even to the consummation of the age* (Matt. 28:20).

45. This having been said, it follows with absolute clarity that Christ was not speaking about the real presence of His body but only about the presence of the deity and the power of His Spirit. Otherwise, He is with us in the same way that He was with the apostles at that time (namely, visibly), since He did not say, *I will be with you* but rather *I am*. Nor is there anything that necessitates a different understanding of the words' meaning.

46. Moreover, it follows that, if He said this with regard to that same real bodily presence, and if this promise pertained not only to the apostles but also to all the other faithful who were on the earth, then Christ did not speak truly. For neither before His death nor after the resurrection was He visibly present with all the faithful who were then in the world and who gathered together in His name.

---

54. *Actu primo* and *secundo*. Muller notes that the "condition of [a being or a substance] simply being what it is with its faculties is the condition of primary actualization; the being or substance is in *actu primo*. Thus the intellect as having the potency to understand is *in actu primo*. The condition of the being in the actual exercise of its faculties is the condition of secondary actualization; the being is considered to be *in actu secundo*. Thus the intellect as actively understanding is *in actu secundo*." *Dictionary*, 166. See also, pp. 11–12. Moreover, "Sometimes the underlying general capacity is called 'first act' (*actus primus*), whereas the concrete, realized act is called 'second act' (*actus secundus*). Thus, in the case of a volition, the capacity of willing opposite acts on the level of the 'first act' is abstracted from the concrete act of will on the level of the 'second act.'" Goris, *Synopsis*, 3:627.

47. For this reason, the doctrine of the real and substantial (but invisible) presence of Christ's body on earth and everywhere else is not consistent with the Holy Scriptures. Instead, it appears to agree with the fancies of the Manicheans, who (as Augustine reports) said that Christ's body hung invisibly from every tree (*Answer to Faustus*, bk. 20, ch. 11).[55]

48. Indeed, the whole church confesses that, before His resurrection and ascension into heaven, Christ did not sit at the right hand in His body. If that confession is correct, then the doctrine of those who teach that, with respect to the flesh He assumed, Christ sat at the right hand of the power of God from the womb of His mother is wicked and heretical.

49. The apostle teaches, the whole of Scripture confirms, and the catholic church confesses not only that Christ sat at the Father's right hand when He ascended into heaven but also that He is present in heaven in a distinct way, for we never read that He sat down at the right hand anywhere but in heaven. If that is true, then is it impossible to say (in accordance with the Scriptures) that Christ sat elsewhere than in heaven at God's right hand. And it is also false that He is seated on earth in such a way that He is really present in the substance of His body in the bread of the Lord's Supper and everywhere else in the same way as He is in heaven.

50. For the apostle contests this elsewhere, especially in Hebrews. There, based on the fact that Christ performs His priesthood sitting at the right hand of the throne of the Majesty in the heavenly places, he denies that He is upon the earth, that is, that He is bodily present (Heb. 8:4).

51. Again, we judge it to be beyond controversy that Christ's sitting at God the Father's right hand is figurative speech, since (properly speaking) God has neither right nor left hand, nor indeed is it correct to imagine anything physical with regard to the seats or thrones on which He is seated in that heavenly kingdom. And often in the Holy Scriptures, besides other meanings, the word *sitting* is used for *dwelling, ruling,*

---

55. *Answer to Faustus*, bk. 20, ch. 11: Augustine, *Answer to Faustus, a Manichean*, ed. Boniface Ramsey, trans. Roland J. Teske, The Works of Saint Augustine: A Translation for the 21st Century I/20 (Hyde Park, N.Y.: New City Press, 2007), 272.

exercising judgment, and *being at peace* [Ps. 107:10; Isa. 6:1; Acts 25:6; Mark 14:62; Heb. 1:3; Mic. 4:4].

52. But it is clearly apparent from the explanation that the apostle provides, besides everything else that has been said, that he does not mean for this phrase to indicate that Christ is truly and substantially present in His body in every place.

53. Indeed, the apostle provides three explanations for Christ's session at the right hand of God the Father. First, Christ was positioned at God's right hand in such a way that He was above every principality, that is, in such a way that no creature is above or equal to Him, not even in heaven. Rather, He is made more exalted than the heavens and all heavenly things. Second, the apostle adds that everything was subjected to Him, that is, there is nothing beneath Him over which He does not have right and authority. Third, it was given to Him to be the church's Head.

54. Moreover, just as we alleged that the apostle's previous statement about Christ's resurrection from the dead and ascension must be understood of Christ according to His human nature, so we (along with the orthodox fathers) judge that this, too, must principally be understood according to that same human nature.

55. Indeed, the human nature in Christ can be understood to have been exalted over all things in two ways. It can be understood with reference to location, just as the passage that says, *He ascended above all the heavens* means that His human nature is geographically located above all created things (Eph. 4:10). Or it can be understood with reference to the excellence of dignity and authority so that it means that, even according to His human nature, Christ was placed in charge of all created things, and to Him was given authority and power in everything. For, in those two ways, something of one kind is said to be over something else, either with regard to place or dignity.

56. So, if it is understood in the second way, then ubiquity cannot be demonstrated because, by His human nature, Christ can exercise this authority over everything even if the substance of His body is not

everywhere. If it is understood in the first way, then it is not everywhere because that which is everywhere is just as much below, with, and among all creatures as it is above them.

57. Moreover, Paul plainly teaches that (as pertains to the human nature) Christ was raised from the dead in such a way that He was no longer among the dead. And He ascended into heaven in such a way that He was no longer on earth. And so, being exalted above all creatures, He sits at the Father's right hand, such that He is not under or among created things, since all of them are placed under His feet.

58. In its substance, a head cannot be said to be where feet are, although its power and influence is in them. And, indeed, a head is as much joined to feet as feet are joined to a head by its substance and by means of nerves and a soul.

59. Moreover, the apostle says that Christ *was given as Head to the church*, namely, according to His humanity [Eph. 1:22]. A head, however, has preeminence over the whole body.

60. Thus, by no means did the apostle intend for his words about the session at God's right hand to imply that Christ's body is present everywhere in its substance. This is the reason why those who attempt to deduce this conclusion from that passage abuse the apostle by their sophistry.

61. On the contrary, no necessary implication of such ubiquity can be demonstrated on the basis of that article of the faith.

62. Indeed, even if it is implied by the session at God's right hand that the human nature in itself became truly omnipotent (which cannot be conceded), nevertheless, unless it were proved that it became omnipotent in such a way that it also became infinite and immense, then proving that Christ's body is present everywhere in its substance is wholly impossible.

63. In fact, this is the only reason why even God is truly everywhere in His substance. This is the case to such an extent that we could not say

that He would be everywhere in His essence were immensity removed from Him.

64. And if you were to forge a body that is infinite and, on that account, ubiquitous, you would still never be able to demonstrate that the whole is simultaneously present in every location unless you also show it to be a most simple essence. For that is the reason why even God is not everywhere in pieces: because He is a most simple essence.

65. This is why it makes no difference what the Ubiquitarians prattle on about, whether they argue from the hypostatic union or from God's right hand or from the words of the Supper or from various modes of being or from the words *All power is given to Me* and similar sayings (Matt. 28:18). Unless they demonstrate by those arguments that the substance of Christ's body became immense and infinite and at the same time also most simple (as God's essence is), they always introduce the *non causa pro causa* fallacy.[56]

66. Yet, we do not on that account deny that, while the body of our Lord Jesus Christ remains in heaven, it is nevertheless truly present with us—not only by its power but also by its substance.

67. But how, or in what way, is Christ's body present? To be sure, His true presence is really in us, but it is present by means of His Spirit in us and by means of our faith. And, if using comparisons is permitted, Christ's body is present just as a head is truly and really present to every one of its members, even its feet.

68. But how are head and feet present to each other? Not by nearness of location—for, in that case, the head of a pigmy would be more present to his feet than the head of a giant—but by the force of the soul's union and the bond of nerves and ligaments.

69. Therefore, since we and our bodies and Christ's body are, according

---

56. A logical fallacy that occurs when one identifies something that is not the cause of a thing as the cause of that thing.

to the Scriptures, simultaneously and truly bound together such that we are one and the same body under one and the same Head, which God gave to the church (namely, Christ), no one can deny this true presence without the greatest blasphemy [Eph. 1:22].

70. Notwithstanding, with regard to the session at the right hand, we believe that by this phrase the apostle intended to indicate that, after having endured (according to His humanity) many very weighty labors on earth and having suffered the pains of death for the sake of our redemption, Christ is now gloriously at peace in heaven. And He, the most Beloved of the Father, lives in the utmost happiness. He appears for us in the presence of God the Father. And His intercession and atonement[57] are altogether pleasing to the Father. He also reigns with the Father, and He has been appointed to be judge, who one day will at last come to administer justice to the living and the dead, and He is established in the heavenly throne.

71. Indeed, as Tertullian taught, to sit is characteristic of one who is at rest [*Against Marcion*, bk. 5, §1].[58] And as Augustine taught, this is characteristic of one who dwells, reigns, and administers justice.[59] Nor are any but greatly beloved and dear friends said to sit at the right hand.

72. To be sure, this is how Augustine interpreted that passage. *Believe this: He ascended into heaven. Believe this: He sits at the right hand of God. By "sitting" you must understand "dwelling," as we might say of a certain man, "He's been sitting for three years in that country."*

And likewise: *Therefore, believe that Christ dwells at the right of God the Father; He is there. Let not your hearts say, "What is He doing?" Do not seek after that which is not given to you to know. It suffices for you that He is there. He is blessed, and the blessedness by which He is blessed is called "the Father's right hand." The name of His blessedness is: the Father's right hand. For if we interpreted this in a woodenly literal way then, since He is*

---

57. ἱλασμόν.
58. [*Against Marcion*, bk. 5, §1]: Tertullian, *Adversus Marcionem*, trans. Ernest Evans, Oxford Early Christian Texts (Oxford: Clarendon Press, 1972), 2:510.
59. See §72 of this disputation.

sitting at the Father's right hand, the Father is at His left hand. Surely it cannot be right for us to arrange them thus—the Son at the right hand and the Father at the left? In that place, everything is on the right hand because there is no misery there. (On the Creed to the Catechumens, bk. 1, ch. 4 [that is, sermon 398.11]).[60]

Again: *Beloved, you should not think of this sitting as arranged for human limbs, as though the Father were sitting on the left so that the Son might sit on the right. Rather, understand that the right hand itself is the power which that Man receives from God to come in judgment, He who previously had come to be judged* (bk. 2, ch. 4 [that is, Quodvultdeus, The Creedal Homilies, §1.7.2]).[61]

Again: *Who is He who sits at the Father's right hand? The man Christ. For insofar as He is God, He is always with the Father and from the Father, and when He advanced toward us, He did not withdraw from the Father. Indeed, this is what it is to be God: to be everywhere wholly. Therefore, the Son is in the Father's presence whole, in heaven whole, on earth whole, in the virgin's womb whole, on the cross whole, in the infernal regions whole, in paradise to which He brought the thief whole. We are not saying that He is everywhere whole at various times or places so that He is whole just now over there and at another time is whole elsewhere. Rather, He is always whole everywhere* (bk. 3, ch. 7 [that is, The Creedal Homilies, 2.7.1–3]).[62]

Again: *But* [the article of the Creed] *that says that the Son sits at the Father's right hand demonstrates that the very man whom Christ has*

---

60. *On the Creed to the Catechumens*, bk. 1, ch. 4 [that is, sermon 398.11]: Augustine, *Sermons*, vol. 10, 341–400, ed. John E. Rotelle, trans. Edmund Hill, The Works of Saint Augustine: A Translation for the 21st Century III/10 (Hyde Park, N.Y.: New City Press, 1995), 452.

61. bk. 2, ch. 4 [that is, Quodvultdeus, *The Creedal Homilies*, §1.7.2]: Quodvultdeus of Carthage, *The Creedal Homilies*, trans. Thomas M. Finn, Ancient Christian Writers 60 (New York: Newman Press, 2004), 40. Quodvultdeus (d. 454?) was a bishop of Carthage who corresponded with and was a disciple of Augustine. He developed a series of catechetical instructions—homilies on the Apostles' Creed—for those preparing for baptism.

62. bk. 3, ch. 7 [that is, *The Creedal Homilies*, 2.7.1–3]: Quodvultdeus of Carthage, *The Creedal Homilies*, 61.

assumed received the power to judge (bk. 3, ch. 7 [that is, *The Creedal Homilies*, 2.7.5]).[63]

Again: *Now the man assumed by Christ reigns at the Father's right hand* (bk. 4, ch. 7 [that is, *The Creedal Homilies*, 3.7.4]).[64]

Again: *In addition, because He is God and is equal to the Father and always judges, He is always present, but as Redeemer He will come in that form in which He was assumed* (bk. 4, ch. 7 [that is, *The Creedal Homilies*, 3.8.2–3]).[65]

73. Therefore, when the apostle spoke of the session at God's right hand, he hardly meant to indicate that Christ is on earth and everywhere else in the substance of His body. Rather, it seems he was teaching the opposite, seeing that the perfect blessedness of men depends only on heaven and not on earth. And it consists in God dwelling in heaven and not on earth. And He is said to reign in heaven rather than on earth. And we believe and preach that Christ is coming not from earth but from heaven to judge the living and the dead.

74. Moreover, just as God's feet are, humanly speaking,[66] said to be on earth and not in heaven—as that passage says, *Heaven is My throne, and the earth is My footstool* (Acts 7:49)—so we are not wrong if we say that His own right hand is located in heaven rather than on earth.

75. We therefore conclude that, just as the ubiquity of Christ's body cannot be demonstrated from the apostolic doctrine of Christ's resurrection from the dead and ascension into heaven but is rather refuted, so neither can it be inferred as necessary from the doctrine of the session at God's right hand.

---

63. bk. 3, ch. 7 [that is, *The Creedal Homilies*, 2.7.5]: Quodvultdeus of Carthage, *The Creedal Homilies*, 62.

64. bk. 4, ch. 7 [that is, *The Creedal Homilies*, 3.7.4]: Quodvultdeus of Carthage, *The Creedal Homilies*, 78.

65. bk. 4, ch. 7 [that is, *The Creedal Homilies*, 3.8.2–3]: Quodvultdeus of Carthage, *The Creedal Homilies*, 78.

66. ἀνθρωποπάθειαν.

76. On the contrary, we say that, if we allow ubiquity of that sort, then all these articles of the faith—concerning the incarnation having taken place specifically in the virgin's womb, concerning true death (that is, true separation of the soul from the body), concerning true resurrection of the flesh, concerning true and visible ascension from earth into heaven, concerning true session in the high heavenly places at the Father's right hand, and finally, concerning the visible return from those places to judge the living and the dead—are not so much undermined as altogether overthrown.

77. For a body that is everywhere is not moved from place to place according to its whole. This is demonstrated by true philosophy and is also confirmed by Christian theology, which teaches that this is the reason why God does not move from place to place. For, since He is immense, He fills all things.

78. Neither can it correctly be said that a ubiquitous body sits either on the right or on the left of another. Rather, it becomes necessary for you to confound the substance of the sitting body with the substance of the right hand at which it sits and with the substance of the one at whose right hand it sits. For it is indeed because Father, Son, and Holy Spirit are one and the same essence that each of them and all of them are everywhere, filling heaven and earth.

79. Finally, we judge that this doctrine of the invisible and intangible everywhere-present flesh of Christ is neither true nor beneficial.

80. Indeed, it is not true because we cannot see it demonstrated either by the manifest testimony of the Holy Scriptures or by necessary consequences following from them. Indeed, we note that, when they have been carefully examined, both the Holy Scriptures and the catholic consensus of the ancient church to the rule of faith expressed by the Apostles' Creed are in conflict with this position.

81. And we observe that it is in conflict with the Scriptures in such a way that you cannot simultaneously accept what the Creed teaches and what

the authors of the doctrine of ubiquity write without getting caught redhanded in a contradiction.

82. It is not beneficial either. For to offer up, believe, or maintain that which does not agree with God's Word as if it were necessary for salvation is a sin. This is in accordance with what the Lord said: *Neither add nor subtract* (Deut. 12:32). And as the apostle said, *Everything that is not of faith is sin*, and *the wages sin is death* (Rom. 14:23; 6:23).

83. Lastly, it is not beneficial because, if that opinion concerning the ubiquity of Christ's body were believed to be true, then it would be a hindrance, keeping one from laying hold of and eating Christ's true body (which exists in heaven) with a mind that has been lifted up on account of Christ. Yet, with regard to this, the apostle and the church call to us, saying, *Lift up your heart*. Again, *Seek those things that are above, where Christ is sitting at God's right hand* (Col. 3:1).

84. Therefore, as for those who regard Christ's flesh as not being in heaven (where it actually is) but who imagine that it is really present everywhere in its substance, there is nothing that they do less than eat Christ's flesh. Aesop's dog, having dropped the real meat, foolishly pursued meat's mere shadow because it seemed to be the bigger scrap of food.

A Question Based on 1 John 4:[2–]3
St. John, describing the Antichrist, says: *Every spirit that does not confess that Jesus Christ* (a true human) *came in the flesh is not from God. And this is the spirit of Antichrist* [1 John 4:3].

But Christ assumed flesh one time, and He never took that flesh off but rather bore it with Him into heaven, and with it He will return in the clouds, visible before all men, to judge the living and the dead. So then, of which spirit are they and by what name should they be called who, with the ancient heretics, do not hesitate to counterfeit for our Lord Jesus Christ I know not what invisible, uncircumscribed, intangible, everywhere-present flesh really existing whole and in its whole substance in the heavens and stars, in the air, on earth, under the earth, in the infernal realms, and in every single part of the world, and every piece of every part, and in the teeniest piece of every particle? And of which spirit are they who do this in opposition to Scripture and the orthodox consensus of the catholic church?

The Dispensation of Salvation by Christ Based on the First Chapter of Ephesians (1580)

1. Our Lord Jesus Christ, in whom we were chosen unto eternal salvation, did not only redeem us once for all, having obtained the remission of our sins by His blood and having gained the victory. He also dispenses and communicates to us the grace of redemption and salvation on a daily basis (Eph. 1:7–8).

2. It is characteristic of the perfect Redeemer not only to redeem by paying the ransom[67] but also really to indicate to the redeemed the redemption accomplished for them and to free them from the hands of the Tyrant. Likewise, it is characteristic of a good head to distribute to its members the life, perceptions, and motion that it has in itself.

3. Moreover, it is customary for Christ to distribute this saving grace by word of the truth, that is, by the gospel of our salvation, to which we join the sacraments as well, as seals and instruments of our salvation (Eph. 1:13).

4. For the gospel makes known to us the mystery of the divine will of our salvation by Christ Himself and the gathering together of all things both in heaven and on earth and their joining together under one Head, Christ (Eph. 1:9–10).

5. He not only makes known the mystery of salvation by the gospel but also effectually calls and draws us unto Himself and unto fellowship[68] with Him, and thus He calls us unto participation in redemption and salvation (Eph. 1:13).

---

67. λύτρῳ.
68. κοινωνίαν.

6. For, ordinarily, it is by the preaching of the gospel that Christ stirs up faith in our hearts with which to believe in Him and by which we are received into His fellowship (Eph. 1:13; Rom. 10[:17]).

7. He even gives us the Holy Spirit, by whom He regenerates and seals us with the stamped image of God to the full possession of an eternal inheritance (Eph. 1:13).

8. By that same Spirit, He stirs up, urges, and guides us into eagerness for a holy life and good works.

9. And if we slip into sin (which is our foolishness), He raises us from there, having granted repentance, and assures us all the more of our remission. And in that way, through the Spirit Himself as though by a deposit, He confirms us in the certainty of our eternal salvation more and more every day (Eph. 1:14).

10. But, without ever utterly forsaking us, Christ grants these benefits to us until, at last, He guides us according to His grace and boundless benevolence toward us (Eph. 1:14). He does this from the first redemption[69] (which is from the guilt and slavery of sin and from the power of the Devil) to the second redemption[70] (namely, preservation,[71] which consists in the complete claiming and full possession of the heavenly inheritance).

11. But just as the Lord Jesus is our Redeemer and the Head of the whole church according to both natures, so He also communicates salvation and eternal life not only as He is God but also as man. This accords with the passage that says, *"Be assured, son, your sins have been forgiven"* [Matt. 9:2]. And then He says, *"That you might know that the Son of Man has power to forgive sins,"* He said to the paralytic, *"Arise, take up your bed, and go home"* [Matt. 9:6]. Each nature is in communion with the other, doing that which is proper to it (Eph. 1:22).

---

69. ἀπολυτρώσει.
70. ἀπολύτρωσιν.
71. περιτοιήσεως.

12. For just as the natures are so mutually united in the one person that, nevertheless, no change or confusion occurs, so the actions are therefore also the actions of one and the same person. Yet, this is the case in such a way that they are truly distinguished among themselves. And they are so distinguished that it would be wrong to say the things that belong properly to the one nature, although they happen by mutual participation with the other nature, happen by (or that Christ does them according to) the other nature.

13. For this reason, just as we approve of the fathers when they say that Christ's actions in redeeming and saving us were and are both divine and human[72] actions, so we also strongly approve of Bishop Leo of Rome's much celebrated saying, and we teach that it should be retained with firm faith: *For each form does what is proper to it, in communion with the other—namely, the Word working that which is of the Word and the flesh carrying out that which is of the flesh* (Letter to Flavian[, ep. 28.4]).[73]

14. For Christ suffered and died and was buried for us according to the flesh. But according to His deity, he gave the grace of meriting and redeeming through the suffering whereby He redeemed us. Moreover, He willed all this according to both natures.

15. Likewise, He rose from the dead and ascended into heaven by a visible and local ascension, having been exalted above all the angels, according to His humanity. But the resurrection itself, the ascension, and the exaltation were performed according to His divinity. He willed, however, according to the wills of both natures (Eph. 1:20–21).

16. We believe that Christ redeemed us according to both natures in accordance with the passage that says, God obtained His church *by His own blood* (Acts 20[:28]). So, in the same way, we do not doubt that Christ, sitting and resting at the Father's right hand in the high heavenlies and ruling over all things with the Father, dispenses and communicates from heaven the grace of eternal redemption and salvation to the whole

---

72. θεανδρικὰς.
73. Letter to Flavian[, ep. 28.4]: Leo I, *Letters*, 97–98 (*NPNF2*, 12:40).

church (which is His body) and to each of His members according to both natures. By the Word, He accomplishes that which is of the Word, and by the flesh that which is of the flesh.

17. For although He uses the ministry of Word and sacrament through men to impart salvation to us, nevertheless, properly speaking, it is Christ Himself—both as God and as man—who calls us, grants faith and repentance, and justifies, regenerates, vivifies, and saves unto eternal life those who believe according to the working of the might of His power[74] [Eph. 1:19].

18. Hence, even the faith whereby we lay hold of salvation in Christ and eternal life ought not look to and rest upon one or the other of Christ's natures separately but rather the whole Christ Himself, just as the Ephesians were also said to have had faith in the Lord Jesus[75] [Eph. 1:15].

19. From this it follows that they cannot become partakers of redemption and eternal salvation who deny either of the natures in Christ or divide the one from the other or confuse the two of them simultaneously in such a way that they do not know Him either as true God or as true man like us in every way except for sin and who, consequently, do not embrace Him as a true and perfect Redeemer of that sort [Heb. 4:15].

20. For just as he who believes in Christ as He is has eternal life, so he who does not believe cannot have life [John 3:36].

Things Predicated of Our Lord Jesus Christ after the Union and How They May Be Predicated, Based on the First Chapter to the Ephesians (1582)

1. The apostle wrote that *Christ has been raised from the dead* [1 Cor. 15:20], and hence He truly died. Indeed, he wrote elsewhere that *the Lord of glory was crucified* [1 Cor. 2:8]. Moreover, we also frequently read that *the Son of Man was handed over to die* [Matt. 20:18]. Yet, in all those statements, the one discussed is always the same person, namely, the

---

74. κατὰ τὴν ἐνέργειαν τοῦ κράτους τῆς ἰσχύος αὐτοῦ.
75. ἐν κυρίῳ Ιησοῦ.

incarnate Son of God. Thus, the person of Christ, who is the subject of these statements, is ordinarily indicated by three types of nouns, namely, those that indicate (1) just the divine nature, with reference to either essence or hypostases (such as *Lord of glory*, or *only begotten Son of God*); (2) in a similar fashion, only the human nature (such as *Man*, or *Son of Mary*); or (3) both natures at the same time (such as *Christ*, *Immanuel*, or *God in the flesh*).

2. But we as well add that Christ's very person is also signified by the nouns designated with reference to the offices of a mediator. For example: Mediator, Redeemer, Savior, Priest, Advocate, and other similar ones. But these can be assigned to the third type because they indicate both natures in one person.

3. When, in statements about Christ, concrete nouns are the subjects whereby natures are denominated—such as *man* for humanity and *God* for deity—then they have two simultaneous meanings: one is formal (as the scholastics say), and the other is material. Of these, the nature itself is indicated by the first; the person (which has the sort of nature being denominated) is indicated by the second.

4. For just as abstract nouns signify only the nature and particular property[76] in something, so all concrete nouns refer to the nature and distinguishing quality[77] in the things as well as the *hypostasin* in which it exists. By way of example, the word *just* simultaneously points to the justice whereby one is just as well as to the one who is just.

5. Thus, sometimes these subject nouns that have their denomination from the natures point to the particular property of the nature indicated, and sometimes they indicate the unity of the person. For this reason, we must understand and explain the subjects with the variety of predicates in view.

6. Indeed, the following phrase must be explained in view of the [divine]

---

76. proprietatem.
77. qualitatem.

nature's particular property: *the Son of God is eternal*. But *the only begotten Son of God suffered* must be explained in terms of the unity of the person. For He who suffered is not only a man but also the God whose deity remains impassable.

7. We do not deny that sometimes we find abstract nouns as subjects (such as *the Light that came into the world*), just as we sometimes find them as things predicated (such as *Christ is the light of the world*, or *our righteousness*, or *our peace*), but that undergoes a change with things pertaining to the concrete (for example, *the Light who comes into the world is He who illumines us*). Thus, to understand such nouns, they must be ascribed to one or another of those three kinds.[78]

8. Again, there are three kinds of attributes that are ordinarily predicated of the very same person of Christ—God and man—by whatever noun it is signified. For certain nouns are proper to the divine nature and, thus, are not really communicable to the other nature (such as *being impassible*, *eternal*, or *immense*). Certain nouns are proper to the human nature and, thus, are in fact utterly incommunicable[79] with the other (such as *to become*, *finitude*, or *passibility*). But other attributes are proper to the whole person, corresponding to both natures, and, thus, are common to both natures simultaneously (such as *to be Mediator*, *Redeemer*, or *Savior*).

9. To this third kind of attribute pertain actions that the Greek fathers called theandric energies,[80] whereby, in the works of redemption, each form works not what is proper to the other but what is proper to it and does so in communion with the other. *With the Word working that which is of the Word and the flesh carrying out that which is of the flesh* [Leo I, Letter to Flavian, ep. 28.4].[81]

10. We find in our own selves an analogy not so dissimilar from these three kinds of attributes. Indeed, certain things in man are proper only

---

78. That is, one of the three kinds of nouns described in §1 of this disputation.
79. ἀκοινώνητα.
80. θεανδρικὰς ἐνεργείας.
81. [Leo I, Letter to Flavian, ep. 28.4]: Leo I, *Letters*, 97–98 (NPNF2, 12:40).

to the soul (such as *to be immortal, to understand,* or *to will*) and some things are proper only to the body (such as *to be mortal, tangible,* or *heavy*). Some things are common to both, such as those works that, in their performance, each part performs in fellowship with the other part (such as *to write, to speak, to run,* or, indeed, whatever bodily occupation is performed only with the power and guidance of the soul).

11. Moreover, a diversity of predication also follows on the basis of what was said about the different subjects and predicates. Therefore, every predication about Christ is either proper and simple or improper and figurative.

12. Proper and simple predication happens in two ways. One is when the things that are proper to one of the natures are predicated of Christ's person. Either they are expressed by a noun from the same nature denominated or a noun proper to the person (such as, *this our God,* or *Christ is omnipotent and everywhere present.* Similarly, *this man,* or *Christ suffered and died*).

The second way is when the things that are proper to the whole person are likewise predicated of the whole person. They are signified by a noun that embraces both natures, like those that pertain to the office of the Mediator and the honor of the Head (such as, *Christ,* or *Immanuel,* or *God incarnate redeemed, sanctified, and saved us; He is King and is to be adored*). These, therefore, are said properly of the person because they cannot rightly be accommodated to either of the natures on its own. But all these expressions are proper and simple because, in all of them, the predicates are joined to subjects that are of the very same kind.

13. Improper and figurative predication is also twofold. First, when things that pertain to the whole person—either to the office of the Mediator or the honor of the Head—are predicated of one nature, signified by an abstract or concrete noun (such as *flesh makes alive, blood washes from sins, God redeemed the church, the Mediator between God and man, the Man,* and so forth). Second, when that which is proper to one nature is predicated of the other nature, signified by a concrete noun and referring to the person (such as *God suffered and died, a Man who, when He was on earth, was simultaneously in heaven as well*).

14. Indeed, in improper propositions of the second sort, idioms or concrete nouns of different kinds are bound together. And, thus, it is improper to say *God suffered* insofar as (according to its proper signification) the noun *God* signifies the divine essence, which cannot suffer. But, with respect to the person referenced, who is indeed a man, the proposition is true, albeit improper. And thus, these propositions are actually spoken of the whole person by way of synecdoche,[82] since they do not in fact correspond to the person except with respect to a single nature.

15. This second kind of improper speech we call the communication of proper qualities.[83] In his explanation of this, Theodoret calls it *a communication or sharing of names*[84] (Theodoret[, *Eranistes*], dialogue 3, p. 68, bk. 3, chs. 3–4 [that is, §226]).[85] And the Damascene calls it *the method of exchange*.[86]

16. Indeed, for Theodoret and the Damascene, the concrete noun ἰδιωμάτων signified the *proper qualities* of a certain nature. And communication,[87] or exchange,[88] was the mutual and reciprocal

---

82. συνεκδοχικῶς.
83. κοινωνίαν ἰδιωμάτων. Muller notes that, for the Reformed, the communication between the proper qualities of the divine and human natures in Christ is "a mutual interchange or reciprocation of names, rather than a transfer or communication of properties; or…a communion of proper qualities by synecdoche. Since synecdoche is a figure by which the whole is named for one of its parts, this *communio* is not merely a human invention but a *praedicatio vera*, a true predication of attributes, but of the person only and not between the natures." Muller, *Dictionary*, 71.
84. κοινωνίαν or κοινότητα τῶν ὀνομάτων.
85. Theodoret[, *Eranistes*], dialogue 3, p. 68, bk. 3, chs. 3–4 [that is, §226]: "We must also be aware of this, that the common sharing of the names did not produce a mixture of the natures. This is why we seek to determine how he is the Son of God, and how the same one is also Son of Man, and how the same one is yesterday, today, and forever; and by means of a pious verbal distinction we find that the opposites are in harmony." Theodoret of Cyrus, *Eranistes*, trans. Gerard H. Ettlinger, Fathers of the Church 106 (Washington, D.C.: Catholic University of America Press, 2003), 219 (*NPNF2*, 3:233).
86. τὸν τῆς ἀντιδόσεως τρόπον. John of Damascus, *The Orthodox Faith*, 170 (*NPNF2*, 9:48).
87. κοινωνία.
88. ἀντίδοσις.

predication of the proper qualities[89] of one of the natures with a concrete noun of the other nature, which referred to the person. So, it is the height of ignorance to imagine that, when the fathers spoke of the communication of the properties,[90] they meant to discuss the essential properties of one nature either really emanating from or being communicated to the other, since they clearly wrote, *The union makes the names common*,[91] but they never wrote that it makes the actions[92] common.

17. For if our discussion concerns the natures themselves that are in Christ, then Theodoret and other fathers teach that we should not say that those things belonging to[93] one nature are also really common with the other. Rather, we should say that we attribute to each nature only those things that belong to it, just as we do not ascribe to the body that which is of the soul. We only ascribe it to the soul, and vice versa. But if we are talking about the person, then we should compose our speech in such a way as to indicate that those things belonging to[94] each nature are also truly and really common to the whole person, just as we also really and in truth attribute the things of the soul to the whole man, as we do the things of the body.

Moreover, these are Theodoret's words after introducing the parallel of the body and the soul and of the whole man: *Then this is how one should speak about Christ. When discussing the natures, we should attribute to each one its proper qualities and realize that some belong to the divinity and others to the humanity. When, however, we speak about the person, we must make the natures' properties common and attribute both types to Christ the Savior. We must call Him both God and man, both Son of God and Son of Man, both David's Son and David's Lord, both Seed of Abraham and Abraham's Creator, and so on in every respect.* (Theodoret[, *Eranistes*], dialogue 3, p. 67B [that is, bk. 2, §139]).[95]

---

89. ἰδιωμάτων.
90. de communicatione idiomatum.
91. ἡ ἕνωσις κοινὰ ποιεῖ τὰ ὀνόματα.
92. τὰ πράγματα.
93. ἴδια.
94. ἴδια.
95. Theodoret[, *Eranistes*], dialogue 3, p. 67B [that is, bk. 2, §139]: οὕτω

Throughout his dialogues, Theodoret supports the same doctrine using the writings of Bishop Amphilochius of Iconium and various other fathers ([*Eranistes,*] dialogue 1, p. 19 [§107]; dialogue 3, p. 17 [§242]).[96]

18. The Damascene also explains the same matter—that is, how the things of the one nature are communicated to the other, to wit, *in the person.* These are his words: *Moreover, the Word appropriates what is human (for what belongs to His holy flesh is His) and communicates His own attributes to the flesh by the method of exchange on account of the parts coinhering in each other and the hypostatic union* [*The Orthodox Faith*, §47].[97]

19. On the basis of this it is clear—and not just a little bit—first, that things of the flesh are attributed to the Word[98] no less than things of the Word[99] are attributed to the flesh. Second, the things of the Word[100] are assigned to the flesh in the same way as things of the flesh are attributed to the Word.[101] Finally, this way is called the method of mutual predication[102]—not simply and with the abstract nouns of the natures but with the concrete nouns that denote the person.

τοιγαροῦν καὶ τοὺς περὶ τοῦ Χριστοῦ ποιεῖσθαι προσήκει λόγουςρ καὶ περὶ μὲν τῶν φύσεων διαλεγομένους ἀπονέμειν ἑκατέρᾳ τὰ πρόσφορα, καὶ εἰδέναι τίνα μὲν τῆς θεότητος, τίνα δὲ τῆς ἀνθρωπότητος ἴδια. ὅταν δέ γε τούς περὶ τοῦ προσώπου ποιώμεθα λόγους, κοινὰ χρὴ ποιεῖν τὰ τῶν φύσεων ἴδια καὶ ταῦτα κἀκεῖνα τῷ σωτῆρι προσαρμόττειν Χριστῷρ καὶ τὸν αὐτόν καλεῖν καὶ θεὸν καὶ ἄνθρωπονρ καὶ υἱὸν θεοῦ καὶ υἱὸν ἀνθρώπουρ καὶ υἱὸν δαβίδ καὶ κύριον δαβίδ, καὶ σπέρμα Ἀβραὰμ καὶ ποιητὴν Ἀβραάμ, καὶ τὰ ἄλλα πάντα ὡσαύτως. Zanchi quotes this passage in Greek. The translation is from Theodoret of Cyrus, *Eranistes*, 118 (NPNF2, 3:194).

96. [*Eranistes,*] dialogue 1, p. 19 [§107]; dialogue 3, p. 17 [§242]: Theodoret of Cyrus, *Eranistes*, 83, 239 (NPNF2, 3:181, 240).

97. [*The Orthodox Faith*, §47]: οἰκειοῦται δὲ τὰ ἀνθρώπινα ὁ λόγος. αὐτοῦ γάρ ἐστι τῆς ἁγίας αὐτοῦ σαρκὸς ὄντα· καὶ μεταδίδωσι τῇ σαρκὶ τῶν ἰδίων κατὰ τὸν τῆς ἀντιδόσεως τρόπον· διὰ τὴν εἰς ἄλληλα τῶν μερῶν περιχώρησιν καὶ τὴν καθ᾽ ὑπόστασιν ἕνωσιν. Zanchi quotes this passage in Greek. The translation is from John of Damascus, *The Orthodox Faith*, 170 (NPNF2, 9:48).

98. λόγῳ.
99. λόγου.
100. λόγου.
101. λόγῳ.
102. ἀντιδόσεως.

20. Later in the fourth chapter, with the following words, the Damascene uses both examples and purpose to explain what the method of exchange[103] is and why it bears that name: *And this is the manner* [or method] *of the exchange, each nature exchanging with the other its own properties through the identity of the hypostasis and the mutual interpenetration of the natures. It is in this way that we can say of Christ: "This God of ours was seen on earth"* [Bar. 3:36, 38] *and came together with men, and: "This human being is uncreated and impassable and uncircumscribed"* [*The Orthodox Faith*, §48].[104]

The examples affixed teach very clearly how the one nature assigns to the other nature the things belonging to[105] itself, and for what reason. For insofar as *God* signifies the divine essence, He was not seen on earth. He was seen, however, but only insofar as the person is signified, which is both God and man.

21. It is for this reason that the traditional account of the communication of the proper qualities[106] is not displeasing: *The communication of the proper qualities is a predication in which properties suitable to one nature are assigned to the person in the concrete because the two natures—the Word*[107] *and the assumed nature—are a single subsisting one.*[108]

22. Therefore, we judge that it is not wrong to define the communication of the proper qualities thus: the communication of the proper qualities is a predication or manner of speaking in which the proper quality (that is, the concrete noun signifying something proper to one nature), having

---

103. ἀντιδόσεως τρόπος.
104. [*The Orthodox Faith*, §48]: οὗτος ἔστιν ὁ τρόπος τῆς ἀνιτδόσεως, ἑκατέρας φύσεως ἐντιδιδούσης τῇ ἑτέρᾳ τὰ ἴδια διὰ τὴν τῆς ὑποστάσεως ταυτότητα, καὶ τὴν εἰς ἄλληλα αὐτῶν περιχώρησιν. κατὰ τοῦτο δυνάμεθα εἰπεῖν περὶ χριστοῦ, οὗτος ὁ θεὸς ἡμῶν ἐπὶ τῆς γῆς ὤφθη, καὶ τοῖς ἀνθρώποις συνανεστράφη· καὶ ὁ ἄνθρωπος οὗτος ἄκτιστός ἐστι καὶ ἀπαθής καὶ ἀπερίγραπτος. Zanchi quotes this passage in Greek. The translation is from John of Damascus, *The Orthodox Faith*, 172 (NPNF2, 9:49). Note that the phrase καὶ τοῖς ἀνθρώποις συνανεστράφη [*and came together with men*], which Zanchi includes, is not in the best manuscripts.
105. τὰ ἴδια.
106. κοινωνίας ἰδιωμάτων.
107. λόγος.
108. ὑφιστάμενον.

been signified by a noun of the other nature, is really predicated of Christ's person. It is, however, nominally predicated of the other nature itself in the concrete on account of the coinhering[109] of the natures and the hypostatic[110] union.[111]

23. But we say that it is the same thing for something to be predicated of the person signified by a concrete noun of the other nature as to be predicated of the concrete noun denoting the person of the other nature, just as, in this matter, the proper quality and the concretized name signifying the proper quality[112] of the one nature are the same thing.

24. For it was not so much with regard to the things themselves as with regard to the Holy Scriptures' ordinary way of speaking about Christ that the fathers set forth this question against the heretics, namely, how these phrases should be understood, since, at one time, it says, *The Lord of Glory was crucified*, and at another, *When the Son of Man was on earth, He was also in heaven*, and other things [1 Cor. 2:8; John 3:13].

25. For no one in their right mind has doubted the proposition that, just as the natures remained distinct, whole, and unconfused in the person of Christ after the union, so also did the essential properties of both natures. Thus, by way of example, the deity did not become passible and local, nor did the humanity become impassible and uncircumscribed as some heretics, perverting the Scriptures, have falsely accused.

26. However, the foundation of this whole explanation was the true and real mutual union of the two natures and their uniting into one and the same person, this being accomplished in an inexpressible way without change, confusion, division, or separation.[113]

---

109. περιχώρησιν.
110. καθ' ὑπόστασιν.
111. Zanchi's draws his language from John of Damascus, *The Orthodox Faith*, 170 (*NPNF2*, 9:48), which he quoted above.
112. ἰδιώτητα. The intended word was likely ἰδιότητα (proper quality) rather than ἰδιώτητα.
113. ἀτρέπτος, ἀσυγχύτως, ἀδιαιρέτως or ἀχωρίστως. This is the language of the Chalcedonian Definition. Schaff, *Creeds*, 2:62.

27. Indeed, John of Damascus explains this after teaching how the things of the flesh are attributed to the Word[114] and how the things of the Word[115] are communicated to the flesh (namely, according to the method of exchange[116]). When he does so, he adds the reason why, saying, *on account of the parts coinhering in each other and the hypostatic union* (*The Orthodox Faith*, bk. 3, ch. 3[, §47]).[117] And later, he says, *This is the manner of the exchange, each nature exchanging with the other its own properties through the identity of the hypostasis and the mutual interpenetration of the natures* ([*The Orthodox Faith*, bk 3,] ch. 4[, §48]).[118]

28. Indeed, the coinherence[119] is the oneness.[120] That is to say, coinherence[121] is the intimate and entire, perfect and absolute union, as the Damascene explained elsewhere, especially in the place where he says, *Rather, once the divine nature had passed reciprocally into the flesh, it also endowed the flesh with an ineffable interpenetration, which indeed we call the union* ([*The Orthodox Faith*,] bk. 4, ch. 19[, §91]).[122]

29. We add to this that that same union is this figure of speech's final cause, seeing that Holy Scripture propounds this reciprocal predication in order to display the true oneness[123] of the natures in the one person

---

114. λόγῳ.
115. λόγου.
116. κατὰ τὸν τῆς ἀντιδόσεως τρόπον.
117. *The Orthodox Faith*, bk. 3, ch. 3[, §47]: διὰ τὴν εἰς ἄλληλα τῶν μερῶν περιχώρησιν, καὶ τὴν καθ᾽ ὑπόστασιν ἕνωσιν. Zanchi quotes the passage in Greek. The translation is from John of Damascus, *The Orthodox Faith*, 170 (NPNF2, 9:48).
118. [*The Orthodox Faith*, bk 3,] ch. 4[, §48]: οὗτός ἐστιν ὁ τρόπος τῆς ἀντιδόσεως, ἑκατέρας φύσεως ἀντιδιδούσης τῇ ἑτέρᾳ τὰ ἴδια, διὰ τὴν τῆς ὑποστάσεως ταυτότητα, καὶ τὴν εἰς ἄλληλα αὐτῶν περιχώρησιν. Zanchi quotes the passage in Greek. The translation is from John of Damascus, *The Orthodox Faith*, 172 (NPNF2, 9:49).
119. περιχώρησις.
120. ἕνωσις.
121. περιχώρησις.
122. [*The Orthodox Faith*,] bk. 4, ch. 19[, §91]: ἀλλ᾽ ἡ θεία φύσις ἅπαξ περιχωροῦσα διὰ τῆς σαρκὸς ἔδωκε καὶ τῇ σαρκὶ, τὴν πρὸς αὐτὴν ἄρρητον περιχώρησιν· ἣν δὴ ἕνωσιν λέγομεν. Zanchi quotes the passage in Greek. The translation is from John of Damascus, *The Orthodox Faith*, 269 (NPNF2, 9:91).
123. ἕνωσις.

of Christ. This is the reason why these verbal predications cannot in any way be deemed hollow or unprofitable, since they have the greatest usefulness: displaying the two natures united in one person without confusion.[124]

30. Again, we say that that same communication of the proper qualities (for the sake of example, in the statement *God was crucified*) pertains to both words and to reality, but in distinct respects. For it is a real predication insofar as it indicates the person, by the concrete expression *God* (who is not only God but also man). But because the person is also man, for that reason He truly and really died. However, insofar as the predication indicates the *deity*, or God simply, by formal signification (as they say), it is a verbal predication and indeed a true one. For God is truly said to have died on account of the person to whom reference is made. Nevertheless, He did not really die—nor could He—because He is God. Notwithstanding, He who is God really died.

31. Having explained these things in this way, it is easy to judge various expressions—which are true, which false, and with what manner of predication they are expressed.

Rule One
Regardless of whether an abstract or a concrete noun is used, neither the one nature nor its properties can be predicated in any way of the other nature when it is signified by an abstract noun. For this proposition: *The human nature is God*, or *humanity is God*, is just as false as this: *Humanity is deity*. And this: *Humanity is immense and infinite*, is just as false as this: *Humanity is immensity and infinity itself*.

Hence, no speech of this kind is found in the Holy Scriptures.

Rule Two
32. When one nature is signified either by a concrete or an abstract noun, the other nature and its properties cannot be predicated in the

---

124. ἀσυγχύτως.

abstract, for both of these propositions are false: *God is humanity*, and: *Deity is humanity*.

Rule Three

33. When either nature is signified by any kind of noun, anything that belongs to that nature may be predicated. It may be predicated of either nature in the concrete but may also be predicated of the divine nature in the abstract on account of that nature's simplicity. For this proposition: *Deity is omnipotent*, is as true and proper as this one: *God is omnipotent*, and even: *God is omnipotence itself*. And likewise: *Humanity is mutable*, and: *Man is mutable*.

Rule Four

34. When the person is described by a proper noun that indicates both natures or by a noun that signifies the office of the Mediator, that which belongs to one nature may be truly and properly predicated of the person. The same is true for that which belongs to the other nature or simultaneously to both natures. For example: *Christ is God*, or: *Christ is omnipotent*. Likewise: *Christ is a man; Christ died*. Likewise: *The Mediator is God, is man, is immortal, died, redeemed us*.

Rule Five

35. When the person is signified by a noun pertaining to one nature, that which belongs to that nature is truly and properly predicated. For example: *This God* (or *the only begotten Son of God*) *is eternal and omnipotent*. Likewise: *This man* (or *the Son of Man*) *was born and died in these latter days*.

Rule Six

36. When one nature is signified by either an abstract or a concrete noun, that which belongs to the whole person cannot be predicated unless a part is taken for the whole synecdochically.[125] For example: *The flesh makes alive*, or: *God redeemed the church*.

---

125. συνεκδοχικῶς.

37. This is the reason behind Leo's claim that *Each form does what is proper to it, in communion with the other* [Leo's Tome, ep. 28.4].[126] The Damascene says the same.[127] We agree with him that, properly speaking, it is Christ who works according to each form. For, properly speaking, actions belong to self-subsisting things or persons.[128]

38. Thus, when John says, *His blood cleanses us from sins* [1 John 1:7], and when Christ says, *My flesh truly is food* [John 6:55], and also when it is said that *His body makes alive* and *His body should be worshiped*, the nouns are taken as concrete nouns. That is, *Christ's flesh* is taken as *Christ incarnate*. And *Christ's blood* is taken as *Christ by His blood*.

39. For the One who said, *He who eats My flesh has eternal life*, also said, *He who eats Me will live because of Me* [John 6:54, 57]. And the same one who wrote, *His blood washes us from our sins*, explained Himself by saying, *Christ will wash us from our sins in His blood* [1 John 1:7; Rev. 1:5?]. And the same ones who determined that Christ's flesh ought to be worshiped gave this reason: not because it is flesh but because it is God's flesh. Thus, properly speaking, Christians are not to adore the flesh but rather the incarnate God[129] (Cyril, *Against the Bishops of Oriens*[, §8]; John of Damascus, *The Orthodox Faith*, bk. 3, ch. 8[, §52] and bk. 4, ch. 3[, §76]).[130]

Rule Seven
40. When the person is indicated by a noun of one nature, that which belongs to the other nature is predicated truly and, indeed, really, but in an improper and figurative way by means of the communication

---

126. [Leo's Tome, ep. 28.4]: Leo I, *Letters*, 97–98 (*NPNF2*, 12:40).
127. John of Damascus, *The Orthodox Faith*, 170 (*NPNF2*, 9:48).
128. This final sentence is absent from the 1599 English translation.
129. θεὸν ἐνσαρκωθέντα.
130. Cyril, Against the Bishops of Oriens[, §8]: Cyril of Alexandria, *A Defense of the Twelve Anathemas against the Bishops of the Diocese of Oriens*, in *Three Christological Treatises*, by Cyril of Alexandria, trans. Daniel King, Fathers of the Church 129 (Washington, D.C.: Catholic University of America Press, 2014), 155–56
John of Damascus, The Orthodox Faith, bk. 3, ch. 8[, §52] and bk. 4, ch. 3[, §76]: John of Damascus, *The Orthodox Faith*, 181–82, 230 (*NPNF2*, 9:52, 74–75).

of the properties. For example: *The Son of Man is simultaneously in heaven and on earth.* Likewise: *The unbegotten One* (or *the Lord of Glory*) *was crucified.*

Rule Eight

41. A second thing follows from this: when one nature is represented by a concrete noun, that which belongs properly to the other nature is indeed predicated truly on the basis of the person denoted. However, it is only predicated nominally, not really. For example: *God* (meant as a formal signification) *died*, or: *Man is eternal.*

42. For this reason, we say that such things are predicated by means of the communication of properties, since they are proper to the one nature but also are made common to the other nature in the concrete by the method of exchange.[131] That is to say, they are made common, provided that they are really attributed to the person of whom each nature is a part.

43. For since Christ is altogether truly and really both God and man, we do not hesitate to say and to predicate with the whole church (for the sake of an example) that *Christ truly and really did indeed suffer*, which is to say that He suffered according to the one nature but did not suffer according to the other nature.

44. And since Scripture says that God is immortal,[132] and also that He died or was crucified, we teach that, in the first statement, the noun is taken of God essentially[133] and that, in the second, it is taken hypostatically.[134] And thus, in speech concerning Christ, both statements are true, but each is asserted about Him with a different mode of predication.

Rule Nine

45. When we read that something was really given to Christ at a point of time after the union, it is really and truly predicated of the person

---

131. ἀντιδόσεως.
132. ἀθάνατον.
133. οὐσιωδῶς.
134. ὑποστατικῶς.

with respect to the humanity and, thus, is really and truly predicated of the humanity itself. However, we should not think that it is to be predicated with respect to the divinity (and pronounced with a concrete noun) except by way of the communication of the properties.

First example: *The Spirit of wisdom will rest upon Him* (Isa. 11[:2]). Second example: *He gave to Him* (that is, to the Son who is from heaven whom God the Father sent) *the Spirit without measure* (John 3[:34]). For insofar as He is the only begotten Son, it cannot be said that He really received the Spirit. This can only be said by way of the communication of the properties.

46. We acknowledge, however, that it was not God's essential properties that were given in this way but only created gifts and habits of grace[135] (as they are called). These pertain in part to the perfection of the human nature in Christ, in part to His executing the office of mediator, and in part to the honor of the church's Head.

47. For God's essential properties are indeed united with the human nature in the one person in a way that is altogether real, but by no means are they really communicated to the human nature in its very essence.[136]

48. For, as Athanasius and Cyril testify—to omit a nearly infinite number of other reasons and testimonies from both the apostles and the ancient fathers—whatever Christ received as man (that is, in the essence[137] of His human nature), He received as Head, so that He might distribute it to His members (Athanasius, *On the Human Nature Taken Up by the Only Begotten Word, against Apollinaris*, p. 531; Cyril of Alexandria, *The Treasury of the Holy and Consubstantial Trinity*, bk. 8,

---

135. *Gratiae habituales*. "A divine gift infused into the soul in such a way as to become a part of human nature," but not in the post-Tridentine sense of an inherent justifying grace. Rather, Zanchi's view seems to accord with the Reformation and Reformed orthodox view of "inherent, or intrinsic, albeit still imperfect" righteousness that was understood to be "a result of the Spirit's work in sanctification." Thus, the "concept of an inward *habitus*, or disposition," arose out of the concept of "the cleansing or renovation of the believer." Muller, *Dictionary*, 146–47.

136. οὐσίᾳ.

137. οὐσίᾳ.

ch. 1).¹³⁸ Indeed, this is why He sanctified Himself, so that we, too, might be sanctified and so that the oil poured out on Aaron's head might run down onto the rest of His members, even to the fringe of His garment [John 17:19; Ps. 133:2].

49. But who, other than a lunatic, would say that God's essential properties are distributed to us?

50. Indeed, according to Cyril, the reason why Christ (as He is God) cannot be said to have received created gifts is that (as He is God) He did not need them (Cyril of Alexandria, *On the Right Faith*, bk. 2, p. 305).¹³⁹ Therefore, if God's essential properties were indeed really communicated to Christ (as He is man), then He should not be said to have received the created gifts of the Holy Spirit. For, why would finite power be given to Him who has really communicated infinite power to Himself?

---

138. Athanasius, *On the Human Nature Taken Up by the Only Begotten Word, against Apollinaris, p. 531*: The first of these works is Pseudo-Athanasian but was included in the 1546 Latin edition of Athanasius's works, which Zanchi cites. "For the Lord of Glory is not glorified, but the Lord of Glory's flesh is what receives glory. It also ascended to heaven with Him, from where He poured out..." *Athanasii magni Alexandrini episcopi opera* (Basel, 1564), 531 (PG, 26:990B).

Cyril of Alexandria, *The Treasury of the Holy and Consubstantial Trinity*, bk. 8, ch. 1: Cyril writes, "The Word of God is always most exalted as God but is exalted as man; as God He lacks nothing but as man He is said to receive; as God He is worshipped always, but now He receives worship as man. If He died as a man, this detracts nothing from the dignity of the Word of God, so it is not an affront if He is said to have received something. For just as He receives the one thing by the humanity, so also this thing. If, as man, He is said to have died while, as God, He is immortal, then He is called exalted as man while He is most exalted as God." *PG*, 75:331C.

139. Cyril of Alexandria, *On the Right Faith*, bk. 2, p. 305: *PG*, 76:1399D–1402B.

Bibliography

Adam, Melchior. *Decades duae continentes vitas theologorum exterorum principum*. Frankfurt, 1618.

Ambrose. *Theological and Dogmatic Works*. Translated by Roy J. Deferrari. Fathers of the Church 44. Washington, D.C.: Catholic University of America Press, 2002.

Ambrosiaster. *Commentaries on Galatians–Philemon*. Translated and edited by Gerald L. Bray. Ancient Christian Texts. Downers Grove, Ill.: IVP Academic, 2009.

———. *Commentaries on Romans and 1–2 Corinthians*. Translated and edited by Gerald L. Bray. Ancient Christian Texts. Downers Grove, Ill.: IVP Academic, 2009.

Asselt, Willem J. van, and Eef Dekker, eds. *Reformation and Scholasticism: An Ecumenical Enterprise*. Texts and Studies in Reformation and Post-Reformation Thought. Grand Rapids: Baker Academic, 2001.

Asselt, Willem J. van, Riemer A. Faber, Andreas J. Beck, and William den Boer, eds. *Synopsis Purioris Theologiae / Synopsis of a Purer Theology: Latin Text and English Translation*. 3 vols. Leiden: Brill, 2014–2020.

Athanasius. *Athanasii magni Alexandrini episcopi opera*. Basel, 1564.

———. *De Incarnatione*. In *Contra Gentes and De Incarnatione*, edited and translated by Robert W. Thomson, 134–277. Oxford Early Christian Texts. Oxford: Clarendon Press, 1971.

Augustine. *Answer to Faustus, a Manichean*. Edited by Boniface Ramsey. Translated by Roland J. Teske. The Works of Saint Augustine:

A Translation for the 21st Century I/20. Hyde Park, N.Y.: New City Press, 2007.

———. *Answer to Julian*. In *Answer to the Pelagians*. Vol. 2, by Augustine, edited by John E. Rotelle, translated by Roland J. Teske, 222–536. The Works of Saint Augustine: A Translation for the 21st Century I/24. Hyde Park, N.Y.: New City Press, 1998.

———. *Answer to the Letter of Mani Known as The Foundation*. In *The Manichean Debate*, by Augustine, edited by Boniface Ramsey, translated by Roland J. Teske, 227–67. The Works of Saint Augustine: A Translation for the 21st Century I/19. Hyde Park, N.Y.: New City Press, 2006.

———. *Answer to the Pelagians*. Vol. 1, edited by John E. Rotelle, translated by Roland J. Teske. The Works of Saint Augustine: A Translation for the 21st Century I/23. Hyde Park, N.Y.: New City Press, 1997.

———. *The Augustine Catechism: The Enchiridion on Faith, Hope, and Charity*. Edited by Boniface Ramsey. Translated by Bruce Harbert. Hyde Park, N.Y.: New City Press, 1999.

———. *The City of God: Books VIII–XVI*. Translated by Gerald G. Walsh and Grace Monahan. Fathers of the Church 14. Washington, D.C.: Catholic University of America Press, 1952.

———. *The Confessions*. Edited by John E. Rotelle. Translated by Maria Boulding. The Works of Saint Augustine: A Translation for the 21st Century, I/1. Hyde Park, N.Y.: New City Press, 1997.

———. *De Doctrina Christiana*. Edited and translated by R. P. H. Green. Oxford: Clarendon Press, 1995.

———. *The Donatist Controversy*. Vol. 1, edited by Boniface Ramsey and David G. Hunter, translated by Maureen Tilley and Boniface Ramsey. The Works of Saint Augustine: A Translation for the 21st Century I/21. Hyde Park, N.Y.: New City Press, 2019.

———. *Grace and Free Choice*. In *Answer to the Pelagians*. Vol. 4, by Augustine, edited by John E. Rotelle, translated by Roland J. Teske, 70–106. The Works of Saint Augustine: A Translation for the 21st Century I/26. Hyde Park, N.Y.: New City Press, 1999.

———. *Homilies on the Gospel of John 1–40*. Edited by Allan D. Fitzgerald. Translated by Edmund Hill. The Works of Saint Augustine: A Translation for the 21st Century III/12. Hyde Park, N.Y.: New City Press, 2009.

———. *Homilies on the Gospel of John 41–124*. Edited by Allan D. Fitzgerald. Translated by Edmund Hill. The Works of Saint Augustine: A Translation for the 21st Century III/13. Hyde Park, N.Y.: New City Press, 2020.

———. *Letter to Catholics on the Sect of the Donatists*. In *The Donatist Controversy*. Vol. 1, by Augustine, edited by Boniface Ramsey and David G. Hunter, translated by Maureen Tilley and Boniface Ramsey, 605–86. The Works of Saint Augustine: A Translation for the 21st Century I/21. Hyde Park, N.Y.: New City Press, 2019.

———. *Letters*. Vol. 1, *1–99*, edited by John E. Rotelle, translated by Roland J. Teske. The Works of Saint Augustine: A Translation for the 21st Century II/1. Hyde Park, N.Y.: New City Press, 2001.

———. *Letters*. Vol. 2, *100–155*, edited by Boniface Ramsey, translated by Roland J. Teske. The Works of Saint Augustine: A Translation for the 21st Century II/2. Hyde Park, N.Y.: New City Press, 2003.

———. *Letters*. Vol. 3, *156–210*, edited by Boniface Ramsey, translated by Roland J. Teske. The Works of Saint Augustine: A Translation for the 21st Century II/3. Hyde Park, N.Y.: New City Press, 2004.

———. *On Christian Belief*. Edited by Boniface Ramsey. Translated by Edmund Hill, Ray Kearney, Michael G. Campbell, and Bruce Harbert. The Works of Saint Augustine: A Translation for the 21st Century I/8. Hyde Park, N.Y.: New City Press, 2005.

———. *Opera Divi Aurelii Augustini episcopi Hipponensis*. 10 vols. Basel, 1528–1529.

———. *Sermons*. Vol. 7, *230–272B*, edited by John E. Rotelle, translated by Edmund Hill. The Works of Saint Augustine: A Translation for the 21st Century III/7. Hyde Park, N.Y.: New City Press, 1993.

———. *Sermons*. Vol. 10, 341–400, edited by John E. Rotelle, translated by Edmund Hill. The Works of Saint Augustine: A Translation for the 21st Century III/10. Hyde Park, N.Y.: New City Press, 1995.

Austin, Kenneth. *From Judaism to Calvinism: The Life and Writings of Immanuel Tremellius (c.1510–1580)*. St Andrews Studies in Reformation History. London: Routledge, 2007.

Bancroft, Richard. *A Survey of the Pretended Holy Discipline*. London, 1663.

Baschera, Luca. "Total Depravity? The Consequences of Original Sin in John Calvin and Later Reformed Theology." In *Calvinus Clarissimus Theologus: Papers of the Tenth International Congress on Calvin Research*, edited by Herman J. Selderhuis, 37–58. Reformed Historical Theology 18. Göttingen: Vandenhoeck & Ruprecht, 2012.

Baschera, Luca, and Christian Moser. "Introduction." In *De religione christiana fides – Confession of Christian Religion*, vol. 1, by Girolamo Zanchi, 1–49. Studies in the History of Christian Traditions 135. Leiden: Brill, 2007.

Beck, Andreas J. "Reformed Confessions and Scholasticism. Diversity and Harmony." *Perichoresis* 14, no. 3 (December 2016): 17–43.

Bede. *Commentary on the Acts of the Apostles*. Translated by Lawrence T. Martin. Cistercian Studies Series 117. Kalamazoo, Mich.: Cistercian Publications, 1989.

Benefield, Sebastian. *Doctrinae Christianae sex capita*. Oxford, 1610.

Beza, Theodore. *A Discourse of the True and Visible Markes of the Catholique Churche*. 1582.

———. *Tractationes theologicae*. 3 vols. Geneva, 1570–1582.

Brakel, Wilhelmus à. *The Christian's Reasonable Service*. Edited by Joel R. Beeke. Translated by Bartel Elshout. 4 vols. Grand Rapids: Reformation Heritage Books, 1992.

Bravi, Giulio Orazio. "Girolamo Zanchi, da Lucca a Strasburgo." *Archivio storico bergamasco* 1 (1981): 35–64.

———. "I riformati bergamaschi Girolamo Zanchi e Guglielmo Grataroli in Italia prima dell'esilio." In *Il dissenso religioso a Bergamo nel*

Cinquecento, edited by Giulio Orazio Bravi, 125–67. Bergamo: Centro studi e ricerche Archivio Bergamasco, 2018.

Bucer, Martin. *Enarrationes Perpetuae in Sacra Quatuor Evangelia*. Strasbourg, 1530.

———. *Praelectiones in epistolam ad Ephesios*. Basil, 1562.

Bullinger, Heinrich. *The Decades of Henry Bullinger*. Edited by Thomas Harding. 3 vols. Cambridge: Cambridge University Press, 1849–1852.

Burchill, Christopher J. "Girolamo Zanchi in Strasbourg, 1553–1563." PhD diss., University of Cambridge, 1979.

———. *The Heidelberg Antitrinitarians: Johann Sylvan, Adam Neuser, Matthias Vehe, Jacob Suter, Johann Hasler*. Bibliotheca Dissidentium 11. Baden-Baden: Koerner, 1989.

Burnett, Amy Nelson. "Basel, Beza, and the Development of Calvinist Orthodoxy in the Swiss Confederation." In *Calvin und Calvinismus: Europäische Perspektiven*, edited by Irene Dingel and Herman J. Selderhuis, 67–84. Veröffentlichungen des Instituts für Europäische Geschichte Mainz 84. Göttingen: Vandenhoeck & Ruprecht, 2013. https://doi.org/10.13109/9783666101069.67.

Büsser, Fritz. "Freedom in Reformed Confessions of the 16th Century (The 'Harmonia Confessionum Fidei' of 1581)." *Zwingliana* 16, no. 4 (1984): 281–300.

Calvin, John. *Commentaries on the Epistle of Paul the Apostle to the Romans*. Edited by John Owen. Edinburgh: Calvin Translation Society, 1849.

Calvin, John, and Jacopo Sadoleto. *A Reformation Debate: John Calvin & Jacopo Sadoleto*. Edited by John C. Olin. New York: Fordham University Press, 2000.

Campos, Heber Carlos de, Jr.. *Doctrine in Development: Johannes Piscator and Debates over Christ's Active Obedience*. Reformed Historical-Theological Studies. Grand Rapids: Reformation Heritage Books, 2017.

Cyprian. *Letters (1–81)*. Translated by Rose Bernard Donna. Fathers of the Church 51. Washington, D.C.: Catholic University of America Press, 1964.

———. *Treatises*. Translated and edited by Roy J. Deferrari. Fathers of the Church 36. Washington, D.C.: Catholic University of America Press, 1958.

Cyril of Alexandria. *Commentary on John*. Edited by Joel C. Elowsky. Translated by David R. Maxwell. 2 vols. Ancient Christian Texts. Downers Grove, Ill.: IVP Academic, 2013–2015.

———. *A Defense of the Twelve Anathemas against the Bishops of the Diocese of Oriens*. In *Three Christological Treatises*, by Cyril of Alexandria, translated by Daniel King, 131–82. Fathers of the Church 129. Washington, D.C.: Catholic University of America Press, 2014.

———. *Dialogues sur la Trinité*. Translated by Georges-Matthieu de Durand. 3 vols. Paris: Éditions du Cerf, 1976–1978.

———. *Select Letters*. Translated by Lionel R. Wickham. Oxford Early Christian Texts. Oxford: Clarendon Press, 1983.

Davie, Martin, Tim Grass, Stephen R. Holmes, John McDowell, and T. A. Noble, eds. *New Dictionary of Theology: Historical and Systematic*. 2nd ed. Downers Grove, Ill.: IVP Academic, 2016.

Dennison, James T., Jr., comp. *Reformed Confessions of the 16th and 17th Centuries in English Translation*. 4 vols. Grand Rapids: Reformation Heritage Press, 2008–2014.

Dingel, Irene. *Concordia controversa: Die öffentlichen Diskussionen um das lutherische Konkordienwerk am Ende des 16. Jahrhunderts*. Quellen und Forschungen zur Reformationsgeschichte 63. Gütersloh: Gütersloher Verlagshaus, 1996.

Donnelly, John Patrick. "Calvinist Thomism." *Viator* 7 (1976): 441–55.

Drake, K. J. *The Flesh of the Word: The Extra Calvinisticum from Zwingli to Early Orthodoxy*. Oxford Studies in Historical Theology. New York: Oxford University Press, 2021.

Erasmus, Desiderius. *Collected Works of Erasmus*. Vol. 34, *Adages: II vii 1 to III iii 100*, translated by R. A. B. Mynors. Toronto: University of Toronto Press, 1992.

———. *Collected Works of Erasmus*. Vol. 56, *Annotations on Romans*, edited by Robert D. Sider. Toronto: University of Toronto Press, 1994.

Euripides. *Hippolytus*. In *Euripidis Fabulae*. Vol. 1, *Cyclops, Alcestis, Medea, Heraclidae, Hippolytus, Andromacha, Hecuba*, edited by Gilbert Murray, G4v–I3r. Oxford: Oxford University Press, 1902.

Eusebius. *Ecclesiastical History, Books 1–5*. Translated by Roy J. Deferrari. Fathers of the Church 19. Washington, D.C.: Catholic University of America Press, 1965.

———. *Ecclesiastical History, Books 6–10*. Translated by Roy J. Deferrari. Fathers of the Church 29. Washington, D.C.: Catholic University of America Press, 1969.

Farthing, John L. "Christ and the Eschaton: The Reformed Eschatology of Jerome Zanchi." In *Later Calvinism: International Perspectives*, ed. W. Fred Graham, 333–54. Sixteenth Century Essays and Studies 22. Kirksville, Mo.: Sixteenth Century Journal, 1994.

———. "De coniugio spirituali: Jerome Zanchi on Ephesians 5:22–33." *Sixteenth Century Journal* 24, no. 3 (Autumn 1993): 621–52.

———. "*Foedus Evangelicum*: Jerome Zanchi on the Covenant." *Calvin Theological Journal* 29 (April–November 1994): 149–67.

Fesko, J. V. "Girolamo Zanchi on Union with Christ and the Final Judgment." *Perichoresis* 18, no. 1 (March 2020): 41–56.

———. "Jerome Zanchi on Union with Christ and Justification." *Puritan Reformed Journal* 2, no. 2 (July 2010): 53–76.

Fulgentius of Ruspe. *Selected Works*. Translated by Robert B. Eno. Fathers of the Church 95. Washington, D.C.: Catholic University of America Press, 1997.

Gallizioli, Giambattista. *Memorie istoriche e letterarie della vita e delle opere di Girolamo Zanchi*. Bergamo: Francesco Locatelli, 1785.

Gibson, Jonathan, and Mark Earngey, eds. *Reformation Worship: Liturgies from the Past for the Present*. Greensboro, N.C.: New Growth Press, 2018.

Gomarus, Franciscus. "Disputationes theologicae." In *Opera theologica omnia*. Vol. 2, 1–155. Amsterdam, 1644.

Goodwin, Thomas. *The Works of Thomas Goodwin*. 12 vols. Grand Rapids: Reformation Heritage Books, 2021.

Goris, Harm, ed. *Synopsis Purioris Theologiae / Synopsis of a Purer Theology: Latin Text and English Translation.* Vol. 3, *Disputations 43–52*, translated by Riemer A. Faber. Studies in Medieval and Reformation Traditions 222/9. Leiden: Brill, 2020.

Gratian. *Corpus Iuris Canonici.* Edited by Aemilius Friedberg. 2 vols. Graz: Akademische Druck- und Verlagsanstalt, 1959.

———. *The Treatise on Laws (Decretum DD. 1–20) with the Ordinary Gloss.* Translated by Augustine Thompson and James Gordley. Studies in Medieval and Early Modern Canon Law. Washington, D.C.: Catholic University of America Press, 1993.

Greenslade, S. L., ed. *Early Latin Theology: Selections from Tertullian, Cyprian, Ambrose, and Jerome.* The Library of Christian Classics 5. Philadelphia: Westminster Press, 1956.

Gregory the Great. *Forty Gospel Homilies.* Translated by David Hurst. Cistercian Studies Series 123. Kalamazoo, Mich.: Cistercian Publications, 1990.

———. *The Letters of Gregory the Great.* Translated by John R. C. Martyn. 3 vols. Mediaeval Sources in Translation 40. Toronto: Pontifical Institute of Mediaeval Studies, 2004.

———. *Moral Reflections on the Book of Job.* Vol. 3, *Books 11–16.* Translated by Brian Kerns. Cistercian Studies Series 258. Collegeville, Minn.: Liturgical Press, 2016.

Gribben, Crawford. "John Owen, Renaissance Man? The Evidence of Edward Millington's *Bibliotheca Oweniana* (1684)." In *The Ashgate Research Companion to John Owen's Theology,* ed. Kelly M. Kapic and Mark Jones, 115–28. Ashgate Research Companions. Aldershot: Ashgate, 2016.

Gründler, Otto. "Zanchi, Girolamo." In *The Oxford Encyclopedia of the Reformation.* Oxford: Oxford University Press, 2005–. https://doi.org/10.1093/acref/9780195064933.013.1544.

Gunnoe, Charles. *Thomas Erastus and the Palatinate: A Renaissance Physician in the Second Reformation.* Brill's Series in Church History 48. Leiden: Brill, 2010.

Heidegger, Johann Heinrich. *Corpus theologiae Christianae.* 2 vols. Zurich, 1700.

Hill, Edmund. "Introduction." In *The Trinity*, by Augustine, edited by John E. Rotelle, translated by Edmund Hill, 18–59. The Works of Saint Augustine: A Translation for the 21st Century I/5. Hyde Park, N.Y.: New City Press, 1991.

Hill, Robert. "The Epistle Dedicatorie." In *Life Everlasting, or The True Knowledge of One Jehovah, Three Elohim, and Jesus Immanuel*, by Girolamo Zanchi, ¶2r–¶4v. Cambridge, 1601.

Hooker, Richard. *A Learned Discourse of Iustification, Workes, and How the Foundation of Faith Is Overthrowne*. Oxford, 1612.

Jerome. *Commentaries on the Twelve Prophets*. Translated by Thomas P. Scheck. 2 vols. Ancient Christian Texts. Downers Grove, Ill.: IVP Academic, 2016–2017.

———. "Jerome's Prologue to the Books of Solomon." Translated by Kevin P. Edgecomb. *Biblicalia* (blog), August 13, 2006. https://web.archive.org/web/20220309114224/https://www.bombaxo.com/2006/08/13/jeromes-prologue-to-the-books-of-solomon/.

———. *St. Jerome's Commentaries on Galatians, Titus, and Philemon*. Translated by Thomas P. Scheck. Notre Dame, Ind.: University of Notre Dame Press, 2020.

John of Damascus. *On the Orthodox Faith*. Translated by Norman Russell. Popular Patristics Series 62. Yonkers, N.Y.: St Vladimir's Seminary Press, 2022.

Justin Martyr. *The First and Second Apologies*. Translated by Leslie W. Barnard. Ancient Christian Writers. New York: Paulist Press, 1997.

Kinzig, Wolfram, ed. *Faith in Formulae: A Collection of Early Christian Creeds and Creed-related Texts*. 4 vols. Oxford Early Christian Texts. Oxford: Oxford University Press, 2017.

Kittelson, James M. *Toward an Established Church: Strasbourg from 1500 to the Dawn of the Seventeenth Century*. Veröffentlichungen des Instituts für Europäische Geschichte Mainz Abteilung für Abendländische Religionsgeschichte 182. Mainz: Verlag Philipp von Zabern, 2000.

Knox, John. "First Book of Discipline." In *The History of the Reformation of Religion in Scotland*, 486–525. Glasgow: Blackie & Fullarton, 1831.

Lasco, Joannes à. *Opera, tam edita quam inedita*. Edited by Abraham Kuyper. 2 vols. Amsterdam: Frederic Muller, 1866.

Leo I. *Letters*. Translated by Edmund Hunt. Fathers of the Church 34. New York: Fathers of the Church, 1957.

Lynch, Michael. "Weird Reformation: Christ the Mediator of Angels?" Davenant Institute, May 25, 2018. https://davenantinstitute.org/weird-reformation-christ-mediator-angels/.

Mastricht, Petrus van. *Theoretical-Practical Theology*. 4 vols. Edited by Joel R. Beeke. Translated by Todd M. Rester. Grand Rapids: Reformation Heritage Books, 2018–2023.

———. *Theoretico-practica theologia*. Amsterdam, 1724.

McDonald, Lee Martin. *The Formation of the Biblical Canon*. 2 vols. London: Bloomsbury T&T Clark, 2021.

McGinnis, Andrew M. *The Son of God Beyond the Flesh: A Historical and Theological Study of the Extra Calvinisticum*. T&T Clark Studies in Systematic Theology 29. London and New York: Bloomsbury T&T Clark, 2016.

Menander. *Menandri sententiae. Comparatio Menandri et Philistionis*. Edited by Siegfried Jäkel. Leipzig: Teubner, 1964.

Merkle, Benjamin R. *Defending the Trinity in the Reformed Palatinate: The Elohistae*. Oxford Theology and Religion Monographs. New York: Oxford University Press, 2016.

Moor, Bernardus de. *Compendium theologiae christianae didactico-elencticum*. 7 vols. Leiden, 1761–1771.

Moore, Norman, and Michael Bevan. "Winterton, Ralph (1601–1636)." In *Oxford Dictionary of National Biography* (Oxford University Press, 2004–). https://doi.org/10.1093/ref:odnb/29776.

Muller, Richard A. *Christ and the Decree: Christology and Predestination in Reformed Theology from Calvin to Perkins*. Grand Rapids: Baker Academic, 2008.

———. *Dictionary of Latin and Greek Theological Terms: Drawn Principally from Protestant Scholastic Theology*. 2nd ed. Grand Rapids: Baker, 2017.

Musculus, Wolfgang. *Common Places of Christian Religion*. London, 1563.

———. *Loci Communes in Usus Sacrae Theologiae Candidatorum Parati*. Basil, 1560.

O'Banion, Patrick J. "Jerome Zanchi, the Application of Theology, and the Rise of the English Practical Divinity Tradition." *Renaissance and Reformation / Renaissance et Réforme* 29, no. 2–3 (2005): 97–120.

Origen. *Contra Celsum*. Translated by Henry Chadwick. Cambridge: Cambridge University Press, 1980.

Pabel, Hilmar. *Herculean Labours: Erasmus and the Editing of St. Jerome's Letters in the Renaissance*. Library of the Written Word - The Handpress World 5. Leiden: Brill, 2008.

Palmer, Benjamin Morgan. "The Relation between the Work of Christ and the Condition of the Angelic World." *Southern Presbyterian Review* 1, no. 1 (June 1847): 34–63.

Polanus, Amandus. *The Substance of Christian Religion*. London, 1600.

———. *Syntagma theologiae christianae*. Geneva, 1617.

Quodvultdeus of Carthage. *The Creedal Homilies*. Translated by Thomas M. Finn. Ancient Christian Writers 60. New York: Newman Press, 2004.

Riches, Aaron. *Ecce Homo: On the Divine Unity of Christ*. Interventions. Grand Rapids: Eerdmans, 2016.

Robinson, Hastings, ed. *The Zurich Letters (Second Series)*. Cambridge: Cambridge University Press, 1845.

Rufinus of Aquileia. *A Commentary on the Apostles' Creed*. Translated by J. N. D. Kelly. Ancient Christian Writers. New York: Newman Press, 1954.

Sallust. *Catiline's War, The Jugurthine War, Histories*. Translated by A. J. Woodman. London: Penguin, 2007.

Salvard, Jean-François, ed. *Harmonia confessionum fidei orthodoxarum et reformatarum ecclesiarum, quae in praecipius quibusque Europae regnis, nationibus et provinciis sacram evangelii doctrinam pure profitentur*. Geneva, 1581.

———, ed. *An Harmony of the Confessions of the Faith of the Christian and Reformed Churches*. Cambridge, 1586.

Schaff, Philip, ed. *Creeds of Christendom, with a History and Critical Notes*. 6th ed. 3 vols. Grand Rapids: Baker Books, 1984.

Schmidt, Charles. "Girolamo Zanchi." *Theologische Studien Und Kritiken* 32 (1859): 625–708.

Scieri, Emanuele. "The Catena Manuscripts on Acts: A Revised Classification." *Vigiliae Christianae* 76, no. 3 (June 2022): 281–305. doi: 10.1163/15700720-bja10042.

Shepherd, Norman. "Zanchius on Saving Faith." *Westminster Theological Journal* 36, no. 1 (Fall 1973): 31–47.

Spijker, Willem van 't. *The Ecclesiastical Offices in the Thought of Martin Bucer*. Translated by John Vriend and Lyle D. Bierma. Studies in Medieval and Reformation Traditions 57. Leiden: Brill, 1996.

———. "Reformation and Scholasticism." In *Martin Bucer (1491–1551): Collected Studies on His Life, Work, Doctrine, and Influence*, edited by Christa Boerke and Jan C. Klok, 61–78. Refo500 Academic Studies 44. Göttingen: Vandenhoeck & Ruprecht, 2018.

———. Review of *De religione christiana fides – Confession of Christian Religion. [Studies in the History of Christian Traditions 135]*, by Girolamo Zanchi, edited by Luca Baschera and Christian Moser. *Church History and Religious Culture* 92, no. 2–3 (January 2012): 377–79.

Sytsma, David S. "Sixteenth-Century Reformed Reception of Aquinas." In *The Oxford Handbook of the Reception of Aquinas*, edited by Matthew Levering and Marcus Plested, 121–43. Oxford: Oxford University Press, 2021.

Tanner, Norman P., ed. *Decrees of the Ecumenical Councils*. 2 vols. Washington, D.C.: Georgetown University Press, 1990.

Tertullian. *Adversus Marcionem*. Translated by Ernest Evans. 2 vols. Oxford Early Christian Texts. Oxford: Clarendon Press, 1972.

———. "Apology." In *Tertullian, Apologetical Works and Minucius Felix, Octavius*, translated by Rudolph Arbesmann, Emily Joseph

Daly, and Edwin A. Quain, 3–125. Fathers of the Church 10. Washington, D.C.: Catholic University of America Press, 1962.

———. *Homily on Baptism*. Translated by Ernest Evans. Eugene, Ore.: Wipf and Stock, 2016.

———. *Tertullian's Treatise against Praxeas: The Text Edited, with an Introduction, Translation, and Commentary*. Edited and translated by Ernest Evans. London: SPCK, 1948.

Theodoret of Cyrus. *Eranistes*. Translated by Gerard H. Ettlinger. Fathers of the Church 106. Washington, D.C.: Catholic University of America Press, 2003.

Thomas Aquinas. *Summa Contra Gentiles: Book Three: Providence, Part 1*. Translated by Vernon J. Bourke. Notre Dame, Ind.: University of Notre Dame Press, 1975.

———. *Commentary on the Letter of Saint Paul to the Romans*. Edited by J. Mortensen and E. Alarcón. Translated by Fabian R. Larcher. Latin/English Edition of the Works of St. Thomas Aquinas 37. Lander, WY: Aquinas Institute, 2012.

Thompson, Nicholas. *Eucharistic Sacrifice and Patristic Tradition in the Theology of Martin Bucer 1534–1546*. Studies in the History of Christian Traditions 119. Leiden: Brill, 2005.

Turretin, Francis. *Institutes of Elenctic Theology*. Edited by James T. Dennison Jr. Translated by George Musgrave Giger. 3 vols. Phillipsburg, N.J.: P&R Publishing, 1992–1997.

Ursinus, Zacharias. *The Commentary of Dr. Zacharias Ursinus on the Heidelberg Catechism*. Translated by G. W. Williard. Phillipsburg, N.J.: Presbyterian and Reformed, 1985.

Velde, Dolf te, and Rein Ferwerda, eds. *Synopsis Purioris Theologiae / Synopsis of a Purer Theology: Latin Text and English Translation*. Vol. 1, *Disputations 1–23*, translated by Riemer A. Faber. Studies in Medieval and Reformation Traditions 187/5. Leiden: Brill, 2014.

Velde, Roelf T. te. "Always Free, but Not Always Good: Girolamo Zanchi (1516–1590) on Free Will." In *Reformed Thought on Freedom: The Concept of Free Choice in Early Modern Reformed Theology*, edited by Willem J. van Asselt, J. Martin Bac, and Roelf T. te Velde, 51–93. Grand Rapids: Baker, 2010.

Vischer, Lukas. "Girolamo Zancho, reformierter Prediger in Chiavenna." *Bündnerisches Monatsblatt* 10 (1951): 289–301.

Vitringa, Campegius. *Doctrina christianae religionis, per aphorismos summatim descripta*. 6th ed. 8 vols. Arnheim, 1761–1786.

Weinrich, William C. "Translator's Introduction." In *Greek Commentaries on Revelation*, by Oecumenius and Andrew of Caesarea, edited by Thomas C. Oden, translated by William C. Weinrich, xix–xxxix. Ancient Christian Texts. Downers Grove, Ill.: IVP Academic, 2011.

Wollebius, Johannes. *Compendium theologiae christianae*. Editio nova prioribus correctior. London, 1760.

Wuellner, Bernard J. *A Dictionary of Scholastic Philosophy*. 1st ed. Milwaukee, Wis.: Bruce, 1956.

———. *A Dictionary of Scholastic Philosophy*. 2nd ed. Milwaukee, Wis.: Bruce, 1966.

Zanchi, Girolamo. *De natura Dei seu de divinis attributis libri quinque*. Heidelberg, 1577.

———. *De operibus Dei intra spacium sex dierum creatis*. Neustadt, 1591.

———. *De primi hominis lapsu, de peccato et de lege Dei*. Neustadt, 1597.

———. *De religione christiana fides – Confession of Christian Religion*. Edited by Luca Baschera and Christian Moser. 2 vols. Studies in the History of Christian Traditions 135. Leiden: Brill, 2007.

———. *His Confession of the Christian Religion*. Cambridge: J. Legat, 1599.

———. *In d. Pauli Apostoli epistolas ad Philippenses ad Colosenses ad Thessalonicenses, commentarij*. Neustadt, 1595.

———. *La fede cristiana. Che precisamente ora, a sessantanove anni d'età, mise alla luce a nome suo e della sua famiglia*. Translated by Emanuele Fiume. Rome: Edizioni GBU, 2011.

———. *On the Law in General*. Translated by Jeffrey J. Veenstra. Sources in Early Modern Economics, Ethics, and Law. Grand Rapids: CLP Academic, 2012.

———. *Speculum Christianum: A Christian Survey of Conscience*. Translated by Henry Nelson. London, 1614.

———. *The Spiritual Marriage between Christ and His Church and Every One of the Faithful*. Translated by Patrick J. O'Banion. Grand Rapids: Reformation Heritage Books, 2021.

Zanchi, Jerom [sic]. *The Doctrine of Absolute Predestination Stated and Asserted with a Preliminary Discourse on the Divine Attributes*. Translated by Augustus Toplady. London: Joseph Gurney, 1769.

Zanchi, Jerome. *The Whole Body of Christian Religion*. Translated by Ralph Winterton. London: John Redmayne, 1659.

Zylstra, Stephen John. "Immanent Causation in Spinoza and Scholasticism." PhD diss., University of Toronto, 2018.

Scripture Index

OLD TESTAMENT

Genesis
1	356
1–2	61, 63, 69
1:1	356
1:28	64
2	69
2:2	65
2:24	112
3:1	69
3:6	69
3:15	79
6:5	75
7:23	207
8:21	75
12:3	314
15	314
15:6	164–65
50:20	356

Exodus
20:1–17	120
20:7	183
21:13	67, 357

Leviticus
25:48–49	359
26:4	356

Numbers
23:19	357

Deuteronomy
4:2	46, 84
5:22	84
5:31	46
6:4	51
8:3	356
10:12	182
12:32	46, 84, 379
13:1–10	222
14:22–29	227
28	178
32:4	356
32:41	357

1 Kings
17:4	356
22:21	63

1 Chronicles
16:34	356
29:11–12	356

2 Chronicles
14:11	357
20:6–12	357

Nehemiah
9:33	356

Job
5	356
9	356
9:4	356
12:13	356
19:25	254
19:27	254
37	356
38	356
39	356

Psalms
1:2	48–49
2	241
2:1–2	241n1
2:10–11	241
2:12	243
5:6	357
8:5	356
8:7–9	64
10:16	181n1
19:1	356
32:1	162
32:6	161, 165
33	356
33:11	356
46:1	357
50:15	17, 181n1
50:16	181
72:18	356
91	356
102:25–26	253
103:20	63
104	356
104:4	356
107:10	372
110:7	33–34
115:3	356
119:91	355, 356
119:176	206
127:1	7
130:3	165
133:2	398
138:8	356
139	356
139:4	355
143:2	162, 165
145:17	356
147	356

Proverbs
8:22	356
16:4	357
16:33	357

Ecclesiastes
7:29	64, 69

Song of Solomon
1:5	199
2:10	199

Isaiah
6:1	372
7:14	79
9:6	315
11:2	99, 397
14:27	356
24:23	253
42:5	356
43:1	356
46:10	356
59:17	357
61	318
65:17	253
66:2	161
66:22	253

Scripture Index

Jeremiah
4:2	182
10:23	356
23:1–2	189
23:6	102
23:21	220
31:18	158
31:34	178
32:17	356
32:20	356
32:40	172, 173
33:3	17
51:15	356

Lamentations
3:37	356

Ezekiel
34:1–10	189

Daniel
4:31	355
4:32	356, 357
7:10	63
12:2	253

Hosea
2:21	356
2:21–22	66
13:9	357

Jonah
4:5–8	26

Micah
4:4	372
5:2	90

Nahum
1:2	357

Zechariah
2:8	356

Malachi
4:1	253

NEW TESTAMENT

Matthew
1:1	90
1:20	79
1:22	381
3	294
3:2	117
3:9	59
3:11	129, 297
4:10	182
5	318
5:6	161
5:7	178
5:16	56, 177
5:34–37	182
5:44	195n1
6:10	61, 356
6:12	165, 246
6:26	356
7:7	17
7:15	20
8:12	252
9:2	381
9:6	381
10:20	41
10:22	25
10:28	357
10:29	356
10:29–30	55, 65, 67, 68
10:32	25
10:33	25
11:27	270
13	192
13:21	154

Matthew (continued)

13:22	308
13:43	262
14:7	183
15:8–9	176
15:11	231
16:18	5, 112, 192, 208
18:15	223
18:15–17	195
18:15–18	234
18:17	203
18:18	223, 247
18:20	191, 370
18:23–35	248
19:9	225
19:11	224
19:14	137
19:17	53, 356
20:18	383
20:25–26	330
22:23–46	318
22:30	63
22:37–39	85
24:1–44	253
24:24	205, 222
24:29–31	257
24:36	253
25:1	192
25:31–33	257
25:34	259, 262
25:34–36	261
25:41	258, 259, 206, 262
26:26–28	80
26:35	90
26:41	19
28	289
28:18	354, 374
28:19	51, 135, 191, 223, 290
28:19–20	139, 194
28:20	118, 208, 233, 361, 370

Mark

1:4	118, 136, 157, 297
1:15	157
8:38	25
9:24	57
13:32	60
14:62	372
16:15	191
16:15–16	106
16:16	130

Luke

1:33	211
1:34	79
1:37	356
2:41–47	318
2:52	99
3:16	297, 298, 303
4:16–30	318
5:20	247
5:21–25	247
6:27	195n1
6:35	195n1
10:7	226
11:17	8
12:6	356
13:3	157
13:5	157
15:7	63
16:9	251
16:19–31	252n2
16:23	252
17:5	154
17:10	178, 179
18:1	17
21:5–36	253
21:34	20, 21
22	355
22:19	128, 148
22:32	172
23:34	247

23:42	61	10:16	188
23:43	251	10:17	34, 360
24:39	101, 363, 365	10:27	192, 206
24:46	67	11:10	205
		13:34	192
John		13:35	18, 195
1:3	211	14:2	61, 367
1:6	182	14:23	107
1:14	90, 91, 99, 272	15:1	112
1:17	121	15:1–7	106
1:18	41	15:5	78, 175, 176
1:29	88	15:6	178
2:19	360	15:15	60
2:21	360	16:33	356
3:6	79	17:19	398
3:13	207, 391	17:21–23	188
3:19–21	205	17:24	252, 254
3:34	99, 277, 397	17:26	60
3:36	383	20:19	363
4	356	20:23	223, 247
5:17	356		
5:21	78	**Acts**	
5:29	253	1:5	296n126
6	285n95, 287, 356	1:7	253, 255
6:22–59	146n9	1:11	260
6:35	146n9	1:25	252
6:52	146n9	2:38	289
6:53	98, 145, 272	2:38–39	291
6:53–54	285	2:42	17
6:54	285, 395	3:21	101
6:55	395	4:12	57
6:56	148, 284	4:28	55, 67, 172, 355
6:57	395	4:32	18
6:63	147	5:29	240
7	356	6:3	215
8:34	70	7:49	377
8:36	169	7:59	181
8:44	62	8:12–16	289
10:3	186	8:13	130
10:4–5	194	8:23	130
10:5	206	10:35	178

Acts (*continued*)
13:48	154
14:16	65
14:22	216
15:18	55
17:27–28	150
17:28	67, 356
19	290n108, 291, 294, 295, 298
19:2	302, 304
19:3	299, 302, 303
19:4	296n126, 300, 302, 303, 304
19:5	135, 138, 289
20:21	118
20:28	90, 98, 216, 382
20:29–30	189
24:2	355
25:6	372
27:23	357
27:31	66
27:35	357

Romans
1:2	118
1:16	118
1:19–20	41
2:5	258
2:24	226
2:28–29	208
3:2	296
3:20	87
4	314
4:3	165
4:5	314
4:7	162
4:8	163
4:25	364
5:12	70, 105
5:15	166
5:19	69, 70, 79, 163, 315
6:3–4	291
6:4	136, 138, 364
6:5	79
6:11	291
6:23	178, 260, 379
7:7	72, 86
7:8	70, 71
7:10	86
7:12	120
7:23	192
8:1	88, 121, 161
8:3	86
8:4	88, 121
8:7	22
8:9	113
8:11	200
8:17	262
8:24	155
8:26	169
8:28	356
8:30	65
8:35	172
8:38–39	58
9:8	165
9:10	356
9:11	56, 262
9:14	68
9:15	59
9:17	356
9:18	59, 352
9:22	56
10:4	88
10:10	1, 24, 155, 233
10:14	182, 191
10:17	49, 120, 126, 154, 381
11:13–14	177
11:17	79, 112
11:33	68
11:36	52, 68
12:1	214
12:5	284

13:1	239, 243	7:39	225
13:1–2	224	9:7–10	227
13:2	240	10:4	133
13:5	224, 239, 240	10:9	93
13:7	239	10:16	141
13:14	355	10:17	284
14:7–8	170	10:31	170
14:23	175, 182, 379	11:20	195
16:1	215	11:23–29	223
16:17	203	11:24	128
		11:26	142
1 Corinthians		11:27	145, 312
1:10	197	11:27–32	307
1:11–13	205	11:29	310, 311, 312
1:14	297	11:30	311
1:16	297	11:31	311
1:30	102, 161, 165, 315, 360	11:31–32	312
1:31	56, 58	11:32	311, 312
2:8	383, 391	12:10	223
2:9	262	12:12	109, 200
2:14	22, 78	12:13	115, 142, 147
2:14–15	171	13:4–7	156
3:4	197	13:12	193, 263
3:5	212	14:26	223, 226
3:9	212	14:28	228
3:12	197	14:33	xxxi, 217
3:22	197	14:40	xxxi, 201, 223
5:4–5	223	15	363, 365
5:11	203	15:20	365, 383
6	305	15:22	70, 253
6:2–3	258	15:28	107, 263
6:11	146, 309	15:36	253
6:15	284	15:40–49	14
6:19	135	15:42	253
7:8–9	225	15:45	120
7:9	224	15:47–48	79
7:14	135, 137	15:48	108
7:15	225		
7:16	177	**2 Corinthians**	
7:29–31	21	1:4	178
7:32–33	225	3:7	120

2 Corinthians (continued)

3:9	120
3:17	169
3:18	121, 356
4:7	4
5:10	179, 258
5:17	56, 166
6:14–17	203
6:16	65, 228
7:10	158
9:7	230
10:4	22
12:2	61, 62, 367
12:4	367
13:5	57, 310

Galatians

1:1	221
1:6–9	205
2:11–14	206
2:11–21	205
2:20	142, 169
3:22	88
3:24	87
4:4	89, 91
4:4–5	89, 315
4:5	90
5:6	18, 154, 156
5:9	24
5:17	87, 172
6:6	223
6:15	56

Ephesians

1:3	262
1:3–4	358
1:4	56, 58, 191, 358
1:4–5	56
1:5–6	358
1:6	358
1:7	102, 359
1:7–8	380
1:8	153, 154
1:9	356
1:9–10	380
1:10	90, 187
1:12	136
1:13	117, 380, 381
1:13–14	186
1:14	381
1:15	383
1:17–18	154
1:19	383
1:20	155, 270, 360
1:20–21	382
1:20–22	369
1:22	99, 101, 189, 191, 373, 375
1:22–23	186
1:23	186, 200, 211
2:1	70, 78
2:3	75
2:9	56
2:10	57, 58, 166, 175, 178
2:12–13	79
2:14	102
2:14–16	111
2:15	114, 194, 200
2:18	194
2:20	9, 194
2:21	112
3:8	68
3:17	112, 129
4	294
4:3–6	201
4:4–6	188, 344
4:5	194
4:10	101, 270, 367, 372
4:11	216, 217, 356
4:12	200, 220, 221
4:15	112, 189
4:16	101

4:24	63	2:3	99
4:30	178	2:8	21
5:22–23	132	2:11–12	137, 291
5:21	324	2:14	246
5:23	189, 211	2:16	229
5:26	136, 143	2:18	176, 182
5:26–27	138	2:23	176, 296
5:27	194, 199	3:1	379
5:30	79, 109, 142	3:1–2	270, 369
5:32	112	3:4	309
6:11–17	22n31	4:14	21n30
6:12	62, 192		

Philippians

1 Thessalonians

1:1	215, 216	3:11	181
1:6	173	4:7	178
1:11	162	4:14–16	257
1:23	262	4:15–16	253
1:29	154	4:16–17	367
2	32	4:17	270, 368
2:1	12	5:6	20, 21
2:6	90, 269	5:12	322
2:6–7	272	5:17	17
2:7–8	32n1	5:21	22, 49
2:8	79		

2 Thessalonians

2:8–9	315	2:9	222
2:8–10	33	2:12	63
2:9	32, 367	2:15	xxvi
2:11	367	2:16–17	181
2:13	65, 169, 171, 176, 211, 240	3:2	28
		3:6	xxvi
3:15–16	197		
3:20	367	**1 Timothy**	
3:21	254, 365, 368	1:5	154, 175, 321
		1:19	19, 179
Colossians		2:2	240
1:10	178	2:5	32n1
1:16	61, 356	3:2	216
1:17	211	3:2–7	220
1:18	189, 200	3:3–8	227
1:19	102	3:8–12	215

1 Timothy (continued)

3:15	205, 206
4:1	231
4:3	231
4:16	177
5:8	27
5:17–18	227
5:17–19	214
5:20	223, 234
6:15	243

2 Timothy

1:6	166, 178
1:10	283
2:13	60
2:16	84
2:19	57, 173, 208
2:25–26	158
3:16	42, 46
4:2	223
4:8	259
4:10	21

Titus

1:1	154
1:2	357
1:6–9	220
1:7	216
1:15	129, 231
1:16	57
2:12	120, 177, 192, 195, 240
2:12–13	119
2:13	155
2:14	166
2:15	216
3:5	56, 136, 359
3:10	203

Philemon

24	21n30

Hebrews

1:1	41
1:2	213
1:3	67, 356, 372
1:6	98, 277
1:7	63
1:14	212
2:3	41
2:12	213
2:14	283
2:16	91
3	356
3:6	211
4:13	55
4:15	79, 90, 213, 383
5:4–5	220
6:1	216, 223
6:4–5	308
6:18	357
8:4	371
9:10	121
10:20	273
10:24	178
11:1	154, 155, 208
11:3	356
11:6	179
11:10	61, 101, 186, 367
12:1–2	25
12:22	187
13:4	224
13:8	133
13:15	229

James

1:13	357
1:14–15	72
2:12	164
2:15–16	156
2:20	154, 179
2:21	162
2:24	167

4:10	357	2:17	26
4:13	170n1	2:19	188, 192
4:15	170	3:4	72, 357
5:12	182	3:7	162
5:14	216	4:2–3	379
5:16	40	4:3	379
		4:7	28, 156
1 Peter		4:8	156
1:4	155	4:10	107
1:10	118	4:13	113
1:21	41	4:16	156
2:13	239	4:19	106
2:24	450	5:7	51
2:25	216	5:11	102
3:17	224	5:20	90
3:19	93		
4:1	101	**2 John**	
5:1	216	6	182
5:6–7	357	10	24, 203, 220
5:7	65		
5:8	19, 20	**Jude**	
		3	xxvii
2 Peter		6	62, 251n1
1:4	107, 109, 169	14–15	253
1:5	175		
1:10	178	**Revelation**	
2:4	62, 251n1, 252	1:5	395
2:5	207	5:9	136, 181
3:3–4	255	13:8	133
3:13	253	14:6	118
		14:13	179
1 John		17:14	243
1:3	115, 141	20:5	101
1:5	357	21:1	253
1:7	138, 395	22:4–5	263
1:8	87	22:9	63
2:2	165	22:11	166
2:16	67, 72	22:18–19	46

Subject Index

abide, 101, 109–110, 114, 147, 197, 222, 368
Adam
    fall of, 55–56, 69–71, 75, 79, 105, 166, 315
    as father, 70–71, 80, 85, 253
    freedom of, 63–64, 69, 72, 86
    nature of, 93–94, 273
adoption, 89–90, 119, 135, 163, 169, 261–62, 358
adultery, 225, 241
advent, second, 16, 155, 254, 257–60, 367–68, 377–79
Ambrose, 41, 214, 289–90, 292–94, 297, 299, 367
Ambrosiaster, 32, 214
Amphilochius, 389
Anabaptists, 6, 139, 184, 244, 260n1, 289n107, 302
angels
    and church, 186–87, 192, 235–36
    as creature, 62–63
    as messengers, 63
    as minister, 212, 231, 257
    nature of, 62
anhypostasis, 91–94, 273, 279–81, 343
Anselm, 282–83

antinomianism, 57, 88, 122, 173
Apocrypha, xxviii, 42–44, 269
apostasy, 6, 202–4, 216, 243, 308
Apostles' Creed, xxvi, 9, 49, 182, 378–79
apostolic succession, xxix, 195–96. *See also* church, as apostolic
Arianism, 6, 11, 22, 53–54, 100, 102, 196, 269, 348, 354
armor of God, 22–23
Athanasius, 53, 91, 93–94, 273, 280, 397–98
atonement, 250, 375
attributes
    communicable, 346, 385
    incommunicable, 52–53, 346–47, 353, 385
Augsburg Confession, xxix
Augustine, xxvii, 11–14, 32, 45, 47–49, 70–71, 76–77, 84n2, 92, 94, 124–27, 130, 143, 147, 150, 171, 176, 200–202, 230, 241, 246, 260n1, 271, 288, 292, 294, 298–99, 371, 375–77

Bancroft, Richard, xvi
baptism
    of believers, 110, 136–37, 291, 294

baptism (*continued*)
  in Christ, 24, 289–91, 293–95, 302–5
  form of, 136–38, 289–90
  as immersing, 136
  of infants, 47n9, 135–37, 139, 291, 294
  as initiation, 133, 142
  and ministers, 139
  mode of, 289
  nature of, 115, 123–24, 136–38
  necessity of, 137
  as ongoing, 138
  and rebaptism, 291–97, 299, 302–3, 305
  of repentance, 297
  as sacrament, 127, 131, 136, 204
  and salvation, 130
  as sign and seal, 135–36, 207, 291
  of the Spirit, 136, 138, 143, 297–300, 303, 305
  as sprinkling, 136
  as washing, 129, 138, 143–44, 297
Bede, 292
Beza, Theodore, xxii–xxiii, 68n2, 266–67
biblicism, xxviii
bishop, xxviii, xxxi–xxxii, 177, 195–96, 205, 209, 216–19, 234, 236, 320–22, 324–28, 330
blasphemy, 24, 68, 103, 115, 118, 226, 241, 243, 250, 341, 349, 375
body
  as creature, 61
  as image of God, 63, 93–94, 114, 272–74, 286–87
  as mortal, 251
  and nourishment, 142
  as physical, 334
  resurrection, 253–54, 363, 368
  as subsisting, 273, 340
  as temple, 231–32
  transformation of, 257, 285
Bonaevall, Benedictine, 147
born again, 70, 78, 169, 171
Bucer, Martin, xxxii, 218n11, 294–95, 316–28
burial, 231–32

Calvin, John, xxx, xxxiin63, 3n1, 68n2, 187n2, 214n4, 289n107
canon, 42–46
catechesis, 9–10, 14, 216, 223, 226, 233, 317–18, 320–23
cemetery, 231
Chalcedon, 11, 16, 37–38, 100, 279n54, 331–32, 351n12, 391
children, 226–27, 231, 242
chiliasts, 260
Christ
  as advocate, 181, 384
  ascension of, 13, 94, 101, 103, 257, 341–42, 365–73, 377–79, 382
  as begotten, 52, 89–90, 117, 277, 285, 332, 352, 397
  blood of, 89–90, 108–111, 113–115, 129, 136, 138, 141–42, 144–45, 147–49, 151, 248–49, 285, 359, 380, 395
  body of, 13, 34–36, 93, 101–2, 108–111, 113–115, 129, 131, 141–51, 254–55, 257, 259, 278, 281, 285, 306–310, 337, 348, 354–55, 360–65, 367–74, 377, 379, 383, 395
  as composite, 272, 280, 347
  as Creator, 61, 211
  death of, 33–34, 67, 79–80, 89, 100–101, 103, 108, 110, 117,

136, 138, 145, 147, 159, 276, 281–83, 291, 315, 333–34, 337, 339, 342, 360–64, 369–70, 375, 378, 382, 393, 396
divinity of, 15, 33, 37–40, 51, 53–54, 79, 90–100, 102, 108, 149, 155, 247–48, 270, 272, 274–82, 284–86, 331–43, 347–49, 353–55, 360–62, 366, 368, 381–82, 384–85, 388–89, 391–98
exaltation of, 32–33, 99, 315, 375, 382
fellowship with, xxx, 126, 129, 132–33, 138, 141–43, 145, 156–57, 186, 188, 380
as forgiver, 18, 96, 100, 247
glorification of, 37, 366, 372, 375
happiness of, 375
as head, 79–80, 90, 101, 105–6, 108–9, 111–112, 114, 149, 161–63, 169, 185–89, 191, 193–94, 199–200, 207, 212, 244–45, 248, 253, 263, 272, 309, 312, 368, 372–75, 380–81, 386, 397
as holy, 119, 194
honor of, 33, 263, 280, 333, 372, 386, 397
humanity of, 15, 33, 37–40, 79, 89–102, 108, 247–48, 254–55, 257, 270, 272, 274–82, 284–86, 331–43, 347–49, 353–55, 360–73, 375–77, 381–82, 384–85, 388–89, 391–98
humiliation of, 32–33, 315, 333
incarnation, xxx, 12–13, 79, 90–93, 105, 107–8, 114, 282–83, 316, 335, 345, 347, 359, 362, 369, 378–79, 395

as institutor, 129, 131, 137–38, 288, 309
intercession of, 25, 94, 101, 109–110, 144, 147–48, 155, 190, 270, 310, 348, 360, 366, 369–79, 382
as judge, 101, 253, 257–58, 260, 311–12, 375–79
as justifier, 87
as lawgiver, 20
as mediator, 32n1, 98, 101–2, 133, 153, 181, 187n2, 237, 247, 248, 282, 283n87, 299, 344, 354, 384–86, 394, 397
as Messiah, 80, 89, 300–302
obedience of, 31–33, 70–71, 79–80, 89, 101, 108, 119, 155, 163, 166, 259, 314–16
as omnipotent, 34, 36, 276, 283, 353, 355, 373, 383
as omnipresent, 34–35, 37, 40, 207, 276, 280, 341–42, 348, 376
person of, 91–92, 277–80, 282–83, 286, 331–32, 337, 339–41, 382, 384–86, 388–91, 394
as priest, 371, 384
as prince, 24
as ransom, 90, 359, 380
as redeemer, 5–6, 79, 83, 87, 89–103, 117–18, 120, 156, 159, 177, 189, 248, 254, 359–60, 377, 380–86, 394
resurrection of, 37, 101, 103, 136, 155, 159, 254–55, 283, 354, 360–65, 368–73, 377–78, 382
as ruler, 101, 211, 223, 372, 376, 382–83
as sacrifice, 89, 103, 108, 121, 147–48, 163, 248
as satisfaction, 159, 163, 246, 248

Subject Index

Christ (*continued*)
- as savior, 22, 57–58, 70, 80, 87–88, 100–102, 155, 263, 359, 384–85, 388
- as single subject, 94–98, 274–77, 286, 332–33, 335, 337, 339, 354, 361, 383–84, 386–89, 391, 394
- as sinless, 89–90, 213
- as Son, 51, 53, 89–94, 97, 107, 110, 117, 159, 212, 244, 270, 274, 283, 300, 304, 332, 342, 345, 359, 365, 375–77, 384, 388
- soul of, 90, 102, 109, 278, 281, 354–55, 360–62
- suffering of, 67, 80, 97–98, 100–101, 103, 110, 339–41, 353, 363–64, 382, 396
- as teacher, 212–13
- union with, xxx, 12, 56, 71, 78–80, 98, 101–2, 105–115, 121, 129, 132, 138, 142, 145, 147, 149, 153, 163, 169, 176, 186, 194, 200, 231, 284–87, 309, 312, 374–75
- unity of, 91–92, 94–96, 107–8, 110, 278, 282–83, 286, 382–83, 385, 392
- as vine, 112–114, 169, 175–76, 284–86, 309
- will of, 95, 98–99, 101, 103, 247, 368, 382
- as Word, 12–13, 35–36, 90–91, 95–96, 107, 272, 274, 277, 279–83, 286, 332–35, 337, 341–44, 348–49, 355, 362, 366, 383, 389

Christian
- affections of, 17–18, 119, 127, 189
- as buried, 136, 291
- and chastisement, 310–12
- and confession, 159, 233–34
- as contemplative, 313
- endurance, 24
- as free, 79
- friendship, 27–30
- glorification of, 79, 107, 359–60, 363, 368
- as good, 169
- as holy, 56, 58, 157, 166, 186–87, 191
- and joy, 127
- as judge, 258
- and law, 87, 119–122, 240
- liberty, 201, 211, 217
- as living, 186
- as new creation, 56, 65, 70, 72, 79, 84–85, 101, 112, 114, 136, 166, 169, 171, 176, 189, 245, 262
- obedience of, 87, 119–21, 177, 186, 189, 191, 195, 207, 233–34, 240, 315
- as righteous, 71, 90, 101, 119, 157, 166, 191
- as sacrifice, 213–14, 229
- and temptation, 172
- and thanksgiving, 142, 177, 208, 213–14
- as united, 8

Chrysostom, 187n2, 292

church
- as apostolic, 9, 17, 24, 49n10, 194–96, 199, 219, 221–22, 236
- assembly, 232, 235, 325–26
- authority of, xxvii–xxviii, 45–46
- as body, 107–9, 111–113, 133, 135, 142, 147, 185–89, 191, 194, 200–202, 207, 211, 236, 291, 373–75, 383

as bride, 194, 199, 263
buildings, 228
as catholic, xxvii, 7, 40, 189, 193–94, 199, 202, 205–8, 265–66, 316
in Christ, 101, 105, 107–9, 111–113
as communion, 14, 17–18, 200, 249
consistory, 232, 242
council, 232
discipline, 192, 195–96, 200, 214, 217, 222–23, 232–35, 242, 324–28
dispensations, 193
divisions, 193, 197–99, 201, 207, 236
as fellowship, 17–19, 135, 141, 156, 186, 188, 207, 228, 249, 261
goods, 227, 242–43
governance, 211–12, 214–15, 217–19, 223, 230–32, 235, 243
as holy, 187, 189, 194, 199, 206–7, 249
as house, 211
and hypocrites, 131, 145–46, 187–89, 192, 197, 205–6, 208, 236, 258, 262, 306–11
as invisible, 208
marks of, 10, 14, 16, 18–19, 194–97, 199, 201, 203, 207, 222–23, 236, 242
members of, 185–86, 188, 245, 261
militant, 186, 190–209, 245
necessity of, 11
officers, 213–17, 316
as one, 188–90, 193–94, 199
preservation of, 205–6, 208, 211, 239
synods, 232, 235, 242, 244, 325–26
as temple, 112
triumphant, 186, 190, 192–93
true, xxxii, 10–11, 14, 126, 194–99, 206–7, 209, 222, 236, 323
as united, 8, 40, 196–203
as visible, 83, 193, 199, 207–8
and visitation, 231
witness of, 45
circumcision, 83, 89, 123, 137, 291
civil disobedience, 240
commonwealth, 5, 83–84, 86, 121–22
communication of attributes, 15, 33–40, 52–54, 60, 91–93, 95–100, 102, 247–48, 269–70, 273–78, 331–44, 348–50, 353–55, 360–62, 370–71, 381–98
confession
  definition of, xxvi
  of faith, 24, 57, 135, 154–55, 194, 309
  public, 24–25, 200, 233, 301, 307
  of sin, 159
  as summary, xxix, 233
conscience
  as cleansed, 129
  and examination, 310
  as free, 201, 230, 232, 236, 240
  good, 18–19, 57, 175, 178–79, 202, 239, 258
conversion, 162, 165
councils, ecumenical, 10–11, 16, 100, 232, 269, 329, 354
covenant, 83, 135, 137, 142, 290–91
creation, 61, 80
creator/creature distinction, 52–54, 272, 346–48, 353
Crisp, Oliver, 275n32

curse, 86, 120–21, 219, 258–59
Cyprian, 11–12, 44, 147, 159, 195–96, 249, 269, 294, 298, 309, 319–20, 326
Cyril of Alexandira, 38–39, 103, 279n54, 284–87, 395, 397–98

damnation, 70, 72, 192, 251–53, 259
Daneau, Lambert, xxxi
deacons, 214–15
death
  as departure, 231–32
  eternal, 70, 72, 87
  as final, 249
  as penalty, 69–70, 80, 86, 105
  as separation, 360–61, 368, 378
Decalogue, as summary, 9–10, 85
decrees, 58, 66–67, 224, 283, 356–57, 359
decretive will, 55–57, 59–60, 66, 380. *See also* predestination; election
demons, 62–63
Devil. *See* Satan
divine properties. *See* communication of attributes; God, essence of
doctrine
  as dogma, 14, 19, 24, 44, 205
  as false, 205
  obedience, 14–15
  as pure, 196–97, 220, 222–23
Donatism, 11, 139, 200, 207, 302
Dun Scotus, 66n1

earth, 61, 252–53, 271
ecclesiology. *See* church
effectual calling, 11, 56
elders, as shepherds, 214, 216–17
Elector Frederick III, xix, 345

election
  and assurance, 57, 178, 205
  in Christ, 11, 56, 58, 90, 105, 120, 186, 191, 193, 199, 248, 258–59, 261–62, 358–59
  means of, 56–57, 66, 132, 178, 309, 356, 358–59
  as reward, 259
  as secret, 208
Elohim, 345–46
end times, 252–55, 257–63
enhypostasis, 91–94, 273, 279–81, 343
episcopy, xxxi–xxxii
eternal generation, 52, 89–90, 117, 277, 332, 352. *See also* Christ, as begotten
Eutychianism, 38–39, 95–97, 102–3, 275, 335–36
excommunication, 24, 195, 233–34
expiation, 100–101, 103, 107, 118–19, 148, 159, 163

faith
  active, 141, 178, 262, 313
  alone, 25, 162, 165, 167, 314
  apostolic, xxviii, xxxiii, 14
  as assent, 153, 308, 313
  assurance of, 57–58
  and baptism, 298–99
  as certain, 154
  in Christ, 57–58, 72, 78, 80–81, 85, 87, 98, 106, 110–112, 114–115, 117–20, 126, 129, 133, 135, 137, 145, 153, 163, 191, 200, 213, 248–49, 252, 261–62, 272, 285, 287, 290–91, 293–94, 301–2, 304–5, 314, 348, 368, 374, 381, 383
  as gift, 45, 56, 106, 120, 153–54, 161, 194, 309, 313, 383

as instrument, 164, 314
and intellect, 313
as knowledge, 153–54, 308, 313
as living, 154, 165, 167, 175, 179, 231, 262, 309, 313
necessity of, 18, 130, 154–55, 179
and Old Testament, 118, 133
as prudence, 153–54, 313
and sacraments, 126–28, 130–31, 145–51
as sincere, 154
testing of, 62, 178
true, 80, 119–20, 137, 145, 154–56, 206, 248–50, 301, 306–9, 313, 348
as trust, 154
weakness of, 126, 132, 154, 172
and will, 313
as wisdom, 153–54, 313
fasts, 230–31, 237, 250
finitum non capax infiniti, 353
flesh, as enmity, 22, 172, 190, 192
foreknowledge, 55, 62–63, 355
forgiveness
    of debts, 158, 245–48, 250, 283n87
    ministerial, 247, 249
    of sins, 18, 90, 159, 161, 163, 178–79, 194, 245, 247–50
Formula of Concord, xxi–xxii
fornication, 225
free will
    of angels, 62
    of Christians, 169–73, 176
    of man, 64–65, 67, 69, 72, 75
    nature of, 75–77
    power of, 76, 78

general revelation, as condemning, 41, 77
Gnesio-Lutherans, 36

God
    as cause, 51, 65–67
    as Creator, 52, 61, 64–65, 69, 91, 158, 366
    energies of, 276, 385
    essence of, 13, 35–39, 51–54, 90, 96–97, 99, 114, 269, 276n39, 278, 301, 338–41, 343–44, 346–50, 352–54, 366, 374, 378, 384, 387, 390, 397
    as eternal, 51–52, 94
    as Father, 40, 51–53, 79, 89–90, 92, 97–98, 101, 107–8, 133, 158, 187–88, 244, 270, 311, 315, 359, 369, 373, 375–77
    as forgiver, 247, 359
    glory of, 7, 10, 25, 56, 85–86, 153–54, 159, 170, 177, 188, 208, 220–22, 242, 263, 315, 358
    as good, 52–53, 55, 60, 64, 158, 164, 346–47, 356
    honor of, 10, 183
    as immanent, 351–52
    as immense, 52, 95, 153, 272, 278, 343, 347–48, 353, 374, 378, 385
    as immutable, 91–93, 350
    as impassable, 385, 390
    as indivisible, 51
    as infinite, 55–56, 60, 95, 270, 272, 281, 343, 347, 349, 351, 353, 360
    as invisible, 41
    justice of, 56, 60, 62, 67–68, 70, 72, 86, 183, 239–41, 246, 253, 258, 350, 356–57
    as living, 51, 60
    love of, 11, 56, 85, 153–54, 358

God (*continued*)
  mercy of, 56, 59–60, 77, 79, 119, 153, 155, 158, 163, 178, 352, 359
  as mysterious, 22, 68, 293, 380
  as omnipotent, 36, 59–60, 65–68, 99, 109–110, 155, 274, 350–53, 355–56, 358, 360, 363
  as omnipresent, 35, 52, 99, 272, 278, 341–42, 347, 374, 378
  as omniscient, 52, 55, 208
  as one, 51–52, 60–61, 345–46
  as perfect, 94, 278, 347
  as simple, 51–53, 94, 99, 272, 278, 281, 343, 346–47, 349–50, 374
  as sinless, 352–53
  as sovereign, 4–5, 65–68
  as transeunt, 351–52
  as triune. *See* Trinity
  as truth, 41, 60, 353
  will of, 56, 59–60, 65–68, 84, 86–87, 107, 119, 132, 164, 171–72, 175, 186, 351–52, 357–58, 380
  as wise, 55, 68, 86, 99, 153, 356
  wrath of, 56, 62, 79, 87, 230
Goodwin, Thomas, xv–xvi
gospel
  definition of, 117–118, 120–21
  free offer, 105, 248
  as instrument, 117, 120, 130, 144, 153, 200, 287
  origins of, 80, 83, 117–118
  of peace, 23
  unity with, xxxiv
Gregory I, 219, 283n86, 292, 328, 364
Gregory of Nazianzus, 280

grace
  alone, 22, 56, 58, 78–79, 119, 247, 287, 294
  and angels, 63
  common, 170–71
  daily, 380
  means of, 17, 57, 117, 124, 132, 216–17
  as unbound, 129–30
  grafted in Christ, 12, 56, 78–80, 106, 111–14, 121, 127, 138, 153, 161, 163, 166, 169, 172, 175–79, 186, 194, 245, 248, 259, 261, 286, 291, 309–310.
    See also Christ, union with
Gratian, 183, 203, 218, 288
Gwalther, Rudolf, xxii–xxiii, xxix

heaven
  as destination, 61, 90, 127, 251–52, 259, 367
  and earth, 61, 252–53, 271
  fellowship, 14
  as inheritance, 90, 101, 118, 155, 178, 188, 191, 251, 261, 358, 381
  as locale, 252, 255, 367, 372, 377, 382
  new, 253
  as third, 61–62, 101
hell, 192, 251–55, 259, 262, 311–12
heresy
  as arrogance, 15, 22
  christological, 102–3, 364, 379–80, 383, 391
  and creation, 64
  nature of, xxvi, 10, 198, 243
  resurgence, 6, 17, 235, 269
  trinitarian, 53–54, 269
holy days, 229

Holy Spirit
  anointing of, 79, 289, 291–95, 397–98
  as author of faith, 45, 78, 106, 108, 111–112, 120–21, 128, 132, 153, 161, 163, 248, 272, 312–13, 381, 383
  as Creator, 61, 91
  divinity of, 51, 53–54, 90, 109–10, 301
  as forgiver, 247
  gifts of, 110, 220–21, 299–302, 322–23, 398
  grief of, 178
  as guide, xxvii, 19–20
  and illumination, 170, 189, 385
  as indwelling, 106–9, 111–115, 145, 169, 173, 175–76, 178, 186, 194, 211, 231, 248, 262, 347, 363, 374
  and inspiration, 41–42, 45
  as regenerator, 106, 158–59, 169–73, 175–76, 200, 381
  as ruler, 211
  and sacraments, 124, 126–30, 135–36, 138, 143, 146–49, 151, 289–95
  as sanctifier, 72, 101, 121, 189, 213, 381
  as seal, 186, 381
hope
  as confidence, 155
  and faith, 155
  future, xxvi, 13n19, 107, 119, 142, 191, 254, 332, 368
  as gift, 133, 155, 185, 368
  nature of, 155, 157
  and salvation, 9, 22, 24, 84, 155, 254, 344
  and temporal blessings, 86
hospital, 227

humanity
  as creature, 61, 76–77
  as finite, 37, 40, 95, 97, 99, 254, 257, 270, 272, 276, 278–79
  and fourfold state, 84–85, 272
  as rational, 76–77
hypostasis, 13, 35, 39n44, 40, 51n1, 272, 275–82, 339–40, 343–44, 390, 392
hypostatic union, 12, 15, 36–37, 90–100, 109, 272–87, 331–44, 353–55, 359–60, 362, 366–70, 381–85, 387–98

idolatry, 63, 84, 115, 148, 184, 199, 203–4, 222, 228, 241, 243
illumination, 170, 189, 385
image of God, 63–64, 69, 79, 84–85
incorporation in Christ, 108, 110, 112, 117, 132, 135, 163, 176, 186–87, 287, 290. *See also* Christ, union with
indulgence, 250
intermediate state, 251–52, 254–55, 368
Irenaeus, 12–14, 73, 124–25, 195, 198–99, 288–89, 310
Islam, 54, 103, 196, 198, 307
Israel, xxxiii, 6, 86, 111, 118–121, 133, 193, 215, 217, 218n10, 241, 345, 370

Jehovah, 52, 90, 102, 345–46
Jerome, 33, 44, 103, 217–18, 269n6, 292–93, 297, 299, 364
Jesus Christ. *See* Christ
John of Damascus, xxviin46, 39–40, 274–77, 280–81, 387n86, 389–92, 395

Judaism, 54, 103, 196, 198, 301, 307
judicial. *See* law, civil
justification
   in Christ, 11, 56, 79, 87, 162–66, 169, 262
   and faith, 80, 145, 157, 162–65, 314
   as fiction, 165–66
   as gracious, 56, 163, 383
   true, 162–63, 165–66
Justin Martyr, 12–13, 38, 273

kingdom
   of God, 9, 76, 90, 137, 171, 186, 191–92, 211–12, 220, 260–62, 329, 371
   of Satan, 90, 190–91, 381
knowledge
   of God, 41, 60, 233, 270
   human, 77
   of Scripture, 221, 233

language, 228, 234, 236–37, 242, 319
law
   abrogation of, 121, 133
   authority of, 10
   ceremonial, 83–84, 121, 291
   civil, 83–84, 121–22
   as commands, 120
   as death, 120
   of God, 18, 72, 83–88, 119, 159, 224–25, 240–41, 247, 357
   and gospel, 119–122, 158, 287
   moral, 83–85, 121
   of Moses, 83–84, 88, 120–21
   of nature, 84, 225
   as perfect, 86
   purpose of, 84, 86–88, 287, 291
   substance of, 291
   as threefold, 86–88
Leo I, 95, 100, 247–48, 283, 382, 395
Libertinism, 6–7, 155, 179
life
   eternal, 31, 56, 79, 98, 101, 117, 119, 163, 178, 231, 249, 260–61, 383
   as gift, 30, 175, 178, 260–61
   as three kinds, 76–77
Lord's Day, and tradition, 47
Lord's Prayer, as summary, 9
Lord's Supper
   bread, 36, 124, 130–31, 142–48, 151, 307–8, 364, 371
   Christ's presence, 36, 123–24, 126–31, 141, 143–47, 149–51, 284–85, 287, 306–9, 364, 371, 379
   fencing of, 13
   as nourishment, 17, 133, 142, 308
   as recall, 142
   as sacrament, 127
   spiritual, 12–13
   and superstition, 148–49, 202
   transformational, 12
   transubstantiation, 12, 150
   wine, 124, 142, 144, 147–48, 151, 307, 364
   and worthiness, 306–7, 310–11
love
   as affection, 17–18
   of enemies, 156, 195
   and faith, 156
   as gift, 156, 189
   of God, 85, 106, 119, 153–54, 156, 170, 189
   as natural, 156
   nature of, 156
   of neighbor, 10, 17–18, 56–57, 85, 119, 127, 154, 156, 170,

177, 186, 191, 195, 200, 208,
    213–14, 231
  of righteousness, 164
Lutherans, unity with, xxxiv

magistrate
  as appointed, 239
  and bishops, 330
  lesser, 243–44
  as pious, 4, 213, 224, 240–43
  and religion, 242–43
  responsibilities of, 23–24, 213,
    224, 230, 235, 239–44
  and submission, 239–40, 243–
    44, 330
  as wicked, 4–5, 224, 239–40,
    244
manducatio impiorum, 306–7
Manicheanism, 64, 73, 78
marriage, 224–26, 236
mass, 250
merit
  of Christ, 31–34, 105, 155, 164,
    178–79, 191, 248–49, 258–60,
    382
  of humans, 158, 179, 249, 359
  imputation of, 259
millennium, 260
ministers
  authority of, 223, 230, 232,
    324–29
  calling, 219–22, 242
  and confession, 159, 223
  and differences, 197–98
  and discipline, 233–35, 321–22,
    324–28
  and duties, 234–35, 317–18
  false, 220, 222
  income, 226–27, 236
  and marriage, 224

and ordination, 220, 222, 242,
    245, 325–27
  and preaching, 213–14, 317,
    321–22
  purpose of, 212–14, 223
  ranks of, 319–23
  and sacraments, 129, 137–39,
    213–14, 223
  as shepherds, 214, 216, 321–22
  as teachers, 212–14, 216, 220,
    317–18, 320–22
  types of, 215–17, 221–22, 316,
    319–28
ministry, summary of, 213–14
miracle, 221–22
modalism, 54
Monophysites, 341–43
Monothelitism, 96
Muller, Richard, xvi, xxxiiin66,
    51n1, 143n7, 275n32, 276n38,
    283n90, 313n182, 370n54,
    387n83, 397n135
murder, 241
Musculus, Wolfgang, 294

Nestorius, 15, 94, 102–3, 275, 286,
    334–36
new birth. *See* born again
Nicene Creed, 10, 15, 100, 218

oaths, 181–84
occasionalism, 68
Oecumenius, 292
Origen, 103, 171, 321–22, 364
original sin, 70–71, 73, 79–80, 105,
    138, 271
overseer, 214n3, 217–18, 223–24,
    227, 325, 328
Owen, John, xvi

pardon. *See* sin, pardoned of

participation
  in Christ, 11, 106, 108, 114–115, 123, 138, 153, 284–85, 380
  in divinity, 107–9, 166, 169
  in heaven, 14
  in sacraments, 125, 129, 131
passion, 32n1, 48n9, 80, 229. *See also* Christ, suffering of
patriarchs, 326–29
patristic witness
  and Christology, 11, 15–16, 38, 53, 93, 95–96, 103, 247, 272–73, 279–80, 282–83, 354, 363–65, 372, 378, 382, 385, 388–91, 397
  and doctrine, 23, 31–32
  and ecclesiology, 195–96, 198, 203, 216–19, 234, 324–30
  and justification, 165, 315–16
  and sacraments, 123–25, 136–37, 292–305
  and Scripture, 44–45
  and works, 170–71, 179
Pelagianism, 11, 73, 78, 167
penance, 159, 233
persecution, 5, 192, 203
perseverance
  of angels, 62–63
  in Christ, 11, 19, 24, 121, 205, 381
  as true, 173
philosophy
  as gift, 76
  true, 324, 362, 378
  worldly, 21, 68, 111, 254
polytheism, 64
poverty, 214–15, 227–28, 233
prayer
  as dependence, 7, 19
  of faith, 17
  as good works, 181

  and magistrates, 240
  as necessary, 17, 233
  object, 9, 19, 181–82, 229
  private, 208
  public, 208, 233
  of repentance, 119, 245–46, 310
  as supplication, 231
preaching
  and faith, 153–54, 381
  gospel, 105–6, 110, 115, 120, 132, 137–38, 153–54, 158, 186, 191–92, 194, 196, 200, 205–8, 213–14, 221–23, 228, 233–34, 242, 248, 293, 317, 381, 383
  and hardening, 307
  law, 158
  as nourishment, 17, 245
  as pure, 19, 205
predestination
  and faith, 56, 154
  as gracious, 56, 105–6, 358
  and love, 56
  and permission, 55–56, 62, 65, 69, 73, 357
  purpose of, 57–58, 186, 357–58
  See also election
presbyters, 218n9, 320–22, 324–26
prescriptive will, 56, 60, 84, 86–87, 175
prince. *See* magistrate
providence, 65–68, 170, 355–58
purgatory, 179, 237, 250–51, 254

reassessment, xvi–xviii
reconciliation, 100–101, 111
redemption, 11, 55, 80, 84, 89, 101–2, 105–6, 121, 186, 248, 259, 262–63, 358–60, 375, 380–85
Reformation, as light, 4–5

Subject Index

regeneration
  and baptism, 133, 136, 138, 143–44
  in Christ, 56, 78–79, 105, 111–112, 169, 199, 262
  of nature, 71–72, 78, 170–72
religion, 41–42, 46–47
remission, 13, 102, 115, 117–118, 130, 136, 138, 142–45, 157–58, 161–67, 230, 245–50, 261–62, 289n108, 291, 297–98, 314, 359, 380–81
repentance
  as change, 158, 214
  in Christ, 56, 117–118, 120, 157–59, 245, 305
  as contrition, 159, 161, 233–34
  as daily, 159, 213, 245, 291
  fruits of, 13, 18, 21, 56, 310
  as gift, 158, 194, 381, 383
  necessity of, 117, 121, 130, 157, 248–49, 310
  as satisfaction, 159
  as sorrow, 119, 158–59
  as turning, 18, 135, 157–59
reprobation, 56–57, 65, 105, 130, 192, 248
resurrection
  in Christ, 11, 155, 364–65
  of Christians, 14, 143, 155, 249, 252–54, 285, 363–65, 368
  as comfort, 368–69
  general, 253–54, 257
righteousness
  of Christ, 71, 87, 102, 105–6, 119, 157, 161–67, 194, 314–15, 385
  as contaminated, 162
  as declared, 176, 248, 260
  of faith, 22, 87, 164–65
  imputation of, 70–72, 80, 119, 161–64, 166–67, 189, 194, 246, 259, 314–15
  inhering, 71, 161–62, 164–67
  original, 80
  as reckoned, 101, 161, 163–65
Roman Catholicism, xxxii–xxxiii, 5–6, 195–96, 203–4, 216, 236, 330
Rufinus, 45n6

Sabbath, 47
sacramental union, 12, 124–25, 131–32, 143, 150, 309
sacraments
  as confirmation, 125–26, 138, 141–42
  corruption of, 202
  as effectual, 128–31, 133–34, 383
  as *ex opere operato*, 129–31
  and faithfulness, 128, 145–47
  as fellowship, 110, 135, 141, 148–49, 151, 228
  as instrument, 117, 126–27, 136, 141–43, 153, 191, 200, 242
  and invisible grace, 288
  as nourishment, 17, 19, 106, 125–27, 245
  Old Testament, 133
  as promise, 123
  as sacrifice, 288
  as seal, 80, 125, 127, 135
  as sign, 123–25, 128–29, 131–32, 136, 151, 289, 306, 308–310
  simplicity of, 127
  substance of, 35, 111, 128–34, 136, 138, 144, 149–51, 306–7, 309–310, 364
  as summary, 10
  as symbol, 123–25, 128–29, 142

sacraments (*continued*)
  and understanding, 127–28, 134, 307–8, 310
  as visible word, 17, 123–25, 132, 142, 144, 150–51, 185–86, 192, 195–96, 208, 287–88
  and words of institution, 126, 143–44, 147, 288
salvation
  as certain, 58, 108, 232
  in Christ, 103, 105–6, 108, 110, 114, 117, 119, 124, 137, 142, 166, 276, 283, 383
  and church, 206–7
  as gracious, 56, 80, 259–60, 359
  of infants, 115, 137, 312–13
  as perseverance, 19, 63, 84, 173
  pre-advent, 80–81, 271–72, 287, 314
  as predestined, 55–58, 105, 161, 358
  purpose of, 177–78
  requirements of, 84, 86
  undivided, 157, 166
sanctification
  in Christ, 11, 79, 189, 348
  definition of, 119
  as mortification, 10, 26, 119, 127, 159, 213, 246, 291, 311
  necessity of, 121, 306
  as vivification, 101, 119, 159, 200, 213, 291, 311, 383
Satan
  as deceiver, 212
  as enemy, 4–5, 20, 23, 70, 192–93, 198, 211, 328
  and heresies, 6, 53, 203, 235, 345
  and hypocrites, 188–89
  as instigator, 69–70, 271
school, 226–27, 242

Scripture
  analogy of faith, xxviii, xxxv, 10, 14, 16, 19, 27, 40, 47, 49, 112, 223, 242, 292, 296–97, 299, 305, 354
  as comfort, 231
  as final authority, xxvii–xxviii, 9, 14, 44–47, 49, 60, 151, 153, 204, 223, 232, 242–43, 262, 299, 305, 316, 354
  as God's Word, 17, 23, 41, 44–45, 49, 60, 153, 175, 204, 222, 262, 313
  as inspired, 41–42, 60
  meditation of, 20
  as necessary, 41, 46–49, 175
  as perfect, 46
  perspicuity of, 46–49, 60, 182
  reading of, 17, 48–49, 234, 317, 319–20, 322
  study of, 234
  as sufficient, 46, 48–49
  translation of, 48–49
Second Helvetic Confession, xxix
sickness, 231
sin
  as absolved, 161, 163, 245
  as actual, 315
  author of, 67–69, 72–73, 271, 357
  as cleansed, 129, 136, 138
  as concupiscence, 57, 70–73, 85–86, 315
  and consequences, 246, 311, 359
  as contrary, 379
  as corruption, 70–71, 75, 78, 159, 162, 248, 271, 315, 359
  and faithlessness, 175, 182, 309
  as forgiven. *See* forgiveness, of sins
  gradations of, 73

and guilt, 69, 72, 119, 158, 163,
    245, 248, 250, 315, 381
hatred of, 159, 161
imputation of, 70–71, 162–63,
    194, 245–46, 315
indwelling, 87, 154, 162, 165,
    172–73, 192, 245, 381
and infants, 271
as lawlessness, 72, 85–87, 357
as offense, 158, 245
original. *See* original sin
origins of, 69–71, 73, 79
as pardoned, 103, 119, 159, 163,
    245–47, 259, 344
and penalty, 245
as privation, 73, 271
as punishment, 70–72, 163
as slavery, 101, 172–73, 381
and sorrow, 18, 119, 158–59
as transgression, 69, 71, 80, 86,
    121, 183, 224, 245, 247, 315
soul
    of believers, 251–52
    as creature, 61–62
    as image of God, 63, 93–94, 109,
        114, 272–73, 286–87
    as immortal, 64, 231–32, 251,
        254
    and nourishment, 148
    sleep, 254
    as spiritual, 334
    as subsisting, 273, 340
    of unbelievers, 251–52
special revelation, as necessary, 41,
    46–48
spiritual warfare, 62
Stoicism, 73
sursum corda, 128

Tartarus, 62, 251–52, 254–55

Ten Commandments. *See*
    Decalogue
Tertullian, 12, 18, 24, 59, 159, 171,
    195–96, 294, 297, 375
Theodoret, 387–89
Thomas Aquinas, xxn19, xxviin47,
    36n21, 66n1, 76n4, 164n1,
    272, 351n12
Tossanus, Daniel, xxii
tradition
    fidelity to, xxvii–xxviii, 10–12,
        14–15, 23–24, 47, 49, 296–97,
        299, 305, 316, 332–35, 378
    and Scripture, 47, 49
transubstantiation. *See* Lord's Supper, transubstantiation
Trinity
    and baptism, 138–39, 289–90,
        292–93, 299–304
    as coeternal, 90
    as consubstantial, 53, 89–91, 99,
        278, 360
    economic, 91
    and personal properties, 52, 99,
        278, 300, 302, 304, 352
    as three persons, 51, 60, 114, 181,
        249, 269, 278, 302, 345–46
    as three subsisting ones, 51, 60,
        99, 269, 278, 302, 346, 378
    and undivided works, 61, 91
Turk. *See* Islam

ubiquity, 35–37, 40, 111, 114, 150–
    51, 341–43, 348, 367, 369–74,
    377–79
Union with Christ. *See* Christ,
    union with
universalism, 260
unregenerate, 77–78, 87, 170,
    175–76
Ursinus, Zacharias, xxii

Vermigli, Peter Martyr, xix
Vigilius, 15, 33–34, 331–44
virgin birth, 79, 89–90, 107, 281, 332, 335, 376, 378
virtue
  Christian, 76–77, 170–71, 178
  as gift, 77–78
  as sobriety, 8, 20–22
  as true, 171
  as vigilance, 19–20, 22
Vos, Antonie, xvi

works
  benefit of, 178
  definition of, 175–76
  as edifying, 177–78
  external, 86, 176
  as fruit, 176–77, 262, 313
  as gift, 166, 175, 179, 259
  and justification, 56, 87–88, 163, 166–67, 176–78, 260, 314
  necessity of, 58, 167, 177
  purpose of, 170, 175, 177–78, 261–62
  rewards of, 178–79, 258–59
  as service, 153–54, 166, 170, 177, 230
  types of, 181
  and unbelievers, 170–71, 175–76
worldliness, 21, 192–93, 227–28
worship
  of Christ, 98, 395
  of God, 85, 98, 188, 233
  liberty of, 201
  and oaths, 181–82
  as praise, 133, 213, 263, 358
  and prayer, 181, 233
  public, 228, 233
  regulation of, 10, 47, 48n9, 63, 181–83, 201, 222, 229–30
  as sacrifice, 229, 288

Zanchi, Girolamo
  biography, xviii–xx, 25–26, 28
  characteristics of, xv
  Confession of the Christian Religion
    content of, xxix–xxxv
    context of, xx–xxv, 27–29, 265–67
    foundation and structure of, xxvi–xxix
  literary work of, xx–xxi
  rediscovery of, xvi–xviii
Zylstra, Stephen, 351n12